Praise for *Save Our Unions*

"It's no secret that organized labor is on the ropes. Steve Early has a keen eye for where and how labor can revitalize itself by exerting its strength in strategic ways. *Save Our Unions* is both analytical and a battle cry. A must read for activists."

—CLANCY SIGAL, author, *Weekend in Dinlock, Going Away,*
and *Hemingway Lives!*

"*Save Our Unions* is a much-needed discussion of problems arising from the corporate-type structure of many U.S. unions. It is hard to fight this war on workers when unions behave like businesses and act like it's all about the money. This book shows why we need a labor movement that represents all working people, not just a few."

—NICHELE FULMORE, Teamsters Local 391 and member,
Labor Notes Policy Committee

"No observer of the current labor scene writes with the cutting edge lucidity of Steve Early. His many years of experience as a national union representative make his work essential reading for anyone trying to build a new type of labor movement."

—ROBERT M. SCHWARTZ, labor attorney and author,
The Legal Rights of Union Stewards

"Unions once had high hopes that the Obama administration would help them resist health care cost shifting. Instead, the Affordable Care Act (ACA) is actually increasing bargaining table pressure for more medical benefit givebacks. As Steve Early documents, labor needs real health care reform— and greater independence from the Democrats—now more than ever before."

—DR. JILL STEIN, 2012 Green Party presidential candidate

Save Our Unions

Dispatches from a Movement in Distress

by STEVE EARLY

For Sister Kshama —
Best wishes
and in solidarity
keep up the transformation
of Seattle!

Steve Early

MR

MONTHLY REVIEW PRESS
New York

Library of Congress Cataloging-in-Publication Data available from
the publisher

—

Early, Steve.

  Save our unions : dispatches from a movement in distress / by Steve Early.

  pages cm

  ISBN 978-1-58367-427-7 (pbk.) — ISBN 978-1-58367-428-4 (cloth) 1. Labor
unions—United States. 2. Labor—United States. 3. Industrial
relations—United States. 4. Strikes and lockouts—United States. I.
Title.

  HD6508.E343 2013

  331.880973—dc23

                          2013041237

Monthly Review Press

146 West 29th Street, Suite 6W

New York, New York 10001

www.monthlyreview.org

5 4 3 2 1

CONTENTS

This book is dedicated to CWA President Larry Cohen,
the best of his generation in labor, and three IBEW union brothers
in Boston—Myles Calvey, Dave Reardon, and Steve Smith.

INTRODUCTION—SAVING OUR UNIONS

In the winter of 2013, when this collection was being assembled, the U.S. labor movement had just been coldcocked—in Michigan of all places. How does a big midwestern industrial state go from being a bastion of blue-collar unionism to another notch in the belt of the National Right to Work Committee, right next to Oklahoma, Texas, and Alabama?

Well, the road back to open-shop conditions in the birthplace of the United Auto Workers (UAW) was paved by earlier labor setbacks in neighboring states. First Indiana, then Wisconsin and Ohio, stripped public workers of their bargaining rights (although the Republican attack on government employees in the Buckeye State was later repelled by popular referendum in the fall of 2011). Then, Indiana followed up with passage of a right-to-work law, forbidding union security clauses in private industry.[1] In November 2012, despite spending millions, Michigan labor lost two ballot questions related to public sector bargaining rights. So the lame-duck GOP legislative assault on union security in the private sector that followed soon thereafter in Lansing should not have been a surprise, given trends in the region.

Amid the resulting political furor, even labor's just reelected "friend" in the White House, Barack Obama, felt compelled to speak out. Obama was visiting Michigan right before GOP Governor Rick Snyder signed his state's "right-to-work" bill into law. "We should do everything we can to

keep creating good middle-class jobs that help folks rebuild security for
their families," Obama told a union crowd in Detroit. "What we shouldn't
be doing is trying to take away your rights to bargain for better wages and
working conditions. The so-called 'right-to-work' laws—they don't have
to do with economics, they have everything to do with politics. What
they're really talking about is giving you the right to work for less money."[2]

Unfortunately, by this point in Obama's presidency, working for less
money, with fewer job rights or benefits and little employment security,
was an experience shared by millions of white-collar and blue-collar
workers. Even those still lucky enough to have union contracts (just 11.3
percent of the workforce in 2012) were battered by the great Wall Street
meltdown and its continuing aftershocks. When push came to shove
in 2008–9, there was much emergency relief for those at the top of our
economic pyramid and far less for the millions of wage earners and homeowners at the bottom. The latter suffered from layoffs, pay cuts, loss of
home equity, and the evaporation of retirement savings. As a result, by
2013, overall employee compensation—including health and retirement
benefits—dropped "to its lowest share of national income in more than
50 years while corporate profits have climbed to their highest share over
that time."[3]

Union members had more protection, of course, but only if their legal
rights were not undermined by friends and foes alike. Just as President
Obama's own tutorial on the politics and economics of "right-to-work"
failed to sway Governor Snyder in Michigan, labor's attempt to enlist
Democrats in a vigorous defense of unionism has been less than successful.
During Obama's administration, the desperate plea, "Save Our Unions!"
fell on deaf ears among labor's supposed allies in Washington and many
state capitals. From New York to California, Democratic governors and
other public office holders often joined the budget-cutting Republican
chorus criticizing teachers and other government workers or seeking to
curb their bargaining rights.

Thanks to this bipartisan hostility and/or indifference to collective
bargaining, U.S. labor can expect little respite from its uphill battles of
the recent past, despite much initial relief over Obama's reelection.
Throughout our last three decades of retreat and defeat, the generally
agreed-upon left-wing formula for turning the tide has been a "to-do"

list more easily recited than implemented. In some combination or fashion, most labor leftists agree that unions should do more systematic and
radical membership education, become internally democratic, engage in
direct action on the job, organize the unorganized (particularly foreign-
born workers), build cross-border solidarity, and get involved in broader
community-labor alliances leading to greater independence from the
Democratic Party.

If this recipe for revitalization was easy, there would have been much
more union reform than we've seen to date. Instead, thousands of dedicated labor activists have toiled diligently, for years, to change their own
small (or larger) corner of the "house of labor," while myriad private and
now public sector enemies have tried to demolish the whole shaky structure. Between 1980 and 2007, I was among these frontline union defenders,
while still on active duty as an organizer and international representative for
the Communications Workers of America (CWA). Many of our collective
standoffs with management, union reform campaigns, and new organizing
initiatives helped slow the process of de-unionization, but they have yet to
reverse the steady decline in membership and bargaining clout.

Unexpected Uprisings

In 2011-12, an unexpected wave of protest movement activity, involving
workers and their allies, inside and outside of unions, bolstered the case
for bottom-up change.

In the year following big midterm Republican legislative gains, the massive public employee uprising in Wisconsin and the much more diffuse
Occupy Wall Street (OWS) movement mounted a long-overdue challenge to working-class disempowerment and the not unrelated growth of
income inequality. From their earliest stage, the mass marches and rallies in Wisconsin sought to unite private and public sector workers, and
thwart Governor Scott Walker's right-wing populist strategy of "divide
and conquer." The demonstrators (and occupiers) included public service
providers and those who rely on tax-supported state and local programs,
working together as allies, not fiscal policy adversaries. Whereas the Tea
Party activity of 2009-10 had scapegoated taxes, immigrants, and big
government, Wisconsin and OWS refocused public attention on the real

threat to all working people, namely the power of big business and the political agenda of those doing its bidding.

Both protest movements also gave our timorous, unimaginative, and politically ambivalent unions an ideological dope-slap, not to mention a much-needed injection of youthful energy and ideas. AFL-CIO union leaders first sought an infusion of those scarce commodities in labor when they jetted into Wisconsin in the winter of 2011. Without their planning or direction, the spontaneous community-labor uprising in Madison managed to reframe the debate about public sector bargaining throughout the United States. So the top officialdom flocked to the scene even though the protests were launched from the bottom up, rather than in response to union headquarters directives from Washington, D.C. Six months later, OWS become another Lourdes for the old, lame, and blind of American labor. Union leaders began making regular visits to Zuccotti Park and other high-profile encampments around the country, offering material aid and union reinforcements for Occupy-related marches and rallies.

Based on this interaction with the 99%, Stuart Applebaum—a New York City union leader whose annual earnings put him near the 1%, income-wise—assured the media that "the Occupy movement has changed unions." The question was, how much? And in what fashion? It would be a miraculous transformation indeed if organized labor, inspired by OWS, suddenly embraced more direct action, greater democratic decision making, rank-and-file militancy, and salaries for officials closer to the pay of workers they represent. It would also be helpful if unions adopted more consistently Occupy's brilliant popular framing of the class divide as a conflict between "them and us."[4] This requires casting aside the crutch of labor's muddled rhetoric about "defending the middle class" and instead championing America's working-class majority against the economic elite represented by Wall Street.

Unfortunately, most unions, pre- and post-Occupy, utilize the same high-priced Democratic Party consultants, focus groups, and opinion polls that fuel the Obama administration's endless conflation of working class and middle class. As labor historian Nelson Lichtenstein argues, "Obfuscation of this sort will only mislead and confuse." The contemporary category of middle class "has no sense of agency, purpose, or politics—while the idea of a working class is (by virtual definition) a font of all of this." Says Lichtenstein:

> We need to construct a sense of class dignity and destiny for all those whose work fails to provide social recognition and economic well-being. We need to restore some definitional precision to those who truly constitute America's working-class majority. Unionists and those who advocate on their behalf need to use the kind of language whose emotive power and historic resonance match the political audacity of those who occupied both the Wisconsin statehouse and the Wall Street parks. To speak on behalf of the working class is to begin to educate millions of Americans to the realization that their future is linked to their own capacity of organization and empowerment.[5]

As educational and empowering as they were, the Wisconsin and OWS protests proved hard to sustain. Both ultimately fell short of achieving their goals, which, in the case of OWS, tended to be far more diffuse than the demands echoing through the Wisconsin state capitol building when it was occupied. In Wisconsin, union-backed efforts to recall anti-union Governor Scott Walker failed at the polls, as did various legal challenges, so the Republican rollback of public sector bargaining rights was still largely intact for the duration of his four-year term, if not longer.[6]

Return of the Strike

In 2012, while Obama's reelection campaign commanded most of mainstream labor's available resources and attention, there were further grassroots stirrings that pointed in a positive direction. The year's biggest strike, by 25,000 public school teachers in Chicago, combined elements of the Wisconsin upsurge with the anti-corporate themes of OWS. Under new and more activist leadership, the Chicago Teachers Union (CTU) also provided a much-needed demonstration of the powerful synergy between union reform, internal democracy, workplace militancy, and effective community organizing.[7]

Prior to the strike, CTU members elected new officers and board members from the Caucus of Rank-and-File Educators (CORE). CORE remained active, as a reform group, after the election of new president Karen Lewis, and its members played a key role in the systematic internal organizing that CTU undertook to rebuild union structures and prepare for 2012 bargaining.[8] CTU activists also did extensive outreach to the community to neutralize, as much as possible, anti-teacher union sentiment whipped up by City Hall, the school board, and corporate-backed "education reform" groups. When the CTU strike began, then Republican presidential candidate Mitt Romney expressed his solidarity with Democratic Mayor Rahm Emanuel, who formerly served as Obama's White House chief of staff. During the nine-day walkout, tens of thousands of students, parents, and other community members struck with the teachers, making it difficult for Emanuel to isolate and demonize the CTU, as planned.[9]

At the same time that the CTU was providing an inspiring example for embattled teachers everywhere, other workers showed that militancy is possible even in the absence of formal collective bargaining. Strike activity in large established bargaining units may have reached a new all-time low, yet, in 2012 and 2013, retail, warehouse, and fast-food workers in Illinois, California, New York, and other states staged a series of walkouts over low pay and employer unfair labor practices that generated national publicity. These protest strikes involved low-wage workers who, in many cases, want a union. Unfortunately, under current legal conditions, they had little realistic chance of winning union recognition in any single work location of their employer. So, they banded together in broader and looser networks, like OUR Walmart or Fast Food Forward, which do not have the short-term goal of unionization. Backed by national unions, like United Food and Commercial Workers (UFCW) or Service Employees International Union (SEIU), and local worker centers, they have picketed, appealed to the public, and petitioned management for better pay and working conditions.[10]

In October of 2012 some Walmart workers walked off the job in thirty stores in twelve states; one month later, store protests by 400 workers and their supporters spread to 1,000 locations, in three times as many states, on "Black Friday," the day after Thanksgiving. In the spring of 2013, Walmart workers and their supporters confronted store managers in 100 locations to keep the pressure on Walmart to make scheduling improvements first promised after the Black Friday protests.[11] Their continuing use of direct action harks back to an earlier era of industrial relations, prior to the passage of the National Labor Relations Act in 1935, and draws on a model of workplace organization that's more typical of the late nineteenth and early twentieth centuries than the last seventy-five years.[12]

In the case of Warehouse Workers for Justice, aided by the United Electrical Workers in Illinois and Warehouse Workers United, a Change-to-Win–assisted formation in California, one protest strike goal has been to force Walmart to take responsibility for the personnel practices (including wage and hour violations) of the logistics chain staffing agencies that it employs.[13] In New York City, fast-food workers used their one-day work stoppage in November 2012 to protest the long-term wage stagnation of the two million workers trapped in these $8 to $9 per hour jobs. Four months later, both Fast Food Forward in New York and the "Fight for $15" campaign in Chicago organized another round of strike activity at McDonald's, Wendy's, Dunkin Donuts, Burger King, Subway, and similar chains. Similar one-day walkouts soon followed in Detroit, St. Louis, Kansas City, Milwaukee, and other cities, leading one close observer of the trend to argue that "these fast-food campaigns, and the recent strike wave against Wal-Mart, represent the most dramatic challenges by the embattled U.S. labor movement to two industries that increasingly define the new U.S. economy."[14] On August 29, 2013, fast food worker protests spread to fifty-eight cities, targeting many new outlets and generating more national publicity about low wages in the industry.[15]

Now, as in the past, the best starting point for broader labor revitalization is not pie-in-the-sky blueprints that have little connection to current reality. Rather, it's the actual worker organizing and strike activity that defies recent labor-relations trends and demonstrates, by example, that another way is possible. Who are the key agents of change on today's difficult workplace terrain? In yet-to-be-unionized work locations, it's the brave individuals who are joining the new retail, warehouse, and food service worker networks. In unionized workplaces, the tens of thousands of shop stewards who still form the backbone of the labor movement remain key to its revitalization today. As illustrated in many parts of this book, their day-to-day organizing activity on the shop floor is what brings unionism to life where it counts the most. And, in external organizing campaigns, nobody can promote the labor movement better than those who have experienced it postively, in their own lives, as a haven in a heartless neoliberal world.

Contents of the Book

In *Save Our Unions*, I've brought together various pieces of journalism that illuminate the challenges facing workers, whether they're trying to democratize their union, win a strike, organize the unorganized, defend past contract gains, develop new leadership, or become more effective in political action. The subject matter includes labor-related books and even a film or two. But, far more than my previous edited collection for Monthly Review Press, *Embedded with Organized Labor*, this book is based on firsthand reporting that describes strikes and picket lines, union conventions and funerals, celebrations of labor's past, and struggles to ensure that unions still have a future in the twenty-first century.

Save Our Unions begins with an assessment of past union reform campaigns, at the local and national level, in the Mine Workers, Teamsters, International Brotherhood of Electrical Workers (IBEW), International Association of Machinists (IAM), and United Auto Workers (UAW). I then consider the state of the strike and workers' right to strike, here and abroad. In Part 3, titled "Organizing for the Long Haul," I examine two overlapping strategies for increasing private sector union density. One involves the training and deployment of inside organizers (or "salts") and the other relies heavily on concerted union activity on a global scale.

In Part 4, "Labor's Health Care Muddle," I describe the continuing problems with job-based medical plans in the United States. The "private welfare state" achieved by some unions through collective bargaining in the post–Second World War era is now shrinking. Workers arriving late at the table, like recently unionized home-based caregivers, find traditional benefit coverage, except in the skimpiest form, beyond their reach. A single-payer system would make medical coverage part of the social wage for everyone. Yet too often today, "Medicare for All" is seen, even by unions that favor it, as "off the agenda," particularly during the phase-in period of the Affordable Care Act (ACA). Unfortunately, the ACA offers union members little or no interim relief from health-care cost shifting and other afflictions of the current system. Unions that continually fail to organize around this issue are doing a grave disservice to their members.

Recent bargaining in telecom, often revolving around "legacy benefit" disputes, is explored at length in the next section, based on my personal experience in this sector. "Telecom Union Troubles," Part 5, includes a case study in strike conflict at Verizon, arising from concession demands and management's systematic drive to marginalize unionized workers. I describe how the deteriorating telecom bargaining climate has spawned some restiveness among CWA stewards and local officers on the front lines of the fight to increase union membership, while defending past gains.

In Part 6, "Is There a Leader in the House?," I consider the challenge of new leadership development in the larger labor movement. At the national level in particular, organized labor still suffers from being a gerontocracy (if less pale and male than before). The commentaries here suggest that forming a "labor House of Lords"—to put more top officials out to pasture sooner—or even a new labor federation does not address deeper, more fundamental problems related to membership involvement and empowerment, or lack thereof.

In Part 7, "Two, Three, Many Vermonts," the collected pieces highlight the experience of progressives in the Green Mountain State as one model for greater political independence by labor. I also explore the struggle in Vermont for a local single-payer system that has become a beacon for health care reformers in other states.

Before each of the seven parts of the book is a brief introduction. Following some individual pieces, I've added a "postscript" on developments occurring since that particular article, review, or essay appeared. Some of the material in *Save Our Unions* has been shortened and/or re-edited to eliminate duplication. In other cases, cuts in the original version (made by an editor for space reasons) have been restored or different versions of the same piece that appeared in multiple outlets have been combined. At the risk of emulating a favorite writer, the late David Foster Wallace, I've also added endnotes to some pieces that were not present in their original published form. These citations provide links to further information, elaborate on the situation described, or reference contrary reports and opinions. (Readers who are not fans of Wallace-inspired references can simply ignore them, all or in part!)

The epilogue to *Save Our Unions* addresses the continuing debate about whether U.S. unions can best survive (and eventually revive) by embracing labor-management cooperation or by adopting a more adversarial stance in the workplace, at the bargaining table, and in politics. It is a postscript of sorts to my book *The Civil Wars in U.S. Labor*, which chronicled California health care union conflict and broader divisions within labor over organizing and bargaining strategy.[16]

Many of the "case studies" or stories of struggle contained herein do not have triumphant or even conclusive endings. Some are sad (but wiser?) accounts of wrong turns or dead ends on the road to labor recovery. *Save Our Unions* also warns of shortcuts and quick fixes, some of which have already fizzled. In several cases, the jury is still out on initiatives that remain promising, in theory and conception, but not without problems in practice.

In regard to all the reporting and commentary that follows, I repeat a caveat from *Embedded with Organized Labor*: The daily work of union bargaining, contract enforcement, organizing, political action, and strike support is not getting any easier. Writing and talking about what unions should do in these areas involves a lot less heavy lifting than actually doing the work itself. Anyone (including me) who offers advice and criticism from the sidelines, however helpful and constructive it may be, should always keep this difference humbly in mind.

A small but encouraging sign on the sidelines is the recent flourishing of online labor journalism, inspired in part by developments like Occupy and the Wisconsin Uprising. Old and new progressive media projects like *In These Times, The Nation, CounterPunch, Alternet, Salon, Daily Kos,* and others have expanded their labor commentary and coverage. These outlets, and the blog established by *Labor Notes,* a reliable source of alternative labor news and views for thirty-five years, have enabled many new voices to be heard. Younger journalists now have more of a platform for labor-related work, which compensates, somewhat, for the near-total disappearance of the "labor beat" in the daily press. These writers are tackling a wide range of topics with a depth, sophistication, and political sympathy sorely lacking in the mainstream media.[17] Without such hardworking (and universally underpaid) "content producers," many of the best labor stories of the current era would remain untold or underreported. So, if any workplace issue of particular concern seems slighted in *Save Our Unions* (and many have been), readers should check out the books or journalism of Dave Zirin, Lee Sustar, Gabriel Thompson, Tracie McMillan, Kari Lyderson, Liza Featherstone, David Jamieson, Micah Uetricht, Sarah Jaffe, Mike Elk, Josh Eidelson, R. M. Arrieta, Michelle Chen, Ari Paul, Brian Tierney, Laura Clawson, Arun Gupta, Mathew Cunningham Cook, James Cersonsky, Joseph Riedel, Andy Piascik, Erik Forman, Ned Resnikoff, Peter Rugh, Ryan Haney, Yvonne Yen Liu, Jake Blumgart, Shamus Cooke, Cole Stangler, Rebecca Burns, Bennet Baumer, Bhaskar Sunkara and his comrades at *Jacobin*, plus all past or present staff writers for *Labor Notes*. (Working with editor Jane Slaughter and director Mark Brenner, the current *Labor Notes* writing team includes Al Bradbury, Samantha Winslow, and Jenny Brown, whose work is often cited herein.)

As noted in my previous MRP book, *Embedded with Organized Labor*, writers like these often face formidable obstacles trying to reach more labor readers. In some cases, that is due simply to union indifference and lack of imagination. If the labor movement promoted more "active literacy"—for example, by encouraging union activists to acquire and read labor-related books—that step alone would enhance rank-and-file participation in debate and discussion about the future of unions. Of course, not everyone in organized labor favors that kind of membership education, information sharing. and involvement. And then there's also the problem of union priorities. The same national unions with tens of millions to spend on political candidates of questionable value rarely have more than a few thousand dollars left for pro-labor media outlets like *In These Times, The Progressive, Workers Independent News*, and others. The task of helping to keep them afloat thus falls, as always, to concerned readers and listeners with more limited financial resources.

Acknowledgments

Writers don't reach readers in any audience, large or small, without editors. For their editorial assistance in the original publication of material in this collection, I'd like to thank the following: Manny Ness at *WorkingUSA*, Wade Rathke at *Social Policy,* Joel Bleifus at *In These Times,* Jeremy Gantz, former editor of *Working in These Times,* and Jessica Stites, current editor of *WITT*, Randy Shaw at *Beyond Chron,* Roane Carey at *The Nation*, Marjorie Pritchard at the *Boston Globe*, Lynn Feekin at *Labor Studies Journal*, Nick Serpe at *Dissent*, Matt Rothschild at *The Progressive*, Jane Slaughter and Mischa Gaus at *Labor Notes*, Jeffrey St. Clair and the late Alexander Cockburn at *CounterPunch*, Michael Albert at *ZNet*, Arun Gupta and Elizabeth Henderson at *The Indypendent*, Jim Cullen at the *Progressive Populist*, Diane Krauthamer at *Industrial Worker*, Chris Sturr at *Dollars & Sense*, Hillary Wainwright at *Red Pepper*, Jason Pramas at *Open Media Boston*, John Russo and Sherry Linkon, former book review editors of *New Labor Forum*, Gregory Zucker at *Logos*, and Ryan Grim, John Celock, Alison Spiegel, and Lucia Graves at *The HuffingtonPost*.

Among rough draft readers, none get pestered more than my wife, Suzanne Gordon, and my longtime Bay State collaborator, Rand Wilson, whose own recollections of Ron Carey are reflected in Part I of this book. Teamsters for a Democratic Union (TDU) national organizer Ken Paff did his usual sharp-eyed vetting of Teamster-related material, after hooking me up with my 2011 Teamster convention roommate, Brother John Lattanzio, from Spokane. In Transport Workers Local 100 in New York City, many thanks to John Samuelsen, Steve Downs, and Nick Bedell.

The organizing and telecom sections of *Save Our Unions* similarly benefited from the information sharing and/or fact checking of various CWA or IBEW brothers and sisters. Most are now much closer to the action than the author (if not always on the same page themselves). They include Larry Cohen, Tony Daley, Ken Peres, Tim Dubnau, Josh Coleman, Erin Bowie, Pat Telesco, Bill Henderson, Glenn Kalata, Cindy Vines-Harrity, Chuck Borchert, Howie Coling, Don Trementozzi, Darlene Stone, Cory Bombredi, Sheila McGillicuddy, Kevin Condy, Al Russo, Pam Galpern, Rich Corrigan, Eddie Starr, John Walsh, Jan Pierce, Louie Rocha, and the still undercover "Woody Klein." In CWA's beleaguered manufacturing sector, I would like to pay additional tribute to Brother Dominic Patrignani, an extraordinary membership mobilizer in the IUE-CWA, and his tireless Albany area helpers Jon Flanders and Mike Keenan.

The "salting" insights provided by Peter Olney, Carey Dall, Agustin Ramirez, Steve Strong, Tenaya Lafore, and "Nick Stoekel" are also much appreciated. Granville Williams from the Campaign for Press and Broadcasting Freedom in the UK gave me a fascinating tour of what's left of the Yorkshire coalfields and pointed me in the direction of the miner's gala in Durham. The Vermont section of the book was assisted by some of the Green Mountain State's finest—Traven Leyshon, James Haslam, Mike O'Day, Morgan Daybell, Martha Abbott, Anthony Pollina, Ellen David-Friedman, Liz Blum, and Phil Fiermonte.

For sage health care reform reality checks, I turned, as usual, to Mark Dudzic, the irreplaceable national coordinator of the Labor Campaign for Single Payer Healthcare. In writing the epilogue (and earlier health care–related sections of the book), I was aided by Sal Rosselli, John Borsos, Rose Ann DeMoro, Marilyn Albert, Fred Seavey, Jon Sternberg, Leighton Woodhouse, Paul Kumar, Paul Delehanty, Cal Winslow, Meredith Schafer, Adrian Maldonado, and a much longer list of courageous NUHW-CNA rank-and-filers, not all of whom are quoted by name, because of the challenges they face and risks they take at work. In the interests of full disclosure, I should note that I have been a volunteer organizer of NUHW solidarity activity since the union was newly formed in 2009.

Last but not least, I want to express my special thanks for the always comradely and reliable MR Press team of Michael Yates, Martin Paddio, and Scott Borchert. Neither this collection nor my earlier one would have been possible without Brother Michael's never-ending editorial encouragement and support. His own writing on labor, particularly his widely read *Why Unions Matter*, should be a model and inspiration for younger voices in the field.[18]

All mistakes of fact or interpretation in the following are mine alone. (And many thanks to my three-time indexer Elliot Linzer for reducing the miscues of the first type.) Readers who catch any errors or who want to file a dissenting opinion are encouraged to do so at Lsupport@aol.com.

PART I

REBELS WITH A CAUSE

The essays in this section have an initial focus on the historic reform movement victories that propelled rank-and-file militants and local union officers into top leadership positions in the United Mine Workers (UMW) in 1972 and the Teamsters twenty years later. I was fortunate to be a close observer of both developments and their aftermath as a national staffer of the UMW in the mid-1970s, a longtime supporter of Teamsters for a Democratic Union (TDU), and a member of Ron Carey's Teamster headquarters "transition team" after Carey was elected International Brotherhood of Teamsters (IBT) president with TDU support.

In the 1970s, shop floor unrest took shape under different social and economic conditions than exist today. It was a period of wildcat strikes and contract rejections votes, pioneering fights over occupational health and safety, and public discussion of worker alienation on the assembly line—"the blue collar blues." Whether large or small, workplace struggles against recalcitrant employers and unhelpful union officials were sustained by what sociologist Rick Fantasia calls "cultures of solidarity."[1] These reflected a labor movement more muscular and self-confident at its industrial base, but already displaying signs of bureaucratic decay. Plant closings and capital flight, deregulation, and de-unionization soon laid waste to that traditional labor landscape.

The resulting decline in union density and rank-and-file militancy (a trend explored further in Part 2) has made it harder for the standard-bearers of reform to prevail over entrenched incumbents, whether at the national or local level in the Teamsters, Electrical Workers, Machinists, or UAW.[2] (Staying on the right track, when and if elected to union office, remains a perennial challenge as well.) Some academics have now concluded that the larger-scale labor insurgencies of the 1970s were just a flash in the pan. In their view, the rank-and-file rebellion of that era left few lasting traces. It was merely the last hurrah of an old industrial working class whose problems were quite different from those facing low-wage earners in today's "postmodern, global age." Others, understandably concerned about labor's current weakness, deem "the call to reform and democratize union governance" to be "less urgent now that the very survival of unions in any form no longer seems assured."[3]

In reality, as shop floor observers like Greg Shotwell report, union structure and functioning continues to affect organizational performance. Employment conditions in restructured industries, like auto manufacturing, or deregulated ones, like trucking, are trending backwards toward those that prevailed in the pre-union era. When the difference between union and non-union shops becomes harder to distinguish, the appeal of unionization begins to dim. When members are angry, alienated, or disengaged, the internal and external organizing needed to strengthen unions is much harder, making overall labor movement survival (not to mention revival) more difficult. Even if the locus of workplace struggle today has shifted from the industrial hot spots of the 1970s to other sectors of the economy, the need for bottom-up change—through the creation of new unions or, where possible, transformation of older ones—is no less urgent.

1—WHEN UNION "OUTSIDERS" WIN

I was welcomed into the labor movement, four decades ago, while watching retired coal miners, stoop-shouldered and short of breath, trudge through a gauntlet of union goons on their way into an American Legion

hall in Tamaqua, Pennsylvania. It wasn't a pretty sight, but it became a
formative experience.

Throughout the coalfields in December 1972 members of the United
Mine Workers (UMW) were participating in balloting for national leaders
of their union held under the supervision of the U.S. Department of Labor
(DOL). The federal government was involved because the incumbent
UMW president, W. A. (Tony) Boyle, had stolen the previous election in
1969. Not only was there massive vote fraud but, shortly afterward, Boyle
also ordered the killing of his opponent, Jock Yablonski, who was shot by
union gunmen in his home, along with his wife and daughter.

In 1972, Boyle was being challenged again, this time by a rank-and-
file slate fielded by the Miners for Democracy (MFD). The MFD was a
grassroots reform group created by Yablonski supporters after his death
to continue the fight against corruption, violence, and dictatorship in the
UMW. Like many other student radicals who have embraced the cause of
labor, before and since, I was drawn to the scene of this workers' struggle—
or at least a small corner of it—by a mixture of idealism and ideology.

The MFD needed poll watchers to help ensure that, even with government oversight, there wouldn't be a repeat of the ballot fraud that marred
the 1969 vote. Inspired by Sixties notions about "participatory democracy," I was committed to the idea embodied by the MFD—namely, that
unions should be controlled by their own members. So I joined several
other law students on a trip from Washington, D.C., to Pennsylvania's
dying anthracite coal region (where pensioners collected $30-a-month
checks) so we could serve as MFD campaign volunteers.

As I tried to distribute MFD slate cards to UMW members at the Legion
hall, it became obvious that the beefy entourage stumping for Tony Boyle
did not appreciate my presence in Tamaqua. The Boyle men were cluster-
ing around union voters as they neared the door, reminding them of past
favors, and escorting them in before they could be solicited by any meddlesome "outsiders." During a moment of downtime from their last-minute
handshaking and arm-twisting, they soon turned their full attention to me.
"Doesn't look to us like you've ever picked slate, have you, sonny?" one
fellow snarled. "What the hell are you doing here?" another asked.

Egged on by a well-dressed UMW International rep—rumored to
be part owner of a local coal mine—the hostile crowd closed in around

me, pushing and shoving, grabbing for my MFD literature, and muttering
darkly about "communists" who wanted to destroy the union. Just as I
seemed destined for the fate of the Molly Maguires (radical miners who
were lynched nearby a century earlier), a far more experienced and aggressive MFD volunteer named Ray Rogers arrived on the scene. He pushed
his way into the middle of the scrum and liberated me from its clutches.
(This timely intervention left me with lasting respect for Ray, whose subsequent career as a pioneering "corporate campaigner" has left its mark in
many other labor arenas.)

Doing the Unthinkable

Later that same month in 1972, the UMW election ballots were counted
by the Labor Department officials. Despite threats, intimidation, and
red-baiting throughout the coalfields, UMW members did the unthinkable. They chose three of their own rank-and-file coal miners from West
Virginia or Pennsylvania to become UMW national officers. The winners
were Arnold Miller, Harry Patrick, and Mike Trbovich. Unlike the brave
Yablonski, these local union activists had never served on the national
union staff or executive board, but they carried the banner of union
democracy and reform as best they could.

The labor establishment was deeply shocked and unsettled by their
election. This kind of thing was just not done. Not a single labor organization (with the exception of the always independent United Electrical
Workers) applauded Tony Boyle's well-deserved defeat in his bid for
reelection as UMW president. Even though Arnold Miller was running, at
the top of the ticket, against a management-friendly incumbent—soon to
be indicted for his role in the Yablonski murders—the MFD slate ousted
Boyle by only 14,000 votes out of 126,700, hardly a landslide.

Then and now, contested elections in which local leaders challenge
top union incumbents are few and far between. Rising through the ranks
in organized labor normally requires waiting your turn, and when you
capture a leadership position, holding on to it for as long as you can,
regardless of the organizational consequences. For trade unionists who
are ambitious and successful, upward mobility usually follows a long
career track that looks something like this: shop steward, local bargaining

committee or executive board member, local union officer, national union staffer, national union executive board member, and then national union officer—president, vice president, or secretary-treasurer.

Aspiring labor leaders can most easily make the transition from membership-elected positions, at the local level, to appointed national union staff jobs if they conform politically. Dissidents tend to be passed over for such vacancies or not even considered for them unless union patronage is being deployed, by those at the top, to co-opt actual or potential local critics. As appointed staffers move up, via the approved route, in the field or at union headquarters, they burnish their resumés and gain broader organizational experience "working within the system."

If they become candidates for higher elective office later in their career, they enjoy all the advantages of de facto incumbency (by virtue of their full-time staff positions, greater access to multiple locals, and politically helpful headquarters patrons). Plus, in the absence of any one-member/one-vote election process, most seekers of union-wide office only have to compete for votes among several thousand usually docile national convention delegates. In unions that provide geographical representation on their board, candidates for regional leadership positions can even get elected, at conventions, with the support of just a few hundred local union delegates. Either way, candidates who are part of an "administration team" usually win over independents and rank-and-file slates, particularly in unions where all board members are elected "at large."

In 1972, the Miners for Democracy (MFD) blazed a trail directly to the top, under admittedly abnormal circumstances. The UMW always permitted direct election of its president (and other top officers) but under conditions reminiscent of Saddam Hussein's Iraq or Syria under the Assad family. Only after passage of the 1959 Landrum-Griffin Act were UMW dissidents able to challenge illegal trusteeships over local unions and entire UMW districts. They also had new legal tools to thwart the expenditure of dues money to help reelect incumbents, and they could seek DOL-supervised voting as a remedy for rigged elections. The MFD cause was much championed by the New York–based Association for Union Democracy, whose network of sympathetic lawyers has helped union members enforce their Landrum-Griffin rights for more than a half-century.[4]

From the vantage point of four decades later, the choice between Boyle and the MFD in 1972 should have been a no-brainer, given all that had transpired beforehand. But in the rough-and-tumble world of trade union politics, the advantages of incumbency can never be underestimated. As a grassroots organizing project, mounting an electoral challenge to any candidate backed by the national union establishment, no matter how discredited, is an uphill fight. Competitive elections—a.k.a. "this is what democracy looks like"—are far more celebrated in the breach than the observance in organized labor. Within labor's top officialdom, there's no announcement more pleasing to the ears than "reelected by acclamation." Whether that's healthy for the labor movement is another question.

Propelled by Militancy

The MFD victory and its tumultuous ten-year aftermath has been variously chronicled by former UMW lawyer Tom Geoghegan in *Which Side Are You On?*, labor studies professor Paul Clark in *The Miners Fight for Democracy*, and journalist Paul Nyden in his contribution to an edited labor history collection titled *Rebel Rank and File*.[5] As Nyden notes, the election that thrust three rank-and-filers into unfamiliar jobs at UMW headquarters in Washington, D.C., "channeled the spontaneous militancy arising throughout the Appalachian coal fields" during the previous decade. In the 1960s, miners staged two huge wildcat work-stoppages protesting national contracts negotiated in secret by Boyle (with no membership ratification); in 1969, 45,000 UMWA members participated in a statewide political strike that accelerated passage of new federal mine safety legislation and creation of the first West Virginia program for compensation of miners disabled with black lung.

Candidates backed by the MFD, a group founded at Yablonski's funeral in 1970, "succeeded in ousting one of the country's most corrupt and deeply entrenched union bureaucracies" because they had key allies inside and outside the union, according to Nyden. In the coalfields, "wives and widows of disabled miners, the Black Lung Association, the wildcat strikers, and above all the young miners who were dramatically reshaping the composition of the UMWA constituted the backbone of the campaign."[6] Also aiding the MFD was a skilled and committed network of community organizers, former campus activists, journalists, coalfield researchers, and public interest lawyers, some of whom would later play controversial roles as headquarters staffers for the union.

The UMW had been run in autocratic fashion since the 1920s when John L. Lewis crushed the last major rank-and-file challenge to his leadership, organized by radical miners like John Brophy, Powers Hapgood, and Alex Howat. (Their failed campaign to oust Lewis in 1926 was waged under the banner of "Save the Union!") When the would-be UMW saviors in the MFD took over forty-six years later, the weight of institutional history was heavy indeed. The ensuing tensions between those newly elected and the working miners who sent them to Washington can best be described now as a smaller-scale U.S. union version of the regional political turmoil that followed Arab Spring overthrows of long-reigning Middle Eastern despots.

The MFD candidates inherited formidable internal and external problems that would have been vexing for anyone in their shoes. They succeeded in the project of structural democratization and, for a time, more competent union administration. But membership expectations in the crucial area of contract negotiations and enforcement were not always met, despite a 1974 agreement with the national Bituminous Coal Operators Association (BCOA) that provided wage increases of 37 percent over three years, a first-ever cost-of-living allowance, improvements in pensions and sick pay, strengthened safety rights, and job security protection. [7]

Within the union, the conservative Boyle forces quickly regrouped and maintained their own baleful, disruptive influence. The three top MFD officers fell out among themselves, with the best and youngest of them— Secretary-Treasurer Harry Patrick—leaving the UMW after a single term of office in 1977. Arnold Miller's weak and erratic presidency became an unmitigated disaster; in 1977–78, 160,000 miners had to battle UMW headquarters and the White House while shutting down the bituminous coal industry for 110 days. Highlights of that struggle included two contract rejections and a failed Taft-Hartley back-to-work order sought by Jimmy Carter.

A Discredited Experiment?

To this day, the MFD experience remains a Rorschach test for how one views regime change in labor, engineered from below. Some MFD veterans, who were ex-coal miners, blamed (and even red-baited) "the outsiders" for what went wrong. By the late 1970s, most of the college-educated non-miners, who were swept into influential positions by the MFD's victory, left in frustration over the failings or political setbacks of their friends and allies. Some went on to work for other unions, most recently the Service Employees International Union.

Labor insiders, including those at AFL-CIO headquarters in Washington, viewed UMW turmoil as proof that "inexperienced" people should never be allowed to run a major union. On the labor left, the shortcomings of the Miller administration have always been attributed to its unwillingness to empower fully the rank and file. If only "the MFD hadn't been disbanded" and top officials had been willing to embrace the right to strike over grievances and employed the militancy of the UMW's wildcat strike culture, rather than clashing with it, the outcome would have been different.

Some semblance of stability and forward motion was not restored until a second-generation reformer, Rich Trumka, took over as UMW president in 1982, after defeating a former Boyle supporter who replaced Arnold Miller when he retired for health reasons in the middle of his second term. Trumka gained valuable experience as a headquarters legal staffer during Miller's first term. He also had the street cred of working underground before and after his initial tour of full-time union duty in Washington. But even with steadier, more skilled hands at the helm and an inspiring strike victory at Pittston in 1989, the union now suffers from severe marginalization; its working membership today is less than 20,000. As former UMW General Counsel Chip Yablonski observes, not all of "its failings are self-inflicted."

The coal industry moved west, principally to the Powder River Basin in Wyoming, where more coal (sub-bituminous) is produced than in all the coal states of the East and Midwest combined and nearly all of that coal is non-union. The UMW was totally unprepared to meet this sea change. Its efforts to organize miners in the West have been anemic, if not absent altogether. In the meantime, the multi-employer BCOA has fragmented, leaving the UMW with fewer and fewer companies with which to negotiate an overarching national contract. Many companies in the eastern coalfields are now operating non-union affiliates or subsidiaries... but are impossible to organize after the givebacks in 1978 and 1981, which have not been reversed.[8]

In the 1970s and '80s, high-profile challenges to the leadership of other, now declining industrial unions did not take the form of pure rank-and-file insurgencies of the MFD sort. Instead, they looked more like the campaign that Yablonski's father courageously waged against Tony Boyle in 1969. In the United Steel Workers and Auto Workers, two dissident regional directors in the Midwest, Ed Sadlowski and Jerry Tucker, challenged their respective union establishments from the inside. Both called for reform while serving as national executive board members, after winning those positions in elections that were initially stolen. Both were forced out of top leadership positions after trying to move up or just get reelected. Tucker fell victim to tight control of convention delegate voting by the UAW "Administration Caucus," which has ruled his Detroit-based union for six decades. With some former UMW reformers assisting him, Sadlowski ran strongly but unsuccessfully for USW president in 1977 balloting involving nearly 600,000 of the union's then 1.4 million members.

The Teamster Reform Opportunity

A campaign like Sadlowski's was impossible in the International Brotherhood of Teamsters (IBT) when IBT leaders were chosen at national union conventions attended by a few thousand delegates and heavily influenced by organized crime. As part of the 1989 consent decree settling a controversial anti-racketeering lawsuit filed by the Justice Department, the IBT was forced to hold its first-ever membership election of officers and board members two years later.

Fortunately, the IBT was the longtime turf of Teamsters for a Democratic Union (TDU). TDU was well positioned to utilize the one-member/

one-vote system it had helped get incorporated into the consent decree. (Some in the Justice Department had originally favored a court-order trusteeship over the union instead.) TDU was launched in the mid-1970s, just a few years after the MFD, as a vehicle not just for electioneering but for long-term rank-and-file organizing.[9] In the IBT twenty-five years ago, there were no credible or trusted dissenters on the national executive board like Ed Sadlowski or Jerry Tucker, but, helpfully, the Teamster "old guard" became badly splintered after the union's settlement with the Justice Department. Two rival slates formed, composed of incumbent IBT executive board members, well-known regional officials, and other principal officers of large Teamster locals.

For fifteen years, TDU had been conducting unofficial, bottom-up "contract campaigns" and helping Teamsters democratize their local union by-laws and run for local office. Yet there were was not a long list of reform-oriented local leaders willing or able to run for national president, now that the "right to vote" had been won. Fortunately, Local 804 President Ron Carey stepped forward, with TDU encouragement, and proceeded to wage a grueling two-year cross-country campaign in hundreds of Teamster work locations. Carey was an ex-Marine and militant leader of United Parcel Service (UPS) workers in New York City; his vocal criticism of Teamster corruption had turned him into a pariah among fellow local union officials (except for the handful who agreed to run with him). Half of Carey's slate for the Teamster executive board consisted of TDU members who had never held any union position above the level of shop steward or convention delegate; others were relatively new local officers.

Carey garnered little delegate support at the Teamster nominating convention in 1991. So most experts in the mainstream media joined the labor bureaucracy in dismissing him as a fringe candidate, a "loner," and an inexperienced "outsider" with little backing among "real Teamsters." They and Teamsters employers were much surprised when Carey won the three-way presidential race with 48 percent of the membership vote. Carey's largely rank-and-file slate swept all but one position on the union's executive board. As *Newsday* labor reporter Ken Crowe recounted in *Collision: How the Rank-and-File Took Back the Teamsters*, the 400,000 Teamsters who cast their ballots in 1991 were participating in the largest government-supervised union vote since the MFD ousted Tony Boyle.[10]

Anyone who had experienced the MFD years at UMWA headquarters and then spent some time in the IBT's "Marble Palace" after Carey became president, could not escape the déjà-vu feeling. Carey inherited a hostile and dysfunctional national union bureaucracy; at the local level, scores of Teamster affiliates were cesspools of corruption, headed by crooks and thugs of all sorts. Like the Boyle forces in the UMW, Teamster regional barons remained bitter foes of the new reform administration. They had been ousted from the executive board, stripped of costly perks, and then deprived of additional paychecks for their multiple union positions by a TDU-backed reformer. Much of the Teamster officialdom, though not corrupt, nevertheless feared and disliked Carey's strong commitment to rallying the rank and file in contract campaigns and strikes. That approach to union bargaining was perceived as undermining "local autonomy"— that is, the ability of IBT officials to negotiate any kind of sweetheart contract with management.

Outside the union, Carey's "New Teamsters" were now feted and applauded in the liberal and labor circles that had largely ignored them in 1991. In 1995, the 1.4 million votes cast by the IBT at the AFL-CIO convention provided the margin of victory for John Sweeney's "New Voice" slate in the first contested election at the federation in one hundred years. Sweeney became the AFL's reform-oriented new president and Rich Trumka was elected secretary-treasurer. Both owed their jobs to the success of the Teamster reform movement.

Counter-Revolution (eith a Brand Name)

A Teamster counter-revolution began brewing from the moment Carey took over. It produced the well-financed 1996 presidential candidacy of James P. Hoffa, a lawyer from Michigan who had never been a working member of the union, except in summer jobs arranged by his father when he was IBT president. Hoffa Senior was one of the best-known labor leaders in the nation before he was imprisoned in 1967, later pardoned by Richard Nixon, then kidnapped and killed by the Mafia in 1975.

Carey defeated Hoffa in 1996—by a mere 16,000 votes—but in a tainted fashion that sadly shortened reform-oriented rule in the Teamsters. Carey's career came crashing down in "Teamster Donorgate," a reelection campaign-financing scandal that ensnared many, inside and outside the union, including Rich Trumka, then secretary-treasurer of the AFL-CIO (and now its president). Trumka took the Fifth Amendment when he was questioned before a federal grand jury about the federation's role in a complicated contribution swap scheme arranged by various Carey campaign consultants, vendors, or union staff members. Those mainly responsible pled guilty, receiving fines and no jail time. One participant in the scheme, the Teamsters' political director, was tried, convicted, and jailed. Carey himself was forced from office by the union's court-appointed overseers in late 1997, later banned from the union, and indicted for perjury. He denied any knowledge of the campaign funding violations and was acquitted in federal court four years after he left office. Carey's lifetime exclusion from Teamster activity remained in effect. Trumka was never charged.

Carey's political demise was a tragedy for some but a propaganda victory for others who feared and opposed him. In the demonology of current Teamster leaders, Carey was a hypocrite who left the union in financial trouble and personal disgrace. Even though he was acquitted (unlike three of his predecessors, including Hoffa's father), Carey's entanglement in the scandal gave his Teamster foes a damaging new storyline, which tapped in to deep wells of worker cynicism and despair. "Mr. Clean" was a "fraud" and a "crook" himself, no better than any other Teamster bad guy ousted from the union, before or since. When the 1996 presidential election was overturned and rerun, Hoffa won the first of his now four presidential campaigns. He has been trying to turn the clock back ever since, although key structural changes made with TDU backing during the Carey era have proven hard to undo.

During his six years in office, Ron Carey was no Arnold Miller, a tortured soul out of his depth and element in Washington. Like Miller, Carey never felt comfortable in his new union headquarters world (where a sycophantic culture of political hustling and unprincipled "consulting" would, in the end, contribute to his undoing). He much preferred hanging out with working Teamsters in Queens, not politicians or the top union officials who mix with them inside the Beltway. He was a workhorse, not a show horse, a hands-on handler of Local 804 members' daily problems. His finest hour came in 1997 when the presence of someone at the top of the union who believed in the power of those at the base made it possible for 185,000 UPS workers to win the biggest nationwide strike in the last thirty years. A key step in building their contract campaign was taking sixteen UPS activists off the job to work as full-time membership mobilizers for a year before the contract expired. Working in TDU activist fashion in UPS hubs and terminals throughout the country, they surveyed members, held parking lot meetings, orchestrated quickie job actions, and expanded the union's existing steward network, even where local officials were hostile to their efforts.

Facing Down "Big Brown"

Carey was at his best during UPS national bargaining because he knew the company like the back of his hand. He went to the table with a team of thirty that included, for the first time, rank-and-filers just off the truck or loading dock. On the other side sat an equal number of arrogant "Big Brown" managers and lawyers. He loved jousting with the top brass, but unlike his tainted predecessors, he was not about bluff and bluster followed by backing down. When UPS wouldn't drop its demand for contract concessions, despite record profits at the time, Carey countered with coordinated Teamster rallies around the country. When there was still no progress in the talks, he broke them off and ramped up the union's carefully planned member mobilization. UPS found itself beset with job actions and negative publicity about its plan to replace even more full-time workers with part-timers, while undermining their defined-benefit pension coverage.

As the contract deadline neared and it was clear that UPS management wouldn't budge, Carey privately agonized about the enormous cost and disruption of a national walkout for UPS workers and their families. He knew that taking on the company was risky and a favorable outcome far from assured. Strike action by such a relatively well-off group could easily have become the focus of much public resentment, just as autoworkers today are being unfairly pilloried for their past gains.

To avert such a backlash, the Teamsters under Carey used direct rank-and-file outreach to friends, neighbors, customers, and local communities to turn their struggle into a popular cause. During the fifteen-day strike, Carey became a convincing national spokesperson not just for his own members, but for all workers concerned about the "part-timing of America." But, with each passing day, the pressure on him was enormous. Internally, many local union officials—more accustomed to accommodation than agitation—were petrified by the tumult around them. Externally, major employers began demanding that the government get a Taft-Hartley injunction to force UPS strikers back to work. Leading Democrats, inside and outside the White House, tried to put the arm on Carey with this threat as well, but he brushed them off and soldiered on, until UPS threw in the towel. The result was a rare strike win, an inspiring victory for all of labor, at a time when workers had little else to cheer about.

To Teamsters for a Democratic Union (TDU) and other members whose votes made him the first directly elected leader of the International Brotherhood of Teamsters (IBT) Carey was a genuine hero. In a union where to this day few local officers dare to cast their lot with the reform movement, the pugnacious ex-Marine and former UPS-driver from Queens was a unique ally of TDU's nearly forty-year campaign for union democracy and leadership accountability. The memory of Carey's contribution to institutional reform and key contract fights is keen indeed among reformers who keep hope alive in the IBT. He will also be long remembered by those who lament that the full potential of democratic unionism—so dramatically on display during the UPS strike—is rarely realized today.[11]

2—SHOP FLOOR PATRIOTISM, RANK-AND-FILE DISSENT

In the 1970s, thousands of recently radicalized Sixties activists decided to "colonize" industrial workplaces under the tutelage of various left-wing groups. They found no tougher nut to crack than military contractors. Not only could the working conditions be as oppressive and dehumanizing as those in any steel mill, auto plant, or coal mine but, as former Raytheon worker Jean Alonso reveals in her memoir, *The Patriots: An Inside Look at Life in a Defense Plant,* assembly-line agitators in this sector also had to confront militarism, misguided patriotism, and more than the usual amount of blue-collar machismo.

Alonso's book and Dana Cloud's *We Are the Union: Democratic Unionism and Dissent at Boeing* provide complementary perspectives on local union politics and the culture of defense industry work.[12] Both authors offer a wealth of instructive detail for academics and activists interested in the mechanics of local union reform in any setting. They also delineate the pros and cons of "cooperative labor relations" as a job security and union survival strategy at firms like Raytheon and Boeing.

Alonso begins her insightful account of factory conditions at Raytheon by describing the tense atmosphere there just before the first Gulf War. The Patriot missiles that she helped to produce, with soldering iron in hand, were much in demand because the United States was about to pummel Baghdad from the air and then evict Saddam Hussein's army from Kuwait, with a ground war launched from Saudi Arabia. Even in liberal Massachusetts, "Yellow Ribbon" fever—pro-war sentiment—was running high among her fellow members of the International Brotherhood of Electrical Workers (IBEW).

Alonso was a Harvard graduate, with a master's degree in English from Tufts, whose personal turn toward the working class was inspired by her "glory days and dark nights in several socialist groups" in the 1970s. By 1990, she was fifty-three, and a financially hard-pressed single mother of two children. Like any other Raytheon worker, she needed a paycheck to support her family. She had been a member of IBEW Local 1505 for thirteen years, long enough for the factory to become "my second home, my second family, my life's work." In a wry description of her in-plant persona, she writes:

I build transformers for missiles and, in my dreams, peace and grassroots rank-and-file power. . . . People like to appraise my politics, which make them both wary and amused. Sometimes, I feel on display—amazing, the pet radical, the only one in captivity, here at least. The one they have personally domesticated, fed, sheltered, and taken civic responsibility to contain. Odd, but theirs, and useful at times. A few years ago, they got fed up with how the union ignored all their grievances, so they voted me in as shop steward. "You're a thorn in their sides, Jean," they would chuckle, knowing that for conservative folks like them to send a radical woman into the ranks of the union officials was a nice shot across the bow.

Saddam Hussein's own shot across the bow in Kuwait had already made things more difficult for anyone dreaming of a more peaceful world back in Massachusetts. The Bay State's own liberal-leaning congressional delegation favored further use of sanctions against Iraq before commencing formal hostilities in the Middle East. But when Alonso made a motion at a local union meeting to support these Democratic critics of the Bush administration, she was roundly booed.

It was not the first time the Boston-based author took a brave stand on behalf of unpopular causes, which were much easier to support in her own inner-city neighborhood. ("At least I'm not a weirdo in Dorchester," she tells a coworker, when discussing her participation in a peace vigil there. "Jeannie, let me give you some advice," her fellow IBEW member said. "Don't try it in the parking lot here, all right?") Outside the plant gate, Alonso's factory had long been picketed by Catholic war resisters and others in "the SANE-Freeze movement." To many Raytheon workers, these protests seemed to target and stigmatize them personally. Even Alonso would at times "feel resentful that the peace people didn't seem to understand the world of working people and our limited options and looked down on us for making weapon parts." Immersed in her new blue-collar world, she also found herself "getting annoyed at middle-class parties. I was resenting privileged types. And one day I awoke to the fact that I had acquired the often disguised, hidden, internal hallmark of many working-class people: a sense of inferiority."

Allies in the Plant

Much of Alonso's book recounts conversations held, over a period of years, with a diverse group of coworkers who met outside the plant to share ideas and experiences, support one another, and better understand the problematic culture and psychology of their own workplace. Members of this racially integrated circle included middle-aged workers and younger men and women, married and single people. For the participants, these consciousness-raising sessions clearly became a haven in a hard-ass blue-collar world, a place of refuge from "narrow-minded, conformist patriotism" in the plant.

Inside the IBEW, simply acting as a free-thinking steward was no day at the beach either. At one "mandatory union retreat for stewards" held on Cape Cod, Alonso was one of only three critics of the Local 1505 leadership among hundreds of stewards attending the training. Before it was over, an IBEW business agent, backed up by another man, pushed her into a dark corner.

> Both started yelling that, with my pro-peace beliefs, I represented a threat to U.S. security just by working at the company. I denied it and excused myself to go into the room where dinner was being served. I chose a table at random and started to sit down, only to have one of the B.A.'s henchman yell, "I won't have Alonso the Red, at my table!" He tipped the table over toward me, sending china and food flying.

Eventually, the company and the union conspired to put Alonso "into receivership as steward," as one worker described her removal from office—because "she spent too much time on the members' grievances." Nevertheless, broader membership frustration over the dysfunction of their local finally reached the boiling point. In 1984, Raytheon workers mounted the first major challenge to incumbent local officers and board members in thirty-five years. Before this electoral campaign, it was just Alonso and a few other dissenters who "elicited shouting about 'commies in our midst' at union meetings when anyone brought up a question." Now, "hundreds of very moderate rank-and-file members also got red-baited, which was downright frightening for most workers." (By the mid-1980s, one key leader of the IBEW at Raytheon had been elevated to the presidency of the Massachusetts AFL-CIO, where he spent much time and energy red-baiting left-wingers in other unions.)

The experience of open rebellion proved to be quite liberating for some of Alonso's friends. They had long chafed under the rule of a right-wing company union that turned a blind eye to contract violations, not to mention racism, sexism, and outright misogyny on the shop floor. As an African American coworker recalls in *The Patriots*, "It was the first time that damn

union ever saw a slate of officers that had black people and women on it . .
. Like we used to say, 'The Union is Us!' All of us, black, white or purple.
Not to mention being willing to strike for the first time in thirty-five years."
Within the local's burgeoning reform movement, members experienced
real solidarity for the first time, while building something new within the
shell of the old. As one younger worker told Alonso:

> Remember how wonderful it felt to go to campaign meetings—no
> intimidation and ridicule like at union meetings. There'd be hun-
> dreds of us from all over who didn't really know each other. But the
> atmosphere of respect was awesome. I think we shared a dream of
> overcoming the low, mean relations [in the plant]. Of creating a new
> little world—we just called it a new union. And we almost had it.

The reformers' bid for office fell tragically short, by a few hundred
votes in 1984. The opposition candidate for business manager—the top
elected position in the local—did not appeal the questionable official
tally. "He decided not to contest the union's many violations of federal
laws governing union elections, knowing that everyone, even management and the incumbents' own supporters, expected him to win the next
election by a landslide."

Death of a Reformer

Sadly, that rematch never occurred. The sudden death of the reform
movement's leader several years later so disheartened some of his
supporters that they just gave up and quit the company. Others who
remained at Raytheon, fell into organizational disarray. Alonso hints
darkly at management's behind-the-scenes role in the resulting "collapse
into frightened silence."

> Our production work was strategic to the power of the State, sup-
> plying the deadly force that underwrote it. Therefore, like certain
> oil-producing regions, we had to be kept under strict surveillance
> and control. The union was too strategic, the guarantor of a no-
> strike, stable and compliant workforce. A reformed union, subject

to the uncertainties of strikes, independent investigations, and participatory democracy, must have been judged to have an unacceptable level of risk.

Four years after the reformers' election defeat, Alonso and others in that campaign regrouped around the more modest demand that IBEW Local 1505 create an official women's committee. This rank-and-file organizing project proved to be no less threatening to the old leadership. So a "guerilla women's group" was formed, which proceeded to bombard "the hall" with "examples of contractual sexual harassment policies from other unions," like the then-smaller "service sector women's unions they were used to lording it over in the state AFL-CIO." Since Raytheon union officials were not about "to insult their skilled trades power base with films or corrective education," Alonso and her female coworkers organized their own program of education about unlawful forms of harassment on the job.

Their unofficial "Women's Action Committee" also surveyed hundreds of female employees about discrimination in pay and promotions. They began agitating for flextime and on-site childcare. In 1989, they won "one big institutional victory—persuading the union to negotiate contract language forbidding sexual harassment." Raytheon's post-contract posting of formal "warnings to men to stop offensive sexual behavior" finally gave women "some backup in departments where it had previously been open season."

Unfortunately, with every step forward, there was always some backsliding as well. In 1990, as Alonso ruefully reports, her women's group "tried cooperation" with a new generation of local union leaders.

We accepted a request not to oppose a slate of officers consisting of the sons of incumbents, in exchange for an official women's committee and a partnership in policy-making. "Let's go forward into the nineties together," they said. When they won, they went back on all those promises. Having exclusive power to appoint all committees under the IBEW's International Constitution, they appointed a women's committee of their allies, which then refused to meet.

In the mid-1990s, several years after Alonso retired, Raytheon recruited the same dutiful "sons of incumbents" to help lobby the state legislature for a big corporate tax break tied to maintaining local employment. The union aided the company because it had already lost thousands of jobs in layoffs, as management moved more of its Pentagon-funded work to a plant in Arizona or lower-cost, non-union contractors. But even after Raytheon got its sweetheart deal, Massachusetts job cuts continued, leaving Local 1505 with only 2,700 members by 1995. (At its peak, the local was more than 10,000 strong.)

In the fall of 2000, under new (and long overdue) reform leadership, IBEW members finally struck the company for five weeks—to resist benefit concessions and further outsourcing. The resulting settlement gave strikers pension improvements, some relief on health care cost shifting, and a new commitment from Raytheon to keep Patriot and Hawk missile production, along with new missile defense work, in its already much downsized Massachusetts plants.

The IAM at Boeing

Dana Cloud's *We Are the Union* is a much larger-scale, more academic case study of similar union controversies at Boeing, the biggest defense contractor in the world. Cloud is a labor historian and professor of communications studies at the University of Texas. For her book, she interviewed would-be reformers (her main focus) and the elected officers and staff members who were often their political adversaries within the International Association of Machinists (IAM) in Kansas and Washington.

Unlike the IBEW at Raytheon in Massachusetts, IAM members have struck Boeing repeatedly in recent decades. Since 1989, Puget Sound aircraft builders have walked out four times and, in 1999–2000, when they didn't, their sister union, the Society of Professional Engineering Employees in Aerospace (SPEEA), staged a forty-day work stoppage. Cloud focuses on the longest of these strikes—a 69-day battle in 1995 that pitted rank-and-file members against management and their own local union negotiators. That walkout began when IAM negotiators recommended rejection of Boeing's "last, best, and final offer"; forty-seven days later, the officialdom was ready to settle short but the strikers were not.

They overwhelmingly rejected a tentative agreement strongly promoted by the union, staying strong on the picket line for another twenty-two days until they got a better deal. This high-profile contract rejection "inspired workers with a sense of their own agency," Cloud argues. "It was an unprecedented moment of rank-and-file self-determination."

At Boeing, like Raytheon, the threat of more radical unionism was suppressed early on, although the challenge of containing indigenous militancy has persisted ever since the 1930s and '40s. In Alonso's book, we learn that some CIO-inspired Raytheon workers wanted to join the "the progressive United Electrical Workers Union," then a powerhouse at General Electric in nearby Lynn, Massachusetts. By the end of the Second World War, the "more cooperative Brotherhood" had gained union recognition instead—"without a fight by the company." After IAM Lodge 751 at Boeing was chartered in 1935, union radicals played a key role in winning a first contract one year later. But, as Cloud reports, the machinists quickly moved to counter the influence of local Communists by expelling fifty Seattle militants from the union and restructuring Lodge 751 "into smaller, atomized lodges that became part of a new District 751."

Six decades later, during the period covered in Cloud's book, the IAM's original top-down structure was still in place, much to the dismay of its modern-day dissenters. Although full-time business representatives, local lodge, and district officers are all chosen by the membership, "stewards in District 751 are appointed, not elected. . . . Similarly, while some unions elect negotiating committees, the negotiating committee is also appointed." If shop stewards were elected, one IAM staffer warned Cloud, "that would be anarchy."

A Patronage Army

Not being able to choose which of their coworkers should be empowered to file grievances and enforce the contract was, of course, a continuing affront to union democrats who, in many cases, were far from being anarchists, socialists, or communists. As Tom Finnegan, an IAM activist in Everett, Washington, explained, a system of appointed stewards takes away "the power of the rank and file on the shop floor to address the issues that we feel are important to us." The union's steward body tends to become part of a patronage army for higher-level elected officials, particularly where "stewards have protected jobs during layoffs" and any display of independence can get them removed from office, as Alonso was in the IBEW. *We Are the Union* further describes various labor-management cooperation programs—particularly in the area of occupational safety and health—that have, in her view, impaired the IAM's ability to improve working conditions on the shop floor. In addition, as in the auto industry, "jointness" has brought "some unionists into quasi-management positions that render the union more aligned with management and leave the union in a weaker position."

Tom Finnegan's opposition caucus—the Rank and File/New Crew at Boeing in Everett, Washington—is one of three local reform groups profiled by Cloud. She also traces the rise and decline of the Machinists for Solidarity, based in Seattle, and the Wichita rank-and-file organization known as Unionists for Democratic Change (UDC). The men and women who risked their jobs and incurred the wrath of Boeing management and the IAM officialdom to build these groups are a thoughtful, formidable, and articulate crew. At critical moments, as Cloud argues, they helped shape "an already palpable rank-and-file upsurge not only against the Boeing Company but local and national union leaders who urged concessions and quietude."

Both Alonso and Cloud deserve many plaudits for bringing these workers' voices so vividly to the printed page, even if the individual and collective stories recounted don't always fit any simple good-vs.-evil narrative about "business unionism" and those bucking it. Both authors make it abundantly clear which side they're on, but, thankfully, let the rank and file do much of the talking. The results are well worth reading, particularly Cloud's extended dialogue (about union reform tactics and strategy) with UDC leader Keith Thomas from Wichita. It's a chronicle of organizational ups and downs, setbacks and successes, personal burnout and some bitterness. But, as Thomas notes, with the publication of *We Are the Union*, "our history isn't forgotten."[13]

3—A DECADE REDISCOVERED (WITH SOME MISSING PIECES)

In his first book, *Capital Moves: RCA's Seventy-Year Quest for Cheap Labor,* Cornell professor Jefferson Cowie used a single compelling case study to illustrate the decline of domestic manufacturing and the rise of overseas outsourcing.[14] Cowie follows RCA's shift of home appliance production from Camden, New Jersey, to plants in Bloomington, Indiana, and Memphis, Tennessee, and then down to Mexico. Not long after *Capital Moves* was published, I arranged for Cowie to speak to a group of shop stewards, including some from manufacturing locals, who were attending a union training program in Ithaca. They were captivated by his account of how corporate globalization affected different groups of workers, here and abroad, in similar fashion. Although quite depressing, Cowie's runaway shop history was a great tool for classroom discussion about the need for global labor solidarity in the face of growing capital mobility and job-killing free trade deals.

Cowie's latest book, *Stayin' Alive: The 1970s and the Last Days of the Working Class,* has been much applauded by fellow academics, but may be more problematic reading for union activists.[15] In 2010, it received the Organization of American Historians (OAH) Merle Curti Prize for the best work published "in American social or intellectual history." According to the OAH, Cowie "moves nimbly between popular culture, campaign and electoral politics, and social science debates to offer a compelling and devastating account of what happened to the working class in the 1970s." However, if I were still bringing CWA members to Cornell, I'd be worried about hosting another book-related talk by Cowie. After all, working-class militants still have to get up the next morning and, as the Reverend Jesse Jackson always helpfully instructed, "Keep hope alive!" The blow to troop morale might be more than any union education program, however book-friendly, could stand.

According to *Stayin' Alive,* blue-collar workers weren't just victims of a runaway shop trend in the 1970s. They actually experienced their "last days" as an entire class. The existence of a working class remains kind of a sine qua non for anyone still trying to mobilize their coworkers or organize new union members (unless all of labor's future recruits are to be found in what the AFL-CIO, with Cowie-like imprecision, calls "the middle class"). For those still on the frontlines of class warfare today, what Cowie's publisher touts as "the definitive account of *the fall of America's working class*" (emphasis added) is deflating reading indeed, since its message seems to be that the union movement's struggle for a better society was defeated thirty years ago. If the contest between capital and labor is already over, a reader might reasonably ask why should workers fight back today, in Wisconsin or anywhere else where their living standards are threatened?

Academics and journalists long overlooked the significance of the 1970s, the decade in which, according to Cowie, "the post–New Deal working class" lost its footing and never regained it, due to the forces of deindustrialization and de-unionization. In the U.S. History section of bookstores, the Seventies used to be sandwiched in, rather thinly, between the much-chronicled era of sex, drugs, rock and roll, and social unrest of the Sixties and the well-known period of conservative backlash in the 1980s dubbed "the Reagan Revolution." But this gap in "periodization" has recently been remedied, for better or worse, by a wave of book publishing, of which *Stayin' Alive* is just one part.

A bellwether of cultural trends, *The Nation* even devoted an entire 2011 cover story to "That Seventies Show." It consisted of a review essay by Rick Perlstein covering fourteen books in addition to Cowie's that analyze the era from various angles. And Perlstein still managed to miss four more, including *Rebel Rank and File: Labor Militancy and Revolt from Below during the Long 1970s*, co-edited by Aaron Brenner, Robert Brenner, and Cal Winslow. As a participant in some of the labor struggles recalled, quite differently, by Cowie and the contributors to *Rebel Rank and File* (of whom I am one), it's hard not to notice that some relevant history is still being downplayed. *Stayin' Alive* is certainly sweeping in scope, often well written, and replete with colorful pop culture references to music, movies, and TV shows that dealt with workers in the Seventies. But the author's account of key union reform struggles launched during that decade is selective, at best, and tinged with cynicism that verges at times on smug condescension.

In my experience, which included Carter-era labor law reform advocacy as a national union staff member in Washington, D.C., workers' struggles in the 1970s were not quite the vessel of the damned and doomed that Cowie makes them out to be today. As the author notes, there was "a national epidemic of industrial unrest in the first half of the 1970s." Hundreds of thousands of workers "fought with supervisors on the line, clogged up the system [of industrial relations] with grievances, demanded changes in the quality of work life, walked out in wildcat strikes, and organized to overthrow stale bureaucratic union leadership." Some of these fights did in fact lay the groundwork for continuing left-labor activism, involving blue-collar workers, many white-collar ones, and younger indigenous militants, still very much alive and kicking today as part of grassroots networks like *Labor Notes*.

In his profiles of "old-fashioned heroes" who led rank-and-file revolts in the United Mine Workers and Steelworkers, Cowie seems intent on proving instead that workplace militancy in the 1970s left "little trace" or "lasting institutional presence in the labor movement." This contention only holds water if you conveniently ignore, as he does, the rank-and-file insurgency with the most durability and organizational impact, Teamsters for a Democratic Union (TDU). Founded in the mid-1970s, TDU was, ultimately, far more of a political force in the Teamsters than either the Miners for Democracy in the UMW or Steelworkers Fightback (the 1976-77 campaign organization of USWA presidential candidate Ed Sadlowski), which *Stayin' Alive* devotes many pages to dissecting, with the help of mainly secondary sources. In 1991, the Teamster reform movement played a central role in Ron Carey's election to the IBT presidency, in the union's first-ever democratic vote; by the mid-1990s, the "new Teamsters" was helping to topple the conservative leadership of the AFL-CIO in the federation's first contested election in one hundred years.

Stayin' Alive's sole reference to this parallel (and much cross-fertilized) "democratization movement" in the Teamsters occurs only in passing during a lengthy discussion of the film *Blue Collar,* Hollywood's rendition of shop floor tensions, union corruption, and racial conflict in the auto industry. TDU itself is never mentioned, either in the text or notes. Cowie's book is supposedly a comprehensive period history. But there is far more in *Stayin' Alive* about *F.I.S.T.*, a clunky Jimmy Hoffa–inspired feature film starring Sylvester Stallone, than there is about real-life Teamsters and their actual union, past or present. Cowie is an enthusiastic Bruce Springsteen

fan and lover of films (like *Saturday Night Fever*) that were far more enter-
taining than *F.I.S.T.* But a reader might ask: if you're a labor historian,
not a rock critic or movie reviewer, why does the depiction of blue-collar
workers by Hollywood (and even Springsteen's stirring ballads about
union men) warrant more attention than 1970s-inspired struggles within
the nation's biggest blue-collar union that had a real impact?

The political lessons and organizing experiences from the 1970s were
not simply forgotten or discarded. Despite the setbacks and defeats suffered by the working class as traditionally defined—predominantly male
blue-collar workers in heavy industry—there was still a "working class"
at the end of the decade. Over subsequent decades, veterans of labor
insurgency continued to promote progressive causes and ideas within the
labor movement, organize union reform campaigns, establish alternative
labor education and media projects, and support successful workplace
organizing and community-labor coalition building that contributed to
union leadership changes at various levels. The union democracy and
reform activity of the 1970s still has influence today in the form of lasting
institutions that were created back then, like TDU. Members of several
unions still benefit from the structural changes secured by internal reform
movements, which used grassroots organizing to give real meaning to the
union members' "Bill of Rights" supposedly guaranteed by the Landrum-
Griffin Act.

As even Cowie admits in his conclusion, there is, in our "postmodern,
global age," an even more exploited "post–New Deal working class." It
includes millions of immigrant workers, displaced from their home countries by civil conflict or the economic forces unleashed by free trade. Their
own impressive insurgent impulses were well displayed on May Day, 2006,
in the largest political strike in recent U.S. history.

Even in some past bastions of racism, sexism, and patriarchy—labor
sins that much preoccupy Cowie—"the times they are a changin'." In the
Teamsters, for example, one challenger for the union presidency is none
other than Alexandra (Sandy) Pope, a product of 1970s labor insurgency
in both the private and public sector and, of course, a leading member of
the unmentioned TDU. Hardly a "one-dimensional working-class hero,"
of the sort that Cowie is prone to caricature and trivialize, Pope is a left-
leaning Hampshire College dropout, a former truck driver and local union

organizer in Ohio, who served with distinction at Teamster headquarters under Ron Carey. She now leads a Teamster local in Queens, New York, that's been very active in defending the rights of the foreign-born.

Forgive me if I'm cherry-picking here—"optimists of the will" tend to do that—but I think there's hope yet for America's battered working class, old and new. It's just sad to see that some of labor's academic historians— and it doesn't have that many—spend so much time at the movies, with their headphones on, trying to figure out which way the wind is (or has been) blowing.[16]

4—*VIVA* LAS VEGAS?

Behind every good man, one finds a good woman, or so we're told. In the International Brotherhood of Teamsters (IBT), circa 2011, this traditional supportive relationship was reversed—at least in Sandy Pope's pathbreaking campaign for the union presidency. At the Teamsters' nominating convention, held in the Nevada desert playground most favored by union meeting planners, it was a small band of good men (plus a handful of their union sisters) who rallied successfully behind this very unusual woman. As a result of their organizing efforts, Pope—the candidate backed by Teamsters for a Democratic Union (TDU)—made it into the final stage of a three-way race that will be decided in mail-ballot voting by 1.3 million IBT members.

Nominated along with Pope, president of Local 805 in New York City, was fellow opposition candidate Fred Gegare, a Teamster regional leader from Wisconsin and dissident member of the union's international executive board. Gegare and Pope each received just over 8 percent of the vote among several thousand locally elected delegates (a minimum of 5 percent was necessary to be nominated). Current IBT president James P. Hoffa and his slate won the backing of more than 83 percent of the participants in a convention clearly dominated and controlled by the incumbent leadership.

Pope is one of only sixteen women now serving as principal local officers in a union with more than 400 local affiliates and 400,000 female members in the United States and Canada. A former executive director of the Coalition of Labor Union Women, she has launched a direct assault on the glass ceiling for Teamster women, drawing on her years of experience as a rank-and-file agitator, local union organizer, labor educator, and tenacious contract negotiator. ("Before cell phones," Pope says, "my CB handle was 'Troublemaker'—and I earned it.") A divorced mother of two adult children, Pope turns fifty-five this year, but looks a lot younger, thanks to her many years of kickboxing and running.

Pledging to restore the "fighting spirit" that she believes has been missing in the IBT since Hoffa took over, Pope has been campaigning around the country. At every stop, she points out that Hoffa's total compensation is now $362,889 a year, at a time when tens of thousands of Teamsters are losing their jobs, pay, or benefits due to the recession and contract concessions. Pope has pledged to take a presidential pay cut, shore up the union's financially troubled benefit funds, and end Hoffa's practice of doling out additional salaries to more than 140 officials who already collect between one and three other union paychecks. According to TDU, this costly form of patronage squanders about $12 million annually. Pope says she would put that money to use in better coordinated national campaigns to organize non-union employers in core Teamster industries.

The Blowout at Bally's

Unfortunately, amid the glitzy distractions of Bally's Hotel and Casino, not too many Teamster convention-goers will pay much attention to Pope or Gegare's critique of business as usual. Instead, the 5,000 delegates, alternates, retirees, wives, and girlfriends will be treated to a five-day-long series of staff- and consultant-crafted speeches, resolutions and video presentations, plus greetings from various celebrities, politicians, and other dignitaries. Their taxing daily work schedule will begin at 9:30 a.m, include a lunch break lasting two hours or more, followed by an afternoon session that ends by 4:30 sharp. By final adjournment, more than $10 million worth of membership dues money will have been spent on a meeting largely devoid of substance.

Just before the official proceedings got under way, several thousand dutiful, placard-waving supporters of Hoffa and his running mate for secretary-treasurer, Ken Hall, packed Bally's palm-tree-lined driveway for a campaign pep rally. Most were wearing the ubiquitous red vests of the "Hoffa-Hall Team," an additional cause of sweating in the already-searing desert sun. Rally organizers used a huge set of speakers to warm up the crowd with a musical soundtrack that ranged from "Viva Las Vegas" by Elvis to Chumbawamba's more contemporary (but equally appropriate) ode to "pissing the night away." Hoffa campaign cheerleaders then led his supporters through a series of chest-thumping chants. The most rousing seemed to be "Don't think small, vote Hoffa-Hall!"—a slogan that clearly resonated in a crowd trending toward Triple X in its T-shirt size.

The stumpy, bombastic seventy-year-old Teamster leader soon took the stage to lead his own cheer: "Five More Years! Five More Years!" President Hoffa announced his great personal satisfaction at seeing, in front of him, nothing but "a sea of red" that was just "unbelievable." This is, he assured his audience, "a great moment in history and you are part of history." He closed his speech with a faintly ominous reminder that it was time to "go in and make sure we kick some ass and win this." (Hoffa was not talking here about any posterior in corporate America, but rather the hindquarters, male and female, of his internal opposition.)

After the sea of red reassembled in the convention center, with a few hundred dissenters now in their midst, the overhead lights were dimmed and the sound of Harleys filled the hall. The huge stage and delegate section in the front of the room were briefly encircled by a Teamster honor guard on wheels, gunning its engines to the sounds of The Who belting out "Won't Get Fooled Again"—an odd selection by an incumbent running for a fourth term. Hoffa then made his own grand appearance to the strains of the Stones' "Street Fighting Man," an even more ironic form of musical accompaniment.

Introductions of the Teamster executive board and division directors provided an opportunity for lusty booing of Gegare, a defector from the Hoffa camp who took more than a decade to discover that just having a famous last name is not a sufficient leadership credential in the Teamsters or any union. One delegate not the slightest bit rattled by this intimidating behavior was John Lattanzio, a mustachioed fifty-seven-year-old freight handler from Spokane. Prior to the convention, he was part of the grassroots network for Pope that helped her sign up 50,000 rank-and-file supporters. "If you got out of line at these conventions in the past," he observed, "they just knocked you on your ass. At least no one is getting beat up this year."

A Rank-and-File Reality Check

Lattanzio works at the troubled Teamster freight carrier known as YRCW. Along with his coworkers, he has suffered a 15 percent pay cut and faces the loss of defined benefit pension coverage and other contract protections as well. So he found the chest-thumping convention rhetoric of top Teamster officials to be out of touch with workplace reality in the trucking industry. "We used to have 2.2 million members," he says with a mixture of wonderment and disgust. "Now we're down to 1.3 million Teamsters and these assholes are bragging about it?" Lattanzio believes that many local union officials are privately "scared to death." "They realize things need to change or we're dead. Even Fred Gegare, who's on Hoffa's own executive board, can see that the union is not going in the right direction."

Lattanzio and his fellow delegates from Spokane got to Las Vegas the hard way, because none of them are full-time union officials. They ran as rank-and-filers, pledged to Pope, and defeated a slate of pro-Hoffa Local 690 officers and executive board members in a Teamster affiliate with 3,000 members. Lattanzio's closest collaborator is fellow TDU activist, Tim Hill who works as a feeder driver at United Parcel Service in Spokane. In Las Vegas, both handed out Pope flyers, talked to other delegates who are working members (a minority of those attending), and posted nightly accounts of their convention activity on YouTube, Facebook, and the "Local 690/Teamsters United" website. At a "Pope for President" fundraiser that raised $15,000 in cash and pledges, Hill donated a week's pay—$800—to the campaign, even though he had worked only five full weeks in the first six months of the year.

Lattanzio is a second-generation TDU member, following in the footsteps of his father, Rocky, a former Local 690 official who is now eighty and suffering from Parkinson's disease. John became a union dissident in the 1970s after returning from a tour of duty in Vietnam and getting a Teamster job. Rocky attended the 1976 Teamster convention in Las Vegas, where Pete Camarata, an early leader of TDU, was beaten by union goons. Camarata had just spoken out on the floor against the inflated and, often, multiple salaries of the Teamster officialdom, a problem that persists today. He then further enraged the leadership by casting the only delegate vote against Frank Fitzsimmons, a member of his own Local 299 in Detroit, who was running for reelection as IBT president.

Four decades ago, the IBT had no well-developed reform caucus yet. There was no direct election of top officers and executive board members, or any type of judicial oversight. The union was a cesspool of mob influence, benefit fund corruption, labor racketeering, and violence against dissidents like Camarata. Among the union gangsters at the 1976 convention were those from Delaware and New Jersey later suspected of killing James R. Hoffa, the convicted felon and former IBT president who sired the current one. Lauded by his son at the 2011 convention as "the greatest Teamster ever," Hoffa senior disappeared without a trace.

Camarata is now retired from the Teamsters after a long career as a rank-and-file activist in Detroit. He was back in Las Vegas as a convention guest and observer. At a dinner gathering with Local 690 delegates, he recalled his first encounter with John Lattanzio's father thirty-five years before. "It took a lot of nerve for Rocky to come up and say he was with us. I had no friends at all at that convention," Camarata said. After witnessing TDU's initial skirmishing with the union leadership in Las Vegas, the Lattanzios invited Camarata to speak in Spokane. Following a script that hasn't varied much since, local Teamster officials tried to red-bait their visitor and his local hosts. Soon the word was out on the street that Pete "Commie-rata," a notorious radical from Detroit, was coming to town.

John Lattanzio's mother was "not afraid of anything," he says. But, knowing what her husband and son were up against in the IBT of that era, even she was worried. "What are you involved in?" she asked Rocky. John Lattanzio had to empty his own personal savings account to line up a hotel banquet room for the local TDU fundraiser and recruitment meeting that featured Camarata. The event was a big success and helped establish the local TDU chapter that, two years later, backed Rocky's successful run for the Local 690 presidency, an early victory for the national reform movement. Now, like his father before him, John Lattanzio is mentoring and supporting younger TDUers in the same local.

TDU's Next Generation

The most active among them is Tim Hill, a thirty-three-year-old with long sideburns, colorful tattoos on both arms, and a political affinity for the Industrial Workers of the World (IWW). Hill's Wobbly ties and active grievance-filing almost got him fired early in his twelve-year Teamster career when he was working as a part-time package sorter for UPS. The charge was sabotage. The supporting "evidence" included IWW tracts downloaded by a UPS labor relations manager and cited at his dismissal hearing. His discharge was changed to a month-long suspension, a result that could have been worse, because the Local 690 business agent who represented Hill was sympathetic to the company's position.[17]

Lattanzio and Hill believe there's a new political opening for the reform movement, locally and nationally. "People are ready for a change," Lattanzio says. "It's a whole lot different because of what's happening in UPS, grocery, and freight. In 1967, the NMFA [National Master Freight Agreement] was so strong, so solid, that everyone got to live a normal home life and we had decent working conditions." Now, at YRCW, "they're able to work us 11 or 12 hours a day continuously," with variable start times, and a backlogged grievance procedure that does little to curb contracting-out and other contract violations.

As Camarata, Lattanzio, Hill, and others similarly adorned in Pope campaign buttons wrapped up their dinner discussion at a watering hole near Bally's, a hulking Teamster delegate, who had been eyeing the group all evening, got up and came over from a nearby table. A prison guard back home, he wanted to wish the Local 690 delegates well. Both he and a heavily muscled companion were troubled by the heavy-handed convention chairing and incessant booing of opposition delegates that made it impossible for Pope or Gegare supporters to be heard on any issue. "We're Hoffa-Hall," he said, with an embarrassed shrug. "But we don't agree with what's been going on. This is America and people have a right to disagree."

Unfortunately, those delegates unafraid to disagree numbered only about 300, supporters of both Pope and Gegare. On Friday morning of convention week, after the two opposition candidates had been nominated, John Lattanzio was among those delegates who joined Pope on stage when she proudly delivered her twenty-minute acceptance speech. The main hall at Bally's was nearly empty. Rather than listening to what Pope and Gegare had to say, all the other delegates walked out, either eagerly or just to be team players, in a final display of convention support for Hoffa.[18]

POSTSCRIPT

When Sandy Pope ran for secretary-treasurer of the Teamsters on a TDU-backed slate in 2006, she and her running mate, Tom Leedham, received 36 percent of the membership vote. Five years later, the combined anti-Hoffa vote among the 250,000 Teamsters who cast ballots was slightly larger—and more than twice the percentage of the delegate vote garnered by Pope and Gegare in Las Vegas. But a three-way presidential race did not favor Pope the way it did Ron Carey in 1991.

The seventy-year-old incumbent was reelected, with 59 percent of the vote, for another five-year term. Under pressure from Pope's candidacy, Hoffa did add two women to his slate for the union's twenty-two-member executive board; both were elected, providing more female representation at the top than before the 2011 election. Campaigning with a near-full slate (which Pope purposely did not do), Gegare got 23 percent and drew more votes away from the reform movement's past base of support than he did from Hoffa's own. The efforts of Gegare's running mates forced many on Hoffa's slate to campaign for their own reelection. This boosted turnout efforts for Hoffa, at the top of their ticket. As a result, Pope placed a disappointing third, with 17 percent of the membership vote.

According to his campaign financing reports, Hoffa raised $3 million, much of that money from Teamster officials who owe their positions to him or benefit from his patronage in other ways. As TDU organizer Ken Paff noted, Hoffa "did multiple mailings to all 1.3 million members, the bulk of them devoted to vicious attacks on Sandy Pope." In contrast, with $200,000 in rank-and-file contributions, Pope could only afford to do targeted mailings to less than 20 percent of the union's membership and relied heavily on volunteer phone banking for her GOTV effort.

5—RAISING HELL ON WHEELS

The rise and fall of union reformers is a familiar story in American labor. It's commonplace enough to make some labor observers rather cynical about the project of union democracy and reform. The day-to-day demands of full-time elected office, combined with heavy pressure to conform to the norms of business unionism, has pushed more than a few rank-and-file heroes down the primrose path, sooner or later. After some opposition candidates get elected, their "Si se puede!" campaign rhetoric has been known to give way to a litany of excuses about why "we can't" empower members, fight the boss, or rebuild the union, as promised before the election.

There are, fortunately, always some committed activists ready to push the boulder of reform back up the hill again, after political setbacks and disappointments. But starting over is never easy. It requires regaining the confidence of fellow workers who may now be angry, frustrated, and disillusioned by the actual or perceived failure of previous union insurgencies. Two iconic labor organizations, Transport Workers Union (TWU) Local 100 and Teamsters Local 804, provide an important case study in how this can still be accomplished through persistent rank-and-file organizing.

TWU represents 38,000 subway worker and bus driver members in New York City. In 2000, a Caribbean-born track worker, bearing the name of a great eighteenth-century Haitian liberator, took office as the presidential candidate of the "New Directions" caucus in Local 100. Roger Toussaint was a battle-tested militant, with a left-wing political background, who had once been fired for his union activity. Toussaint's allies in New Directions had contested many earlier elections, less successfully. They had also spent two decades or more trying to strengthen the union, from the bottom up, through workplace agitation and organizing, a story well told in *Hell on Wheels*, a TWU reform movement history penned by Steve Downs, a train operator and now a member of the Local 100 executive board.[19]

Once Toussaint took office, as Downs recounts, it didn't take him long to create a personal patronage machine, rather than "the democratic, member-run union that New Directions and thousands of the local's members had fought for." Reform of the local became "a top-down, staff-driven process.... Officers and members who pushed for a more participatory approach were frozen out." As a result, Local 100 was in weak organizational shape when it skimped on contract campaigning in 2005 and then conducted a brave but bungled strike against the Metropolitan Transportation Authority. The dispute ended with much internal discord, costly fines for both members and their union, and loss of automatic dues deduction. Toussaint himself was briefly jailed, another unfair consequence of Local 100's violation of the New York State law banning public sector strikes. The contract settlement, which included benefit give-backs, was rejected narrowly by the membership but later imposed by an arbitrator.

The combination of worker dissatisfaction, organizational disarray, and a temporary "open shop" (due to the punitive suspension of TWU's dues check-off deal) led to nearly 50 percent of the MTA bargaining unit no longer being in good membership standing after the strike. The local's deeply eroded and demoralized stewards' network, long neglected by Toussaint, was unable to hand-collect dues effectively or do much else to enforce the contract, except in remaining pockets of workplace self-organization and activity. Four years after the subway walkout, as many as 17,000 former strikers still owed as much as $900 in back dues and were no longer eligible to vote or attend union meetings because they couldn't or wouldn't pay what they owed.

Meanwhile, one year after the strike, the increasingly unpopular Toussaint had to rely on a divided field of challengers to win reelection with only 43 percent of the vote. Rather than work to reunify and rebuild the local, his administration continued to remove staff and sideline elected Local 100 officials who dared to express dissenting views about the direction of the local. Some of those pushed out began to plan for the next election, three years away.

A Teamster Legacy Tarnished

In Teamsters Local 804, based in Queens, the trajectory from militancy to complacency, demobilization, and ineffectual unionism occurred in lower-profile fashion. Local 804 is the home local of Ron Carey. In the 1970s and '80s, under Carey's leadership, the local was a formidable island of rank-and-file resistance to the largest Teamster employer in the country, United Parcel Service. In those days, Local 804 members were surrounded by mobbed-up Teamster locals in New York City and New Jersey; even those Teamster affiliates without such problems tended to be overly cozy with UPS management, to the detriment of their own dues payers.

In 1989–91, Carey joined forces with Teamsters for a Democratic Union (TDU) to wage a successful grassroots campaign to oust old-guard officials at the national union level. Carey's six tumultuous years as Teamster president in Washington culminated with the union's 1997 strike victory over UPS. Shortly thereafter Carey was forced to step down from office in a reelection campaign fund-raising scandal, which also led to his indictment. Acquitted of all charges in 2001, Carey remained painfully banned from having any contact with his former coworkers in 804, until his death from cancer seven years later.

Over time, Carey's successors in the leadership of this 7,000-member UPS local drifted into the camp of current Teamster president James Hoffa. This defection did not sit well with longtime TDU activists and Carey supporters in the local like UPS driver Tim Sylvester. In 2007, Local 804 officers gladly went along with a Hoffa-engineered UPS contract settlement that gave away contract language, won ten years before under Carey, that forced management to convert thousands of part-time jobs into full-time ones. So Tim Sylvester and other dissidents campaigned successfully for membership rejection of the Local 804 local supplement to the UPS national contract. Management was forced to resume negotiations, locally, and put a better offer on the table for 804. The final deal with UPS in New York City reversed a 30 percent pension cut, stopped a proposed wage reduction, and saved the "25 & Out" retirement option that was the key legacy of the Carey years.

Carey's benighted successors did not handle this situation gracefully, since it didn't bode well for their own reelection prospects in 2009. When Carey died of cancer in December 2008, Local 804 officials made the further mistake of failing to attend his wake or even send flowers to the funeral home. At a TDU-organized memorial service several months later, hundreds of UPS workers showed up, angry and determined to avenge the slight and take back their union.

Take Back Our Union

In Local 100, that's exactly what the reorganized reform forces called themselves—Take Back Our Union (TBOU). By the time balloting was held in Local 100 in late 2009, Roger Toussaint had fled for a high-paid staff job with the TWU's not very helpful national organization. In his previous incarnations as a rank-and-file militant and, briefly, reform leader of Local 100, Toussaint had been a big critic of TWU headquarters in Washington, which failed to support the 2005 strike. Now he worked to ensure that someone aligned with the national union succeeded him.

Standing in the way of that plan was John Samuelsen, a stocky, stubborn Brooklyn-born Local 100 vice president with a long history of activism around track safety issues and the fight against contracting out. In December 2009, Samuelsen's multiracial TBOU slate won all four local-wide officer positions, including the presidency and four out of seven VP slots. In his own race for the top job, Samuelsen won by nearly 900 votes out of more than 10,000 cast. That same month, more than 1,000 voters than ever before showed up to help elect Local 804's new officers and executive board members. The TDU-assisted "804 Members United" slate, headed by Tim Sylvester, won all eleven seats, by a two-to-one margin.

In both races, the reform agendas were strikingly similar. Samuelsen stressed the need for an "open, democratic union," "member-driven, clean of corruption," and "single-minded in its resolve to break the cycle of concessionary bargaining." Noting that "we're not going to be able to fix all the problems overnight," Sylvester outlined a ten-point program "to build a stronger Local 804 by tapping the power of an informed and organized membership."

Unusual among U.S. trade union officials today, Samuelsen has a singular focus on "building rank-and-file power and reestablishing union strength in the workplace." At a day-long transition planning discussion, held with ninety TBOU supporters before he took office, Samuelsen kept returning to the theme that Local 100 wouldn't become a "powerhouse" in New York City labor again until it first rebuilt "layers of density" on the shop floor, fought to "control the pace of work," and tackled, rather than ignored, day-to-day problems like the "disgusting condition" of subway employee bathrooms.

Samuelsen also talked about the centrality of elected shop stewards who can't simply be replaced with "loyal bums" at the whim of a local union president. He believes stewards should be trained and encouraged to deal directly with management as "on-site dispute handlers" and key contract enforcers. In the legislative/political arena, Local 100 should rely less on high-priced lobbyists and consultants or union check-writing to politicians. He wants more rank-and-file members to run for office themselves and pressure public officials directly, in their own neighborhoods and communities.

Only forty-two when he announced his candidacy—and thus young by U.S. union leader standards—Samuelsen is very concerned about the challenge of reaching and engaging younger, newly hired transit workers. In one campaign message directed their way, he warned that MTA management has "stepped up its abuse of our members and routinely violates our contract." The local's post-strike abandonment of "any real attempt to mobilize the membership to defend our jobs" has produced a union "in full retreat on safety, discipline, job picks, and seniority rights."

Now charged with the task of actually stopping that retreat and going on the offensive, Samuelsen and Sylvester will need all the help they can get from rank-and-filers, young and old, in their respective big city locals.[20]

Postscript

Three years after first gaining office, both John Samuelsen and Tim Sylvester won second terms in contested elections. In December 2012, Samuelsen's "Stand United" slate swept all the Local 100 races, six of seven departmental vice presidencies, and won thirty-seven of forty-nine executive board seats. While still in the middle of a protracted struggle for a new contract with the MTA, Samuelsen was reelected president by a margin of 7,153 to 4,975. He declared the vote to be "validation that the members wholeheartedly support our determination to resist the concessions agreed to by state employee unions." A month after the Local 100 election results, Sylvester and his "Members United" running mates defeated two competing slates, composed of former 804 officers, in what is still one of the largest UPS locals in the country and the biggest with TDU leadership. According to UPS package-car driver Ken Reiman, "Members United won because, at contract time, we want an executive board that will keep us informed, tell the truth, and stand up to the company."

6—*LIVE BAIT & AMMO*

The tradition of radical pamphleteering in North America is as old as Thomas Paine and his distinguished predecessors in the struggle for democratic rights in a world dominated by monarchs and theocrats. More than a few modern-day purveyors of "common sense" have penned their denunciations of the powers-that-be in rank-and-file newsletters, the shop floor alternative to official labor publications. Their critique of the workplace status quo has been no less welcome than the writings of Paine, a corset-maker by trade, who dared to challenge royal authority in England and its rebellious colonies in the late 1700s.

During his three decades as a machine operator in Michigan, Greg Shotwell was never once asked to contribute to his national union magazine, *Solidarity*, which serves as a glossy mouthpiece for the United Auto Workers (UAW). So Shotwell, a brilliant wordsmith and working-class humorist, launched a lively shop paper called *Live Bait & Ammo* for the edification of his coworkers at General Motors and Delphi. It contained all the news and commentary that *Solidarity* didn't see fit to print. Thanks to the Internet (and much to the chagrin of UAW leaders), *Live Bait & Ammo* was soon circulating in many other auto plants. This made Shotwell widely read, if not more popular, at Solidarity House, the now sadly misnamed headquarters of a national union more devoted to dividing and conquering its own members than uniting them in fights with management.

Fortunately, Haymarket Books and labor journalist Lee Sustar, who assisted the author, realized that Shotwell's broadsides contained unique insights and deserved a larger audience. Repackaged in a collection titled *Autoworkers Under the Gun: A Shop-Floor View of the End of the American Dream*, the author's urgent dispatches from the front lines of labor-management conflict are no less fresh than when they were first read by UAW members in auto plant break rooms, bathrooms, parking lots, and other places of refuge from the assembly line.[21] As the late Jerry Tucker, a former UAW executive board member, notes in his introduction to Shotwell's book, "The UAW has, during the past thirty years, presided over the most destabilizing job and income loss in our industrial history." Its "forced march to the rear" has elicited the "organic, pained protests of individual UAW members and self-organized groups of rank-and-file workers" but few have matched the force and clarity of Shotwell's "call for a democratic union and collective struggle against concessions and the culture of 'joint-ness' that envelops the UAW today."

Tucker was no stranger to this struggle. He began his career as a local officer in the Midwest and supporter of Walter Reuther, whose "Administration Caucus" has dominated the UAW since the late 1940s. After he was appointed to the UAW international staff, Tucker promoted the use of "in-plant campaigns" to win good contracts in manufacturing units where strikes would not have been as successful. He decided that UAW was dangerously adrift under Reuther's successors and needed "new directions." Together with a network of rank-and-file supporters and local officers, he organized an opposition caucus under that name.

Tucker's bid to become director of the UAW's 90,000-member Region 5 was illegally thwarted by UAW headquarters, which favored the incumbent. After Tucker declared his candidacy, he was fired from the Region 5 staff and lost the election by 0.16 percent of the vote at the UAW's 1986 convention. A successful two-year fight by union democracy lawyer Chip Yablonski, son of the murdered UMW dissident, forced the Labor Department to conduct a rerun. Tucker won and served the eight months that remained in his three-year term, only to face constant undermining and interference from UAW headquarters.

While briefly on the UAW board, Tucker continued to criticize the union for being too "top-down" and cozy with management. In retaliation, General Motors barred him from its largest plant in Region 5 when he campaigned for reelection in 1989. UAW retirees were mobilized by Solidarity House to protest his appearance at a *Labor Notes* conference and similarly organized as a voting bloc to deprive him of reelection. Nevertheless, Tucker's New Directions movement continued to contest UAW policies—including the lack of a referendum vote for its top officers—well into the 1990s.[22]

Inspired, in part, by Tucker's example, Shotwell helped launch a later grassroots protest movement called Soldiers of Solidarity (SOS). These

UAW members objected to the union's handling of the 2005 bankruptcy proceeding initiated by Delphi, a parts manufacturer spun off from GM. As Shotwell notes, the company's court filing sparked a revival of grassroots activism, "not just among longtime militants, but among hundreds of workers new to union activity." SOS was forced to confront both the aggressive new management of Delphi and a UAW leadership little inclined to support membership mobilization against further concessions. In *Autoworkers Under the Gun*, Shotwell argues that an effective Jerry Tucker–style "work to rule" campaign could have been organized, as part of a larger community-based defense of Delphi jobs and past contract gains.

That was not the path taken by Solidarity House. Shotwell's account of the resulting layoffs, forced transfers, reduced pension and health coverage, two-tier wages, and deteriorating working conditions makes for painful reading. "The corporations sense the labor movement's weakness," he writes. "They are determined to decimate and throttle the working class while we are down and in disarray. . . . UAW strongholds have been strip-mined and abandoned. Union families have been severed from their communities, their history, their sense of belonging and continuity."

Notwithstanding his understandable disenchantment as a UAW member, Shotwell knows that even a debased union is better than none at all. In 2004, he traveled at his own expense to the Toyota factory in Georgetown, Kentucky, at the invitation of workers trying to unionize their "Japanese transplant." Finding these volunteer organizers to be "some of the finest, bravest, toughest union men and women" he had ever met and the "real prizefighters of the labor movement," Shotwell helped them rebut anti-UAW propaganda disseminated by union foes in Kentucky. Overcoming the "lies, manipulations, and fallacies" of open-shop auto companies, in the South or anywhere else, won't be easy, the author suggests. But "the truth hits you on the nose every day you go to work," which is why, according to Shotwell, "there's a fire that burns in the hearts of workers that can't be snuffed out." [23]

PART II

STRIKING BACK OR STRIKING OUT

The decline of conventional strike activity since the mass firing and defeat of air traffic controllers in 1981 is one major sign of U.S. labor's current weakness. Later in the 1980s, in Britain, the labor movement suffered a similar setback when the Thatcher government won a lengthy struggle with the National Union of Mineworkers. This part of the book examines the legal and organizational context for the erosion of workers' right to strike and what it would take to revive the strike weapon.

As noted in the Introduction and later in this book, more work stoppages in the United States now tend to be shorter, taking the form of one- or two-day protests rather than open-ended strikes.[1] Such strike activity may be related to an unresolved union contract dispute or orchestrated by union-backed worker centers and associations not seeking union recognition as their immediate goal. As one service sector organizer observes, "The short strike works well, offering exciting actions that both pressure employers and educate the public. 'What's new is that the strike is being embraced by a lot of groups as the central point of their strategy.'"[2]

Meanwhile, in long-established bargaining units (with a thousand workers or more) more employers are landing the first blow by locking their employees out until they agree to contract concessions. In

2011, there were seventeen lockouts in the United States, representing a record 90 percent of all major work stoppages. Among the union members locked out were professional basketball and football players, Steel Workers at Cooper Tire in Ohio, Teamsters at Sotheby's in New York, and Bakery and Confectionery Workers at American Crystal Sugar plants in Minnesota, Iowa, and North Dakota. Even in more labor-friendly Canada, Caterpillar used the lockout tactic to defeat the Canadian Auto Workers.[3]

A century after labor's much-celebrated strike victory in the textile mills of Lawrence, Massachusetts, both immigrants and their native-born coworkers have the deck stacked against them. Those seeking "bread and roses" today must find creative ways to confront business owners whose global reach makes them formidable successors to the "lords of the loom" in New England. And sometimes that means embracing, as the Lawrence strikers did, new forms of workplace organization better suited to current industry conditions.

7—LESSONS OF LAWRENCE

One hundred years ago, thousands of angry textile workers abandoned their looms and poured into the frigid streets of Lawrence, Massachusetts. Like Occupy Wall Street in our own Gilded Age, their unexpected protest in January 1912 cast a dramatic spotlight on the problem of social and economic inequality. In all of American labor history, there are few better examples of the synergy between radical activism and indigenous militancy.

The work stoppage now celebrated as the "Bread and Roses Strike" was triggered, ironically, by a Progressive-era reform that backfired.[4] Well-meaning state legislators had just reduced the maximum allowable working hours for women and children from fifty-six to fifty-four hours per week. When this reduction went into effect, workers quickly discovered that their pay had been cut proportionately, and their jobs speeded up by the American Woolen Company and other firms.

Their mass walkout created political tremors far beyond the Merrimack Valley. The shutdown of mills in Lawrence forced a national debate about factory conditions, child labor, the exploitation of immigrants, and the free exercise of First Amendment rights during labor disputes. The strikers' appeals for solidarity and financial support also created a stark "Which Side Are You On?" moment for mainstream unions and middle-class reformers, both of whom were nervous about the role played by "outside agitators" in Lawrence.

On one side of the class divide in Lawrence were rich, arrogant and out-of-touch WASP manufacturers. Their "1%" sense of entitlement led them to spurn negotiations with "the off-scourings of Southern Europe," as *New England Magazine* disdainfully called the strikers. Instead, mill owners relied on rough policing by fifty state and local militia units (including a company composed of Harvard students who were offered course credit for their attempted strikebreaking). Two workers were shot or bayoneted to death, and many others were clubbed and jailed. Three union organizers were falsely accused of conspiracy to murder and faced the electric chair before their post-strike acquittal.

Arrayed against American Woolen and its heavily armed defenders was a rainbow coalition of recently arrived immigrants—low-paid workers from thirty countries, who spoke forty-five different languages. They were welded together into a militant, disciplined, and largely nonviolent force, through their own efforts and the extraordinary organizing skills of the Industrial Workers of the World (IWW), which began recruiting in Lawrence many months before the nine-week walkout.

Unlike the elitist and conservative American Federation of Labor (AFL), the IWW championed the working poor, both native- and foreign-born. "There is no foreigner here except the capitalists," thundered IWW leader "Big Bill" Haywood, in a speech to the Lawrence strikers. "Do not let them divide you by sex, color, creed or nationality." Many on the picket lines in Lawrence were teenagers or women. Their mistreatment at work, miserable living conditions, malnutrition, and other health problems soon became a national scandal. When a delegation of sixteen young strikers appeared before a House committee hearing in Washington, D.C., the wife of Republican President William Howard Taft was among those attending who were shocked by their account of factory life in Lawrence. These child laborers put a human face on the strikers' now famous demand for "bread and roses." They wanted more than just a living wage; they sought dignity, respect, and opportunities for personal fulfillment denied to those employed in the mills at age fourteen or even younger.

Today, the Bread and Roses Strike is feted by all of organized labor. But at the time, the work stoppage upstaged and embarrassed the American Federation of Labor (AFL), because Lawrence workers rallied under the banner of an organizational rival. IWW members fiercely criticized the AFL for keeping workers divided in different unions, based on occupation. Women, non-whites, and recent immigrants—particularly those deemed to be "unskilled"—were largely excluded from the alliance of craft unions derided by the IWW as "the American Separation of Labor." The AFL, in turn, dismissed the IWW's quest for "One Big Union" and worker control of industry as a left-wing fantasy.

AFL president Samuel Gompers was particularly grumpy about the Lawrence strike. Gompers saw the Lawrence uprising as just "a passing event" and the work of agitators more concerned with promoting a "class-conscious industrial revolution" than advancing "the near future interests of the workers." However, when the mill owners finally capitulated, the strikers won most of their immediate demands—an outcome that vindicated their embrace of the IWW rather than the feeble AFL-affiliated United Textile Workers. The strike settlement, reached in March 1912, provided wage increases, overtime pay, and amnesty for all strikers.

On the other hand, as many labor historians have noted, the IWW's political influence in Lawrence proved to be short-lived. Industrial unionism didn't gain a firmer footing in the Merrimack Valley until the 1930s and the great wave of Depression-inspired organizing by the Congress of Industrial Organizations. Even that later labor movement success was eroded over time by mill closings and the relocation of textile manufacturing from New England to the non-union South. The Merrimack Valley entered a period of steady decline.

In recent years, Lawrence's long depressed neighbor to the west, the city of Lowell, has experienced an economic revival, due to public investment in higher education there, a convention center, and other facilities; it's now widely hailed as a model of mill town reinvention and cultural diversity. Tourists flock to its museum of industrial history, run by the National Park Service.

Lawrence remains a city of the working poor, better known for its substandard housing, high unemployment, political corruption, and troublesome street crime. Ninety percent of its public school students are Hispanic, and few speak English as a first language. Although not condemned to factory work at an early age, these children struggle to learn under tenement-like conditions. A recent report by the teachers' union describes "crowded classrooms and physical infrastructure in distress: leaking roofs, poor air quality, persistent mold problems, crumbling walls and rodent infestation." Demoralized teachers have been working without a new contract for two years; student performance is so dismal that a state takeover of the school system has been actively considered.

When worker solidarity prevailed over corporate power in the icy streets of Lawrence a century ago, it made the promise of a better life real for many. The 1912 uprising became a consciousness-raising experience, not only for textile workers and their families, but the nation as a whole. Nevertheless, at strike centennial events in Lawrence, it was hard not to notice that many immigrant workers there still lack "bread and roses"—in the form of living-wage jobs, affordable housing, and decent schools. That injustice will not be cured until U.S. workers and their allies, in Lawrence and elsewhere, find a way to make history again, not just celebrate it.[5]

8—THE GOLDEN AGE OF FACTORY UNREST

In 1968, the world was transfixed by global student unrest. Less attention was paid to factory uprisings that overlapped with campus protests in places like France. In one small corner of the Ford Motor Company's huge production complex in Dagenham, England, several hundred women did their part in the "year of revolt." Toiling in their own sex-segregated department, the only females in a plant of 55,000 had walked out many times in the past over strike issues dear to their male coworkers. Now, it was their turn to shut down sewing machines, stop production of seat covers, and picket Ford over a pay dispute with broader social implications.

The film *Made in Dagenham* is the story of their strike, born of working-class feminist consciousness in a labor movement even more dominated by "the lads" forty years ago than it is today, in Britain or the United States.

Directed by Nigel Cole, the film is schmaltzy, upbeat, and quite out of sync with our current picket-line gestalt of hopelessness and defeat. It is, by far, the best popular depiction of union activism and rank-and-file leadership development since *Norma Rae*, Martin Ritt's 1979 movie about southern textile worker organizing, and Ken Loach's more recent *Bread and Roses,* about the mobilization of immigrant janitors in Los Angeles. But don't hold your breath waiting for most unions to use *Made in Dagenham* as they should, in training programs for their new shop stewards and bargaining committee members. It much too accurately captures the frequent tension between full-time union officials and working members when they try to work together on contract negotiations and strikes.

The Dagenham strike leader played by Sally Hawkins is a very British version of the southern textile worker portrayed so famously by Sally Field in *Norma Rae*. Rita O'Grady is not even a union steward in the film's early scenes of shop-floor life and work. She steps into that role only because her older coworker, Connie (played by Geraldine James), is dealing with the suicidal depression of her husband, a damaged survivor of wartime duty in the RAF. Unlike the mill where Norma Rae toiled, the Dagenham plant is completely organized. Unfortunately, with the exception of Albert, a loveable chief steward ally (wonderfully portrayed by Bob Hoskins), the union, which is a composite of several actually involved, seems to function as an arm of Ford's HR department, a labor-management relationship not unknown to American autoworkers today.

The political traditions of British labor give this arrangement humorous left cover. In one memorable scene, a clutch of worried trade union officials, in jackets and ties, are trying to talk Rita out of strike action that might upend some murky, big picture strategy the leadership is pursuing. While condescending to the only worker in the room, they address each other as "comrade" and invoke Marx as the final authority on what should or should not be done.

Rita's first bargaining session is a face-to-face meeting with Ford managers about their misclassification of the sewing machine operators as "unskilled labor." Both Rita and Connie get a day off from work and overdress for the occasion. Monty, their full-time union representative (played by Kenneth Cranham), first takes the two rank-and-file women out for a well-lubricated lunch, a perk designed to put Rita and Connie in his debt.

Monty has obviously been off the job and out of the plant for years; his main preoccupation now seems to be eating and drinking at dues-payer expense, dressing nicely, and seeing the company's side of things.

When the union delegation finally sits down with management, Monty does all the talking and fails to give Ford a firm deadline for fixing the pay inequity problem. Shocked by the incompetence of her own union rep, and his obvious coziness with Ford HR men, Rita commandeers the meeting. She interrupts Monty and pulls out samples of the seat covers stitched by the workers in her department. She explains the complexity of the labor process involved and insists that Ford properly reward the skill and experience necessary for the job. The scene is a great tutorial in how to make effective job-upgrade presentations—and, believe me, that kind of labor relations lobbying is always best done by those who actually do the work. The Ford bosses are so taken aback that one can only respond by threatening to discipline Rita for lifting the fabric used in her impromptu demonstration.

The ensuing radicalization of Rita is very inspiring, and true-to-life. Hawkins's character in this film is no Poppy, the loopy Cockney she played in Mike Leigh's *Happy-Go-Lucky*, which earned her a Golden Globe and a slew of other awards in 2008. Rita is a mother with two children, working the proverbial "double shift" in a traditional marriage to a fellow Dagenham worker (played by Daniel Mays) who is sweet but weak-willed. She's a woman previously lacking in personal self-confidence, a stranger to public speaking, and bereft of "political experience" (as Ford officials discover when they scour her file expecting to find evidence of left-wing party connections). Under the tutelage of Albert (a more avuncular version of the male union mentors played by Ron Leibman in *Norma Rae* and Adrien Brody in *Bread and Roses*), Rita finds her own voice, a streak of determination, and the powerful capacity to move others.

As in many strikes, rank-and-file unity is stronger at the beginning than later on. As the job action spreads, thousands of Dagenham workers are idled, with no direct stake in the outcome, so the recriminations begin to fly. For some union members, organizing strike relief, attending rallies, maintaining picket lines, and meeting workers from other plants for the first time is a learning experience, liberating and even euphoric. Others—in this case, mainly fearful or disgruntled guys—slink away to the pub. There, they watch strike coverage on the telly and grouse about the economic hardship inflicted on the real bread-winners in the community (namely, themselves) by a handful of unreasonable and uppity women.

Rita's own *Norma Rae* moment occurs at a union conference, not standing up on a workbench brandishing a union sign in her factory. Monty and the other "comrades" have scheduled a vote, among the entirely male conference delegates, that will end this costly "industrial action" at Ford, without a favorable resolution of the job-grading issue. Rita and her roving pickets are the only women at the meeting. Rita takes the stage and delivers a moving but simple speech recalling the wartime courage of her coworker's husband, the now deceased RAF veteran.

"Men and women, we are in this together," she tells the stone-faced crowd. "We are not divided by sex. Only by those willing to accept injustice." Moved, shamed, and/or inspired by her message, the delegates vote to continue union backing for the Dagenham strike, which by then was creating widespread disruption of Ford production. The company responds by sending a hard-nosed executive from Detroit to read the riot act to Britain's then-Labour government. If the strike is not ended, Ford strongly hints, it might shift Cortina production to a land where the blokes and birds aren't so strike-happy.

The prime minister at the time was the wishy-washy Harold Wilson, beset by industrial unrest on all sides. His First Secretary of State was Barbara Castle, a longtime member of Parliament (played with flair by Miranda Richardson). She takes charge of the Ford problem when Wilson doesn't. In the film, after conferring with a delegation of Dagenham strikers, Castle waves her magic wand, transforming an otherwise obscure dispute over the proper pay grade for a single auto plant job classification into a broader feminist demand for "equal pay."

Parliament did not pass legislation against pay discrimination based on gender until several years after the Dagenham strike. The walkout by sewing machine operators there was settled with a wage increase that still left them earning less than men in the same job grade. The new equal pay law was not fully implemented nationally until 1975. In the meantime, UK labor relations reality was also a bit more complex, as radical historian Sheila Cohen and other British reviewers of the film have noted.

In real life, the friendly Labour Party cabinet member who collaborates with Rita and her coworkers in the film soon thereafter triggered a trade union backlash by issuing a white paper titled "In Place of Strife." It sought to curb workers' rights and contributed to Labour's electoral defeat in 1970. Known later in the House of Lords as "Baroness Castle of Blackburn," Castle tried to quell the broader strike wave that brought the women of Dagenham to her doorstep, after they surfed it themselves so impressively.

The finer points of strike history aside, *Made in Dagenham* is in the great tradition of *Brassed Off*, *Billy Elliot*, and *The Full Monty*. These earlier films movingly depicted the industrial struggles, job displacement, and personal dramas of miners and steelworkers. The female sewing machine operators who take center stage in *Dagenham* may not have been prototypical British working-class heroes, but they were no less skilled in the hard work of building union solidarity. Lyrics for the film's theme song are performed by protest singer Billy Bragg, who has a street in Dagenham named after him, and sung by former Dagenham worker Sandie Shaw. More labor films, based on a real-life struggles, should end on such a high note.[6]

9—STRIKING IN PATCO'S SHADOW

In the summer of 2011, labor unrest on both coasts provided a sharp rebuttal to the widely held view that the strike is dead (and buried) in the United States. Even as veterans of the Professional Air Traffic Controllers Organization (PATCO) gathered in Florida to commemorate the thirtieth anniversary of their historic defeat, a new generation of strikers was taking on big private-sector employers like Verizon and Kaiser Permanente. In August 2011, 45,000 Verizon workers walked out from Maine to Virginia in the first stage of a protracted struggle against contract concessions. One month later, they were joined by 20,000 nurses and other union members opposed to similar benefit givebacks sought by Kaiser Permanente in California. Both of these struggles came shortly after the year's biggest upsurge, the massive series of public employee demonstrations in Wisconsin that included pivotal strike activity by Madison schoolteachers.

Of course, just the year before, there were only eleven work stoppages involving 1,000 workers or more in the entire country. And the year before that, as PATCO historian Joe McCartin notes in *Collision Course: Ronald Reagan, the Air Traffic Controllers, and the Strike that Changed America*, the federal government reported only five major work stoppages involving a mere 13,000 workers in all.[7] This total is only slightly more than the number of workers who walked off the job, in airports around the country, in a single, momentous strike on August 3, 1981. McCartin's book and the two others under review remind us what strike activity looks like, whether it occurs in a single union bargaining unit or becomes part of a broader, more amorphous protest movement.

A professor at Georgetown University, McCartin describes what happened when a tightly knit union brotherhood (there were only a few female air traffic controllers in 1981) assumed, mistakenly, that it was irreplaceable. President Ronald Reagan's retaliatory firing of 11,345 PATCO members cast a long shadow over collective bargaining in the United States, and provided inspiration for the more recent union-busting activities by Wisconsin governor Scott Walker and others. PATCO's destruction ushered in a decade of lost strikes and lockouts, triggered by management demands for pay and benefit givebacks. Given renewed momentum by our latest recession, this concession bargaining trend continues unabated today, in both the private and public sector.

Yet, just twenty-five years after PATCO lost, hundreds of thousands of foreign-born workers participated in political strike activity on a scale rarely seen in the United States, even in the late nineteenth and early twentieth centuries. In their edited collection, *Rallying for Immigrant Rights*, sociologists Kim Voss and Irene Bloemraad describe the series of one-day protests that culminated in a massive work stay-away on May 1, 2006.[8] Both union members and an even larger number of non-union workers took to the streets in major cities across the country, along with their family members and community supporters, to protest Republican legislation that would have made it a federal crime to live in the United States illegally. Known as the Border Protection, Antiterrorism, and Illegal Immigration Control Act, this bill was adopted by the House but died in the Senate, thanks, in large part, to the grassroots movement against it.

It is left to Joe Burns, a labor lawyer and longtime union activist in Minneapolis, to imagine how the bitter lessons of past defeats—and inspiring examples of community-labor solidarity (like the immigrant worker protests in 2006)—can become the basis for "reviving the strike." In his highly readable call to action, *Reviving the Strike,* Burns argues that American unions must regain the will and ability to strike or they face further withering away.[9] According to Burns:

> If the labor movement is to rise again, it will not be as result of electing different politicians, the passage of legislation, or improved methods of union organizing. Rather, workers will need to rediscover the power of the strike. Not the ineffectual strike of today, where employees sit on picket lines waiting for scabs to take their jobs, but the type of strike capable of grinding industries to a halt— the kind employed in the first half of the twentieth century.

As McCartin recounts in *Collision Course*, the groundwork for PATCO's fight-to-the-death with the Federal Aviation Administration (FAA) was laid by changes in the system of federal employee labor relations in the early 1960s. After several false starts, the controllers were able to create a real union to replace an ineffectual, management-dominated professional association. PATCO's emergence was part of "the largest surge in unionization since the emergence of industrial unions in the 1930s. By 1967, teachers, social workers, firefighters, police officers, sanitation workers, and others were raising a cry for 'trade union rights to public employees NOW!'" Like state, county, and municipal workers in many parts of the United States, air traffic controllers ended up with the ability to negotiate on some employment conditions, but without any legally sanctioned right to strike.

Nevertheless, PATCO members engaged in a series of militant job actions, including slowdowns, sick-outs, and work-to-rule actions, that helped build their new organization and gave them confidence in its muscle. When PATCO walked out in 1981, its leaders firmly believed that the airline industry would, indeed, grind to a halt. The union's previous (albeit smaller-scale) confrontations with the federal government had ended favorably, leading the controllers to conclude that the results would be the same, with no greater risk to themselves. Between 1962 and 1981, there were thirty-nine recorded work stoppages by all types of federal employees; as McCartin notes, "in only eight were any strikers discharged and, in those cases, firings were targeted, not imposed in blanket fashion."

Nine months earlier, PATCO had endorsed Ronald Reagan's presidential candidacy, believing that he would be more controller-friendly than Democrat Jimmy Carter. PATCO strategists were "sure Reagan would not fire more than ten thousand skilled specialists that the government had spent hundreds of millions of dollars and many years to train—not when they were seeking only improved working conditions and fair compensation after years of seeing their salaries lag behind inflation, and when dismissing them would ultimately be far more costly than meeting their demands." But after giving them forty-eight hours to return, the former California governor and one time leader of the Screen Actors Guild dismissed the FAA employees who struck illegally at 400 airports and air traffic control centers. They were soon replaced by 800 military and 8,900 civilian controllers (supervisors, picket-line crossers, and new hires), a cobbled-together workforce that cost taxpayers $2 billion to recruit, train, and deploy. Commercial aircraft continued to fly despite a post-strike FAA staffing shortage that persisted for years.

An Existential Threat

Neither the AFL-CIO nor, more important, other airline industry unions displayed the kind of strike solidarity necessary to meet Reagan's existential threat. PATCO's most significant aid came from abroad, in the form of a two-day boycott by Canadian air traffic controllers; they risked disciplinary action for refusing to handle flights to or from the United States, until, under government pressure, their union lifted the ban. Meanwhile, top U.S. labor officials, from right to left, dithered about what to do, ultimately leaving it up to individual unions to decide. (The Carpenters did not even disinvite Reagan as a speaker at their national convention one month after he fired the controllers. His speech, defending his actions, also failed to elicit any boos; instead, union delegates "sat respectfully if uncomfortably through his remarks.")

Per usual, Lane Kirkland, the conservative cold warrior then heading the AFL-CIO, found lots of reasons for inaction. Among them, "PATCO had not warned or consulted the AFL-CIO," which was preoccupied at the time with plans for "a massive September 19 'Solidarity Day' march on Washington in protest of Reagan's social and economic policies and program cuts." International Association of Machinists (IAM) president William Winpisinger, "an avowed socialist known for his fiery rhetoric," lectured his Executive Council colleagues about the need to resist Reagan. But Wimpy, as he was nicknamed, "stopped noticeably short of saying he was ready to pull machinists off their jobs." McCartin quotes a federal transportation official as saying that if IAM-represented airline mechanics and baggage handlers had respected PATCO picket lines, "we couldn't have withstood it. It would have closed every single airport."

The president of the Air Line Pilots Association (ALPA), also turned his back on PATCO, leaving other AFL-CIO Council members to conclude, privately, that the controllers' walkout was a "no-win situation" created by "botched negotiations." J. J. O'Donnell, then president of ALPA, publicly declared that the post-strike skies were safe. His own union's safety committee disagreed, and its findings, if backed by ALPA, could have been the basis for more individual pilots refusing to fly. In 1982, after being voted out of office, O'Donnell was named to a top Labor Department post by Reagan. In contrast, PATCO strikers remained under a lifetime presidential ban from federal employment as controllers until 1993, when the Clinton administration finally allowed a small trickle of them to return to their old jobs.

The strikers themselves were unlikely martyrs to labor's cause. The vast majority, as McCartin points out, were "suburban-dwelling military veterans" who went directly from the service into the rigid, hierarchical culture of the FAA. "Although they were breaking federal law in an unprecedented effort to shut down the nation's air travel, they were hardly radicals," as demonstrated by PATCO's ill-fated endorsement of Reagan. Internally, they were extremely well organized and disciplined, with an elaborate, military-style blueprint for their work stoppage that contrasted sharply with the far-sketchier strike plans of other unions, before or since. Providing fascinating detail that is typical of his exhaustively researched book, McCartin reports:

In April 1980, PATCO distributed a fifty-five-page strike planning booklet to members. In the months that followed, the union

prepared as though it was going to war. Strike planners developed
"clusters" of locals that could coordinate their activity during
the anticipated strike, independent of national direction should
PATCO's leaders be arrested. Clusters had established secret "safe
houses" from which local strike efforts could be directed in the
event that union headquarters were raided. Strike planners urged
local clusters to set up decentralized calling trees to pass information and recommended that members use phone booths or friends'
phones when communicating vital strike information.

But systematic internal preparation was not supplemented by pre-strike
outreach to other potential allies. In this regard, breaking ranks with the rest
of organized labor in the 1980 presidential race was not the controllers' only
pre-strike mistake. PATCO members also failed to build cross-union ties
with the pilots, mechanics, flight attendants, and baggage handlers whose
backing was desperately needed when push came to shove. According to
McCartin, the pilots in particular viewed the walkout as "a threat to their
livelihoods" because of the thousands of furloughs it would produce.

The Reagan administration, on the other hand, "knew that winning the
cooperation of major airlines was essential" to withstanding the pressure
of a strike in a period of rising fuel prices, deepening recession, excess
capacity, and other "ongoing turbulence unleashed by the 1978 airline
deregulation act." The FAA's strike contingency plan was sold to the Air
Transport Association, the national trade group for carriers, as "a way for
airlines to shed their least profitable routes without fear of aiding their
competitors." The ATA's "staunch support was a crucial component of
PATCO's defeat," McCartin concludes. PATCO's subsequent bankruptcy
and decertification, in turn, strengthened the hand of airline management
in its own future showdowns with ALPA, the IAM, the Flight Attendants,
and other unions at Continental Airlines, Eastern, TWA, and Northwest.

Nevertheless, as court injunctions, $32 million in fines, and criminal
indictments (against seventy-eight strike leaders) piled up around the
country, the PATCO strike became a labor cause célèbre. As McCartin
notes, "Many activists were angry with their national leaders for failing to do more for PATCO." At the local level, there was a tremendous
outpouring of support for the strikers, despite media vilification of their

contract demands as greedy, irrational, and "unpatriotic." Viewed from the perspective of the last three decades—with its real-wage stagnation, longer working hours, and shrinking pensions—PATCO's proposals do seem "unrealistic" today. But that is a sad commentary on how far union bargaining has gone in the wrong direction, and how worker expectations have been lowered in the process.

Thirty-one years ago, the stressful working conditions in air traffic control, which adversely affected FAA employees' health and longevity on the job, led PATCO negotiators to seek a shorter work week (equal to the reduced hours of controllers in other countries) and better early-retirement benefits. Today, in many industries, early retirement is under assault, curbs on mandatory overtime have been weakened, and exhausting twelve-hour shifts have become the norm. Campaigns for reduced work time are few and far between, in the United States at least. At the FAA, modern-day controllers have been skirmishing with management about the problem of safety errors made as a result of sleep deprivation. Once again, controllers have union representation; in 1987, striker replacements and others hired, post-strike, formed the National Air Traffic Controllers Association (NATCA) and won a union certification ballot, even before Reagan left office.

A "Day without Immigrants"

If air traffic controllers, circa 1981, were unfairly depicted (and sometimes publicly resented) as an overprivileged group of "labor aristocrats," it was pretty hard to make the same claim about the foreign-born workers who rose up, so unexpectedly and impressively, in 2006. Twelve-million-strong, these undocumented immigrants did not have to stop work to break the law: under U.S. immigration rules, it is "illegal" for them to be working. (For the best political critique of that problematic conceptualization of their status, see David Bacon's *Illegal People*.) [10]

The draconian legislation pushed by right-wing Republican Congressman James Sensenbrenner in 2005–6 had a galvanizing effect on recent immigrants because it threatened to make their already precarious employment situation here even worse. Kim Voss and Irene Bloemraad, the editors of *Rallying for Immigrant Rights*, estimate that 3.7 to 5 million people joined the escalating protests held in March, April, and May

2006 in 160 cities. On May Day that year, as many as 700,000 marched in Chicago and Los Angeles, where taking off from work to participate in the "Day without Immigrants" was most widespread. The *New York Times* noted the resulting impact:

> Lettuce, tomatoes and grapes went unpicked in fields in California and Arizona, which contribute more than half the nation's produce, as scores of growers let workers take the day off. Truckers who move 70 percent of the goods in ports in Los Angeles and Long Beach, Calif., did not work. Meatpacking companies, including Tyson Foods and Cargill, closed plants in the Midwest and the West, employing more than 20,000 people, while the flower and produce markets in downtown Los Angeles stood largely and eerily empty.[11]

What Voss and Bloemraad call the "fight for inclusion in 21st century America" could not have been waged so effectively without prior grassroots work by national and local coalitions composed of unions, the religious community, and immigrant rights organizations. In his contribution to their collection, Bay Area community organizer and housing lawyer Randy Shaw credits the Immigrant Workers Freedom Ride (IWFR) as an important antecedent. Organized by UNITE HERE, the Service Employees International Union (SEIU), and the AFL-CIO three years before, "the IWFR largely escaped national consciousness at the time, but it played a critical role in reenergizing and broadening America's immigrant rights movement, setting the stage for the mass marches of 2006."

The editors, joined by political science professor Taeku Lee, describe how the defeat of Sensenbrenner's bill in the Senate did not translate into further progress for advocates of immigrant rights. Groups pushing for more restrictive immigration policies simply shifted their focus from Congress to the states, first under George Bush and now under Barack Obama. In the wake of the protests, there were continuing workplace raids by Immigration and Customs Enforcement (ICE) agents. There was also a sharp increase in the number of deportations in 2007 and 2008. More undocumented workers rounded up by ICE were also charged with felony violations of identity theft and forgery laws. Now, under the not-much-kinder-or-gentler Obama administration, the use of no-match letters has become the enforcement tactic of choice, triggering large-scale workplace purges by low-wage employers across the country. All of this has "had a chilling effect," Voss, Bloemraad, and Lee argue. In addition, "the type of organizations that initially facilitated the protests" contributed, in various ways, to "the rapid demobilization of the movement following spring, 2006."

> For some organizations, such as schools, churches, hometown associations, and the ethnic media, protest activity is peripheral to their primary mission and thus they are poorly equipped to support a long-term social movement for immigrant rights. The organizations that were of a type that might sustain a movement, tended to be smaller, with limited funding. While such organizations continue their activities into the present, the immigrant rights movement also has, like many other social movements, been divided by strong internal disagreement about tactics and goals.

For their part, the two unions most supportive of the foreign-born—SEIU and UNITE HERE—fell out among themselves in 2009–10, moving from "strong internal disagreement" (about issues unrelated to immigration) to public feuding over national union funds, jurisdiction, and membership. This internecine conflict proved to be a costly distraction from grassroots campaigning for health care and labor law reform during Obama's first two years in office; it was also no boon to immigration reform, a cause with almost as many political enemies as the Employee Free Choice Act.

Rebuilding Strike Capacity

In his book, Burns praises the more freewheeling "social movement" character of the immigrant-worker upsurge in 2006 and its middle-American counterpart in Wisconsin five years later. "Reviving solidarity requires new approaches to unionism based not on workers focusing on narrow battles with individual employers but, rather, on fighting for larger issues and causes," Burns argues. He notes that, in France, "workers respond to attempts to eliminate social programs not through letter or email campaigns to politicians, but through direct action involving millions of workers," struggles that look more like the "Day without

Immigrants" or the anti-Walker mobilization in Wisconsin than conventional union walkouts.

One big obstacle to the latter, and a major reason that strike activity has shrunk statistically, is the legal straitjacket imposed on U.S. labor. As Burns documents well, the most effective strike tactics and forms of workplace solidarity have been outlawed in the private sector by legislative fiat and/or court decision. The high-water mark of labor efforts to restrict the debilitating use of permanent replacements in private sector strikes occurred nearly two decades ago during the Clinton administration. Introduced in 1993 as the "Striker Replacement Act" (and later renamed the Worker Fairness Act), this legislation was quickly passed in the Democrat-controlled House, but blocked in the Senate by a Republican filibuster. When labor law reform was revived in 2007–10, in the form of the Employee Free Choice Act (EFCA), the continuing problem of striker replacements was not even addressed for fear of arousing even greater conservative opposition.

Meanwhile, in government employment, only a small number of workers are permitted to strike legally. Public workers who ignore strike bans risk paying a heavy financial price, as PATCO members did thirty years ago and New York City transit workers did after their work stoppage in 2005 (for which they were heavily fined, individually and organizationally, and their union was stripped of its ability to collect dues via payroll check-off). The recent attacks on public sector collective bargaining in the Midwest, where unions have been fairly well entrenched, has reframed the workers' rights debate even more narrowly. Today unions are fighting for the mere existence of contract negotiations and against bipartisan legislative attempts to limit the scope of bargaining with state, county, or municipal agencies. In mainstream union circles, strengthening the right of teachers or state workers to strike has become as unthinkable as repealing the Taft-Hartley Act.

Taft-Hartley's restrictions on secondary strikes and boycotts—that would make primary walkouts more effective—are backed up by provisions that subject unions to employer damage suits and fines. For example, the United Mine Workers (UMW) racked up $64 million worth of fines during its 1989 contract dispute at Pittston, which featured a rare plant occupation. The UMW contract campaign at Pittston is among those cited by Burns as a successful example of "membership mobilization and a refusal to play by the rules that favor management." Using such case studies, and a mixture of historical and political arguments, Burns seeks to dispel what McCartin calls the "dispiriting psychological impact" that labor's poor won-lost record, in major strikes, has had on members and leaders alike.

Reviving the Strike is thus a provocative, well-argued, and much-needed polemic. Burns bravely takes fellow labor progressives to task for being too adaptive to the "new conservative reality" facing unions today. He chides proponents of "social unionism" whose organizing, bargaining, and coalition-building strategies have "functioned comfortably within the existing structures imposed by management and the legal system." My only quibble with the author's approach is a tendency to idealize some open-ended strikes or lockouts that settled into siege warfare and ultimately did not end well for the union side. Heroic struggles like the Hormel strike in the 1980s or the Staley lockout in the 1990s certainly raised worker consciousness, and even radicalized some participants. However, there is no getting around their tragic denouement, aided and abetted in both cases by national union hostility and treachery.

Burns's useful, if overly brief, discussion of "quickie" or intermittent strikes may be more persuasive and relevant to the situation of unions seeking to reduce the cost and risk of walking out without abandoning that strategy altogether, as too many have done by not even maintaining adequate strike funds. A lawyer and negotiator for the Association of Flight Attendants, an affiliate of the Communications Workers of America, Burns describes how their members developed a contract campaign and selective strike plan called CHAOS (Creating Havoc Around Our System). This was a response to the failed full-scale airline worker walkouts of the 1980s and involved the threatened use of intermittent job actions directed at individual flights. While legally entangling in other ways, the Railway Labor Act that governs airline industry labor relations is less restrictive in this area, so, "unlike in other industries, CHAOS can inflict major economic harm upon an employer" while minimizing flight attendant exposure to management retaliation.

The fundamental lesson of all these books is as old as unions themselves: an injury to one is an injury to all. No labor movement can long survive, much less thrive, without a strong culture of mutual aid and protection that facilitates, when necessary, the withdrawal of labor from the production of goods or providing of services. When labor organizations practice solidarity some of the time, rather than all of the time, they do a grave disservice to their members. And they also contribute to the worsening of employment conditions for the working-class majority that lacks even the limited job clout of the union-represented.[12]

10—THE BROKEN TABLE IN DETROIT

The continuing contraction of the newspaper trade and related job insecurity among print journalists is of understandable interest to individual and institutional survivors in the field. In mid-2012, the *New York Times* reported that a much-respected regional paper, the *Times-Picayune* in New Orleans, was trying to stay afloat by publishing less than once a day.[13] Six other newspapers, in the United States and Canada, had previously announced plans to reduce their print schedule and rely on Web editions the rest of the time.

As the *New York Times* account noted, "The decision to reduce print papers is usually accompanied by cuts on the newsroom side as well." The quality of daily coverage, already eroded due to industry-wide editorial staff downsizing, suffers accordingly. "Staff members at the *Times Picayune* expect that about one-third of the roughly 140-person newsroom will be cut." Reporters "have been told that their priorities will shift to writing for the web." According to one past editor: "They want them to produce more blog posts a day and not worry about putting things together in a more thoughtful package. The *Times-Picayune* has a sterling tradition of enterprising journalism. That tradition is being thrown under the bus."

Among the daily papers joining this unhappy trend are the *Detroit News* and *Detroit Free Press*, now owned by the Detroit Media Partnership. Since 2010, the *News* has "printed Monday through Saturday but delivers papers only on Thursday and Friday (with a special section delivered with the *Free Press* on Sundays)." In the mid-1990s, close coordination between the same two dailies—then owned by Gannett and Knight-Ridder respectively—laid the groundwork for labor's biggest media industry defeat in the last several decades. When Detroit newspaper management succeeded in throwing 2,500 employees "under the bus"—by replacing them during a strike—it not only sacrificed the quality of local journalism.

It dealt a grievous organizational blow to my own union, the Newspaper Guild/CWA, one of six labor organizations involved in the 583-day ordeal recounted in *The Broken Table: The Detroit Newspaper Strike and the State of American Labor*.[14]

An Extreme Case?

Written by Fordham University professor Chris Rhomberg, *The Broken Table* provides valuable historical context for this pivotal mid-1990s conflict. He describes the obstacles that strikers faced, how they tried to overcome them, and what consequences their defeat has had, locally and nationally. Rhomberg's in-depth study should be required reading for anyone attempting a newspaper shutdown in the future. It should also be consulted by labor organizers before staging a work stoppage, of any size, in any other venue where the employer has deep pockets, lots of other revenue-producing properties, and the same management-friendly private sector labor law on its side.

By virtue of our steadily declining rate of major job actions, the strike against the *Detroit News* and *Free Press* was, as the author notes, "an extreme case." Some might even view it as an outlier, harking back to an earlier era of no-holds-barred industrial conflict in Detroit. The walkout was "larger than 97 percent—and longer than 99 percent—of all private-sector strikes from 1984 to 2002." It also involved multiple bargaining units aligning their contract expiration dates and acting simultaneously against a common employer, the Detroit Newspaper Agency. The product of a controversial Justice Department–approved joint operating agreement (JOA), this corporate entity allowed Knight Ridder and Gannett to merge their production, circulation, advertising, accounting, and marketing operations in the city, while maintaining their separate newspaper brands.

Elsewhere in the same industry, a corresponding display of coordination and unity within labor has frequently been thwarted by craft union divisions. In Detroit, the Metropolitan Council of Newspaper Unions (MCNU) that successfully welded the strikers together covered "white-collar professionals, blue-collar laborers, and skilled crafts-persons"—a relatively rare occupational mix on U.S. picket lines, now and in the past.

Siege Warfare in the Midwest

Yet the Detroit strike remained much a product of recent labor relations trends that are well described by Rhomberg and have become even more pronounced in the last decade of concession bargaining and declining strike activity in the private sector. The Detroit strike settled into the same mode of siege warfare familiar to those brave manufacturing workers who tried to resist contract concessions on other midwestern battlefields in the 1980s and '90s. As the union-backed alternative newspaper spawned by the strike explained to readers of its inaugural issue, the conflict was never really "about money or even about the number of workers to be bought out or laid off."

According to the *Detroit Sunday Journal*, management was demanding or had already implemented "policies that would virtually wipe unions off the playing field by denying representation to hundreds of employees or denying unions the ability to negotiate wages and other substantive issues." As Detroit Guild attorney Duane Ice told Rhomberg: "After decades of bargaining, nobody could recall any instance when these employers, or any other newspapers in Detroit, had bargained to impasse and . . . basically declared an end to collective bargaining. It meant the unions had no role in the outcome. Basically, an employer could go through the motions, declare impasse, and say, 'Well, here are the terms and conditions. We're done.' "

No less than Detroit strikers in the mid-1990s, government employees in Wisconsin realized in 2011 where such an employer stance leads. So they acted accordingly, taking to the streets and occupying the state capitol, when their unions were similarly menaced, unexpectedly, by GOP Governor Scott Walker, after fifty years of public sector contract negotiations in the Badger State. Equivalent bad faith bargaining, and union-busting intent, triggered a two-week strike by 45,000 Verizon workers not long afterward.

In Detroit, union resistance to labor cost reductions and workplace restructuring took the form of an open-ended work stoppage. Unfortunately, as Rhomberg concludes, the strike "never fully succeeded in halting the production and distribution of the newspapers." Tacitly acknowledging their inability to stop production, union leaders "relied instead on circulation and advertising boycotts and on their legal case" at the National Labor Relations Board (NLRB). Whatever disruption and extra costs they had to endure in Detroit, Gannett and Knight Ridder were both secure in the knowledge that the revenue generated by their many other newspapers (both unionized and non-union) would continue to flow their way.

Profiles in Rank-and-File Courage

Rhomberg begins his impressive case study with chapters describing the new structure of newspaper industry ownership that has adversely affected labor relations within media giants like Gannett, the changing socioeconomic terrain of Detroit as a "union town," and the "daily miracle" of how a newspaper is produced, a process much changed since the heyday of the national unions involved in the strike. Fortunately, *The Broken Table* is not just about the larger forces reshaping newspaper workers lives, on the job and in the community.

The book also includes memorable sketches of—and well-deserved tributes to--strike activists like Michigan Journalism Hall-of-Famer Susan Watson, a *Free Press* features writer fired for participating in civil disobedience at the *News* building on Labor Day weekend in 1996; Barb Ingalls, an autoworker's wife, who "had never been very involved in her own union before the strike," but then became a leader in community-labor outreach around the country, work she continues today for antiwar and labor-religion coalitions in Detroit; and Teamster organizer Mike Zielinksi, who enlisted fifty locked-out or fired union members in a Workers Justice Committee that functioned as a "flying squad that could be mobilized on short notice for any kind of action." (In 1999, Zielinksi was fired himself when, according to Rhomberg, newly elected Teamster president James P. Hoffa decided "to clean house of supporters of his predecessor, Ron Carey, and bring the Detroit struggle to an end.")

And, finally, there is mailroom worker Ben Solomon, whom we meet at the beginning and end of the book. Bloodied but not bowed, he won a rare $2.5 million court judgment against the Detroit newspapers and their municipal government allies for conspiring to deprive him and other strikers of their constitutional rights. During a heavy-handed crackdown on mass picketing at a printing plant in Sterling Heights, Michigan, Solomon

was pepper-sprayed, clubbed, then maced again and jailed without treatment, in a shocking display of the police brutality experienced by many.

Rhomberg's modern-day tale of worker solidarity and personal transformation is no less dramatic or colorful than the storyline of *Newsies*,
although an adaptation of *The Broken Table* is not likely to be seen anytime soon on stage or screen. Mixing fiction with a few facts about an
actual strike a century ago, *Newsies: The Musical* has become a hugely
popular New York City stage production. It pits Manhattan newsboys
against Joseph Pulitzer, a publishing magnate who unilaterally cuts their
pay by raising the wholesale cost of their papers. In the course of their
work stoppage, the strikers face beatings and arrests by the cops, suffer
divisions within their own ranks due to leadership wavering, but succeed
in launching a strike paper and gaining the support of their counterparts
elsewhere. That labor unity, plus the friendly intervention of Governor
Theodore Roosevelt, leads to a favorable settlement with Pulitzer. The
strikers reclaim their now more fairly compensated jobs—a Hollywood
ending for sure, albeit it on Broadway (and lifted from a twenty-year-old
Disney movie by the same name).

Let Down by the Law

Rhomberg's narrative is, of course, more complex and the denouement
of the Detroit strike nothing to sing or dance about. In real-life newspaper strikes, politicians don't come to your rescue, although many public
officials in Michigan were initially persuaded not to grant interviews to
newsroom scabs. Sadly, in February 1997, after nineteen months on the
line, the Detroit unions made unconditional offers to return to work.
The *News* and *Free Press* offered to "take back only a fraction of the striking workers, as new vacancies allowed," because they wouldn't send any
of their hired scabs packing. Four months later, an administrative law
judge from the NLRB upheld the unions' claim that their walkout was an
unfair labor practice strike. "The judge ordered the companies to rein-
state striking workers, displacing, if necessary, the replacement workers
and making any strikers not reinstated eligible for back pay." Two days
after that encouraging decision, the AFL-CIO hosted a belated demonstration of national union solidarity with Detroit newspaper employees.

More than 60,000 union members marched, rallied, and cheered the latest legal developments.

Unfortunately, NLRB case appeal procedures are a monument to "justice delayed, justice denied." The two newspapers refused to comply with the ALJ's decision and the Labor Board failed to get a federal judge to issue "an interim injunction requiring that all strikers be returned immediately to their jobs" while litigation continued. A year later, in the summer of 1998, the board in Washington, D.C., unanimously upheld the ALJ's ruling, setting the stage for a further company appeal to the U.S. Court of Appeals. In the meantime, more than 400 former strikers remained locked out or fired, including five of the six local union presidents involved.

One hundred million dollars in back pay was riding on the appellate court's decision. On July 7, 2000, the back pay and reinstatement hopes of many were dashed when the prior NLRB rulings were overturned. Rhomberg describes what happened next:

> Deprived of their legal leverage, the unions were forced to accept contracts on management's terms. The last of the six unions settled in December, 2000, and, more than five years after it began, the Detroit newspaper strike was over. . . . The agreements offered no amnesty provisions for fired strikers, including prominent writers and columnists who had participated in non-violent civil disobedience.
>
> The newspapers refused to take those employees back, and further legal appeals went on for several more years. Finally, most of the individual strike-related civil rights suits were dismissed or settled out of court.

In one other not legally insignificant footnote to the strike, President George W. Bush named a new chairman to the NLRB in 2002. He chose Robert Battista, the Michigan attorney who served as lead counsel for the *News* and *Free Press* in their ultimately successful defense against bad faith bargaining charges.

As Rhomberg notes, the Detroit newspapers did pay a price for "their scorched earth policy toward the strikers in a community that placed a high value on unionism." He estimates their direct strike-related losses to be $130 million, because a third of all subscribers walked away too. "Circulation fell at eight times the rate for the industry as a whole between 1995 and 1999, and dozens of veteran journalists left the papers and the city, taking with them years of knowledge and public memory." In 2005, after nearly seven decades in Detroit, Knight Ridder sold the *Free Press* to Gannett. The latter then abandoned Detroit too after unloading both papers on a national suburban newspaper chain called MediaNews Group, Inc. By 2011, MNG had 500,000 fewer readers than the *News* and *Free Press* did when the previous owners tamed the unions in 1995.

Some members of the inevitable strike diaspora—union activists who refused or were unable to return to work—"went on to pursue their version of justice in various ways," Rhomberg reports. Among them are Guild members, Teamsters, printers, and others who remain active to this very day as union newspaper editors or writers, labor organizers, or solidarity campaigners elsewhere. In 1999, the *Sunday Journal*—launched as a 48-page weekly tabloid for Detroit readers boycotting the two struck papers—ceased publication. In its first year of operation, the *Journal* reached peak circulation of 300,000, unprecedented success for a labor-backed strike paper. But as former strikers were called back to the *News* or *Free Press* or left town for journalism jobs in other places, the *Journal*'s coverage shrank, its circulation declined, union financing was curtailed, and the paper died.

The *Journal* wasn't alone in not living to see the paltry contract settlements finally reached in late 2000, under duress and after labor's legal defeat. At the better-late-than-never AFL-CIO solidarity rally in June 1997 MCNU leader Al Derey brandished a list of more than a dozen strikers—printers, press operators, reporters and others—who had died from various causes during the first two years of the walkout. To rousing cheers, Derey declared that "not one of them crossed the line!" But, as Rhomberg sadly notes in *The Broken Table*, "their rights were truly scattered to the winds."[15]

11—A RED DAWN OVER DURHAM?

Although their histories are quite different, the British Labour Party and our U.S. Democrats have one thing in common: both like to avoid too

much public cuddling with workers—particularly, any sector of the organized working class whose militant struggles with management might
force them to reveal which side they're really on.

In the United States, the Democratic Party's long-standing treatment of
labor as just another "special interest" has set the stage for endless political
disappointment. In the United Kingdom, distancing yourself from the traditional culture of unionism is harder, but not impossible for a center-left
politician to do, as former prime minister Tony Blair demonstrated when
he campaigned successfully as the leader of "New Labour" in the mid-
1990s (and then proceeded to tarnish that brand as well).

Three million workers are still formally affiliated with Blair's party, via
their own national unions, and the word "labour" has yet to be excised
from its name. So, here, trade unionists still expect some loyalty from the
party that has traditionally spoken for them—whether in government or in
opposition when Parliament is controlled by the Tories (who rule today in
shaky coalition with the Liberal-Democrats).

For much of the twentieth century, party leaders paid dutiful homage
to Labour's working-class roots by joining the annual pilgrimage to the
Durham Miners' Gala. Also known as "The Big Meeting," the gala has
been held for the last 128 years on a grassy racecourse in this beautiful
cathedral town on the banks of the wandering River Wear. The event
remains the largest single union-sponsored gathering of working-class
voters in the UK and a very moving celebration of coal-mining history, art,
culture, and music.

In Durham, the last deep mine closed two decades ago. So here and
elsewhere, the National Union of Mineworkers (NUM), like the United
Mine Workers of America (UMWA), is a sad shadow of its former organizational self. Only a few thousand underground miners remain in a handful
of surviving pits. But, every summer, thousands of NUM retirees and their
families, affiliated with the union's still-functioning lodges, parade beneath
their eighty elaborately illustrated banners through the narrow streets of
Durham. As always, marching tunes are provided by community-based
brass bands, fifty of which participated in the 2012 procession.

The power of their music was well captured in the 1996 film, *Brassed
Off*, starring Pete Postlethwaite and Ewan McGregor. It deals with the
struggle to keep colliery musicians together, after a mine closing in the

depressed, black lung–ridden community of "Grimley," a thinly disguised version of the real-life village of Grimethorpe in South Yorkshire. At the gala, visiting coalfield bands even play in the city's magnificent cathedral at a memorial service for the many men killed or injured since underground mining began. During this unusual, mid-afternoon ceremony, one can listen to the mournful strains of "Gresford," the miners' hymn, while the Bishop of Durham blesses any NUM banners brought, for the first time, to the Big Meeting. The new ones consecrated in 2012 included a just-completed panorama by artist Andrew Turner, honoring the work of "Women against Pit Closures," the organization of miner's wives, girl-friends, and daughters founded by Anne Scargill, Betty Cook, and other coalfield feminists.

Avoiding Photo-Ops with Arthur

Three decades ago—before the coal industry downsizing depicted in *Brassed Off*—the UK employed 170,000 miners in more than 180 collieries. Its solidaristic communities were soon convulsed by the epic strike battle between Conservative prime minister Margaret Thatcher and the NUM, headed by Arthur Scargill, then husband of Anne. The Iron Lady was bent on taming the NUM and phasing out most domestic coal production if that's what it took to curb the power of Britain's most radical union, long allied with Labour.

As *Guardian* columnist Seumas Milne recounts in *The Enemy Within*, his definitive study of NUM-busting by the Tories, then-Labour Party leader Neil Kinnock—a putative foe of Thatcherism—was also discomfited by the blue-collar militancy of the miners. According to Milne, Kinnock "felt impotent and humiliated during the 1984–85 strike." He viewed Scargill "as a deeply unwelcome presence in the new-model Labour Party he was trying to create" more than a decade before Blair had better luck with the same modernizing project.[16]

The fainthearted Kinnock made his last appearance at the Miners Gala in 1989—when a crowd of 50,000 jammed the Old Racecourse. (Some estimates put the 2012 total turnout at twice that number.) After that, he and his successors—John Smith, Tony Blair, and Gordon Brown—all avoided Durham like the plague, so they wouldn't be trapped on the balcony of the County Hotel, reviewing the troops with Scargill and other left-wing union generals. Such carefully calculated snubs were, in Milne's view, designed "to bury the spectre of class politics and trade union militancy which haunted Labour's effort to construct a post-social democratic electoral machine."

A Miliband Not to Be Confused with Ralph

In 2010, the party picked Oxford-educated Ed Miliband, a former TV journalist and Labour Party researcher, to replace Gordon Brown as its new leader. But gala-wise, there was no change of heart one year later. Miliband skipped "The Big Meeting" in 2011 because Bob Crow, of the National Union of Rail, Maritime, and Transport workers (RMT), was also scheduled to attend. Such close proximity to the colorful and controversial Crow, who proudly proclaims the RMT to be a "socialist union," was apparently more than Miliband could bear, public relations-wise, so early in his leadership career.

Where Ed grew up, there was less wariness about working-class heroes. His father, Ralph, was a Belgian-born Marxist academic and internationally known figure in the British New Left who is now buried in Highgate Cemetery not far from Marx himself. Miliband's mother, Marion Kozak, campaigned for human rights and nuclear disarmament. Drawing further attention to this distinguished family tree, Ed became party leader two years ago by defeating his equally ambitious older brother, David, a fellow member of Parliament. To get a feel on our side of the Atlantic for this particular family fissure, imagine the governors of Texas and Florida squaring off against each other in the 2000 Republican primaries, with no Poppy Bush to mediate.

Miliband père's best-known book, *Parliamentary Socialism,* was a sharp critique of Labour policy and practice, circa 1961.[17] A few years later, the author let his own membership lapse and described Prime Minister Harold Wilson's backing of the Vietnam War as the "most shameful chapter" in party history. Writing in *The Independent,* journalist Andy McSmith has noted, accurately, that the elder Miliband's public life had a "nobility and drama" often missing from the "steady, pragmatic political careers" of his two sons.[18]

Why the Coast Was Clear

Bob Crow was not on the speakers' program for the 2012 Big Meeting, although he attended as an honored guest. He was accompanied by a group of rank-and-file members, who marched behind the RMT's own banner, and then gathered at a union information booth set up in a black tent. The tent was adorned with a big picture of Arthur Scargill along with a quote from one of his fiery syndicalist speeches. The now retired miner's leader reminded gala-goers that "what we need is not marches, demonstrations, rallies . . . what we need is DIRECT ACTION!"

In the run-up to the gala, local miners' association official Dave Hopper expressed retroactive relief that Tony Blair, unlike Miliband, had never darkened Durham's door during the party leadership's long boycott of the event. "Blair spent his time starting wars and wrecking the health service," Hopper said. "He would have besmirched the platform." Hopper praised the current leader's display of "courage" in coming and promised, as chair of the event, to ensure a polite reception. "You can't stop people who don't want to listen," the retired miner noted. "But let's hear what he has to say." Hopper predicted that most gala attendees would be "quite pleased" to have Miliband since "the County Council has been Labour-controlled for 93 years, all borough councils have vast Labour majorities, and every constituency regularly elects Labour MPs." Even in two neighboring counties, "the Tories and the liberals were obliterated," Hopper boasted. "They represent the interests of big business and capitalism and we want no truck with them!"[19]

A "Friend" among "Comrades"

In *The Guardian*, Lady Warsi, a baroness born in Pakistan and national co-chair of the Tories, seemed equally enthusiastic about Miliband's mid-July travel plans. Calling him "Red Ed," she hailed the end of "23 years of silence from the Labour leadership at the Gala," and predicted that his appearance there would "drive the Labour Party away from the centre ground of British politics" (where it's not clear she resides either). She accused Miliband of "cozy[ing] up to his militant, left-wing union paymasters."[20]

Seated among the speakers at the gala, Miliband was definitely rubbing elbows with top officials of the General, Municipal, and Boilermakers Union, the Public and Commercial Services Union, and the shrunken NUM, not to mention two Spanish miners who came directly from Asturian highway blockades and left with 10,000 English pounds to support their pit-closing resistance.

Neatly attired in a red tie and dark suit, the slim, dark-featured forty-two-year-old party leader looked every bit like an up-and-coming young London banker or accountant, who had strayed, by accident, onto a country fairgrounds filled with tens of thousands of white working-class northeasterners. Few of the latter were dressed like anyone on the platform, with the exception of the T-shirt–wearing Spaniards and eighty-seven-year-old Tony Benn, the now retired tribune of Labour's parliamentary left, who kept his rambling wear on, instead of displaying his Sunday best.

On the perimeter of the Old Racecourse, I could see many people enjoying themselves on the Ferris wheel and Helter-Skelter ride, at the Fun House and Crazy Circus, and inside an attraction called "Jungle Madness." But thousands also stood stock-still in front of the speaker's platform, listening to two hours' worth of verbal barrages against the "Con-Dems" in Westminster. At one point, Dave Hopper, who was chairing the event, seemed to take notice of the different sartorial tastes of those on the platform as opposed to the thousands of Labour loyalists standing patiently before them on the grass. "We're getting surrounded by lawyers and barristers up here," he joked.

Restoring the Right to Strike?

Fortunately, one member of the bar, who spoke before Miliband, did what no union official on the platform dared: he directly challenged the new party leader to strengthen national labor law when and if Labour defeats the Tories. Longtime NUM lawyer John Hendy, QC, displayed a sharp wit in his open-air tutorial on the current state of collective bargaining in Britain. First, he turned to Miliband and cheekily told him to get his pencil out so he could "take a note" on what was being said. Then he informed the appreciative crowd: "I want to talk about trade union rights, and I will be short because we don't have any."

The tall, white-haired Hendy quickly chronicled the disastrous decline in collective bargaining coverage, from 80 percent of the workforce in 1979 to 30 percent today. He blamed not just Thatcher but Blair for "British laws on trade unions that are now the most restrictive in the Western world." He effectively linked declining union density to the UK's increase in poverty, income inequality, and various social ills. He pointed out that workers' rights "are human rights guaranteed in international treaties, and binding on this country."

"What we need," Hendy concluded, "are trade union rights, like the right to strike, the power to take industrial action." And then, turning to Miliband again, he said: "Ed, you now have a respectable, unimpeachable, legal argument for reinstating these rights."

Next Battle of Britain?

Miliband's own Obama-esque oration was a mere eleven minutes long. His prepared text contained no mention of collective bargaining, and he never deviated from it, in response to Hendy. His carefully scripted cadences elicited only a few scattered catcalls from within the vast crowd, which he addressed as "friends," not "comrades," the old-school saluta-tion favored by other speakers. As Miliband summed up Labour's destiny, it is "to rebuild our country . . . on the values of the people of Britain: responsibility, community, fairness, equality, and justice. That's our mis-sion, that's our task, that's the battle we can win together."

His only slightly less vague agenda for "day one" of a future Miliband government included breaking up the banks and/or taxing bankers' bonuses, ending "energy rip-offs," and curbing the power of press moguls like Rupert Murdoch. To whet the appetite of those present, he invoked the memory of past Labour PM's like Attlee and Wilson, wisely leaving Blair off his list.

As local party officials and visiting union dignitaries filed off the stage, an impressive throng of spectators surrounded Miliband, shaking his hand, patting him on the back, and thrusting program books his way to be autographed. While he made his way slowly to the Labour tent, I took the opportunity to shake hands with Tony Benn instead. The aging lion of the British left had just spent his fifty-first "Big Meeting" hunched over in a folding chair near the edge of the platform, smoking his pipe, and seem-ingly lost in thought. A former Labour cabinet member and MP for half a century, Benn was introduced to the crowd only in passing. As he walked away unsteadily, with the help of a young assistant, he was greeted rever-ently by a handful of other longtime fans.

As barrister Hendy departed the stage, I asked him what Miliband's non-response portended for labor law reform in the UK. "His pencil must have been blunt," he said with a smile, adding that "we're still working on it and we'll get there in the end." At a post-gala screening of a documentary called *Will and Testament*, which chronicles Benn's career, the old social-ist was similarly upbeat, but more protective of the new boy who had failed to pick up the gauntlet thrown his way.

In a Q&A session after the film, I queried Benn about Miliband's performance. He agreed that "the rights of trade unionists need to be restored" and that Hendy's points were "powerfully made." But, in his view, Miliband had shown adequate union sympathy at the gala. According to Benn, if the party leader addresses workers' rights in the future, he will "be taking on some formidable opponents and he knows it."

But overcoming such foes won't be possible without mobilizing Labour's traditional base, plus many new recruits to the Party. If Miliband isn't even willing to pander, Obama-style, to a pro-union crowd—by applauding collective bargaining—he's certainly not going to defend the practice before a national audience or make strengthening unions a post-election priority. And the result of that political positioning will be exactly what workers have gotten in the United States from their own "friend of labor," President Obama, since he entered the White House in 2008.[21]

POSTSCRIPT

At the Durham Miners' Gala just a year later, Ed Miliband's honeymoon was clearly over.[22] In 2013 the leader of the Labour party was MIA again, but much criticized in absentia. Len McCluskey, leader of the 1.4 million-member Unite, warned that Miliband's organization "has no 'God-given eight to exist' and its survival depends on remaining the voice of ordi-nary people." McCluskey was strongly applauded when he noted that the parliamentary party was becoming the preserve of an "out-of-touch elite—who glide from university to think tank to the green benches of the House of Commons without ever sniffing the air of the real world." [23]

In a pre-gala interview, the irrepressible Bob Crow claimed that "the whole program of Labour now is to try to sneak back into government by default on the basis of a manifesto that could trade under the title, 'Carry on Cutting.' Our job is not to prop up the political class behind this racket; our job is to sweep it away." The RMT general secretary "issued a call to the trade union movement to support the creation of a 'new party of Labour' to challenge the pro-business, anti-worker agenda of the Tories." Said Crow: "Clinging to the wreckage of a Labour Party that didn't lift a finger to repeal the anti-union laws despite 13 years in power is a complete waste of time." [24]

PART III

ORGANIZING FOR THE
LONG HAUL

This section of *Save Our Unions* considers the challenge of union organizing in the United States. During the four decades that I've been involved in labor activity, union density—the percentage of the workforce with bargaining rights—has steadily declined to an ever more perilous level. In 1983, forty-two states had at least 10 percent of their private sector workforce covered by union contracts. Today, that's down to just eight states as overall union membership has dropped to 6.6 percent in private industry.

As a national staff member for the Communications Workers of America (CWA), I participated in many attempts to overcome employer resistance to unionization. CWA was not alone in trying to find new ways to help workers win. The AFL-CIO, Change to Win, and other independent unions have waged "strategic campaigns" that seek to neutralize management interference through various forms of external pressure. And some, along with the Industrial Workers of the World (IWW), have tried to strengthen their inside organizing by "salting" non-union workplaces such as Starbucks with younger activists recruited and trained to assist union building as rank-and-file workers, rather than as full-time staffers.

In earlier periods of labor history, like the 1930s and the 1970s, these inside organizers were known as "colonizers." They often had ties to left organizations with a broader and more explicit political agenda than the unions employing "salts" today. Both approaches described in the following reports—colonizing and cross-border campaigning—require much organizational patience, persistence, and long-term focus. Unfortunately, these qualities are not always present in U.S. union recruitment efforts, even where labor's corporate adversaries display great staying power and long-term planning capacity of their own.

12—SALTING TO THE RESCUE?

In the 1970s, as in the 1930s, left-wing activists who wanted to become working-class organizers mainly headed for auto assembly lines, trucking company loading docks, coal mines, shipyards, or steel mills. In all those gritty blue-collar venues, rank-and-file militancy was on the rise and the prospects for labor "radicalization" looked good.[1] Three or four decades later, young American radicals similarly inclined to "industrialize" often found themselves in very different workplace circumstances. The real action was no longer in America's traditional proletariat; it was among the "precariat," the millions of native-born and immigrant workers who lacked collective bargaining rights, fringe benefit coverage, and any semblance of job security.[2]

This change of scenery reflected, in part, a much-noted intervening shift from traditional blue-collar employment to service sector jobs. By the beginning of the new millennium, the once commanding heights of the "old economy" had been reduced, in many midwestern cities, to a sad pile of post-industrial rubble. By 2012, there were 5.5 million fewer factory jobs than in July 2000, and those that remained, in the auto industry, were paying $14 an hour for new hires, about half the wages of newly hired workers only a decade before.[3]

One by-product of manufacturing downsizing is our current shrunken, disheartened, and marginalized industrial union culture. Within the United Auto Workers, Steel Workers, Teamsters, and other onetime midwestern union giants, little remains of the labor left's once active shop floor presence. Labor insurgency today is more likely to be found among workers making closer to the minimum wage, in fast food or retail jobs, than bottom tier pay in auto plants. And these struggles, while backed by some traditional unions, are being waged by less formal, community-based workers' organizations.

In 2005, the small left group known as Solidarity published a well-crafted appeal addressed to "young radical activists" contemplating entry into some sector of labor. It urged them to work for "change from below"—always a good place to start—by "taking jobs in targeted workplaces to organize." This course of action was projected as an alternative to using prior campus experience as a labor ally to get hired, after graduation, as a full-time staffer for a worker center or union. *Radicals at Work: An Activist Strategy for Revitalizing the Labor Movement* was carefully ecumenical on the question of whether former students should seek employment in non-union shops or "go into already organized ones to build workplace organization"[4]

The latter route was much preferred by members of the same group when they belonged to the International Socialists (IS) in the 1970s. The IS encouraged the formation of Teamsters for a Democratic Union (TDU) and other shorter-lived union reform caucuses in several industries. In a 2002 internal document, Solidarity continued to argue that political work among "unionized industrial workers is essential to the revitalization of the labor movement and the socialist project."[5] However, as a guide to personal career planning, this assertion proved to be less persuasive in the early twenty-first century than in the last quarter of the previous one. "With only 6 or 7 percent of the workforce organized in the private sector, rank-and-file caucuses aren't the answer for a lot of people," admitted one young Solidarity member, who had cast his own lot, bravely but atypically, with TDU.[6]

Far more veterans of recent campus activism have embraced the challenge of organizing the unorganized on the new frontiers of the service sector. There, some national unions have been eager to train and deploy underground organizers—now more commonly known as "salts," rather than as "colonizers," with its Old Left connotation of having a political agenda broader than just union building.

It's also a sign of the times that employment in the service sector, retail, and hospitality industries may be easier to obtain without concealing, via a falsified job application, your educational background as a four-year degree holder. In today's world of downward mobility, no one seems to be "overqualified" anymore—a tip-off that once enabled HR managers to finger New Left infiltrators, with college experience, who made a beeline for traditional blue-collar jobs in the 1970s. But serious workplace organizing is never for dilettantes, in any era. As the personal stories below confirm, recruiting coworkers into a union from the inside can be more challenging and complex than the better-known role played by full-time professionals operating on the outside.

Adding More Salts

One promoter of the inside approach is Peter Olney, who dropped out of Harvard (like Bill Gates, he notes) and later worked as an elevator operator and refrigeration mechanic at a unionized hospital in Boston. In the 1970s, Olney belonged to a "vanguard party" that encouraged its members to become coal miners, steel workers, and other kinds of industrial workers. In the 1980s, he moved to the West Coast and became a full-time union organizer, ending up on the staff of the International Longshore and Warehouse Union (ILWU). The ILWU has a long history of support for progressive political causes, from its founding in the 1930s to the present day. Unfortunately, like many other blue-collar unions, its core membership has aged and shrunk due to technological change, industry restructuring, and job elimination through attrition. After Olney became the union's organizing director, he invoked the lessons of labor history when he called for "a broad-based plan that emphasizes 'salting' or planting organizers in key workplaces and industries" to help unions rebuild their lost strength. Olney argued:

> Salting was one factor in much of the labor upsurge of the 1930s
> when communists, socialists, and other progressives "industrial-
> ized" to build worker power in the mines, mills, and fields. This,
> more than hiring young people as organizers, is the way to promote
> large-scale organization. Nothing can replace the presence of these
> politicized organizers in the workplaces of America. Nothing can
> replace this experience in teaching young organizers, largely from
> a non-working-class background, what the working class is about

and how to talk and especially listen to workers. Salting needs to become fashionable again for young people politically committed to reinvigorating the labor movement.[7]

Carey Dall and Jono Cohen are two young organizers mentored by Olney. They agree that "systematic salting of key industries can force changes in the labor movement, specifically around the question of how best to organize."[8] In their view, too much new member recruitment is "heavily reliant upon staff organizers and virtually incapable of developing rank-and-file leadership." Instead, it just "helps reinforce the seemingly universal notion that unions are myopic insurance agents."

In the late 1990s, both Dall and Cohen got jobs in San Francisco's courier industry, "under the strategic direction of the ILWU," just as workers there were showing signs of interest in organizing. Courier companies employ radio-dispatched bike messengers and local delivery drivers to transport legal documents and other time-sensitive materials from one corporate client to another. Among their job-related complaints were "low wages, poor health benefits (if any at all), long hours, without legally required overtime, and terrible working conditions."

Both in their mid-twenties, Dall and Cohen dived into the "dangerous, physically exhausting, and psychologically taxing" bicycling end of this business, in part because "two college-educated leftist white guys" wouldn't stand out so much in a San Francisco workforce that was "male, white, single, and between the ages of eighteen and thirty." Most "same-day delivery" drivers, in contrast, tend to be first-generation immigrants from Mexico, Central America, China, and South Asia with families and mortgages. They are thus far "less likely to be part of the messenger social scene," a "tight community of athletic young men" in which a shared interest in "punk rock and beer" played no small part.

Organizing Bike Messengers

Dall and Cohen found that organizing bike messengers was "like herding cats." Becoming part of their community was essential to the process of "having meaningful conversations about the pros and cons of unionism."

The messenger world in San Francisco operates on the fringes of a number of young and rebellious cultural movements. It is virtually impossible to determine where the shared work experience ends and the social bonding begins. . . . Many in the industry would not have thought of being messengers without having met at punk shows or parties. . . . Giving personal advice, offering a couch to crash on, loaning money, and drinking ourselves legless are all part of instinctive bonding among fellow workers.

In Dall and Cohen's opinion, "a salt is, well, not worth his or her own salt if the relationships he or she builds with coworkers are not real friendships, independent of the union organizing." Without the "support and friendship of coworkers, many of whom will never know that we got jobs as messengers to organize, we would not have found salting sustainable," the ILWU organizers report. "Salting is not a form of labor activism that everyone can sustain. Adding to the ever present stress of organizing, including all the after-work and weekend meetings, is the constant fear of being found out and fired by your boss."

In the San Francisco bike messenger drive, participants met quarterly to analyze their industry and plot strategy through a citywide Courier Organizing Group (COG). As ILWU organizer Augustin Ramirez recalls, Local 6 officers and national union staff members

had to adjust to and respect the traditions and customs of the bike messengers. We had meetings in extremely loud bars, meetings at the union hall were very, very animated and sometimes chaotic, but, at the end, we got things done. Every action we did during this campaign involved bike messengers riding from point A to point B.[9]

The messengers themselves set the agenda, ran their own meetings, and tried to reach consensus on next steps in their campaign. According to Dall and Cohen, the "deliberations of the COG followed the traditional ILWU method: the rank and file makes the decisions, and the attending labor bureaucrats help to carry them out." Dall and Cohen contrasted this approach with that of a union using a salt "as it would a staff organizer, where the activist is given instructions and must toe the line of the union's organizing policy."

During the nearly five years that Dall worked at two non-union messenger companies, there was considerable worker-initiated strike activity over management unfair labor practices and fair labor standards violations. In 2000, the bike messengers secured the first of two union contracts, via NLRB elections and the leverage provided by wage and hour complaints to the state labor commissioner. About 130 workers were covered in all. At a third company, called DMS, a strike by the workers led to negotiation of a card check and neutrality agreement. But after a majority of workers signed up and union recognition was demanded the company closed its doors.

The COG's original objective of organizing industry-wide and winning a master contract was never achieved due to a number of inhibiting factors. The dot-com bubble burst, reducing messenger service business among San Francisco's high-tech firms. Then Arnold Schwarzenegger was elected governor, which led to weaker state enforcement of state wage and hour laws. Within the ILWU, Warehouse Local 6, which had been supporting the bike messengers' campaign, became paralyzed by internal factional strife and dysfunctional in the area of organizing.

Although no courier firm in the Bay Area is unionized today, several veterans of the organizing a decade ago created small bike messenger collectives, which wooed clients away from mainstream firms and continue to function today. Carey Dall became a welder and a working member of Local 6 in an established bargaining unit. He continues to work as a "lost-time" or member organizer, as needed by his local or the International union. Jono Cohen became a labor lawyer, now practicing in Southern California.

The UNITE HERE Model

Far more than the West Coast–based ILWU or any other union, the Hotel Employees and Restaurant Employees (known since a 2004 merger as UNITE HERE) has developed an ongoing national program of salting. Using careful targeting, training, and support, UNITE HERE has steered scores of "interns," as the union euphemistically calls its salts, toward non-union workplaces in the hospitality industry. There, inside organizers coordinate their work closely with union staffers operating on the outside. The best and most persistent of the UNITE HERE salts spend many months, even years, building personal relationships with coworkers who may eventually become public supporters of the union.

As UNITE HERE's organizing program evolved in the 1980s and '90s under the leadership of John Wilhelm and other veterans of student and union activity at Yale, the union also became well known for hiring Ivy League (and other college) graduates as corporate campaign researchers, boycott coordinators, and full-time staff organizers.[10] But not all ex-Yalies have taken that route. Nick Stoeckel (a pseudonym), a former graduate student at the university, explained that he much preferred working as a "salt." In his first union job as a poorly trained organizer for the Service Employees International Union (SEIU), Stoeckel's attempt to build inside organizing committees in nursing homes "basically crashed and burned" because he had "no clue about how to talk to workers."

After switching to a UNITE HERE affiliate on the West Coast, Stoeckel spent six months on internal organizing projects, working with shop stewards in unionized hotels. Then he decided to better develop himself as "an organizing leader" by going to work at a non-union Westin Hotel, where salting contributed to a successful unionization drive. For the next three years, he learned the issues, built relationships with coworkers, and recruited other "interns" for a local union that, at one point, had twenty-five participants in its citywide salting program, some with prior hotel worker experience and others with none.

"There were people who said, 'I'd rather get a staff job' because they didn't want to go from college to working in a hotel and then have to worry about what their parents would think," Stoeckel recalls. "For me personally, it was a matter of learning how to relate to people in a confident way to function as a workplace leader. I was more of a heady intellectual type before, very passionate, but not necessarily that great an organizer even as a student."[11]

Puttin' on the Ritz

Ritz-Carlton's Huntington Hotel (now known as the Langham) in upscale Pasadena seemed like an equally dramatic change of venue for former campus organizer Steve Strong when I met him there in late 2007. Just nine miles from downtown Las Angeles, the 107-year-old Ritz advertises itself, with pride, as "a Southern California classic." It's a sprawling, palace-like building, salmon-colored with a red-tile roof and a central courtyard with a sun-dappled fountain. Palm trees surround its twenty-four beautifully manicured acres, and, in the distance, one can see the San Gabriel Mountains. The hotel's gilt-trimmed ballrooms are used for lavish weddings and receptions; on weekdays, its conference rooms are used for meetings and seminars held by brokerage firms, media companies, and high-tech industry sales managers. When these and other well-heeled guests break for lunch on the terrace, they can sample specialties of the house like a $125 caviar crepe appetizer. After work, the Ritz offers a further "world of well-being"—ranging from California's first Olympic-size pool to "all embracing featherbeds." In the seventeen treatment rooms of its Spa, guests get to choose from "a full menu of massage therapies, facial treatments, and salon services," all promising "relaxation and restoration of body, mind, and spirit."

I first encountered Steve Strong at a meeting of United Students against Sweatshops (USAS) in 2002, when he was still an undergraduate at Fordham University and working as a USAS regional organizer.[12] The son of an IBM worker from Fishkill, New York, Strong had read about the experience of radicals involved in the great industrial union upsurge of the New Deal era. "What inspired me," he explained, "was the Communists in the 1930s—students dropping out of school, getting jobs, and organizing in the plants."[13] His original postgraduate goal was "just taking a job and working with a socialist organization" that was trying to influence the direction of an established union. But then he decided that the best way to acquire organizing experience was "to get a job in a non-union workplace and learn there."

Now the slender, fair-haired Strong greeted me in the Ritz lobby, clad in the brown uniform of a bellman, his job for the previous four years. With only a few minutes to spare on his break, he proceeded to brief me on what hotel work can do to the "body, mind, and spirit" of those waiting, hand and foot, on Ritz customers. "Working here has radicalized me even more," Strong said. "I've been abused and disrespected by some of the richest people in the world!" When we met in Pasadena, the "underground" union organizing committee that Steve had been patiently trying to build had just surfaced publicly (but only partially) several months before, putting him in the unwanted spotlight as a ringleader.

In August of 2007, 12,000-member Local 11—the UNITE HERE affiliate seeking to represent Ritz housekeepers, dishwashers, cooks, servers, and front-desk staff—had called a press conference outside the hotel to denounce "an anti-union campaign that include[d] interrogation of employees, threats of retaliation, and the offering of incentives to prevent employees from engaging in union activity." The union's labor and community allies picketed in protest while its lawyers filed unfair labor practice charges against the Ritz at the National Labor Relations Board in Los Angeles.[14]

The union's now public campaign was still primarily directed at the hotel's owner, the Los Angeles County Employees Retirement Association (LACERA), a $40 billion public employee pension plan. UNITE HERE's campaign strategy was to get the unions represented on LACERA's board to insist that the management company employed by the fund, Marriott International, stop its illegal intimidation of workers and agree to negotiated ground rules for union recognition. Marriott fights unionization both in the hotels it owns directly and the ones it manages for others—acting as "the Wal-Mart of our industry," Strong explained. Unfortunately, UNITE HERE's bid for an "organizing rights" deal in Pasadena became more complicated when LACERA decided to sell its hotel there. This development threatened to undermine the union's "leverage campaign" at a stage when majority support for unionization might still be hard to demonstrate, inside the hotel, even if management's anti-union behavior could be curbed.

UNITE HERE had proceeded methodically over the previous four years to create a network of hotel workers willing to seek unionization, an effort that, in its final stages, also required putting pressure on putative allies at the ownership level to impose a policy of neutrality on Ritz management. Some form of negotiated "card check and neutrality" was necessary because winning a contested NLRB election would have been problematic, even if it were not union policy to avoid such representation votes, wherever possible. As is common now in the "hospitality industry," the hotel no longer had a workforce that fit the traditional Labor Board

definition of an appropriate "wall to wall" bargaining unit.[15] More than
four hundred workers performed various tasks in the Ritz, but many were
not direct employees of the hotel. In a fashion invisible to guests, and even
to one another, workers in some departments, like housekeeping and valet
parking, were actually employed through temporary agencies.

Contracting out not only gave the hotel an additional legal tool for
dividing and conquering, it also helped reinforce the usual racial division of labor between the "front of the house" (predominantly white) and
"back of the house" departments (largely non-white), where lower pay
and bad working conditions led to higher turnover. Due to the prevailing "fear factor," Strong made no direct effort to recruit coworkers to the
union cause when he was first hired. Instead, he discreetly gathered the
names and addresses of various people he met who might be receptive
and passed this information along to Local 11's outside organizing team.

UNITE HERE is "very good at building tight structure, through one-
on-one organizing," Strong said. So his individual assessments of Ritz
employees were double-checked by UNITE HERE staff members who
visited these same workers at home. To avoid alerting hotel management
to the fact that a union probe was under way, even the first round of house
visits was conducted under cover. When they knocked on doors, Local
11 organizers did not disclose their real organizational affiliation. Instead,
they pretended to be canvassing the neighborhood on behalf of some
other labor or community issue to justify the visit, hoping to engage Ritz
workers in any living-room conversation that might reveal their attitude
toward collective action in general.

Inside Committee Building

Over time, the union's inside and outside organizers were able to pull
together a small but well-trained and trusted committee that included up
to twenty-five public supporters.[16] The personal courage and commitment
of this "militant minority" at the Ritz was a continual source of inspiration
for Strong, particularly during the long weekends and evenings he spent
visiting hotel staff members at home. "Sometimes when some of my friend-
liest coworkers opened their door, it was as if the cage of a trapped animal
had just been opened," Strong recalled. At other Ritz workers' homes the

reception wasn't so friendly. Strong learned to accept door slamming in his face and, sometimes, workers reporting back to management that he had been canvassing for the union.

On the job, Strong found the workplace environment in some parts of the hotel to be "very sexist and homophobic." On campus, he had been sheltered in the more tolerant world of progressive student activism. However, "in a hotel, you can't just write off people who talk about 'bitches' and 'fags' when your goal is to get everyone to come together in the union." After a while, however, he was able to get other organizing committee members to join with him in discouraging comments that were demeaning to women and gays. Because he won their respect and helped them to develop an understanding of what it takes to build workplace unity, he even succeeded in getting "the very masculine bellman department to stop talking about faggots."

Some of Strong's foreign-born coworkers had prior union or political experience that proved to be helpful in the campaign. But Strong also learned that the experience of past union failures or "revolutions that left behind broken hopes and promises" could be an impediment to activism. One coworker from Iran—his closest personal friend at the Ritz—was particularly distrustful of union bureaucracy and reluctant to put himself forward as a leader in the campaign. Only belatedly did Strong discover that the man had nearly been killed when he and his father were fired on by government troops during a rally against the Shah in 1979. After the Islamic revolution, his father, a prominent judge, received death threats when he dared to criticize the new regime for allowing the U.S. embassy hostage taking, a violation of international law. Family members were eventually forced to emigrate. Over time, Strong learned that "whether we change a workplace or not depends more on anger, fear, trust and respect, rather than telling facts or showing union contracts—some of the things my coworkers would say they needed to get involved, but which usually turned out to be part of a litany of excuses. . . . More than reason or theory, winning the union comes from the gut."

Other union committee members at the Ritz also had firsthand exposure to economic hardship, political unrest, or government repression in their native lands. "When we feel like it's really tough," Strong told me, "they remind themselves of how things are comparatively easier here." To boost his sometimes sagging spirits, he would recall the experience of an ex-guerilla he once met, who spent eight years on the same little mountain working as a radio operator during El Salvador's civil war. "This hotel is my mountain," he told himself, "and I too have my little role in a world-wide struggle."

When the Ritz campaign went public, management's divide-and-conquer strategy intensified. Recalls Strong: "They threatened the 'back of the house'—all immigrant, primarily Mexican, Salvadoran, and Filipino—while trying to buy off the more privileged 'front of the house' workers, who tend to be more formally educated, English-speaking, and from more middle-class backgrounds." In a bid to co-opt him, management made Strong a "Quality Leader." In a leadership training class, mainly composed of executive management and hotel supervisors, he was given a mirror that said "I am a hero" on it. He joked later that "they were trying to remind me, 'hey, you're white . . . you're on the wrong side, what are you doing?'" Meanwhile, on the job, the youthful Ritz bellmen built solidarity among themselves in a playful way, right under the noses of the "Ritz Crackers," as they called the managers. "We jokingly created a union 'gang symbol' with our hands that we increasingly found unexpected coworkers discreetly flashing back at us."

It was Strong's job as an inside organizer to talk to groups here and there throughout the hotel, and remind them that, for the time being, it was okay to stay *bajo de agua* (underground) because there was "a tidal wave of backlash coming and it's okay to duck under and hold your breath, until you're ready to find you strengths, confront your fears, and stand up to change your life." Housekeeper Elvia Alonzo was one of the open union supporters brave enough to join Strong at the August 2007 press conference that accused Ritz managers of violating wage and hour laws, plus engaging in racial discrimination. The day before Alonzo spoke out publicly, three managers brought her into their office. They interrogated her about union activity, and warned that she might lose her job because of it. Backed by members of the clergy and community organizations, she told the press the very next day how she proudly took off her apron and threw it at them, saying if they wanted her to leave she would and they could clean her fifty rooms themselves.

At an employee meeting called by the general manager of the Ritz to rebut union charges, Strong and other organizing committee leaders took the floor to challenge the hotel's mistreatment of its staff. Their statements received "thunderous applause from coworkers, including some of the most scared and anti-union critics among them." Local 11 encouraged its public supporters to engage in a series of "shop floor fights" that would build solidarity, develop rank-and-file leadership, and win concrete gains even before the union was recognized. With Strong's participation and encouragement, delegations of up to fifteen workers tested the limits of the Ritz's "open door" policy by using their breaks to present "group griev-ances" to the hotel's human resources director, and then escalating their complaints directly to the general manager.

Solidarity Divided?

Unfortunately, the higher-ranking labor officials on LACERA's board dis-played far less spunk. When Strong finally had an opportunity to address "the owners of our hotel," he and other Ritz workers ended up being rather disappointed with their response. "Support from the LA county unions—SEIU, AFSCME, the Firefighters—was lukewarm, with the Firefighters union leadership outright opposing us," Strong recalls. SEIU's represen-tative on the board did vote in favor of the card check/neutrality agreement that UNITE HERE was seeking to impose on the anti-union managers of the Ritz. But, according to Strong, even his union's Change to Win ally "didn't want us to tell our war stories about oppression in the hotel." The Ritz's subsequent sale to the Langham Hospitality Group, a luxury hotel chain owned by Hong Kong investors, ended up making the old owners' views on management neutrality irrelevant.

Developments at the Ritz had forced the union to go public with its inside committee building before a broader, more representative group could be established. Yet, by using a combination of legal and publicity tactics, the "militant minority" of union supporters was able to secure a commitment that the pay and benefits of the existing workforce would survive the ownership transfer intact. At that point, Strong and two other inside organizers left the hotel to join the UNITE HERE staff and work on other campaigns. "If the committee that was public wanted to push forward with Langham, and if the underground committee was bolder and angry enough to go public, more might have been possible," Strong believes.

Continuing the drive proved to be impossible after key inside leaders left and many other workers adopted a wait-and-see attitude toward the new owners when the hotel was changing hands. Twenty years earlier, the same hotel had been unionized, as part of the Sheraton chain; the facility was then closed for renovations and reopened, non-union, as the luxurious Ritz. So the 2008 ownership change in Pasadena was not the first to produce a union setback.

Strong went on to organize full-time for UNITE HERE in Hawaii and Texas, before leaving the country in 2010 to pursue graduate studies and research on bank worker unionism in Brazil. Upon his return to the United States, he aided an internal organizing drive at a Xerox-run E-ZPass call center on Staten Island in New York City. There, anti-union workers had won a Labor Board vote to "de-authorize" the union security clause negotiated by the Communications Workers of America, the first step toward a management-backed decertification effort. In late 2012, the bargaining unit was saved in part because of Strong's systematic UNITE HERE–style approach to inside committee building.

Reflecting on his varied organizing experiences, Strong is critical of his old union's "limited political program" and what he perceives as overinvolvement with the Democratic Party. But he gives UNITE HERE much credit for "appreciating people who have the ideological commitment necessary to spend four and a half years in a hotel" as a salt. During that period in his life, Strong found there was little room left for any outside political activity, including his own continuing self-education about radical theory. "In the real world of organizing, your time and energy has to go so much into the day-to-day work," he said.

Undercover in Northern California

California native Tenaya Lafore got her first union experience helping to organize cafeteria workers at Brown University in the early 1990s. Two years after graduating, she became a private and public sector union organizer in Vermont. In the Green Mountain State, she learned firsthand "how business unions worked and don't work." The government employees' association that hired her had very few stewards, and didn't train or support them well or encourage collective activity on the job.

Instead, "all the knowledge and control remained with the full-time staff." Working as a servicing rep was "like doing social work," Lafore found. She summed up the union's organizational philosophy as follows: "We're the experts—we get things for the members because they're not capable of doing it for themselves."

Lafore left her union staff job and got involved with the Vermont Workers Center (VWC). She helped the VWC and the United Electrical Workers (UE) launch an experimental organizing campaign in Vermont's state capital. Like the ILWU's bike messenger drive in San Francisco, the Montpelier Downtown Workers Union (MDWU) tried to build a direct action-oriented union, based on existing social networks of young workers who moved from one low-wage job to another in local bars, restaurants, retail stores, and Montpelier's main hotel. But even organizing full-time for the VWC in the freewheeling youth culture of central Vermont, Lafore experienced "the limitations of being a staff person." She was not a retail worker herself, yet it was her job to encourage union supporters to take leadership roles in their workplaces, which led, inevitably, to several being fired for organizing activity. "Because I became an organizer straight out of college and never had to work in any of these crappy service sector jobs myself, I felt it was a little hypocritical to push people to do something I hadn't done," Lafore told me. "As a member of a union, I also thought I'd be in a better position to organize my coworkers to fight for democratic control of the organization."

Lafore returned to California where her first job in food service was an eighteen-month stint at the Cheesecake Factory, where Young Workers United (YWU), a San Francisco worker center, was conducting a protest campaign over wage and hour law violations by the non-union restaurant chain. (YWU eventually helped Cheesecake Factory employees win a $4 million settlement of unpaid overtime claims.)[17]

In San Francisco, 80 percent of the restaurants were once unionized. Now, only a few outside of unionized hotels are—and Local 2 of UNITE HERE can afford to focus its resources on organizing restaurant workers only as part of hotel-wide campaigns. This left YWU free to engage in shop floor agitation among non-union workers while cooperating with Local 2 on political initiatives like a campaign to enact a municipal ordinance requiring local employers to provide paid sick leave. The fluid organizational structure of YWU was an advantage, Lafore found, because "unions often have such institutional baggage and workers' centers can start from scratch and use creative alternative tactics and strategies."

Unfortunately, like most worker centers, the YWU had few dues-paying members and was heavily dependent on outside funding—at the time, about $100,000 in foundation grants. The main contribution of its fifty activists was their own time and energy. But there was not, according to Lafore, "much accountability to the membership. When members pay dues they can demand more accountability."[18]

Hoping to play a role in more structured, larger-scale workplace campaigns, with stronger outside support, Lafore applied for employment in both union and non-union hotels. She landed a job as a cocktail waitress at a San Francisco Hilton that was among the hotels involved in Local 2's 53-day lockout in 2005–6. The result of that epic struggle was a widely praised citywide master agreement with good wages and benefits, plus strong "successor clause" language protecting workers if their hotel was sold (in a deal like the one that derailed organizing at the Ritz in Pasadena).[19]

Strategically Smart

Lafore freely praised the UNITE HERE leadership for being "so strategically smart" and building the membership mobilization capacity necessary to fight employers locally and nationally. But she faulted Local 2 for not putting sufficient emphasis on new member orientation, steward training, and internal organizing between contracts. She argued that all unions, including her own, needed more membership involvement in organizational decisions about what job-related issues to take up during the life of the contract and in negotiations.

Like Steve Strong, Lafore also felt that organized labor, including Local 2, was too focused on conventional forms of political action. "When unions spend so much time on their political programs, their workplace organization suffers," she said. "For most members, their best experience of the union is going to happen at work."[20]

Local 2 officers, staff, and rank and file were very committed to "new organizing, but they don't leave behind a strong internal structure that enables existing members to enforce their contract." At the Hilton, when Lafore worked there, a unionized workforce of 800 had only five functioning shop stewards and, unlike in many unions, workers didn't have the right to elect them. Local 2 members can nominate a coworker to serve as steward, but the local itself makes the appointment. In Lafore's experience, "Local 2 picked who they wanted with no shop floor input at all. I never saw stewards get nominated." There was also a reluctance to hold general membership meetings, except when major contract fights were under way and the rank and file needed to be mobilized. As one Local 2 rep explained to her: "We don't have regular meetings. They're a pain in the ass. Members just come and complain."

On the job at the Hilton, Lafore found that "problems came up all the time, violations of the contract that I personally observed, but when workers called the union rep, they wouldn't always get a call back." Lafore didn't become a steward herself because she wanted to encourage other Hilton workers to step forward and get involved in shop floor action on contract issues. In the Hilton kitchen, Local 2 did take up the case of a cook passed over for promotion. "We held a union meeting during worktime, all the cooks stopped work to participate," she recalls. "It lasted more than fifteen minutes and was essentially a work stoppage, so there is this level of militancy that the union will support on certain issues that they want to organize around."

But, on other occasions, Lafore felt that the full-time union rep assigned to the Hilton discouraged rank-and-file initiatives rather than supporting them. When the hotel refused to pay server staff the new city minimum wage, which was higher than the contract rate, the union wouldn't back the servers who organized around this issue, with Lafore's help, for a number of months. "I learned on a non-intellectual, emotional level what it's like to stand up to your boss. When someone has power over you, it's scary—even if you have the option of leaving, which many workers can't do as easily as I could."

Strategy Differences

In late 2007, Lafore left the Hilton to take a job as the lone "salt" in a non-union hotel in San Francisco's financial district. Working as a cocktail waitress again, her initial task, like Strong's at the Ritz in Pasadena, was to assess which coworkers might be receptive to a discreet home visit from a Local 2 organizer. "Being a rank-and-file activist again, I have more space," Lafore told me at the time. "I get to talk to workers and organize in the way I want to. Because I'm actually doing organizing that's useful to the local, it's less frustrating for me and less threatening for them."

As her work progressed, Lafore was able to identify and cultivate the natural leaders in different hotel departments. Working with outside organizers, she helped pull together an inside committee that went public in 2008 when its members petitioned the hotel for management neutrality and a commitment to union recognition based on majority sign-up (a "card check"). Like at the Ritz in Pasadena, this proposal was spurned, which led to a new division of labor between workers on the inside and their full-time helpers operating on the outside. Local 2 staffers now tried to round up support for the union's organizing demands among other labor organizations, local clergy, public officials, and community leaders.

According to Lafore, she and her coworkers were asked to participate in this outreach campaign, but were "not at the center of it." At one public rally, this became so apparent that a committee member turned to Lafore and remarked, "You know, we're just a pretty face for the union." After much arguing with the lead organizer assigned to the campaign, Lafore and other inside committee members were finally allowed to coordinate an action of their own, a confrontation with management at a "town hall" meeting of all employees within the hotel.

Because of this and other strategy differences, Lafore became more critical of UNITE HERE for its "very hierarchical, military-style of organizing. They expect you to follow the program and the program is decided by the staff, not the workers." Despite the personal connections and friendships she developed with coworkers, Lafore was never supposed to reveal her secret connection to Local 2. Effective salting, as defined by UNITE HERE, required "lying to your coworkers," and this was difficult for her to accept. It became just one more small "reflection of a union model that doesn't sufficiently respect workers' knowledge, experience, and ability to run their own organizations."

Like Strong, Lafore eventually left her inside organizing job and began work on a master's degree, which she completed. In 2012, after having a baby, she became a staff organizer for a university employees' union. The San Francisco hotel that she worked in as a salt remains non-union like the Ritz in Pasadena.

From the IWW to CWA

Twenty-four-year-old Woody Klein (a pseudonym) worked as an inside organizer in retail outlets of two brand-name companies—Starbucks and T-Mobile. While still a college student, Klein got a job at the coffee shop chain so he could help recruit coworkers into the 108-year old Industrial Workers of the World (IWW). Employed after graduation in the wireless industry, Klein began salting for the Communications Workers of America as part of its decade-long campaign to unionize German-owned T-Mobile, an effort that has employed few other inside organizers with Klein's political background in the IWW and Occupy Wall Street.

The IWW organizing effort that Klein assisted has been chronicled by one of its key organizers, Daniel Gross, in a pamphlet about "do-it-yourself workplace organizing," co-authored with labor historian Staughton Lynd. *Solidarity Unionism at Starbucks* "makes the audacious argument that workers themselves on the shop floor, not outside union officials, are the real hope for labor's future." [21] As Gross and Lynd recount, IWW activity at Starbucks began in 2004 among New York City "baristas," most of them part-timers, who were "fed up with living in poverty and being mistreated."

According to the authors, workers at Starbucks are not, as a practical matter, able to seek NLRB-sponsored elections "even if they wished to do so," because the company "maintains that the appropriate bargaining unit for employees would be a prohibitively large multi-store unit." In addition, many in the IWW have a political bias against "using the statutory mechanism designed to produce exclusive bargaining representation" because, when U.S. unions get legally certified, they gain "the power to bargain away members' rights to engage in concerted direct action." The IWW has used the NLRB repeatedly to challenge the retaliatory dismissal of its supporters, and other forms of management interference with union activity.

Instead of seeking formal bargaining rights via a Labor Board election, or an organizing rights agreement that would enable their union to demonstrate majority support through a "card check" procedure, IWW supporters tried to extract concessions from local management through solidarity activity on the job, combined with creative public protests and embarrassing publicity. Collective activity is central to the IWW organizing model, although, as we've seen above, it's also part of the committee-building method in long-term strategic campaigns conducted by UNITE HERE, in which there is a much more dominant role played by outside union strategists. As a sign of IWW campaign success, Gross and Lynd cite wage increases introduced by Starbucks, in response to New York City barista agitation, which "increased pay almost 25% in a period when retail wages in the city were essentially stagnant."

In Massachusetts, an IWW-assisted online petition campaign and a threatened strike by shift supervisors won concessions from management worth a million dollars annually in bonuses and raises. Starbucks had responded to a recent legal decision by excluding the shift supervisors from sharing in tips, which translated into a 20 percent pay cut for some. The supervisors sought help from the union, for a protest campaign that led to an increase in their hourly wages from $11 to $13.59 and additional bonuses of $350. "I think this is the shape of things to come," predicts IWW organizer Erik Forman. "Workers deciding to take action on the job [because] capital is destroying the legal framework that unions have existed under in the U.S. since 1935—in the public and private sector. But that doesn't mean the end of workers' struggle. In fact it probably means we're about to see the beginning of an entirely new wave of rebellion. I think it's important for us, as people who've had experience organizing, to be there for workers who are starting to fight back."[22]

When he became a Starbucks salt, Klein got what he calls "first-rate training from the IWW," which emphasized the importance of one-on-one worker organizing. Before he was fired on trumped-up charges of tardiness, Klein succeeded in recruiting seven other workers into the IWW in a Starbucks outlet that employed thirty. After a series of skirmishes over various issues, management began to weed out other militants as well. Klein discovered that "most people, even if they fully agree with you, don't want to be fighting all the time. So it's hard to sustain a full-scale class-struggle approach." In the IWW, he recalls, "we could at least say, truthfully, that there's no fat-cat union bosses at the top, that all decisions are made by the workers." The IWW's downside was that Klein had to do all the inside and outside organizing work—setting up meetings, compiling lists, making phone calls, etc.—while working and going to school.

> When you're the rabble rouser at work, it sometimes helps to be able to show that there's a whole organization out there, with money and more of a national structure, that's done this kind of thing before. Every outside person from the IWW was someone who looked like an anarchist—now that's cool with me. But tattoos and dreadlocks may not go over so well with all your coworkers, even at Starbucks.

Going Mainstream

After taking an online test and getting his T-Mobile retail store job with CWA help, Klein joined a more mainstream union campaign, which also has "nontraditional" elements. While *Solidarity Unionism* argues that "the IWW's orientation to worldwide class solidarity makes possible organizing that traditional unions eschew," Klein found that the CWA heartily welcomes German-union solidarity at T-Mobile. CWA's protracted campaign among 20,000 T-Mobile technicians, call-center workers, and retail employees involves a close working partnership with *ver.di*, a two-million member German labor organization. In the United States, T-Mobile union activists organize around and attempt to influence personnel policy issues, company-wide. With help from outside CWA organizers, they also seek to build, where possible, pro-union workplace majorities through IWW-style local agitation and collective action.

Klein joined the staff of a big-city T-Mobile store with only eight non-management employees. Most of his coworkers were black or Hispanic. Selling on a commission basis for the cellular company is a better job than working at Starbucks, Klein believes, because "people earn more money, they feel like they're going places, and moving up in the world." Unfortunately, as one CWA organizer notes, "T-Mobile is still a crappy place to work," with 40 percent annual turnover in some retail stores and call centers. "Everybody is pissed off at the company, so convincing people that management is out to screw them is easy," Klein said. "The problem is that nobody feels like they're going to be here forever. It feels like a temp job."

By the end of 2012, Klein was publicly wearing a union pin and, with the help of a full-time CWA organizer, beginning to make contacts in twenty other retail locations. In his own store, he had tried to initiate group activity around issues like scheduling and a cut in weekly hours. He participated in regular conference calls with other union supporters at T-Mobile locations around the country and has met with *ver.di* visitors from Germany. This CWA-assisted national and international networking "has given me more energy and enthusiasm," Klein says. "Being part of the bigger picture is very encouraging when you're mainly confined to organizing in a single store."

In early 2013, however, Klein was summarily dismissed, along with twenty-three coworkers and six store managers in a controversy over deceptive sales practices, long sanctioned by local management and protested by workers under pressure to meet their quotas. As CWA pointed out in a press statement, calling for the reinstatement of Klein and others:

> These T-Mobile workers, like others in the U.S. without a union, are considered at-will employees and don't have the right to claim wrongful discharge. With a collective bargaining agreement, workers who knew that fraud was ongoing would have been heard.

Klein was hired by CWA to work full-time on the T-Mobile campaign for three months, after which he planned to go back to work as a rank-and-filer at another non-union company.

Conclusion

Whether on the margins of organized labor or within its mainstream, salting has yet to become sufficiently fashionable again to make the more widespread contribution to union growth that some organizing strategists hoped it would. Nevertheless, the presence of politically committed young people, working on the inside, rather than just functioning as full-time union staff members, can help launch and sustain strategic organizing efforts whose life span is measured in years, not weeks or months. The embattled workers they befriend and assist get the benefit of on-the-job allies who would otherwise be more removed from the day-to-day fray of union building.

In the process, the inside organizers acquire workplace experience invaluable in their later union careers. Former California farmworker Agustin Ramirez, who assisted the ILWU's bike messenger campaign, came away with the strong belief that "joining the workforce is great training for young organizers." As Ramirez observes, "Many are into strategy and tactics and other idealistic things . . . but they need to spend more time with workers one on one and create personal bonds with them. They'll see how difficult it is to move workers even on the inside. If you get easily discouraged on the micro level, you are not going to be able to motivate workers from outside on the macro level."[23]

13—GOING GLOBAL AT T-MOBILE

When telecom technician Werner Schonau first came to Nashville, it wasn't for a fun-filled vacation, inspired by any Teutonic affection for country music. Instead, Schonau, an elected member of the works council at Deutsche Telekom (DT) in Neunkirchen, was part of a fact-finding mission in 2012 that included twelve other German workers, union leaders, and parliamentarians. In Nashville, this foreign delegation, organized by Germany's largest union, *ver.di*, bypassed the Grand Old Opry and went directly to the customer service center operated by T-Mobile, the nationwide wireless carrier wholly owned by DT. In a pattern that was repeated at other stops on their U.S. labor rights tour, the Germans tried to meet with T-Mobile workers, in non-work areas during non-work times, only to be barred by company managers and private security guards at every facility.

In Frisco, Texas, call center supervisors acted like kindergarten teachers, hurriedly closing all the window blinds to prevent customer service reps from seeing those gathered outside, under a union banner. The center director sent his entire staff an email reassuring them that this attempted European invasion was just a "publicity effort." He also reiterated the company's long-standing position that, in the United States, "it is better for both T-Mobile employees and our business to maintain a direct working relationship between management. The vast majority of our employees have chosen not to be represented by a union."

Where Schonau comes from, 75 percent of the parent company's workforce is union-represented, including all T-Mobile technicians, retail salespeople, and customer service reps. Thanks to Germany's sixty-year-old system of "co-determination"—a product of U.S. occupation after the Second World War—telecom workers there maintain a "direct working relationship" with management through local and national works councils, plus elected labor representation on the company's Supervisory Board, which is equivalent to the board of directors in U.S. firms. The German government, even when headed by a conservative prime minister, has retained ownership of one-third of DT's stock.

Despite interference by local management last winter, the Deutsche Telekom delegation was able to hold rallies, press conferences, and after-work meetings with many T-Mobile workers who have become fellow union supporters within the same global firm. Over the last two years, about 1,000 have signed up to become members of TU, an unusual cross-border organization jointly sponsored by *ver.di* and the Communications Workers of America (CWA). In Connecticut, TU has already won bargaining rights and a first contract for fifteen T-Mobile workers, out of 20,000 thought to be union eligible, after eleven years of international campaigning against the company's union busting.

Schonau says that learning about T-Mobile's resistance to unionization and the high levels of job stress and insecurity faced by its U.S. workforce "moved me deeply, even made me angry." In a well-documented post-trip report, Schonau and his fellow travelers expressed shock and dismay at the wireless worker abuse they discovered in the land of the free and home of the brave.[24] What disturbed Schonau most was the "degrading" practice known, in T-Mobile lingo, as "decision time." As Schonau reported: "Before an employee is threatened with dismissal for alleged 'poor performance,' he or she has to go home, sometimes write an essay, but always return to his/her supervisor to describe 'why the company should keep me, why I want to keep working at the company.' The supervisor will then decide whether he/she stays or leaves."

Schonau found this exercise of arbitrary power by first-line supervisors to be "absolutely unbelievable." DT's disciplinary procedures in Germany include the right to union representation and a fair hearing. Layoffs can't occur without a lengthy process of negotiation and guaranteed eligibility for jobless benefits that are much more generous than unemployment insurance anywhere in the United States.

As a longtime T-Mobile technician in Germany, Schonau was "always proud to be an employee there." But now, he says: "I have my doubts regarding the company. That the company can treat people like that—I guess it's just because they can. We need to fight this behavior by management in Germany and around the world. It is unacceptable!"

Germany's Dr. Jeykll and Mr. Hyde

That message, much appreciated by CWA and pro-union T-Mobile workers, has been delivered by two-million member *ver.di*, publicly and within Deutsche Telekom, for more than a decade. Unfortunately, DT is a modern-day Dr. Jeykll and Mr. Hyde, mild-mannered and well-behaved at home, but hostile and aggressive in its labor relations abroad. The protracted struggle to get a major German employer to adhere to the higher labor standards of Western Europe when operating in the low-road environment of the United States illustrates many of the challenges facing other cross-border union campaigns targeting similar firms.

DT is a global telecom giant with a presence in more than thirty countries. It gained entry to the U.S. wireless market twelve years ago, after acquiring VoiceStream Communications, a past foe of CWA organizing. T-Mobile has since become the fourth largest American cellular company, after heavily unionized AT&T, and the almost entirely non-union Verizon Wireless and Sprint Nextel. It has a workforce of about 30,000, more than 33 million customers, $20 billion a year in revenue, and sales that currently amount to 25 percent of the parent company's worldwide total.

In 2000, some American conservatives opposed the VoiceStream takeover because of the German government's continuing role in Deutsche Telekom. The firm's partial public ownership was cited as a possible threat to the security of our national telecommunications network. Both the CWA and AFL-CIO disputed this claim and went to bat for DT in Washington. Organized labor urged Congress, the Clinton and then Bush administrations, and the Federal Communications Commission to approve the VoiceStream purchase.

In his personal lobbying, then-AFL-CIO president John Sweeney praised DT's enlightened, cooperative labor-management policies, noting that they stood "in stark contrast to the behavior of U.S. firms which actively fight workers' efforts to improve their lives." Then and later, DT claimed to respect International Labor Organization (ILO) standards for securing "rights at work through collective bargaining" and pledged, in its own "Social Charter," to recognize "legitimate employee representation." The company's CEO at the time, Ron Summer, personally promised then CWA-president Morton Bahr that DT would apply German standards of labor relations to its U.S. workforce.

Once the sale of Voicestream was approved by federal regulators (and the business rebranded as T-Mobile), DT's U.S. managers proceeded according to a different maxim: "When in Rome, do as the Romans do." As a result, there has been very little German-style "social partnering" with American labor since then. Instead, T-Mobile has invested heavily in a nonstop program of "union avoidance" more typical of homegrown southern union busters like Arkansas-based Wal-Mart.

Creating Fear at Work

T-Mobile's ensuing unfair labor practices have been well documented in various National Labor Relations Board (NLRB) proceedings and reports by Human Rights Watch, American Rights at Work (ARAW), and the Trade Union Advisory Committee of the Organization of Economic Cooperation and Development. (An OECD complaint against the company, filed jointly by *ver.di* and CWA, is still pending.)

One initial bad sign was DT's hiring of the Burke Group, a notorious union-busting consultant, to help defeat wireless worker organizing in England seven years ago. Similar anti-union lawyers or consulting firms have been utilized, on a regular basis, to prepare all T-Mobile USA supervisors for their role in monitoring, reporting, and actively discouraging any signs of organizing activity.

As San Francisco State University professor John Logan found in his study for ARAW, titled "Lowering the Bar or Setting the Standard?," local managers "have deliberately and systematically instilled fear in their workforce, engaging in repeated incidents of anti-union harassment and intimidation throughout the country." In 2005, Logan reports, Union Network International (UNI), a global federation of telecom and other service sector unions, interceded with top DT officials in Germany. UNI's then–general secretary Phil Jennings even announced that a breakthrough was impending, in the form of a new global agreement by DT, that "there will be no more intimidation; no bullying, and no firing of people that stand up and decide to join the union."

Seven years later, DT still has not signed any organizing rights deal with UNI and, according to Logan, "its anti-union policy in the United States stands out as the single major obstacle in the path of such an agreement."

Other Industry Models

In other market settings during the same period, some European-based firms have made different calculations than T-Mobile about the cost and benefits of facilitating rather than resisting unionization. In 2004, for example, the Teamsters and Service Employees enlisted the help of the British Transport and General Workers to persuade First Group, based in Scotland, that it needed to better align its behavior in the United States with its global mission statement about "corporate responsibility," which, like similar DT documents, references international human and labor rights standards.

First Group is the United Kingdom's largest rail and bus transportation company. Its subsidiary, First Student, is the biggest operator of privately contracted school bus services in the United States and employs a work-force there of 60,000, which it initially tried to keep entirely nonunion.

The First Group campaign was a multiyear effort, involving public protests, negative publicity, and legislative inquiries on both sides of the Atlantic. In the United States, SEIU and the Teamsters tried to demonstrate that labor's local political clout and community allies could be deployed to help or hurt First Student when it was bidding for new contracts with school boards around the country. Brandishing both carrot and stick, labor first obtained a "neutrality" pledge that was often violated and proved to be unenforceable. So the joint union agitation and pressure continued.

In 2008, stronger organizing rights language was negotiated. Since then, 20,000 First Student bus drivers and other workers have voted to be represented by the Teamsters and other labor organizations (the agreed-upon recognition procedure is not tied to a single union). In 2011, First Student and the Teamsters even agreed on a "master contract," which has helped to raise wage and benefit standards in IBT-represented bargaining unions throughout the United States.

An AT&T Solution?

In the very different setting of the U.S. wireless industry, where the largest union lacks similar political leverage, large-scale organizing has been possible only at the firm now known as AT&T-Mobility. Under CWA's "card check and neutrality" agreement with AT&T, which took many years of struggle to achieve, management has recognized union card-signing majorities in scores of previously agreed-upon bargaining units. The American Arbitration Association (AAA) expedites the card count and then certifies the results. AT&T Mobility supervisors are not allowed to interfere with union committee building or card signing activity, as T-Mobile managers routinely do. Management must provide CWA with employee information and workplace access that is beyond the bare minimum obtainable under NLRB election rules.

In one eighteen-month period, in 2005–6, 20,000 new CWA members were recruited, doubling the size of the union's total wireless membership, because AT&T-Mobility, then known as Cingular, acquired a national competitor and CWA was able to extend its organizing agreement to cover that firm's previously non-union workforce. If CWA had been forced to petition for NLRB elections instead, and management had resisted unionization, most of these call center and retail store workers would never have won bargaining rights.

With this same scenario in mind, CWA strongly supported AT&T's proposed acquisition of T-Mobile two years ago. The union argued that this $39 billion deal was good for workers and consumers, citing AT&T's pledge to bring 5,000 customer service jobs back to the United States that T-Mobile had outsourced overseas. Unfortunately, AT&T's takeover bid was rejected, on antitrust grounds, by the Obama administration. Some consumer groups regarded this as a great victory, but it was no boon for "the good union jobs in the wireless industry" that CWA was seeking to protect and create.

Just the prospect of an AT&T–T-Mobile merger led to a sudden flurry of organizing among cellular technicians in the Northeast. In the summer of 2011, T-Mobile technicians actually won a representation election in one of three contested units in Connecticut and New York. After signing up majorities in all three groups, union organizers withdrew their election petition in upstate New York, were defeated 9 to 6 on Long Island, and won by a margin of 8 to 7 in Connecticut. In the New York City–area unit, T-Mobile management dragged out the board's unit determination hearings for four days. The actual vote was then delayed for another ten months while the NLRB considered, and finally rejected, the company's weighty legal claim that "TU"—the union entity backed by T-Mobile workers on their signed authorization cards—didn't qualify as a "labor organization" under the National Labor Relations Act.

Meanwhile, T-Mobile flew in top HR officials to lavish attention on the small number of techs involved, wooing them with free dinners, Mets game tickets, picnics, barbecues, and more costly bribes like new trucks, raises, and promotions. The long delayed election that was lost on Long Island occurred right after the merger with AT&T was scuttled, a case of bad timing made even worse.

With the deus ex machina of amalgamation with AT&T no longer on the horizon, it was time for renewed German engagement with the T-Mobile campaign. So, in March 2012, *ver.di* and CWA paid for a full-page ad in the *New York Times* to administer a public dope slap to wayward German companies with subsidiaries in the United States. In this high-profile appeal, a distinguished group of labor law academics and former government officials in Germany urged multiple firms, including T-Mobile, to respect workers' freedom of association and their right to engage in collective bargaining. Among the signers were representatives of all four major German political parties, spanning the left, center, and right.

Later that same month, T-Mobile laid-off 3,300 workers and closed seven call centers in six states. To add insult to injury, the company then tried to prevent its former employees from qualifying for trade adjustment assistance (TAA), even though they were casualties of expanded overseas outsourcing (which T-Mobile denied was the cause).

A TAA Victory

CWA immediately sought a U.S. Department of Labor (DOL) ruling that these displaced workers were eligible for TAA benefits, which include extended unemployment checks, subsidized COBRA coverage, job retraining help, and other allowances. In July 2012, based on evidence gathered by T-Mobile activists, the AFL-CIO Solidarity Center—which helped develop information sources within the overseas call centers where T-Mobile work was moved—and CWA researchers like Tony Daley, the DOL found that the "foreign country services" utilized by management to handle more domestic customer calls "contributed importantly to worker separations at T-Mobile USA." In one internal memo, CWA estimated that, if all eligible U.S. workers availed themselves of this great legal victory, the "total benefits per worker would exceed $72,000 over two years for a total of $244 million."

T-Mobile's shifting of work to Honduras, Guatemala, and the Philippines, followed by its Scrooge-like stance on TAA benefits, boosted the union's standing in surviving customer service centers. "All of those people who didn't pay attention to the union before were forced to acknowledge its positive role," Daley says. The DOL's T-Mobile case decision was the largest single TAA determination involving the service sector, and an important precedent for the future.

Back in Germany, a report in *Der Spiegel*, the mass circulation newsweekly, accused T-Mobile officials of submitting false information to the DOL to thwart TAA approval. A headline in the *Suddeutsche Zeitung* declared: "U.S. Department accuses T-Mobile of lying." *Ver.di* leader Lothar Schroder noted that the company had "lied to its employees and to the public" as well.

In the summer of 2012, with *ver.di* representatives at the bargaining table, CWA Local 1298 finally negotiated a first contract for T-Mobile techs in Connecticut—ratified just in time to avert a management-backed decertification vote. "The only reason we got that contract is because of the Germans," asserts CWA Organizer Tim Dubnau. "In other parts of the country, there has been enough juice from Germany to discourage the firing of more workers for union activity."

Unfortunately, the initial agreement in Connecticut consists of little more than the existing T-Mobile employee handbook, signed by both parties, with a grievance and arbitration procedure attached. "We had no power to get anything more," one union negotiator lamented.

Strengths of the Campaign

According to Daley and other CWA activists, their union's partnership with *ver.di* has several distinctive features. These include its durability, the progressive deepening of the bilateral relationship between the two unions, and the unusual degree of rank-and-file engagement and direct contact that has resulted at T-Mobile.

CWA has no international affairs director because its current president, Larry Cohen, plays that role himself. This lack of delegation has an upside, however. Cohen's many trips to Germany and extensive personal involvement in the campaign have been critical to forging strong personal ties with *ver.di* officials like Schroder. Cohen also worked closely with top-level German union leaders during his activist stint as president of UNI's telecom division between 2000 and 2007.

One weakness of many well-intentioned global campaigns is that cross-border contacts are limited to the officialdom on either side, like the four full-time staffers that CWA has working on the campaign. International union "solidarity" is too often demonstrated just by attending conferences, making speeches, passing resolutions, issuing press releases, and engaging in "online" activity, at best. Meanwhile, not enough organizational resources are devoted to driving things down to the shop floor level, so direct exchanges can take place between working members. When that difficult work is done, over a period of many years, there's a far better chance that the solidarity campaign being waged will more accurately reflect the day-to-day concerns of workers and their willingness to take risks and escalate the struggle, as needed.

In addition to past visits to Germany and the United States by rank-and-file delegations, TU has used an online forum to facilitate regular information sharing between T-Mobile employees in each country. Unionized call centers in Germany have been encouraged to adopt a counterpart facility in the United States. In Tennessee, three hundred T-Mobile call center workers are now twinned with customer service reps who work in Düsseldorf; others in Charleston, South Carolina, maintain regular contact with *ver.di* members in Berlin.

Participants in these "sister call center" relationships use the Internet, conference calls, and a shared shop newsletter to keep in touch and coordinate activity.[25] "Hello, Düsseldorf Works Council," said one recent interoffice communication. "The TU workers here in Nashville welcome your help forming a union. We believe that working together with you can help us get to this goal." What followed was a detailed report on local working conditions and organizing progress, plus short personal bios on individual union activists.

Connecticut T-Mobile technician Chris Cozza traveled to Frankfurt, Berlin, and Cologne two years ago to help mount a challenge to CEO Rene Obermann at DT's annual meeting. Cozza met with fellow field techs, *ver.di* shop stewards, and works council members who participated in the shareholder meeting protest against T-Mobile's "Wild West" labor policies in the United States. As Cozza notes, "They have things a lot better over there than we do here—but it's not because T-Mobile there is any nicer than in the U.S. It's because they have a strong union."

T-Mobile Today

After T-Mobile walked away from its failed marriage with AT&T, the company was $4 billion richer (due to a negotiated penalty payment), but still needed to find another partner to strengthen its own market position. Unfortunately, for its employees and the CWA–*ver.di* campaign, T-Mobile decided to merge with a smaller, urban-based cell phone service provider called MetroPCS. That $30 billion deal combines T-Mobile's 30,000 employees and 33 million customers with MetroPCS's 3,700 workers and 9.3 million customers.

CWA lobbied against the transaction, in part, because MetroPCS has contracted out all of its customer service and billing work to firms like Telvisa, which operates call centers in Mexico, Antigua, Panama, and the Philippines. Many MetroPCS retail outlets are run by "authorized agents" and also have no direct employees of the company.

CWA warned the Federal Communications Commission (FCC) that if T-Mobile pursues further Metro PCS-style outsourcing of its "customer care" work, there will be more call center jobs eliminated in the United States. The union recruited sixty-two U.S. House members, 18,500 individual consumers, many state and local public officials, as well as organizations like the NAACP, Sierra Club, and AARP, to contact the FCC during its merger review and urge protection for U.S.-based jobs. In March 2013, T-Mobile issued a press release claiming to "have no plans to move call centers offshore or reduce employment levels."

A few days later the FCC went ahead and approved the deal but, according to CWA, "failed to incorporate enforceable job protections for T-Mobile and Metro PCS workers."

The union committee building that has been strengthened in Nashville, Wichita, Charleston, and other locations since the T-Mobile layoffs in 2012 would be disrupted again if T-Mobile changes its plans. "There's a lot of fear about the merger and where it will lead," one CWA organizer told me. "Plus, it's not good news that T-Mobile's new CEO, John Legere, is a well-known outsourcer too." Legere's résumé includes a controversial ten-year stint as CEO of Global Crossing, during which time he presided over a bankruptcy that cost thousands of of telecom workers their jobs and 401(k)-based retirement savings. As one young worker in New York observed, T-Mobile is already "a crappy place to work," with 40 percent annual turnover in some retail stores and call centers. If conditions worsen, getting coworkers to stay and fight will only become more difficult, he believes. "Everybody is pissed off at the company, so convincing people that management is out to screw them is easy, " he said. "The problem is that nobody feels like they're going to be here forever. It feels like a temp job."

Another, older union activist, still trying to hang on to his T-Mobile job, described the daily management pressure like this: "I walk around with a target on my back. They make your life a living hell until you're forced to leave."

Pressure from Abroad?

CWA's interest in sustaining this struggle is pretty obvious. *Ver.di*'s stake is a little different, more long-term. German telecom unionists are motivated by a genuine concern that what they've seen in the United States might be a glimpse of their own future, if American labor practices were ever exported back to Europe. That's why *ver.di* has helped generate the negative press coverage in Germany that reached its crescendo with a November 2012 *Der Spiegel* indictment of the "brutal psychological terror" inflicted on T-Mobile USA staffers.

In that investigative report, based on interviews with TU supporters and German union officials, the magazine also highlighted T-Mobile's questionable sales practices and pressure on customer service reps to meet unreasonable quotas. In Chattanooga, *Der Spiegel* noted, some T-Mobile workers even had dunce caps placed on their heads as punishment for not "meeting their numbers." In 2010, T-Mobile ranked as the most customer-friendly wireless company in the United States but now lags behind its three largest competitors.

Ver.di has had its own struggles with DT about call-center staffing, pay, and other conditions that affect the quality of customer service. The union has succeeded in pressuring management to return some T-Mobile customer service work to Germany that was outsourced to Eastern Europe. Dealing with such problems closer to home will always be a higher *ver.di* priority than rocking the boat over T-Mobile misbehavior in the United States, particularly if that might expend organizational capital (or endanger relationships with management) necessary to defend German workers. As one CWA strategist acknowledged, "If it's hard to for us to do something that might run against the interests of our own members, why shouldn't they display a certain caution?"

CWA's German partners might well wonder how the additional "juice" needed to win organizing rights at T-Mobile is going to be generated by them from afar, when CWA has not been able to apply enough pressure on Verizon (VZ), via its own members employed by that company in the United States, to prevail in an eighteen-year fight for an AT&T-style union recognition procedure at Verizon Wireless (VZW). VZW's non-union workforce is now as large as VZ's total landline union membership, making it increasingly difficult to maintain better pay, benefits, and conditions for the latter.

In 2000, after much internal education and discussion about the threat posed by de-unionization within Verizon, 75,000 members of CWA and the IBEW walked out for two weeks over wireless worker organizing rights and other issues. They returned with what they thought was a workable four-year card check and neutrality deal. It covered VZW employees in call centers, technical units, and retail stores from Maine to Virginia.

Double-Breasting at Verizon

On the Verizon side, however, there proved to be no willingness to implement these unionization ground rules, as negotiated. Between 2000 and 2004, an agreed-upon process for arbitrating bargaining unit determination disputes was obstructed and delayed. While this foot-dragging continued, VZW closed three northeastern call centers in which union organizing was under way and moved the work performed by those 1,500 customer service reps to North and South Carolina, states not covered by the agreement.

Elsewhere, management threats, harassment, and firing of union activists continued at VZW, with no recourse for workers or their would-be union other than utilizing the feeble and ineffective NLRB. (VZW was at the time still partially owned by Vodafone, a UK company equally opposed to unionization there.)

Verizon's long-term, and so far successful, strategy of "double-breasting" depends on maintaining what CWA calls "the wall" between the company's shrinking landline business and its ever expanding wireless side. "Tearing Down the Wall" was stressed in some union contract campaigns at Verizon over the last twelve years. But unfortunately it receded as an issue during the strike and bargaining ordeal involving 45,000 CWA and IBEW members in the Northeast in 2011–12.

As these landline workers came under siege, their local unions and community allies gathered at VZW retail outlets for nationwide protests against the wage and benefit givebacks sought by Verizon. The company's long record of worker mistreatment in its wireless subsidiary—not much different than T-Mobile's track record—was less frequently stressed in appeals to labor and consumers.

So, if there are demonstrable limits or obstacles to what U.S. workers will do—or what their national union can try to mobilize them to do—against union-busting within their own company in the same country, what can be expected of a foreign union in a T-Mobile-type situation?

So far, *ver.di*'s much valued and very necessary solidarity on behalf of T-Mobile workers in the United States has mainly taken the form of symbolic protests, press conferences and reports, shareholder meeting interventions, complaints to DT management within the works councils and supervisory board, and considerable rank-and-file fraternization. To a degree unusual among European unionists, key *ver.di* activists have experienced firsthand, and now better understand, what one CWA organizer calls "the war on workers" here.

But none of this laudable activity approaches the level of direct action, of a more disruptive sort, that might put long-established German collective bargaining relationships and "social dialogue" in jeopardy. As one CWA campaigner said, "*Ver.di* lives in a labor relations environment where consultation is the rule. That's why its first impulse is to talk, rather than to act, like we do, because no one will talk to us here."

The Problem of Enforcement

This cultural and political difference has created "a not-so-secret tension between U.S. and European unions" that "limits the possibility for outright industrial action against European firms," according to Cornell professor Lance Compa and former NLRB general counsel Fred Feinstein. In a recent survey of cross-border campaigns, where direct action was employed or threatened in some fashion, Compa and Feinstein concluded:

> Many European unionists who see fruitful dialogue with top corporate officials think their U.S. counterparts go too far with what they see as the latter's overly confrontational, company-bashing campaigns and expectations that European unions should be equally belligerent in attacking management. European union leaders will go so far as to distribute literature and put some members in front of corporate headquarters holding signs, but they see their real point of influence in private meetings with top company officials to persuade them to rein in their U.S. managers.[26]

But what happens when many years of private labor-management meetings, accompanied by publicity, political pressure, and symbolic expressions of worker solidarity, fail to "rein in" U.S. managers who remain, as Dubnau described them, "ideologically and culturally anti-union" and free to act accordingly?

Even where sustained cross-border campaigning has created sufficient leverage to secure a signed "international framework agreement" (IFA), unions still face the challenge of enforcing such pacts when multinational employers renege on them, as Verizon did with its 2000–2004 wireless organizing deal with CWA. While international labor law experts like Compa, Feinstein, and others debate the best methods for securing management compliance in various legal venues, global labor federations like the newly created IndustriAll already face this problem on the ground.

IndustriALL is the recently rebranded global federation of manufacturing, mining, textile, and chemical unions. Along with the German Metal Workers, a key affiliate, and the Siemens Works Council, it negotiated an IFA that all the labor signatories assumed would apply to a pending NLRB election campaign in Maryland. Like Verizon Wireless, Siemens management proceeded to flout their parent company's commitment to neutrality by fighting the organizing drive of the United Steel Workers (USWA). According to USWA Organizer Phil Ornot, over a six-week period prior to the vote, "Siemens supervisors and consultants held daily captive audience meetings where workers were told that it would be futile to join the union and that the company would lose customers if the union won the election." The result was predictable—a 24 to 15 vote against collective bargaining.

A Siemens Setback

This NLRB election debacle occurred only weeks after the central management of one of Germany's most important global firms promised not to oppose unionization in its overseas facilities. Right before the vote, as the USWA's "card majority" was being eroded, IndustriALL issued a statement pointing out that "the spirit and actions" of Siemens management in Maryland "totally breach the commitments made in the Framework Agreement." This same press release called for "swift intervention from the company."

In a personal letter to Siemens president and CEO Peter Löscher, IndustriALL general-secretary Jyrki Raina demanded the termination of two outside union-busters hired for the Maryland campaign. Raina urged Siemens to convene a meeting of the affected workers, with USW representatives present, so local management could "inform them that the company will take a neutral position, cease all anti-union activities, take no reprisals against employees on the basis of their union advocacy, and afford the USWA reasonable access to the plant to communicate with employees."

When none of these steps were taken and the union was defeated, IndustriALL said it would back USWA's post-election objections, aimed at overturning the results and getting another NLRB vote. As one European HR organization speculated in its membership newsletter, some in the global federation may question the value of this new IFA with Siemens "if it is unable to prevent management at a single US facility from running a robust 'union-free' campaign."

No Shortcuts to Success

The day-to-day representational activities most consequential to union members remain largely confined to the boundaries of a single nation-state. Many American trade unionists, particularly those who hold local union leadership positions, still view the world through the prism of their traditional core jurisdiction, which is often tied to a single domestic industry, or several industries, or a particular occupation, craft, or line of business. As in telecom, where wireless is the future but "landline" is where most remaining members are found, local union priorities may not always be properly aligned with the strategies necessary for long-term organizational survival.

Overcoming barriers created by organizational bureaucracy, geography, nationalism, or language is much harder for trade unionists than for corporate managers. Big global companies are able to marshal and deploy resources on a transnational basis, in a top-down fashion, with speed, discipline, and coordination. Any merger, acquisition, or joint venture they undertake can quickly change the contours of the playing field, while the affected workers, who find themselves "restructured," must scramble to catch up with their employer's latest *Star Trek*–like shapeshifting.

There aren't any shortcuts to successful cross-border campaigning. Building labor solidarity and unity requires patient personal networking and relationship building, information sharing, and escalating workplace activity among the diverse national unions or labor federations that may represent some portion of a reconfigured employer's worldwide workforce. Commitments made by firms headquartered in Europe to meet the higher labor standards of that continent, when they operate elsewhere, won't count for much unless global union partners can make labor disruption and lost business a real threat to promise breakers.

In Western Europe, regional economic integration has forced national labor movements to become less parochial and more accustomed to working together through European Works Councils and the international trade union secretariats based in Geneva, although many political tensions and differences remain. Recent anti-austerity strikes have been coordinated throughout Europe on a scale rarely seen within the United States, except in the great immigrant worker protests of 2006.

Durable and effective forms of international labor solidarity are not created through mere organizational rebranding, such as "TU" or "IndustriALL." As the long, hard union slog at T-Mobile has shown, it also takes years of bottom-up organizing to make a difference, if one can be made at all.[27]

Postscript

In 2013, CWA's cooperation with *ver.di* focused on a cross-border campaign to protest the firing of TU activist Josh Coleman, a T-Mobile customer service rep in Wichita, Kansas, which is twinned with a DT facility in Dortmund.

Coleman was a top sales performer but his networking with German trade unionists and Facebook postings critical of T-Mobile personnel practices resulted in his May 2013 dismissal from the company. Four months later, thousands of *ver.di* members at more than twenty Deutsche Telecom locations protested this retaliatory firing by reporting to work in a t-shirt that proclaimed (in German): "I am Josh Coleman."

Their "day of action" was followed by some party-crashing in Berlin, where twenty similarly attired German telephone workers approached Rene Obermann, CEO of DT, at a social event and demanded Coleman's reinstatement. The union's message of solidarity was also projected on an outside wall of the building where Obermann was confronted. Back in the

U.S., a regional office of the National Labor Relations Board failed to issue a complaint against T-Mobile over Coleman's discriminatory discharge, a decision appealed by CWA to the NLRB in Washington, D.C.

On September 25, 2013, workers at a Metro PCS retail store in New York City participated in a secret ballot election conducted by the NLRB. Despite intensive anti-union campaigning by top T-Mobile executives, the vote was 7 to 1 in favor of representation by CWA.

PART IV

LABOR'S HEALTH CARE MUDDLE

Like many labor negotiators, I looked to health care reform for legislative relief from endless haggling with management over the costly details of employee medical plans. My own union and others greeted passage of the Affordable Care Act (ACA) with much cheering, despite its failure to remove insurance benefits from the bargaining table, as a Medicare-for-All/single-payer system would do.[1]

In 2010, union members were told, correctly, that President Obama's plan would expand Medicaid access for millions of lower-income Americans and make private insurance coverage more consumer-friendly for everyone else. Organized labor also expected the new law to aid union functioning by leveling the playing field among all employers, much like the statutory minimum wage and other protective labor legislation does. Unions hoped that the ACA would restrain medical cost inflation and reduce conflict over premium sharing, a continuing cause of strikes or union contract rejections at big firms like Verizon Communications, Kaiser Permanente, or United Parcel Service.[2]

Instead, just a few months before key ACA provisions became effective, Obamacare was backfiring, in very damaging fashion, on an already battered labor movement. Contrary to repeated White House assurances, many unionized workers were facing more, rather than fewer, health insurance-related problems and costs. Alarmed by Obama administration decisions and ACA provisions unfriendly to labor, top union leaders openly expressed concern about the "nightmare scenarios" unfolding for millions of workers, retirees, and their families.[3]

In anticipation of the law, smaller firms were outsourcing so they can keep their total head count below fifty and not be covered by ACA requirements.[4] Larger ones, like Wal-Mart, plan to hire more part-timers and schedule existing employees for less than thirty hours a week so they won't have to cover their non-full-time workforce.[5] Even unionized retailers like Stop & Shop, faced with higher ACA-imposed medical plan costs, have adopted the same tack in bargaining. Their proposed solution is to "eliminate coverage for thousands of part-time workers," creating what one United Food and Commercial Workers official described as his most difficult negotiations in forty years.[6]

More employers may terminate their medical plans entirely, in response to the ACA. An estimated four to seven million people will be thrown into state health insurance exchanges as a result, greatly adding to the cost of public subsidies authorized by the ACA.[7] Income-based subsidies for workers who wish to keep employer-provided individual benefits won't be available to maintain family coverage. This "strict definition of affordable health insurance...will deny federal financial assistance to millions of Americans with modest incomes who cannot afford family coverage offered by their employers."[8] Even lower-income participants in multi-employer plans, jointly run by labor and management, will be disadvantaged if ACA rules don't permit them to qualify for subsidies on the same basis as non-union workers without any employer coverage.[9]

The presidents of three national unions, representing three million workers, raised many of these concerns with Democratic congressional leaders in July 2013. In an open letter, they warned that the ACA was threatening "to shatter not only our hard-earned benefits, but destroy the foundation of the 40 hour week.... Time is running out: Congress wrote this law; we voted for you. We have a problem; you need to fix it. The unintended consequences of the ACA are severe. Perverse incentives are already creating nightmare scenarios.[10]

Not even mentioned in their desperate appeal (but criticized in an AFL-CIO convention resolution several months later) is Obamacare's 2018 excise tax on so-called "Cadillac coverage." [11] As intended, this part of the law is already having a negative impact on workers with better insurance long before its actual implementation date. In mid-2013, the *New York Times* found that "companies hoping to avoid the tax are beginning to scale back the more generous health benefits they have traditionally offered." But this was hailed as good news by White House advisor Jonathan Gruber, an influential MIT professor who believes that the Cadillac tax is one of the "most significant" provisions of the ACA.[12] At the same time, "cities and towns across the country are pushing municipal unions to accept cheaper health benefits" in anticipation of the tax as well. According to Gruber, this will "shift compensation away from excessively generous health insurance toward wages," a prediction that seems highly unlikely in the current climate of concession bargaining across the board.[13]

What is to be done about this dangerous muddle? The reporting and commentaries collected here suggest that unions need to get back to the basics of fighting for fundamental change. The political challenge for Labor for Single Payer campaigners is how to move beyond the ACA while the new law proves itself to be "simply incapable of doing what it is supposed to do—provide nearly universal care at an affordable and sustainable cost."[14] In the meantime, the nation's existing public health care programs must also be defended against piecemeal dismantling by Democrats and Republicans alike. Although Medicaid will be greatly expanded under Obamacare, it too will be partially privatized like Medicare was under Bill Clinton, costing taxpayers far more than the traditional form of coverage provided through the original program.[15] Among union members, the fight for real health care reform still starts at the bargaining table.[16] In the health care industry itself, that means challenging the misbehavior of big employers like Kaiser Permanente, instead of partnering with them on programs that are detrimental to caregivers and health care consumers, among whom are other union members. As reported in this section, "corporate wellness" is one such initiative. Where labor is acquiescent (or workers have no bargaining rights), wellness penalties will lead to disparate treatment different from, but no less divisive than existing "two-tier" arrangements.

Two-tiering today results in less pay and inferior pension or medical coverage for newly hired workers. As wellness programs take root, employees on the payroll longer—but less fit or otherwise non-compliant with employer-imposed standards—will be forced to pay up to 30 percent more for their insurance than younger coworkers not yet beset by the chronic conditions of middle age. It's bad enough that Obamacare encourages this trend—for labor negotiators to embrace it as a cure for medical cost inflation verges on union malpractice.

14—HEALTH CARE FOR SOME OR HEALTH CARE FOR ALL?

When 3,000 General Electric factory workers rallied outside GE's Lynn, Massachusetts, plant in mid-2003, one question preoccupied the crowd: Would there be another strike over health care? Five months earlier, these same workers, members of Local 201 of the International Union of Electronic Workers-Communications Workers of America (IUE-CWA), walked out as part of a company-wide protest against higher medical co-payments. In 2002, GE made $15 billion in profits, while its health care expenses increased less than the national average. Nevertheless, company negotiators insisted that 25,000 unionized employees pay more for their doctor visits, hospital stays, emergency room care, and prescription drugs.

By the time their 2003 bargaining was over, GE unions were able to blunt management's drive for givebacks, averting a second work stoppage. But the threat of further health care cost shifting was only banished for the four-year term of the contract. In other unionized workplaces across the nation, the pressure for concessions continues unabated. Where workers have no union, and 87 percent do not, the burden of medical cost inflation is shifted from management to labor with little fuss for the former, regardless of the financial pain inflicted on the latter. In the unionized sector, industrial strife about health insurance is spreading.

Since 2001, state employees in Minnesota, teachers in New Jersey, janitors in Massachusetts, candy makers in Pennsylvania, food processors in Wisconsin, uranium-plant workers in Kentucky, truck builders in Tennessee, and aerospace workers in Texas have all experienced health care–related strikes or lockouts—and several are still going on. Major contracts in the telephone and auto industries are also up for renegotiation. If management tries to reduce health coverage for the hundreds of thousands of workers and pensioners at General Motors, Chrysler, Ford, or Verizon, even greater confrontations lie ahead.

How unions in the United States respond to this challenge has important implications for the future of health care reform. The actions of organized labor at the negotiating table or on the picket line can become a rallying point for all Americans ill-served by our current system of private, job-based medical benefits. When unionized workers resist benefit cuts in a way that projects the broader demand for health care for all, they help generate pressure for a political solution to the larger problem: how, as a nation, to create affordable health coverage. If organized labor settles for piecemeal change and refuses to challenge the link between medical insurance and employment, it will miss the chance to connect with millions of poorly insured and uninsured workers who have no union. "We need a universal, comprehensive single-payer health care program to cover every man, woman and child in the United States," says United Auto Workers president Ron Gettelfinger. "You can't fix the health care crisis in America at any one bargaining table, with any one employer, or within any one industry."

The last time labor had an historic opportunity to shape the health care reform debate, it made a promising start, and then blew it. In the late 1980s and early '90s, medical cost inflation was reaching double digits, as it now is again. Health care disputes were causing four out of every five strikes. In monumental battles like the Mine Workers' year-long walkout at Pittston, unions that successfully resisted concessions did so by forming alliances with community groups and other unions seeking health care reform. Some AFL-CIO affiliates began to do systematic member education about why a tax-supported universal health system like Canada's would be better for workers than the current patchwork quilt of Medicare, Medicaid, and myriad private plans. A number of big unions endorsed single-payer legislation and joined grassroots coalitions like Jobs with Justice to campaign for fundamental change.

Just as this effort was gaining momentum, the AFL-CIO abruptly switched course. The labor federation embraced Bill and Hillary Clinton's Health Security Act, an ill-fated scheme that preserved the role of private insurers and was so convoluted that few unions could even explain it to their members. The Clinton bill represented a step backwards for labor, mirroring conservative mandated-benefits legislation developed by Richard Nixon in the 1970s to fend off universal coverage based on the model of Medicare. Nevertheless, by 1993, most unions and Democrats were rallying around this approach, which sought to shore up a private, job-based benefits system.

Obligating employers to pay for a portion of their employees' health costs was strikingly out of sync with recent workforce trends. Millions of Americans now rely on part-time, temporary, and "independent-contractor" jobs offering little or no health coverage. As Marie Gottschalk shows in her incisive study, *The Shadow Welfare State: Labor, Business and the Politics of Health Care in the United States*, labor's willingness to settle for the Clinton plan reflected crackpot realism at its worst, for the whole "system of employment-based benefits . . . was crumbling just at the moment when organized labor sought an employer-mandate solution."[17]

After the Clinton initiative failed, most firms with health plans devised their own managed-care fixes. Many imposed new limits on employee choice of doctors, hospitals, and treatment options. When annual premiums continued to rise anyway, they passed along the increased costs to their active and retired workers. Private health insurance for 16 million retirees is a primary management target now, particularly in troubled industries like steel, where companies blame such "legacy costs" for landing them in or near Chapter 11. Twenty-five years ago, more than 80 percent of all medium- and large-sized firms offered medical benefits to retirees. Now only 40 percent do. Successful union resistance to cost shifting in the past is thus no guarantee that the same group of workers won't face benefits cuts in the future, even when they retire from a profitable company. Fourteen years ago, a four-month strike preserved fully paid health coverage for workers at NYNEX; now its successor firm, Verizon, wants to cap all retiree medical contributions, a move that would adversely affect many now-retired veterans of the 1989 walkout.

The challenge facing unions today is how to defend medical coverage for active and retired workers, when more than forty million Americans have none at all. If struggles against cost shifting are framed narrowly—as in "Hands Off My Benefits!"—workers who have good insurance run the risk of being depicted as just another greedy, "special interest" group. However, if union resistance to concessions is perceived as being integral to the struggle for a broader political solution benefiting everyone, it will attract much more labor and community support.

When GE workers struck nationwide in early 2003, their savvier local unions met this challenge in communities where a blue-collar job at GE is among the best compensated locally. In Lynn, IUE-CWA Local 201 joined forces with Jobs with Justice, the Massachusetts Nurses Association, Mass Senior Action, and low-income groups to hold a community rally for health care reform. Speakers highlighted the medical coverage problems of everyone from immigrant workers to the self-employed to retirees who get bounced around from one Medicare HMO to another. Pat Lawrence, a member of the Lynn Health Care Task Force, told the crowd: "We're here to support the GE workers because you will bring attention to those who have no insurance—the elderly, the disadvantaged and the homeless—through your strikes and walkouts."

Engaging this broader public during benefit disputes requires more union acknowledgment of what should be obvious: bargaining solutions are limited at best. This is particularly true when a unionized workforce is transient, part-time, low-paid, and lacking in strike leverage. In Boston, for example, a city-wide strike by 3,000 immigrant janitors began to falter after only a month in 2002, despite a great outpouring of community support. The walkout ended unhappily for many workers because larger wage increases were sacrificed by their union to pay for expanded medical coverage. The insurance plan change helps about 1,000 part-timers, but not 8,000 others. Given the nature of building services and other low-wage sectors, it's doubtful that collective bargaining there will ever produce the comprehensive medical coverage achieved in manufacturing, utilities, and construction, when they were bastions of union strength.

In trucking and the building trades, there's an additional complication: many labor officials don't want to forsake job-based medical coverage, no matter how tattered, because they're in the benefits business themselves. As Gottschalk notes, these labor conservatives have impeded past efforts to get the AFL-CIO solidly behind single-payer. The multi-employer Taft-Hartley funds they administer jointly with management representatives cover half of all union members and a higher percentage of private sector ones. In the building trades unions, they have long been defended as a way to promote union membership and loyalty. Unfortunately, by aligning the interests of union officials with private insurers, the Taft-Hartley funds give one wing of organized labor what Gottschalk calls "a vested interest in maintaining the status quo."[18] It also leads to AFL-CIO pronouncements that appear to be a balancing act between single-payer advocates, at the grassroots, and union affiliates more inclined to partnerships with employers that would preserve and extend job-based coverage.

Such internal divisions are reflected in the mixed bag of labor-backed legislative proposals now being pushed in ten or more states. In Ohio, leading unions and the state labor federation are uniting with health care professionals and community groups to build the Single Payer Action Network, a coalition seeking a comprehensive solution to the state's health care crisis. In California, unfortunately, the AFL-CIO threw its weight behind a far less ambitious "pay-or-play" bill. This would require employers to offer health insurance or pay into a state-operated pool that would provide alternative coverage. The problem with "pay or play," says California Health Care for All chairperson Dan Hodges, is that it "creates a two-tiered system in which people covered through their jobs might have adequate benefits but those who get public coverage will receive an explicitly bare-bones package. Since those with the public package will more likely be people of color, the two-tiered system will have a racial character as well." HCA and the California Nurses Association support an alternative bill that would establish universal, publicly funded coverage for all Californians.

The finer points of such policy differences are usually lost on most union members. That's partly because unions tend to leave health care strategy and lobbying in the hands of in-house experts. In contract talks, negotiators desperately seek new cost-containment schemes to sugarcoat medical plan changes. Meanwhile, labor policy wonks organize events like the current series of AFL-CIO Regional Health Care Conferences, open only to union officials and too narrowly focused on "recent best practice given the current climate." This top-down, overly timid, and technocratic approach fails to address the need for massive workplace education and debate about health care reform. Because that's been so neglected, too many trade unionists with decent negotiated coverage still think of "universal health care" as something that would benefit someone else. The term "single payer" often draws blank stares (and, understandably so, since how many people refer to our current mess as a "multi-payer" system?). Despite the popularity of Medicare among seniors, the concept of a government-run insurance plan strikes some union members as a formula for longer waits, inferior care, and higher taxes, rather than cradle-to-grave health security and greater cost increase protection.

One group trying to change health-reform thinking in labor is Jobs with Justice. In June 2003 the group organized a statewide Health Care Action Day in Massachusetts, endorsed by more than fifty unions and community groups. Sponsoring organizations distributed more than 65,000 stickers demanding "Health Care for All" and then did the workplace mobilization necessary to get workers to wear them on the job. Participants included nurses fighting staffing cuts, state workers facing benefit givebacks, and utility workers threatened with reduced retiree health insurance coverage. Their coordinated workplace activity was accompanied by rallies and informational picketing that demanded health care reform that "covers everyone, is publicly financed, and saves money . . . by reducing bureaucratic waste."

The biggest turnouts were among workers facing strike deadlines at GE and Verizon. If 75,000 members of CWA and the International Brotherhood of Electrical Workers (IBEW) walk out again at Verizon, among the strike risks they'll be taking is possible termination of their employer-paid health coverage. But even this management countermeasure could have a consciousness-raising upside. "When a boss cancels everyone's insurance during a work stoppage, it's a teachable moment," says Rand Wilson, a staffer for the Service Employees International Union in Boston. "It really gets people thinking about what's wrong with having medical coverage tied to their job. The financial risks and penalties of getting laid off, changing jobs, working part-time or retiring early—not to mention going on strike—would all be greatly reduced if we had a Canadian-style system."

Other unions, like the United Electrical Workers (UE), are following up Health Care Action Day with bargaining table challenges to management. UE negotiators routinely seek management signatures on an "employer pledge" that offers two choices: either join labor in lobbying for real health care reform or continue to pick up the tab for the present for-profit system, with its increasingly high costs and shabby care. In Canada, where unions are fighting for adequate funding of a thirty-year-old national health insurance program, the Canadian Auto Workers (CAW) has won business backing for sticking with the single-payer approach, rather than privatizing the system (as Canadian conservatives would like to do). In a recent joint letter, CAW, GM, Ford, and Daimler/Chrysler demanded that Canada's "publicly funded health care system be preserved and renewed, [based] on the existing principles of universality, accessibility, portability, comprehensiveness, and public administration."

Not surprisingly, Jobs with Justice didn't attract this kind of corporate support, south of the border, for its Health Care Action Day. But the diversity of the event's labor endorsers shows how much of a problem cost-shifting has become in every sector of the economy. As such benefit disputes intensify, more trade unionists are reaching the conclusion that status quo solutions aren't the answer. As Colin Gordon concludes in *Dead on Arrival: The Politics of Health Care in Twentieth-Century America*, "Employment-based health insurance, floated as an alternative to public insurance in the middle years of the [last] century, is now little more than a leaky life raft for politicians clinging to budget-neutral solutions and workers with nowhere else to swim."[19]

Growing budget deficits, legislative gridlock, and huge military expenditures create a daunting context for new health care initiatives that would expand public coverage at the state or federal level. Despite these obstacles, mounting employer attacks are forcing unions to fight back in a more political way for what their members really need, instead of what some leaders think they can get. In the process, organized labor could become a far better champion of all workers, not just those with a union card.[20]

15—FROM ROMNEYCARE TO OBAMACARE

When Massachusetts labor activists supported health care reform in their state legislature in 2006 and then in Congress four years later, they hoped there would be less cost shifting. Unfortunately, President Obama's Affordable Care Act (ACA) has the same bipartisan flaws as the Massachusetts plan enacted when Republican Mitt Romney was governor. Neither Obamacare nor its Bay State inspiration, Romneycare, do much to restrain medical cost inflation. And both legislative schemes leave most union members with existing coverage no better off at the bargaining table.

The ACA and its Bay State predecessor do benefit private insurers, whose role remains costly, wasteful, and completely unnecessary. Both Romneycare and Obamacare require individuals to have insurance or be subject to fines, while providing insufficient financial incentives for employers to maintain existing coverage for their employees. Subject to new federal standards, companies with medical plans will still exercise complete control over them, unless workers have collective bargaining rights. For workers in employment-based plans and those shopping for their own coverage in ACA-created state "insurance exchanges," the cost of premiums, co-payments, and deductibles will continue to be a barrier to care. To make health care more "universal" and "affordable" within this dysfunctional framework, hundreds of billions of federal tax dollars will be spent on private insurance subsidies.

The plans available through the Massachusetts "Health Connector" avoid higher costs by shifting charges onto patients.[21] There is little evidence, based on the Massachusetts experience so far, that individual mandates and insurance market restructuring will make the bargaining climate better for unions, in either the private or public sector.[22] In

Massachusetts, the state hailed for its model system of universal coverage, Democratic Governor Deval Patrick and the Democrat-dominated legislature have now passed legislation restricting the scope of health care negotiations by municipal employees. In New Jersey, Republican Governor Chris Christie isn't waiting for relief from the ACA either. Christie wants to take cost-sharing decisions off the bargaining table entirely so public sector employers in his state can impose costly medical plan changes unilaterally. His proposed legislation would shift $3 billion in health care costs to state and municipal workers over the coming decade.

Private sector firms, even those with little basis for claiming inability to pay, are continuing to scale back their benefits. In current negotiations with the Communications Workers of America, United Electrical Workers (UE), or other unions, giant firms like General Electric and Verizon are seeking health care concessions. GE has already burdened its salaried employees with sky-high deductibles and co-pays; now it wants to make similar medical plan changes for its hourly workers. The impending benefit imbroglio at Verizon illustrates how the ACA itself may be adding to labor's troubles, even at hugely profitable firms. In a message to all of its union-represented "associates" in the Northeast, Verizon informed them that cost shifting is necessary *because* of Obamacare: "Under the 2010 Patient Protection and Affordable Care Act, an excise tax will be levied on health care plans with very generous plan design components (so-called Cadillac plans). . . . This excise tax is projected to cost the company as much as $200 million in 2018 when the tax is imposed; however, Verizon is required to account for this cost now. Accordingly, we will need to modify plan designs to avoid the impact of this tax."[23]

During the 2009–10 debate about health care reform, Obama and leading Democrats helped pave the way for this Verizon bargaining push by popularizing the idea that union-negotiated benefit plans, regarded by workers as a "Chevy," actually provided them with "Cadillac" coverage that encouraged overconsumption of medical services. According to the Obama administration, such "luxury plans" had to be taxed to discourage their overuse, restrain rising health care costs, and raise more federal revenue to help pay for private insurance subsidies and the

ACA's much-needed expansion of Medicaid. So Congress created an unprecedented 40 percent excise tax that will apply to more expensive plans beginning in 2018. "Instead of setting a new, higher standard," labor journalist Roger Bybee noted, the law "effectively serves to reinforce a new lower standard of 'acceptable' coverage."[24]

Organized labor tried, but failed, to get this tax eliminated. Instead, thanks to leading Democrats like Max Baucus, Harry Reid, and Obama himself, the "Cadillac" levy was only postponed and the threshold amounts, triggering the tax, were raised.[25] Pro-labor health care experts warned, correctly, that the tax would give employers, like Verizon, an additional incentive to curtail benefits and shift costs to workers, as they attempt to keep premiums below the tax threshold ($27,500 a year for family coverage). As Mark Dudzic from the Labor Campaign For Single Payer points out, "If Verizon was really concerned about the well-being of its 'associates,' the company would work with its unions to transform the ACA into an improved and expanded 'Medicare for All' program. More practically, they could set up joint committees to work on plan design and cost savings to keep under the 2018 excise tax triggers." Instead, Verizon maintains its fierce ideological opposition to any single-payer legislative proposals. And, in contract bargaining, the telecom is intent on forcing active and retired workers to pay more for their existing plan.

As Dudzic notes, it's becoming increasingly difficult for unions to defend benefit packages that only those with remaining bargaining clout or strike capacity still have. "We've got to find ways to turn around this race to the bottom and do what our brothers and sisters in the rest of the industrialized world have already done—remove health care from the bargaining table and establish it as a birthright for everyone in America," he said. "In the meantime, we need to inspire all workers to fight for Verizon-quality benefits, rather than resent those few who have fought and sacrificed to maintain them."

Unfortunately, passage of the Affordable Care Act has created a new challenge for union activists trying to use contract struggles to build broader political support for a single-payer system. Many union members got the message that "health care for all" has been achieved. Most AFL-CIO and Change to Win affiliates hailed Obamacare as a great legislative victory, despite the excise tax that will target their own higher-end plans, the absence of any "public option," and the ACA's failure to lower the age for Medicare eligibility. After mobilizing others in labor against the new tax on benefits, even CWA downplayed the ACA's limitations or possible negative impact. In a January 2010 message to local leaders, the union argued that postponement of the excise tax would "give us one, and in some cases, more than one round of bargaining to address the impact on our members." The outcome of 2011 IBEW-CWA negotiations with Verizon will be one good test of that overly optimistic claim.

In the past, the national health care reform picture was a little clearer because the demand for "universal coverage" had yet to be met, in any fashion. Telephone union activists could use their high-profile struggles to educate and mobilize members, plus appeal to the public, about the need for Medicare-style social insurance covering everyone. Membership expectations about the impact of health care reform were still in the process of being raised rather than lowered. In states where organized labor remains strong, single-payer initiatives, like the enabling legislation passed in Vermont in early 2011, are no less urgent.

In bargaining everywhere, the most effective union response to management demands for cost shifting is what's worked in the past. Link membership resistance to concessions to political education and action seeking state or federal legislation that goes beyond the ACA. If that proactive response seems inconsistent with past union praise for Obamacare, it's better for labor to address the law's shortcomings now before rank-and-file disillusionment really sets in, an outcome that is almost guaranteed.[26]

POSTSCRIPT

Several hundred of organized labor's most active proponents of "Medicare for All" met in Chicago in early 2013 under the auspices of the Labor Campaign for Single-Payer Health Care. Their mission was to recalibrate union-based single-payer campaigning during the period when Affordable Care Act implementation became a popular excuse for not pursuing more systemic reform.[27] More than fifty unions and ten city or state labor councils were represented at this conference. Participants made plans for "educating unions about the impact of the 2018 'Cadillac tax' on employer provided benefits." They also saw new opportunities for wooing unions previously wedded to multi-employer Taft-Hartley welfare plans because Obamacare has become such a booby-trap for them.[28] A keynote speaker at the conference was Chicago Teachers Union president Karen Lewis who likened her union's strike defense of quality public education with the fight labor still needs to wage for publicly funded universal health care.

Later in 2013, the Labor Campaign collected hundreds of signatures on an "Open Letter to the AFL-CIO from Concerned Trade Unionists" that was distributed at the federation's convention in Los Angeles. Said the letter: "We would not be in this boat if the crafters of the ACA had looked to the labor movement for guidance rather than relying on insurance industry lobbyists whose business model relies on a failing employment-based system and whose profits depend on shifting costs onto the backs of workers while reducing choice and quality of care."[29]

16—CAREGIVERS WITHOUT COVERAGE

One of the cruel ironies of America's health care system is how poorly it covers caregivers themselves—particularly those who toil, without professional status, in hospitals, nursing homes, and home health care. More than 2.5 million people now work in this last field. Home health aides (or personal care attendants, as they are sometimes called) are mainly low-income, often non-white, female, and, in some states, foreign-born. Their contingent labor is largely invisible as well as undervalued. Even with union representation, the work pays little more than the minimum wage and lacks significant benefits. Already the second-fastest-growing occupation in the country, home health and personal care jobs are expected to double by 2018.

The good news is that homecare has been an area of explosive union growth in the last two decades, as Eileen Boris and Jennifer Klein report in their new book, *Caring for America*.[30] The bad news is that recent union gains are being rolled back in big states like Wisconsin,

Ohio, and Michigan. There, Republican governors have undone the union organizing deals made by their Democratic predecessors that created new bargaining units composed of home health aides and, in some states, child care providers also. As a result, nearly 50,000 newly organized workers have lost their precarious toehold at the bottom rung of public employment.

Prior to the wave of 2010 GOP gubernatorial victories in the Midwest, the Service Employees International Union (SEIU) and at least four other unions had managed to win bargaining rights for more than half a million home-based workers. Previously—and to this day in most places—home health care aides and home day care providers were unfairly classified as "independent contractors." They had no organizational voice and, in some cases, the "nontraditional workplace" where they cared for children, the aged, or disabled was their own home.

In return for union recognition from union-friendly Democratic governors and legislators, SEIU, the American Federation of State, County and Municipal Employees (AFSCME), the American Federation of Teachers (AFT), the Communications Workers of America (CWA), and the United Auto Workers (UAW) all agreed that their new home-based worker bargaining units would not be covered by existing state worker medical or retirement plans. In labor's latest successful campaign, 11,000 Medicaid-paid personal care attendants and state-funded day care workers gained bargaining rights in Connecticut, thanks to new Democratic Governor Dan Malloy. But they, like their counterparts elsewhere, will be negotiating health insurance quite different from the coverage enjoyed by state employees unionized for decades.

In key midwestern states, the right to bargain itself is being lost, along with some fragile first and second contract gains. In Michigan, 40,000 child care workers represented by the UAW and AFSCME won bargaining rights in December 2006 through an executive order. In early 2011, Republican Governor Rick Snyder cut pay by 25 percent and terminated union dues collection for more than 16,000 of these workers. In Ohio, GOP Governor John Kasich similarly rescinded contract coverage for 14,000 recently unionized child care and home care workers. Another group of 4,000 home health care aides in Wisconsin failed to win legislative approval of the $9 per hour minimum wage they negotiated in 2010. Then, as part of Governor Scott Walker's broader attack on public employee bargaining in the state, he abolished the Quality Home Care Authority created in 2009 to facilitate personal care attendant unionization.

Multiple lawsuits have been filed by right-wing groups opposed to any expansion of public sector bargaining, particularly by executive order. Three legal challenges were mounted in Connecticut to thwart Malloy's initiative. In Missouri, SEIU and AFSCME engineered a statewide referendum authorizing home care unionism in 2008. But, even after the two unions later won representation votes among 13,000 workers, conservative foes stalled first contract negotiations for nearly four years, until the state supreme court finally upheld SEIU-AFSCME certification. In California, Jerry Brown—a governor elected, like Malloy, with strong labor support—vetoed a bill passed by state legislators that would have allowed thousands of child care providers to unionize more easily, through a card check process. Citing fiscal constraints, Brown balked at extending bargaining rights to the same kind of workforce that is union-represented in New York, New Jersey, Oregon, and now Connecticut.

In these states and others run by Democrats, direct care providers will lose their jobs due to budget cuts affecting home-based child care and health services. Since these programs often involve "the poor caring for the poor," as Boris and Klein note, when funding is reduced, hours cut back, or employment eliminated entirely, low-income Americans suffer as both workers and clients. While not threatening their collective bargaining rights, new Democratic governors are squeezing benefits that affect unionized caregivers. In New York State, Governor Andrew Cuomo's proposed budget for 2011 slashed more than $2 billion from education and health care spending. New York City–based 1199 SEIU, which represents 70,000 home care workers, remained hopeful that its members will be protected. "Delivering state savings without disruption to Medicaid beneficiaries and their caregivers is an enormous feat," union president George Gresham told the *New York Times*.

As 1199 pointed out in late 2010, "State Medicaid funding to the home health services sector has been cut 9 separate times in just the last three years." As a result, nearly half of the union's home care members, who often make less than $15,000 a year, lost their coverage under the 1199 health care trust. In addition, to protect the medical benefits of working members who still qualify for health care, thousands of dependent children have been dropped from the union plan because of a reported shortfall between employer contributions and the higher premiums now being charged by its insurance provider. (Most of the children affected are eligible for alternative coverage through New York State's Children Health Plus program.)

In California, spending reductions announced in 2011 by Brown included nearly $3 billion worth of cuts in Medicaid and welfare-to-work programs. Several hundred thousand unionized caregivers are employed in California's county-administered but state-funded In-Home Supportive Services program. Many will feel the impact of this budget crunch. In ten other states where home care unionism is a much newer phenomena, similar reductions in jobs, hours, or compensation can be expected. As *Caring for America* documents, the deepest economic crisis since the Great Depression, public sector budget crises everywhere, and right-wing ascendancy in some state capitals has exposed an "Achilles' heel of the organizing model established by SEIU and copied by other unions."

In their book, Eileen Boris, who is chair of the Feminist Studies Department at UC Santa Barbara, and Jennifer Klein, a history professor at Yale, describe the contested terrain of home-based labor, now and in the past. The authors provide valuable historical background on the development of various forms of privately and publicly funded home care work. They also offer a balanced assessment of the strengths and weaknesses of recent union growth in this sector, which has at times been accompanied by considerable inter-union competition and conflict, particularly in California and Illinois. *Caring for America* includes detailed case studies of successful home care organizing, often aided by experienced community and labor organizers from ACORN. This part of their book is a useful reminder of what that organization helped the working poor accomplish before it was weakened by internal dysfunction, demonized by the right, defunded by its foundation friends, abandoned by labor, and then dismantled as a national entity.

Two-thirds of the 2.5 million workers who provide direct care in clients' homes are still awaiting action by their supposed friends that would finally give them coverage under the federal Fair Labor Standards Act (FLSA). As Boris and Klein wrote in *Labor Notes* during the 2012 presidential race, the U.S. Department of Labor has been dragging its feet on a rule-making initiative to extend FLSA minimum wage and overtime law protections to home health aides. "The home care franchise industry, estimated to be worth $84 billion, has mobilized its defenders against the new rule. The Obama administration, meanwhile, has been thrown off balance by pushback from . . . some disability advocates who fear they will have fewer funds available if their attendants must be paid overtime." Even with the possibility of the White House changing hands, the Obama administration has yet to finalize this critically important rule change. As Boris and Klein note, "If Mitt Romney wins not only will this initiative be dead in the water but the Republicans in Congress have already introduced bills to permanently classify aides and attendants as 'companions' rather than as workers" entitled to normal FLSA coverage."[31]

The authors believe that top-down union organizing victories, achieved through political deals with labor-friendly politicians, will remain vulnerable because home care employment is still "insecure and unstable, with constant turnover." Home-based worker unionism will not survive, they fear, unless "workers themselves have been able to build their union" through "member-to-member organizing." Much more must be done to develop rank-and-file leadership after union recognition, promote "mobilized political action," and encourage the creation of "social bonds" within a workforce otherwise atomized and isolated. The authors argue that home care unions

> must have social depth and a culture that enables them to live on when workers (or leaders or staff) move in and out and that sustain political activism at the state house where the budget and wages take shape. Those who do the work have to be at the table and part of the process. And when political deals fall through, there has to be power on the ground.

Though appreciative of the modest economic gains made for home care workers in New York, California, and Illinois, the authors warn about the tendency toward a "bureaucratic unionism that reinforces the old racialized gender distinctions of care work and stymies the advancement of rank-and-file women." Building real grassroots organization among home-based workers lacking traditional union structures (like a shop steward network) has never been easy. But according to the authors, this work is now more necessary than ever to avert further membership losses in the only occupation where there has been any large-scale union growth.

Of course, in the view of Republicans like Indiana Governor Mitch Daniels, unionization has transformed public employees into "a new privileged class." Decades of union bargaining in a slight majority of states have indeed provided millions of public sector workers with the kind of job-based health insurance and retirement coverage that all Americans should enjoy. But many others in the private and public sector don't have such benefits, and some are resentful about picking up the tab as taxpayers for those who do. That's why Daniels in Indiana, Kasich in Ohio, Snyder in Michigan, and Walker in Wisconsin have all tried to pit workers in private industry against those on public payrolls to build support for their agenda. Teachers have been the main target of this multistate assault, along with state, county, and municipal workers of all kinds. Even public safety officers, although exempted from Walker's anti-union legislation, have been scapegoated along with everyone else in other states. Per usual, labor's counter-campaign has been a defense of the "middle class."

Meanwhile, home care workers, the one group of public employees most at risk because of their recent arrival at the bargaining table, are not "privileged," by any standard. As *Caring for America* confirms, the working poor who care for other poor people (and many of us in other classes) haven't made it far enough up the economic ladder to be considered middle class either. Their paltry pay, lack of benefit coverage, limited training and promotional opportunities all belie the importance of the work they do every day, in difficult non-institutional settings. Organized labor would do well to put their continuing plight front and center because there are no union "fat cats" anywhere to be found in the fields of home care and child care in twenty-first century America.[32]

POSTSCRIPT

A month after this review essay appeared, voters in Michigan rejected a statewide ballot initiative that would have permitted SEIU to continue representing that state's 45,000 publicly funded home care workers. Despite heavy union spending on its behalf, the measure was defeated by a margin of 57 to 43 percent. After seven years of union representation, the workers now stripped of any bargaining rights were still earning only $8 an hour, not much better than the minimum wage. Their statewide bargaining unit was originally created when Michigan had a Democratic governor; it has now been dismantled by Rick Snyder, the Republican governor who also attacked the newly acquired union rights of state-funded child care providers.[33]

When President Obama was reelected in November 2012, he managed to carry Michigan. Many months later, the rule-making process that would guarantee home care workers minimum wage and overtime protections was still bogged down in his White House Office of Management and Budget. On March 1, 2013, a *New York Times* editorial warned "of a real danger that in this late round the long fight to extend basic labor protections to home care workers could be lost." The *Times* urged Obama to end "the companionship exemption" because it "amounts to an institutionalized from of sexism, racism, and exploitation."[34] On Sept. 18, 2013, the U.S. Department of Labor finally announced that it was "extending minimum wage and overtime protections to the nation's nearly two million home care workers . . . who usually earn $8.50 to $12 an hour."[35]

17—PICKETING VS. PARTNERING

In California, the Kaiser name has long been linked to innovations in work organization, personnel practices, and health care delivery. During the Second World War, industrialist Henry Kaiser built America's largest shipyard, virtually overnight, in the city of Richmond facing San Francisco

Bay. That now famous facility turned out scores of "Liberty" ships, using new production techniques, female welders—as in "Rosie the Riveter"—and African Americans who had also been previously excluded from such higher-paying blue-collar jobs. Kaiser's wartime experimentation with a pioneering group health plan, tied to hospitals in Richmond and Oakland, paved the way for prepaid medical coverage of millions of workers and their families.

In its modern-day incarnation, Kaiser Permanente (KP) now operates the largest network of unionized hospitals in the country. It has 7 million enrollees in California, where it has become the state's largest Health Maintenance Organization (HMO). In the managed care field, Kaiser has long been known as "the HMO that labor built." In the mid-1990s, Kaiser formed a much-heralded Labor Management Partnership (LMP) with the Service Employees International Union (SEIU) and other unions to make its labor relations less adversarial. Through the LMP, Kaiser employees were promised a greater workplace voice so they could improve patient care. Their unions, in turn, won the right to organize non-union KP workers without management interference—a "neutrality" deal that helped boost their membership. By 2007, there weren't many other health care employers that seemed as labor-friendly. So American Rights at Work, the union-backed lobbying group, bestowed its annual Eleanor Roosevelt Human Rights Award on Kaiser at a gala reception in Washington, D.C., attended by top union officials. Like ARAW, the AFL-CIO continues to applaud the HMO's "shared purpose" and "partnership approach."

Outside the Beltway, Kaiser has been attracting more picket lines than plaudits, from workers who know it better. In late September 2011 more than 21,000 Kaiser employees conducted the largest work stoppage in California health care history. Four months later, they bested that record by walking out again, in slightly larger numbers. These strikes protested contract concessions sought by Kaiser despite profits of $5.7 billion since 2009. They also exposed organizational rifts within the ranks of labor about when, how, or even whether to resist health care givebacks.

The strikes were organized in response to stalled negotiations involving 4,000 mental health professionals, optical workers, and nurses who left SEIU to join the new National Union of Health care Workers (NUHW). They were supported both times by 17,000 RNs who belong to the California Nurses Association (CNA), which also refuses to participate in Kaiser's labor-management partnership. Joining them in January 2012 were 650 members of Stationary Engineers Local 39, who maintain the hospitals' air conditioning, refrigeration, and physical plant. Local 39, like CNA, struck in sympathy with NUHW and helped picket other building trade workers off the job at Kaiser construction sites.[36] Other AFL-CIO and Change to Win affiliates refrained from participating or publicly criticizing the HMO in any way. SEIU's United Health Care Workers-West (UHW) even urged its 45,000 Kaiser dues payers to cross picket lines set up by their own coworkers—advice that was ignored by some dissident rank-and-filers who favor NUHW. By NUHW's estimate, about 1,000 of them stayed away from work as well, during the September and January work stoppages.

In Kaiser's bargaining with NUHW and another independent union, the Guild for Professional Pharmacists, the hospital chain seeks to eliminate retiree health coverage and force active employees to pay more for their medical benefits. It also wants to replace defined-benefit pensions with individual retirement accounts. Howard Hertz, vice president of the Guild for Professional Pharmacists, finds these concession demands to be reprehensible in light of past collaborative "efforts [that] have given Kaiser ever greater profits and membership growth." Says Hertz: "The benefit changes Kaiser is trying to impose punish people for their past loyalty. . . . They are not just wrong but immoral."

Zenei Cortez, co-president of CNA and a twenty-nine-year Kaiser veteran, believes that if management gets concessions from other unions, nurses will have a much harder time defending their own health coverage and pensions when their contract expires in 2014. A dialysis nurse at Kaiser Sunset Medical Center, who belongs to NUHW, reports that some of her more experienced coworkers "are already contemplating taking early retirement and leaving nursing practice" before any pension changes take place. "Kaiser will save a lot of money," she pointed out, "because they will hire new nurses and start them at a lower pay rate," a trend she and others fear will exacerbate the problem of understaffing.

At Kaiser hospitals and clinics throughout the state, the strikes did more than call attention to deteriorating labor relations. They also highlighted how patients and their families are being negatively affected by Kaiser's own cost cutting. NUHW released a whistle-blowing report titled "Care Delayed, Care Denied: Kaiser Permanente's Failure to Provide Timely and Appropriate Mental Health Services," which is based on information provided by union-represented psychologists and social workers, plus outside experts. The report documents Kaiser's "systematic" failures to observe "recommended clinical standards" and meet the mental health needs of patients with autism, anxiety, depression, schizophrenia, suicidal ideation, and bipolar disorder. NUHW accused Kaiser of non-compliance with state laws requiring HMOs to provide "timely access" to appropriate care. The union demanded an immediate investigation of the largest provider of mental health services in California to avoid further harm to patients.

Kaiser spokesman John Nelson insisted that the HMO has "appropriate staffing levels to meet our members' needs." According to Nelson, Kaiser is merely trying "to find ways to contain costs in partnership with our unions. Both management and labor have a stake in the financial challenges we face and meeting rising health care costs and costs of pension benefits." Nelson was particularly critical of NUHW members, saying it was "disappointing that they have chosen to strike instead of engaging in constructive action." According to SEIU spokesperson Elizabeth Brennan, labor unrest at Kaiser was occurring because some workers had mistakenly joined "a weak, ineffective group" instead of sticking with SEIU. "While NUHW is facing major take-backs, SEIU-UHW members are now preparing for bargaining next year to extend good raises and lock in all of our benefits, pension and job security through 2015 and beyond," she said.

Both Kaiser and SEIU have tried to squelch support for NUHW, which was formed in 2009 after SEIU put UHW in trusteeship and removed its elected leadership. In late 2010, the National Labor Relations Board obtained a rare federal court order forcing Kaiser to provide $2 million in back pay that was illegally withheld from 2,300 workers who voted to replace SEIU with NUHW in the first wave of

post-trusteeship defections at Kaiser. In October 2010, NUHW failed
to oust SEIU in Kaiser's statewide service and technical unit. But that
vote among 44,000 employees was later overturned and a new election
ordered after the NLRB found that SEIU's illegal campaigning, along
with Kaiser's earlier unfair labor practices, "interfered with the exercise of a free and reasoned choice among employees."

In an attempt to discourage further joint strike activity by NUHW
and CNA, Kaiser dragged the nurses' union into arbitration after its solidarity picketing in September 2011. Kaiser alleges that CNA members
violated the no-strike clause in their contract, despite legal precedents
that have established their right to honor other workers' picket lines.
SEIU has interpreted its own no-strike clause just like management
has the CNA's. When SEIU-UHW board member Shawna Stewart
started getting calls from members at Kaiser in Modesto about honoring picket lines, Stewart sent an email to everyone at her facility, citing
their contract's no-strike clause. Stewart also argued that service and
technical workers should not respect the picket lines of other Kaiser
unions because "this is not our fight."

Taking aim at NUHW in particular, Stewart claimed that its members "put themselves at risk" of contract concessions when they
decertified SEIU and joined the new union. "Now they have to fight
for everything they *already* had," she said. "If they want our support,
they would need to sign a card saying they want to come back and then
they can keep what they had." Advised Stewart: "It's always best to
stick with the winning team."

At Kaiser in Richmond, NUHW members seemed to think sticking together was the best way to win. Wearing their crimson NUHW
t-shirts, Larry Parker, Sonia Minor, and their Kaiser coworkers joined
the strike in January to support their elected negotiating team. Parker
has spent twenty-eight years with the health care chain. "If Kaiser gets
takeaways from us," he said, "they're just going to do the same thing
with everybody else." Minor has sat at the bargaining table for NUHW
and heard Kaiser negotiators demand that defined-benefit pensions be
eliminated—while CEO George Halvorson is receiving nearly $9 mil-
lion a year and gets multiple retirement plan coverage. "It's not about
the purple and the red," she said, referring to the signature colors of

SEIU and NUHW. "At the end of the day, we all work for Kaiser and we all need to stand together to protect our benefits."

A very different union stance was emerging from the private deliberations of SEIU and other partnership unions in early 2012. Their more conciliatory bargaining strategy was shaped by Dave Regan, the $300,000 a year leader of SEIU-UHW who was installed in 2009 by SEIU's then national union president, Andy Stern. At one pre-bargaining meeting of SEIU-UHW delegates in San Jose, Regan suggested that "if we're not careful," Kaiser might end up like a Detroit auto manufacturer because of its rising health care costs. According to Regan, there is indeed a "train bearing down on us" in the form of a Kaiser management attempt to "take our stuff . . . our things," as he called the benefits negotiated by the union.

Regan argued that the Coalition of Kaiser Permanente Unions (CKPU) just needed to give Kaiser a "push to a higher place" to avoid concessions. The health care cost-saving destination he has in mind is an employee "wellness" program—of the sort SEIU has already helped other employers introduce. These programs essentially blame the personal habits of workers for medical cost inflation, and penalize, via individualized cost-shifting, those who fail to shape up. As Regan explained in San Jose: "if you're overweight, you pay far more for your health care. If you smoke, you pay 20 percent more. If you do this or that, you pay more. That's what's going on out there."

Regan, who serves as an executive vice president of the SEIU, proposed tying workers' bonuses "to how we use health care to get healthy." This approach, he claimed, will "protect what we have," while improving the public image of unions. The UHW president was joined on stage by John August, a fellow high-paid proponent of "twenty-first-century unionism" who lavished praise on the "clarity" of Regan's "vision." August directs the CKPU and oversees Kaiser's $16 million labor-management partnership budget. A former organizer for SEIU/1199 and later the Teamsters, he announced that the other partnership unions were fully behind Regan's "Let's Get Healthy" plan.

By email, a member of the SEIU-UHW bargaining committee, who listened to these speeches and surreptitiously taped them, accused Regan and August of trying to soften up the membership. "They never talk about the fact that Kaiser is rolling in profits, that the CEO got a $1 million raise, and that other unions are fighting Kaiser's cuts. Instead, they try to scare us that we're going to turn into the UAW and Kaiser will turn into General Motors unless we let Kaiser cut our benefits. They tell us: 'You're lucky to have a job.'" According to a Kaiser worker, who insisted on anonymity, "You know it's total BS when union leaders start telling us we need to be 'innovative' and 'transformational.' Apparently, 'twenty-first-century unions' don't actually fight for their members, they just climb in bed with the bosses and gut our pensions and health insurance in secret. These are benefits that some of us have worked for decades to have.

"Even a half assed union would have a plan to fight cuts in workers' pensions and health insurance," he observed. "But it's clear SEIU and John August have no plan at all to fight. In fact, Regan told us that we can't just show up at the bargaining table and say 'no' to the cuts. Instead, he says we have to 'get out in front of the cuts' by offering our own. . . . They claim that if we eat cuts on a wellness plan then Kaiser will be satisfied and won't try to gut our health insurance. That's their genius bargaining strategy."

The ongoing struggle over which path to take—resistance to concessions or the "non-adversarial" approach embraced by SEIU—will only intensify in the future. When the 44,000 service and technical workers at Kaiser finally get another NLRB vote, Kaiser and its preferred negotiating "partner" may have a harder time peddling "Let's Get Healthy," not to mention health care givebacks, as a "win-win" for everybody.[37]

POSTSCRIPT

In March 2013, shortly before the long-awaited Kaiser election rerun, the California Department of Managed Health Care (DMHC) confirmed the validity of NUHW's strike-related whistle-blowing in 2011. As the *San Francisco Chronicle* reported, "State regulators reprimanded Kaiser for mismanaging its mental health services, making patients wait excessively long periods between appointments and offering members inaccurate information that may have dissuaded them from receiving long-term individual therapy." The DMHC cited Kaiser for multiple failures to meet state standards and referred the case to its Office of Enforcement, for imposition of financial penalties and other legal remedies. In June 2013, the DMHC imposed a $4 million fine against Kaiser for limiting patients' access to health care—the second largest enforcement action in the agency's history.[38]

One month later, NUHW wrote to state officials questioning why Kaiser, the biggest HMO in the state, should be allowed to participate in California's new insurance exchange, set up under the Affordable Care Act, after violating DMHC regulations and incurring penalties that jeopardized its "good standing" as a "qualified health plan." NUHW argued that "the unambiguous language in the insurance exchange's contract clearly disqualifies Kaiser." In August 2013, NUHW also asked the state attorney general to investigate disciplinary action taken against a union-represented clinician who attempted to document an instance of mental health treatment delay at Kaiser.[39]

18—THE CORPORATE WELLNESS SCAM

When it comes to health-related "sin taxes," don't ask for consistency from Corporate America. Whenever there's a public policy initiative that would add a few cents to the cost of surgary drinks to discourage overconsumption and reduce the risk of obesity, PepsiCo spends millions of dollars making sure it's defeated.[40] Yet, like a growing number of U.S. companies, this giant purveyor of junk food has no problem using far greater financial penalties in its own health care plan to encourage weight loss, lower cholesterol and blood pressure levels, or smoking cessation.

Despite protests by the Teamsters union, hundreds of PepsiCo drivers and warehouse workers in upstate New York now face $50-a-month payments if they use cigarettes or have weight-related medical conditions such as hypertension, high blood pressure, and diabetes. As one PepsiCo official explained, these penalties will "enable our associates and their families to have a healthier lifestyle." PepsiCo's professed concern about the "wellness" of its workers is shared by thousands of other firms who are now remaking their medical plans so noncompliant employees end up paying more out-of-pocket for their coverage.

Companies, large and small, have long been shifting the burden of medical cost inflation to their workforce, across the board.

Cost-sharing negotiated with unions or, more commonly, imposed unilaterally by non-union firms has raised labor's share of health insurance premiums to an average of 18 percent for individual coverage and nearly 30 percent for families. Workers or their dependents who utilize plan benefits also face escalating deductibles, co-pays, and co-insurance, which can add hundreds or thousands of dollars more to their annual health care spending.

Now, under the banner of health promotion, management is also making some workers pay more for their insurance based on individual differences in their medical condition or lack of adherence to "wellness" standards. This new, more individualized, form of cost shifting threatens to stigmatize and penalize the chronic health conditions of millions of workers, expose some to job discrimination, and undermine labor solidarity in the process. In addition, workplace privacy advocates are warning about the invasiveness of the personal "health risk assessments," now commonly required in corporate wellness programs, because these surveys probe off-duty behavior related to sex, drugs, and alcohol.

Under the federal Health Insurance Portability and Accountability Act (HIPAA), management can already compel some workers to pay up to 20 percent more than others covered by the same medical plan. According to Lewis Maltby of the National Workrights Institute, "all that is required is that the penalty be 'designed to promote good health.' The employer is not required to demonstrate that the amount approximates the increase in cost due to an employee who engages in any unhealthy behavior." When President Obama's Affordable Care Act goes into effect in 2014, Maltby predicts that wellness program abuses will increase "because the penalty employers can charge without justification increases to 30%."[41] New rules implementing the ACA may soon permit a 50 percent difference in what workers pay, depending on their use or non-use of tobacco.

Among the other groups sounding the alarm about this trend are Families USA, Georgetown University's Health Policy Institute, the American Cancer Society, and the American Heart and Diabetes Associations. A report by the HPI at Georgetown calls for new federal and state standards that will protect consumers from "programs that inappropriately punish workers in poor health, are overly coercive, or create perverse financial incentives that result in poorer health outcomes." As Cancer Society lobbyist Dick Woodruff told National Public Radio, "The whole point of health care reform is to make sure that everyone gets insurance. And if people have to pay more because they're unhealthy, that's a barrier. It defeats the whole purpose."

California Nurses Association copresident DeAnn McEwen, a nurse for nearly forty years, sees great risk of "discrimination through backdoor redlining for individuals with preexisting conditions and disabilities." She points out that the workers "more likely to have the health conditions that wellness programs target are low-income individuals and racial/ethnic minorities." By no coincidence, she says, they also "face barriers to health such as unsafe neighborhoods, poor air quality, substandard, decaying housing, and lack of access to affordable, healthy food."

Despite these warnings, many other unions are buying into wellness schemes under management pressure for more costly contract concessions. Employers and their consultants pitch these programs initially as a way to provide "discounts" for workers who sign up for annual health evaluations, subsidized gym membership, smoking cessation classes, or other forms of health counseling. In Chicago, for example, the Chicago Teachers Union (CTU) returned from their inspiring seven-day strike in 2012 with a freeze on insurance rates but a new wellness plan similar to that covering 38,000 other city employees. According to one top CTU official, it "was definitely one of the least popular parts of the contract settlement" because of "concerns that what we're seeing is just the thin edge of the wedge."

The teachers' program begins with biometric testing for cholesterol, diabetes, blood pressure, weight, and body mass index (BMI). Teachers with an identified problem will be assigned a health coach who works for a third-party vendor. All must log into a wellness website, every month, earning points for reading articles or watching videos; the penalty for failing to do so will be a $50 monthly fine. A family with two adult members that opts out of the program entirely will pay $1,200 more annually for their insurance. In the union's next round of bargaining, this CTU leader worries that management "may try to attach penalties for being overweight or a smoker" in a profession where "many negative health outcomes have a lot to do with job stress."[42]

Efforts to promote better eating, more walking, bike-riding, or working out at the gym would be quite positive—and far more effective—if they were part of a broader campaign that addressed the societal roots of bad nutrition, obesity, and diabetes. Companies like to blame bad choices by individual workers or their families, when some, like PepsiCo employees, may just be showing the side effects of consuming their own employer's heavily marketed sugary drinks or salty, high-fat snacks. In addition, as CNA's McEwen points out, many chronic health conditions have socioeconomic causes, including exposure to hazardous workplace environments.

In California, some of the same hospital chains now pushing for "wellness" penalties don't want to make changes in working conditions that would reduce job stress, fatigue, unsafe workloads, and other causes of occupational illness and injury. Better nurse-patient staffing ratios, limits on forced overtime, guaranteed lunch and break time, and more lift equipment to reduce back injuries would all contribute to employee "wellness," and they would also lower health care costs by increasing patient safety. Instead, Kaiser Permanente, Sutter Health, Dignity Health, and Daughters of Charity Health Systems want to shift the focus in bargaining from their own unhealthy practices to the off-duty behavior of individual employees.

At Daughters of Charity, the new "wellness program" negotiated in April 2012 by SEIU's United Healthcare Workers-West comes, per usual, with more familiar forms of cost shifting. Three thousand UHW members at five hospitals will now pay 25 percent of the monthly premiums for PPO coverage that was previously fully paid by their employer. Out-of-pocket costs for medical plan utilization (doctor visits, prescriptions, etc.) will double and the premiums of workers who fail to meet new standards for personal healthiness will be 20 percent higher than those for their coworkers. To get these concessions approved, UHW conducted a rushed two-day ratification vote that began less than twelve hours after a tentative agreement was reached. The SEIU constitution requires three days' advance notice of ratification votes; workers at Daughters of Charity got only nine hours. According to workers who complained, in writing, to SEIU president Mary Kay Henry, UHW reps refused to provide them with copies of the agreement they were voting on.

Workers at Seton Medical Center, a Daughters of Charity facility near San Francisco, were already so disgruntled that they had petitioned for an election to switch from UHW-SEIU to the National Union of Healthcare Workers, which is now affiliated with the California Nurses Association. In a unit of 750, NUHW lost by just six votes. In January, 2013, the National Labor Relations Board decided that widespread election misconduct by management and SEIU could only be remedied by holding another vote, a ruling now being appealed.

NUHW leader John Borsos is particularly critical of the wellness plan at California's largest health care employer, Kaiser Permanente. KP's "Total Health Program" was negotiated in 2012 by SEIU and other unions involved in Kaiser's Labor-Management Partnership (LMP). Just as at Daughters of Charity, the same contract settlement contained other changes in the medical plan. At Kaiser, retirees previously had the same coverage as active employees. Now, SEIU-UHW has agreed to a freeze on Kaiser's retire health care payments starting in 2017. This concession will save the employer an estimated $1.8 billion but it means that, as premium costs rise, union pensioners will be paying much more for health care out of their fixed incomes. UHW justified the change based on trends in the industry—that is, retiree health care cost shifting elsewhere—and the need for Kaiser to remain "competitive."

The partnership unions similarly tout "Total Health" as "a long-term business strategy" for giving Kaiser a "competitive advantage" over other health maintenance organizations. If wellness-based cost savings are achieved, Kaiser promises a monetary bonus for work groups that complete an annual health assessment, update their "biometric risk screenings," and "maintain or make steady improvements on key biometric risks (weight, smoking, blood pressure, and cholesterol)." [43] Individual compliance will be "encouraged" by a network of "Wellness Ambassadors," derided as "wellness cops" by the NUHW, who will get paid time off from Kaiser for their activities. Borsos predicts that

Kaiser personnel who decline to participate "will be subject to enormous pressure from coworkers when a portion of their future pay is tied to everyone's participation."[44]

The danger of a membership backlash to punitive or intrusive wellness plans is very real. In 2011, labor organizations represented on Oregon's Public Employee Benefits Board (PEBB), agreed to a new "Health Engagement Model" (HEM), that required mandatory "risk assessments," including waist measuring, plus penalties for noncompliance. According to one labor educator in the state, the HEM "riled up many workers, who turned their fury and frustration on the unions." SEIU was among those soon apologizing for "a poorly communicated change to our health plans that included a punitive surcharge" and "got us started on the wrong foot." Labor officials later persuaded the PEBB that non-participants "in health engagement" should no longer be subject to the surcharge; instead, participants should be rewarded with an additional $17.50 per pay period. However, the health plan now forces non-participating workers and their families to pay $100 to $300 more in deductibles, a "punitive aspect" still opposed by their unions.

A survey of 355 private companies by Towers Watson, a leading HR consultant, showed a 50 percent increase in their use of such financial incentives and penalties between 2009 and 2011. Thirty-eight percent of these firms reported further plans to penalize workers who fail to meet health improvement goals tied to their cholesterol levels or body mass index. Clearly, if unions don't get their act together on "wellness" (and, in some cases, remember which side they're on), their members are going to get rolled, one way or another.[45]

A better labor response than just acceding to these schemes would be to shift the terms of the wellness debate, at the bargaining table and in public policy arenas. Unions need to take a more holistic approach to their members' health problems, one that doesn't let Corporate America off the hook for its role in producing the social determinants of poor health, including poverty, inequality, and unhealthy jobs.

Labor should also make wellness controversies a teachable moment for workers upset by punitive medical plan changes but not previously supportive of or well informed about single-payer health care. "Medicare for all" would eliminate job-based benefit coverage and the new forms of cost shifting and differential treatment now being introduced under the guise of "getting healthy." In nations with social insurance systems, health outcomes are better, in part, because achieving public health goals, like reduced obesity, isn't left to companies more concerned about their bottom line than workers' waistlines. American workers who don't want their boss playing "wellness cop" need both short-term legal protection and a longer-term political solution.[46]

POSTSCRIPT

Shortly after this article appeared in *The Nation*, *Health Affairs*, a leading academic journal on health policy issues, published a research paper titled "Wellness Incentives in the Workplace: Cost Savings through Cost Shifting to Unhealthy Workers." The three authors "reviewed results of randomized controlled trials and identified challenges for workplace wellness programs to function as the [ACA] intends," without "health-based discrimination." Their paper acknowledged "valid reasons, beyond lowering costs, to institute workplace wellness programs." But the authors "found little evidence that such programs can easily save costs through health improvements without being discriminatory. Our evidence suggests that savings to employers may come from cost shifting, with the most vulnerable employees—those from lower socioeconomic strata with the most health risks—probably bearing greater costs that in effect subsidize their healthier colleagues."[47]

In May 2013 the Rand Corporation released a wellness program assessment commissioned by Congress and delivered to the Department of Health and Human Services. Rand researchers found that any cost savings achieved by employers were statistically insignificant and that only 2 percent of the 600 firms surveyed even had detailed savings estimates. As *Forbes* magazine reported, "The scientific evidence to support real efficacy just isn't there."[48] Unfortunately, that hasn't stopped the corporate wellness trend from becoming a $6 billion-a-year industry, composed of more than 600 vendors peddling a product that promotes health care cost shifting.

On opening day of the 2013 AFL-CIO convention in Los Angeles, Kaiser was scheduled to give several presentations about "instant recess," a component of its workplace wellness program. Leafleting and picketing threatened by Kaiser workers represented by the National Union of Healthcare Workers led to the cancellation of Kaiser's role at the convention. In a letter to AFL-CIO President Rich Trumka, the workers questioned why the federation was "in effect holding Kaiser up as a model employer" given its "multiple and serious violations of federal labor law" and attempt "to sharply cut the health and retirement benefits for thousands of workers despite the company's record profits."[49]

PART V

TELECOM LABOR TROUBLES

This section draws on my personal experience assisting strikes, organizing, contract negotiations, and, more recently, union reform campaigns in the telecom industry. One common thread here is the steady de-unionization of Verizon, the second-largest firm in the industry, and the scene of many past labor struggles that ended more happily than the strike and contract campaign of 2011–12.

The first big telephone walkout that I witnessed during my three decades with the Communications Workers of America was a three-week national strike on a scale unimaginable today (but, hopefully, not forever). It occurred in 1983 when the three unions then representing AT&T workers had 700,000 members and CWA's share of that workforce was half a million. A year later, the nationwide regulated monopoly known as the Bell System was broken up, spawning separate companies to manufacture and install phone equipment or provide local and long-distance service. This turned telecom bargaining into a far more fragmented, not always well coordinated, and ever smaller series of regional or local contract fights. The combined forces of AT&T divestiture, deregulation, non-union competition, technological change, and workforce restructuring, including overseas outsourcing of manufacturing, have greatly weakened CWA and the International Brotherhood of Electrical Workers (IBEW). CWA's total telecom membership is down 50 percent in the last decade, to about 200,000. The IBEW, a union traditionally dominated by construction electricians, has a telephone worker division numbering only about 25,000 today. The largest telecom strike in recent years involved only one-seventh of the workers who walked out at AT&T thirty years ago. Yet, by 2011, even a work stoppage by 45,000 CWA and IBEW members at Verizon in the Northeast was big for the industry and, of course, increasingly rare elsewhere.

As U.S. telephone workers struggled valiantly to defend past contract gains in the new millennium, they swam against the tide of concession bargaining that has now spread to the public sector. During the public employee uprising against Republican Governor Scott Walker's attempt to repeal collective bargaining, a few unions involved in or aiding that struggle argued against making contract concessions in Wisconsin or anywhere else.[1] But the parameters of organized labor's mainstream "discourse" about takeaways was considerably narrower. As the *New York Times* reported, the multistate assault on public employee wages and benefits mainly produced a debate about "what to give to save bargaining." Even putative friends of labor, like MIT professor and union consultant Tom Kochan, counseled union leaders to recognize reality and accept what AFL-CIO president Rich Trumka calls "shared sacrifice."[2] According to Kochan, "There has to be a new bargain . . . on pension costs and health care costs . . . that helps [unions] take that issue off the table and focus on the issue of workers' rights and the attack on unions."[3]

In telecom, the multipronged corporate offensive against fully paid health insurance, defined benefit pensions, and workers' rights on the job is not so easily differentiated and defused. Union retreat on some contentious issues, like medical care or retirement security, does not necessarily lead to greater management acceptance of unionism per se. For cable TV companies like Comcast, Time Warner, and Cablevision, which are almost entirely non-union, and the fast-growing non-union subsidiaries operated by Verizon, a parent company still saddled with much higher levels of unionization, the preferred labor relations environment is the one offering maximum flexibility, which means no collective bargaining at all. Further state and federal deregulation, the predominance of wireless communication, and joint marketing of "bundled services" offered by past business competitors threaten to erase whatever labor relations differences might have previously distinguished the cable TV–based sector of the industry from the traditional telephone side.[4] As CWA reports, "Union density in the converged telecommunications sector has dropped significantly" and the "historic base of our membership, landline telephone service, is shrinking dramatically" as customers choose to go wireless or "Voice over Internet" (VoIP) through their cable TV or Internet provider.[5]

The main union defenses of the past have included systematic membership education and mobilization based on high-functioning steward networks, aggressive contract campaigns, community-labor coalition building, IBEW-CWA unity, "bargaining to organize," and open-ended strikes. These fortifications may not hold unless there is continual reassessment of what works and what doesn't, followed by better organizational adaptation to an ever-changing industrial battlefield.[6] When national or local union hierarchies fail to provide the coordination and institutional support necessary for new or old forms of resistance, more union reform initiatives of the sort described in this section will be necessary, if not always sufficient, whether they succeed initially or not.

19—REQUIEM FOR A TELEPHONE WORKER

In December 1989 the large Dorchester, Massachusetts, clan of Jerry "Judgie" Leary was, like many other telephone worker families in the Northeast, not exactly flush with cash for Christmas presents. Jerry and 60,000 other members of the Electrical Workers (IBEW) and the Communications Workers (CWA) had just spent four grueling, impoverishing months on the picket line battling NYNEX, the regional telecom giant now known nationally as Verizon.

Participants in that strike still bitterly recall first-time-ever visits to food banks, the company's cutoff of job-based medical benefits, and the dismissal, suspension, or arrest of hundreds of union activists in New York and New England. In Westchester County, New York, a CWA picket captain with several young children was hit by a car driven by a scab and later died of brain injuries. In New Hampshire, one striker from the IBEW was killed in an industrial accident while trying to do an unfamiliar factory job to support his family.

But during that whole long ordeal, the local union that Jerry Leary served for many years afterward, as vice president and business agent, made many new friends. IBEW Local 2222 became well known in the local labor movement and in political circles, far from the predominantly Irish-American neighborhoods that once produced the bulk of Boston's police, firefighters, telephone, and utility workers.

The critical issue in 1989 was health care cost shifting. CWA and IBEW strikers parried the company's proposed givebacks by demanding "Health Care for All, Not Health Cuts at NYNEX!"—a slogan emblazoned everywhere, one that linked workplace and political struggle in a resonant way. The unions argued that forcing workers with better health coverage to pay more for their benefits would do nothing to curb medical cost inflation or alleviate the plight of millions of uninsured and underinsured Americans. Projecting this message with the help of health care reform groups enabled the strikers to publicly position themselves as fighters for universal coverage, not just the maintenance of their own better-than-average medical plan.

They soon had Reverend Jesse Jackson at their side, plus striking coal miners and Eastern Airlines pilots. The NYNEX strike support effort in Boston became a "rainbow coalition," ranging from the National Organization for Women to Physicians for a National Health Program. In a rare role reversal for the 1980s, the strikers actually won and the company lost. To this day, in recognition of the role that solidarity played in that victory, Local 2222 remains an active participant in both the Boston Labor Council, where Jerry Leary was a longtime delegate, and in the more eclectic labor-community coalition known as Jobs with Justice.[7]

Thanks to their sacrifices twenty years ago and a willingness to fight in subsequent rounds of bargaining (which included a fourteen-day strike in 2000), Verizon workers in the Northeast still don't make any premium contributions for their individual or family coverage (as of 2009). But that's an arrangement now enjoyed by only a fraction of the labor force.[8] And some Senate Democrats and the Obama Administration believe that such "Cadillac coverage" should be disparaged and taxed as part of their misbegotten health care reform scheme in Washington, D.C.

Jerry Leary never owned a Cadillac, but he did need good union-negotiated benefits when he was diagnosed with Stage 4 lung cancer in the spring of 2009. That unexpected blow to a seemingly hale and hearty NYNEX strike veteran didn't stop him from being much involved in preparations for a big anti-layoff march a few months later that brought nearly a thousand union members to the front door of Verizon's headquarters and other protest targets in downtown Boston, like the Hyatt Hotel. But Jerry's condition did lead to medical complications that imposed considerable financial and emotional strain on his wife, six children, and large extended family.

To show members' appreciation for Jerry's many years of service to the union and "his lifelong commitment to Dorchester and its various sports, civic, neighborhood, or religious organizations," Local 2222 set up a fund-raising website. The local's mobilization coordinator, Donna Bohan, began making plans for a benefit party at Florian Hall, operated by Firefighters Local 718 and the site of numerous mass meetings during the 1989 walkout. Unfortunately, the fundraiser was held without the guest of honor. On December 11, 2009, Jerry Leary died at the age of 57.

In many unions, it's not uncommon to toast, at great dues-payer expense, some higher-ranking member of the labor officialdom or to shell out big bucks for a politician's "time" (as their year-round fundraisers are called in Boston). But just as Jerry was known, far and wide, for his self-less volunteering, the benefit organized for the Leary family is a typical expression of IBEW caring for those in need, regardless of rank or title in the union. In the last few months alone, due to Donna's tireless efforts, tens of thousands of dollars have been raised for one Local 2222 member left crippled after surgery and the family of another who died in a skiing accident. In myriad ways, large and small, the local is always extending a helping hand and leaving a lasting impression.

Jerry's close friend Myles Calvey, business manager of Local 2222, attends as many wakes as a Catholic priest, where his comforting presence is always appreciated by bereaved family members and friends. Local president Ed "Eddie Fitz" Fitzpatrick, another 1989 strike leader, is a legendary figure in 2222's "employee assistance" program; his personal interventions have saved the lives, marriages, and phone company careers of countless workers caught in the grip of substance abuse. And, of course, a legion of other IBEW business agents and stewards, like the recently retired '89 strike veteran Dave Reardon and organizer Steve Smith, have devoted thousands of hours to answering phone calls, filing grievances, and resolving problems related to the Verizon contract and its hard-won safety net of medical and pension benefits, disability coverage, and family and medical leave protections.

All of the above and many more were at Jerry Leary's funeral at St. Anne's, the parish in Dorchester where he was born, raised, and lived his whole life. After Mass, a long line of cars headed down Neponset Avenue, past the Boston Firefighters honor guard and the Local 2222 union hall in Lower Mills where Jerry, Myles, Fitz, Dave, Steve, Donna, and others have long served the membership. Our destination this time was Cedar Grove Cemetery, a mile or so down the road.

How many people have ever been interred, there or anywhere else, after passing under the raised and arched booms of two telephone company bucket trucks, with a union banner strung between the two? I don't know. But my guess is that Verizon CEO Ivan Seidenberg, big company man that he is, won't be laid to rest in similar fashion when his number is up. Ivan's $20 million a year in salary, bonuses, and stock options will buy a different kind of sendoff. It will probably be far less reflective of real life at the phone company, like the biting cold at Jerry's gravesite that was a familiar companion for those who spend every New England winter climbing poles or splicing cable underground.

In the face of the grotesque caricatures of trade unionism projected by Verizon and other firms today in their unrelenting campaign against the Employee Free Choice Act, it's easy to forget (or never know) what being a rank-and-file member means in the culture of mutual aid and protection, solidarity and friendship that exists in the best local unions. As Chicago labor lawyer Tom Geoghegan noted years ago in his book *Which Side Are You On*, that organizational connection doesn't just provide much better-than-average pay and benefits. For union activists, it makes you part of a distinct counterculture that continues to contest, however imperfectly, the dominance of competitive individualism. Big business, Verizon included, hates and fears this counterculture, far more than any stereotypical working-class Joe might have disliked the Woodstock generation forty years ago.

Strong unions are deeply rooted in the workplace and community; simply by negotiating and enforcing contracts, they "interfere" with "management of the business." That's why employers see them, as top Verizon managers have long viewed 2222, as an unwanted rival for the loyalty of the workers they call "associates." And that explains why Verizon has done so much to downsize, dislocate, and contain the workforce represented by this stalwart defender of "legacy contracts" and the job rights that go with them.

The collective ties that bind coworkers "on the property," as they say at 2222, are allegiances forged over many years of helping each other out, in countless ways, on the job and off. They represent a standing rebuff to the demands for corporate loyalty and obedience from Seidenberg and his army of headquarters bean-counters. To see the difference, in death as well as life, one needed to look no further than the huge crowd of mourners, many with IBEW Local 2222 stickers on their cars, accompanying Brother Jerry Leary to his final resting place. His son Patrick's moving recollections from the altar of St. Anne's about a life well spent—about a father doing good for his family, his neighborhood and city, and his beloved community of Boston telephone workers—brought tears to the eyes of many. The back of the church, filled with hundreds of people, was lined with "outside plant" techs attending in their winter work clothes.

Until recently, Patrick Leary was one of them, too. But now Jerry's son is no longer on the Verizon payroll, a victim of layoffs this fall in New England. That steady downsizing, on the landline side of the business, represents a mortal threat to telephone labor as a union-organized entity in the Northeast. It deprives both IBEW and CWA of the bargaining clout they need to defend past gains, not to mention younger members able to fill the big shoes left behind by the likes of Jerry Leary.[9]

20—SAVE OUR UNION, 2011

Arriving right after the Teamsters left town, local union delegates from the Communications Workers of America (CWA) came to Las Vegas in July

2011 to pick their own national officers and executive board members for another four years. In CWA, unlike the Teamsters, only these 1,100 voters, rather than the entire membership of 500,000, gets to choose the union's top leadership. Yet compared to the razzing—and, in the past, roughing up—that Teamster dissidents could expect, the culture of CWA conventions is relatively civil, democratic, and respectful of minority viewpoints.

If you're a local union officer running for national office, you may still get chewed out privately by higher-ups in the union for being such an audacious upstart. And the convention election process will certainly be tilted in favor of better-known incumbents who have CWA headquarters connections and backing. At least that was the experience of Don Trementozzi when he became the first CWA local leader in thirty years to run for a top headquarters position. In this rare contested race, delegates cast ballots for secretary-treasurer based on the membership strength of their locals. The winner was Annie Hill, the far better-known executive vice president of CWA since 2008. She received 276,769 votes, while Trementozzi, coming out of nowhere, got 94,733, or 25 percent of the total.

A fifty-two-year-old native of Rhode Island, Trementozzi is a former activist in AFSCME, who worked for years in a state mental hospital. As a machinist before that, he spent several years on strike against Brown & Sharpe, in one of the biggest anti-concession battles of the early 1980s in New England. After he became a Verizon customer service rep in Worcester, Massachusetts, Trementozzi and his coworkers organized a reform campaign in 2002 to oust the president of CWA Local 1400. More than twenty years in office, this founding member of the local had become distant from the rank and file and too cozy with the company. When Trementozzi challenged her, she first tried to get him fired by Verizon. Then she stole the election, which had to be rerun, under more neutral national union supervision. Three years later, Trementozzi was narrowly defeated when he ran for reelection. He immediately returned to his old job in a call center and became an active Local 1400 steward again. In 2008, he regained the presidency by a large margin.[10]

Trementozzi's four-state local now includes both AT&T and Verizon workers, plus those employed at a Verizon spin-off in northern New England called FairPoint. He currently serves on the CWA committee trying to negotiate a new contract covering 45,000 workers at Verizon from Massachusetts to Virginia. When Trementozzi announced his unexpected race for secretary-treasurer, he declared that CWA "needs more people in the top leadership who can better reflect the perspective of those of us closest to the membership, who must deal with rank-and-file concerns every day." He called his low-budget campaign "Save Our Union 2011." He created a website and enlisted others to help him post a series of detailed position papers on various issues facing the union and its diverse membership. Telephone workers who supported him tended to be still upset about how his opponent handled negotiations with CWA's largest employer, AT&T. In 2009, AT&T won health care concessions that are now being sought, in "me-too" fashion, by its main competitor, Verizon.

The victorious Hill is a former Pacific Northwest Bell technician and two-term local union president in Oregon. Union career-wise, she has spent a much smoother last twenty years, first on CWA's national staff, then as a regional vice president, and most recently in Washington as executive vice president. In her campaign literature, Hill didn't highlight her dealings with AT&T but emphasized instead that she has raised "almost $500,000 in new COPE money" and built a "Legislative Political Action team structure that has done incredible electoral and legislative work." Her CWA executive board supporters, like Association of Flight Attendants president Veda Shook, even credit her with a "critical role in passing health care reform in America" (laurels generally bestowed on higher-profile labor figures in Washington).

The Hill-Trementozzi contest was the first competitive election for a top officer in CWA since 1998, when the union's executive board split over a bid by Larry Cohen, then CWA's organizing director and now its president, to become executive vice president. Cohen defeated his conservative female opponent, with only 52 percent of the vote, after campaigning on a platform of stepped-up membership mobilization and external organizing. These are union priorities he has stressed throughout his thirty-six-year CWA career, which began in the public sector in New Jersey. Cohen remains widely respected, inside and outside the union, for his progressive leadership. He was reelected by acclamation at the 2011 convention and has indicated that this will be his final term as president. Even Trementozzi supported the top of the Cohen-Hill ticket, while arguing that Cohen could use "a stronger partner in Washington than he's going to end up with for the next four years if Annie Hill becomes secretary-treasurer."

Hill became a lightning rod for criticism when CWA unity unraveled at AT&T in 2009–10. As Local 1298 business agent Chuck Borchert recalled that experience in *Labor Notes*: "Bargaining took place simultaneously at five locations around the country, as each region has a separate contract. The plan was to bargain locally and then, if problems came about, we could all stand together at the national level and be 120,000 strong. Before long, other CWA districts started to fold, one after another, and accept subpar contracts. The smallest bargaining unit, ours—with only 4,000 members—was left standing alone in Connecticut."[11]

In a flyer distributed to convention delegates, Local 1298 president Bill Henderson and two other telecom local leaders also faulted Hill for letting "AT&T finalize a contract deal covering 40,000 wireless workers when linking their struggle to CWA's overlapping landline contract mobilization would have given us all much more leverage. . . . New and old members could have struggled together, built a stronger union, and even closed the contract gap between landline and wireless conditions." When he nominated Trementozzi for secretary-treasurer, Henderson lamented this "breakdown of union solidarity" and received much delegate applause. "The impact of our separate AT&T contract settlements is now being felt at Verizon-East," he told the convention. "If we don't draw a line in the sand here in Las Vegas, I fear we are doomed in CWA's flagship industry."

Anetra Session, president of CWA Local 6327 in Ohio, seconded Trementozzi's nomination. She expressed concern that contract concessions by AT&T or Verizon landline employees, combined with lax enforcement of the union's AT&T Mobility contract, will just make it harder for the union to organize the unorganized. "We need the right hand of the president to be the voice of the people we already represent. If we don't protect our base then anything we grow will collapse upon itself," Session predicted. Unfortunately, CWA convention rules limited Henderson and Session to speaking a grand total of four minutes on Trementozzi's behalf. There was no time allotted for either secretary-treasurer candidate to address the delegates after being nominated and before the convention recessed so secret balloting could begin.

Before the vote and during his six-month campaign, Trementozzi emphasized his own track record as a CWA progressive. In 2004, he was among those delegates who worked with U.S. Labor Against the War to pass a CWA convention resolution calling for an immediate troop withdrawal from Iraq. Local 1400 strongly supports Massachusetts Jobs with Justice, and its members in Vermont have helped campaign for single-payer health care there. Along with others in his local, Trementozzi has participated in past national conferences sponsored by *Labor Notes*.

Unfortunately, his appeal for Cohen-Hill "ticket-splitting" as "the way forward in CWA" failed to sway delegates from the union's flight attendant division, Newspaper Guild, or manufacturing sector locals. Public employee bargaining units in New Jersey that Cohen helped organize three decades ago also stuck with Hill. In these and other parts of CWA, Hill benefited from the long coattails of her running mate and the understandable desire to have women equally represented in the top ranks of the union. At the convention, delegates voted to eliminate Hill's old EVP position, a previously proposed cost-saving move that made finding her a new position, as secretary-treasurer, necessary in the first place; her predecessor in that post announced his retirement in 2010, clearing the way for her job switch.

Save Our Union primarily drew support from telecom locals and IUE-CWA dissenters in upstate New York and New England. They were joined by disgruntled AT&T local officers in other parts of the country, including leaders of the largest telecom local in Texas. In his bid for Canadian delegate support, Trementozzi praised the direct election method that gives CWA dues-payers in Canada the right to vote on their national director. A similar one-member, one-vote system is still used to elect the Newspaper Guild leader who serves on the CWA executive board. Trementozzi called for a study of substituting direct elections for convention voting on other national union positions.

In Las Vegas, Hill showed her distaste for contested elections of any sort when she boycotted a candidates' forum, set up so she and Trementozzi could finally have a face-to-face exchange of views and take questions from delegates before they voted. Prior to the convention, she consistently refused to appear with her opponent before any group of delegates still pondering whom to endorse. She also ducked any joint conference calls set up for the same purpose. At the convention, Hill handed out a long list of "Cohen-Hill supporters" that paraded her insider ties; among them were more than seventy union staffers, lawyers, and executive board members who were not even delegates or eligible to vote.

In CWA, it's less difficult for someone like Trementozzi, who has never served on the national union staff, to run just for a seat on the executive board. The union's fourteen geographical districts or occupational groupings are all headed by national vice presidents elected from these separate constituencies. The odds of a local union candidate winning get better when there's a vice-presidential vacancy, like the spot filled in 2011 by Claude Cummings, the African American president of a large telephone local in Texas. He defeated a top assistant to the previous executive board member from CWA District 6, which covers a five-state area in the Southwest. Two other incumbent CWA board members survived election challenges in their respective districts. Carl Kennebrew, an independent candidate for one of four diversity seats on CWA's recently expanded board, attracted 133,000 votes, but lost to a candidate aligned with Cohen-Hill who received 234,856.

Some critics of new secretary-treasurer Hill fear that she may have her eye on the CWA presidency in 2015 when Cohen plans to retire. Trementozzi backers hope to keep their Save Our Union website up and running as a source of information about CWA struggles and a vehicle for building a wider network of like-minded activists. In Hill's acceptance speech, she never mentioned her opponent but did admit that "mistakes" had been made in the union's last round of bargaining with AT&T. She informed delegates that a "Committee of Eight," composed of four CWA executive board members and four local presidents, including Save Our Union supporter Bill Henderson, would meet soon to plan better coordination of AT&T negotiations in 2012.[12]

Postscript

AT&T is now the biggest firm in telecom, with 2011 operating revenue of $127 billion and profits that same year of $7.2 billion. The coordination of CWA's 2012–13 negotiations with that company started off better but, in the end, "the 4,000 AT&T inside and outside technicians, service reps, and operators in Connecticut were again left holding the short end of the stick," according to Local 1298 business agent Chuck Borchert.

Between April of 2012 and February 2013, nearly 65,000 AT&T landline workers in other parts of the country settled separately with the company, as did CWA's wireless bargaining units. AT&T locals in California and Nevada continued to hold out until their members finally accepted a new contract in April 2013 after an earlier tentative agreement was voted down and then renegotiated. In May 2013 the Connecticut AT&T workers finally settled too. In August 2012 the 20,000 AT&T workers in the West and New England managed to coordinate a two-day strike.

Critics of this balkanized bargaining process believe that CWA lost another critical opportunity to resist concessions from a position of greater union strength. According to Borchert, AT&T was able to achieve more of its objectives, such as health care cost shifting, further implementation of two-tier wages and work rules, and restricting sick time, and weakening protections against movement of work.[13] Local 1298 and others want to see a return to the kind of national union unity demonstrated in June 2004, when 100,000 CWA-represented employees of the same company, then known as SBC Communications, staged a four-day, thirteen-state walkout that successfully resisted concessions.

The 2013 CWA Convention voted to create new telecom bargaining councils for better coordination of future negotiations. These bodies will be empowered "to designate national issues that cross bargaining unit lines at the same company" and encourage a more united stand by the various CWA board members and elected regional bargaining committees that deal with common employers like AT&T. According to an official post-convention report, "This change recognizes the frustration that members, locals, and bargaining committees experience when employers refuse to bargain at a national table," a characterization that shifts the onus of responsibility from the union's own organizational functioning to management's predictable stance on the matter.[14] One convention delegate summed up the situation differently: "Companies are united in how they bargain but we are divided. We need to bargain with one voice."

21—TIME FOR NEW STRIKE TACTICS?

The culture of "no contract, no work" is almost extinct in the United States, where strike activity has reached an all-time low. Among telephone workers in the Northeast, at Verizon (VZ) and AT&T, this union tradition remains strong, based on successful walkouts by the Communications Workers of America (CWA) and the International Brotherhood of Electrical Workers (IBEW) in 1983, 1986, 1989, 1998, 2000, and 2004. In the longest of their joint struggles, 60,000 CWA and IBEW members struck for four months against health care cost shifting at NYNEX, the New York and New England company that later became Verizon.[15] Only in 2003 did VZ workers, then still 75,000 strong from Maine to Virginia, stay on the job after contract expiration to avoid being ensnared in a carefully prepared management plan to replace thousands of strikers with contractors.

On August 6, 2011, CWA and IBEW agreements expire in the same regional bargaining unit, now shrunk to 45,000 by buyouts, attrition, contracting out, technological change, and the contested sale of Verizon landline operations in four states. In negotiations this year, workers face unreasonable concession demands and a tough decision about how to resist them most effectively. As CWA District 1 official Bob Master explains, "Verizon has put on the table the most aggressive set of contract demands we've ever seen," with the goal of turning tens of thousands of secure jobs with good benefits "into lower-wage, much less secure jobs."

Like General Electric, which just wrested more givebacks from manufacturing workers represented by CWA and other unions, Verizon "isn't under any financial stress," according to the *Wall Street Journal*. The company reported $10.2 billion in profits in 2010, and its net income for the first half of this year was $6.9 billion. Over the past four years, Verizon earned nearly $20 billion for its shareholders. This record of profitability has enabled five of its top executives, including new CEO Lowell McAdam, to collect $258 million in salaries, bonuses, and stock options during the same period.

Like GE, but not quite as successfully yet, Verizon has pursued a systematic and long-term strategy of de-unionization. It has thwarted organizing at its fast-growing and hugely profitable cellular subsidiary, Verizon Wireless (VZW), while steadily eliminating unionized jobs on the traditional landline side of its business. The company now has reduced its union-represented workers to about 30 percent of the total Verizon workforce. In 2011 bargaining, management seems determined to close the gap between the wage and benefit standards created through seventy years of collective bargaining and those implemented unilaterally at VZW and other non-union divisions since the mid-1990s.

Verizon's proposed takeaways target what it calls "legacy" benefits. As a result of winning the NYNEX strike in 1989 and continuing to fight ever since, CWA and IBEW members make no premium payments for individual or family coverage. According to VZ, "current average annual medical coverage" costs the firm nearly $14,000 per year, "twice the average for comparable companies in the eastern U.S. whose employees make contributions toward their health care." As management pointed out in a recent message to its "associates," even "the CWA recently confirmed that 99 percent of companies now charge for family health care coverage." Under Verizon's proposal, this disparity would be corrected by forcing workers with dependents to pay $1,300 to $3,000 a year for family coverage.

In addition, and no less alarming, existing group pension coverage would be frozen and eliminated entirely for new hires, who would be covered by 401(k) plans instead. Sick days would be limited to five per year, job security language gutted, raises tied to performance reviews, and more customer service reps put on commission pay. To add insult to injury, Verizon even wants to take away Veterans Day and Martin Luther King Day as paid holidays. Not surprisingly, when supplied with this list of takeaways, estimated to cost Verizon workers $20,000 apiece, more than 90 percent of the workers polled by CWA and IBEW voted to authorize a strike.

Workplace mobilization activity, a long tradition among CWA and IBEW members in the region, has accelerated in recent weeks, after a later than usual official start. Ten thousand workers rallied at Verizon headquarters in New York City and big crowds are expected in Philadelphia and Boston two days before contract expiration. Thousands of rank-and-filers have signed up to become part of national union or locally initiated e-networks to share information about smaller-scale protests and expressions of workplace solidarity throughout the region. On their own initiative, union activists in New England created a very interactive Facebook group that neither IBEW nor CWA controlled. It's called "We

Are One! Ready to Strike at Verizon 2011 (IBEW-CWA)" and has more than 5,000 participants.[16]

Many of the IBEW and CWA stewards most "ready to strike," and with the most strike experience, are wary of any union response that falls short of an all-out work stoppage. Yet a traditional, open-ended strike could be a perilous exercise at Verizon, if it doesn't have sufficient disruptive impact on the company's operations. In 1989, it took more than two months of mass picketing and other forms of pressure before NYNEX began feeling any noticeable pain, at a time when union members still represented a majority of the overall workforce. Two union members died directly or indirectly as a result of that struggle. Scores were arrested; more than 250 were fired or suspended; and all employer-paid health insurance was cut off by NYNEX, to pressure workers and their families into a concessionary settlement. Over the past two decades, due to automation, de-unionization, and its nationwide growth, VZ has developed far greater capacity to weather a lengthy conventional walkout.

To do struck work, Verizon can draw on a much larger, non-union workforce today. It has more managers who can be transferred from states where IBEW or CWA have contracts (covering another 10,000 workers) that don't expire at the same time. Verizon is now better prepared to use its wireless call centers for landline customers or outsource customer service work entirely, to an extensive network of contract call centers. Located both in the United States and abroad, these centers are already diverting large amounts of bargaining unit work under "shared call" arrangements that the Verizon unions want to curb.[17] Verizon also retains the ability to hire scab contractors, with their own trucks, to perform the outside plant maintenance and repair work that NYNEX, its predecessor, deployed them to do in 1989 in New York and New England.

Only one of the Verizon unions, CWA, has a national strike fund able to provide fixed weekly benefits for thousands of strikers. CWA's $400 million war chest was created after the NYNEX strike bankrupted its old $30 million defense fund. The union's newer Member Relief Fund now pays $200 a week initially, and then $300, if a walkout continues beyond several weeks.[18] The IBEW has no automatic, well-funded mechanism for providing similar financial assistance to all strikers. Unlike CWA, it makes no provision for subsidizing COBRA coverage for strikers and their families in the event of a medical benefit cutoff, which is likely to occur much sooner than in 1989. Ad hoc fund-raising, assisted by CWA, helped IBEW members survive the NYNEX strike. And it should be noted that in the course of that ordeal twenty-two years ago, even the better-prepared national union ended up borrowing $15 million from the Japanese telephone workers' federation when its own strike funds were exhausted.

In 2011, there may be a lower-risk, higher-impact strategy for Verizon activists to consider. That is the alternative approach of working without a contract while using accompanying opportunities for direct action that would be both legally protected and potentially disruptive. In a letter to both unions from its top negotiator, Verizon has declared its opposition to any 2011 contract extension. The company warned that "if we don't reach agreement by August 6th, the arbitration provisions of the various labor contracts would not be in effect for grievances that arise after the collective bargaining agreements expire." Thereafter, CWA and IBEW "will not be able to grieve and/or arbitrate any discipline, terminations, or contract violations."

Laying out this post-expiration scenario was supposed to be a threat. It was a misleading one at that, since it's not the unions' ability to present grievances at the earlier steps in the procedure that would be curtailed, just arbitration as the last step. Legally, management could also suspend automatic dues deduction when the contract expires, a financial blow to both unions, although less so than 45,000 workers being on strike and none of them paying dues. All other terms and conditions of the old contract would remain in place while the parties continued to negotiate. One major, if largely untested, advantage for CWA and IBEW is that neither union would be bound by their "no strike" pledge, that is, their promise not to organize work stoppages over contract violations during the life of the agreement. Only unions with a rare open-ended grievance procedure, one with no binding arbitration clause, are able to retain the right to strike over unresolved grievances under normal circumstances.

When CWA Local 1298 in Connecticut was faced with Verizon-style concession demands by AT&T in 2009, its 5,000 members worked without a new contract or a formal extension of the old one for eighteen months. Techs and service reps continued to mobilize on the job and in the community; union negotiators skillfully avoided bargaining to

impasse; and Local 1298 won a series of NLRB cases challenging unilateral changes and disciplinary action that management tried to take against
union activists. Local negotiators were finally forced to accept some premium sharing, based on the contract pattern already established elsewhere
at AT&T in 2009. Meanwhile, Local 1298 members and their families
avoided paying several thousand dollars for their benefits during the long
period when the old medical plan provisions remained in effect, while
negotiations continued.[19]

If Verizon continues to insist on health care cost shifting and other
givebacks, a CWA-IBEW decision to continue working would enable
members to pursue the higher impact strategy of striking selectively over
unresolved grievances. Any group of workers—in a single garage, call
center, department or larger part of the bargaining unit—would be free to
engage in carefully planned grievance strikes of varying duration after the
third and final step of the contract grievance procedure, which remains in
effect, has been exhausted. These job actions would have to be unrelated
to issues unresolved at the bargaining table.

Fighting back in this fashion requires discipline, flexibility, creativity,
and a widely shared rank-and-file understanding of why it's necessary.
Staying on the job and using the right to strike over grievances throws the
company a curve ball that management hasn't seen before. The unions
would be free to escalate their anti-concession contract campaign in
public, building additional support from labor, consumer, and political
allies around the country. Most members could continue to work in the
meantime, but would have to be encouraged to pay dues directly, by credit
card or bank draft, if payroll deduction was suspended.

Working without a contract in this fashion minimizes the cost and risk of
striking, while keeping the company guessing about what part of its operation might be affected next. It might even give Verizon greater incentive
to settle than if everyone walks out together and an army of replacement
workers, already in place, is able to maintain customer service with little
or no interruption.[20]

22—THE ACHILLES' HEEL OF TELECOM UNIONISM

The two unions on strike at Verizon in August 2011 made it clear, from the outset, that their members might return to work without a final contract settlement if management was willing to "get serious" in bargaining. Back to work on this unusual basis after a two-week walkout, the 45,000 former strikers would do well to remember the words of Verizon's Marc Reed when picket lines were withdrawn. Said Reed: "We remain committed to our objectives."

The company's vice president for human resources wasn't just referring to Verizon's current giveback demands. They'll still be on the table, even if winnowed down, when bargaining with the Communications Workers (CWA) and Electrical Workers (IBEW) starts again. Reed's remarks have a deeper meaning because he is a major architect of Verizon's long-term de-unionization strategy. Under his guidance, Verizon has already achieved the "objective" of cutting union density in half since the 1990s. And that's not as low as the company would still like to go.

The continuing failure to unionize more than 50,000 workers at VZW and other new subsidiaries is the Achilles' heel of organized labor at Verizon. The givebacks management still wants to extract from IBEW-CWA, when negotiations resume, mirror the conditions unilaterally imposed on the non-union majority of Verizon employees. These "associates" have "merit" pay, costly medical benefits, and no pensions, job rights, or grievance procedure. For Reed and new CEO Lowell McAdam, these are the employment conditions that union-represented employees, retirees, and new hires should have in some form as well on Verizon's declining landline side, along with greatly weakened unions.

During this work stoppage, just as in past contract fights at Verizon and its predecessors like NYNEX, telephone strikers were unfairly stigmatized as greedy and unreasonable. Why? Because, for one thing, they don't want to make costly payroll deductions for their health care like non-union employees and managers do at Verizon, along with almost everyone else in the country. Unlike in 1989, the unions made no attempt to link the Verizon dispute to the continuing need for universal health care that would benefit all workers and remove this issue from the bargaining table. Instead, in a fashion common within labor these days, union PR people told the press that the strike was a "fight to defend middle-class jobs." This framing of their union goal prompted Verizon to respond that the $75,000 a year or more earned by telephone technicians made them part of the "upper middle class," and thus presumably unworthy of sympathy from other working- class people whose jobs produce family incomes much lower.

In a post-strike phone briefing by CWA, strikers were informed that their picketing at Verizon Wireless stores had been effective. According to documents filed by the company, to support its requests for anti-picketing injunctions, sidewalk protests by the strikers did curtail customer traffic at a number of VZW retail stores. The strike also generated a flurry of calls to CWA from non-union employees in those stores. This wireless worker response was an encouraging sign, if true. In past strikes, like the four-month walkout at Verizon's predecessor NYNEX in 1989, the picket-line hassles endured by 2,500 non-union customer service reps in New England made subsequent recruitment overtures to them more difficult. In fact, it took another five to ten years for these call center workers, serving landline customers, to be recruited by CWA and IBEW, even with the help of negotiated neutrality, an uncontested National Labor Relations Board (NLRB) election, or a "card check" process, all favorable conditions very much missing at Verizon Wireless today.

VZW History

CWA and IBEW made "organizing rights" a big part of the two-week work stoppage by 75,000 Verizon workers in 2000. Their joint contract campaign that year effectively highlighted management's record of union-busting in wireless call centers and retail stores like the ones picketed during the latest strike. By the mid-1990s, top Verizon officials began to make it clear that collective bargaining had no place in their share of America's fast-growing and hugely profitable wireless market. Verizon Wireless now has 90 million subscribers.[21] Amid the corporate mergers and restructuring that led to its creation, two IBEW wireless bargaining units in Boston were destroyed. In New York City, a seventy-five-member CWA cell site technician unit, originally organized in 1989, managed to survive this concerted assault, but it remains the only unionized portion of a VZW workforce that now numbers about 85,000 (including managers).

In 2000, after much intensive membership education about the implications of "the wall" Verizon was erecting between its landline and wireless operations, CWA and IBEW struck not just to defend the pensions, health benefits, and job security of existing members. They also tried to win contract language that would restrain Verizon's aggressive and often illegal interference with wireless worker organizing. During preparations for the 2000 strike, I helped a group of VZW workers build a CWA organizing committee at a 400-worker customer service center in Woburn, Massachusetts. Workers there faced illegal threats, harassment, and surveillance of their activities, as later confirmed by the NLRB, which issued an unfair labor practice complaint against the company, one of many over the years.

The Verizon strike eleven years ago was settled with what we thought, at the time, was a major breakthrough: card-check recognition and management neutrality for any future organizing at VZW locations from Maine to Virginia. As Marc Reed explained the four-year deal: "Our agreement simply provides an expedited procedure for employers to make an informed choice"—between unionizing and staying non-union.[22] Verizon quickly reneged on its written commitment, in ways that "expedited" nothing and thwarted employee free choice at every turn. Follow-up negotiations on appropriate bargaining units for VZW retail store employees in a twelve-state region quickly bogged down in a morass of arbitration proceedings that made NLRB elections almost look better than "card check."

The Verizon Wireless call center in Massachusetts was shut down, along with two others in New York and New Jersey where CWA also had active committees. The work handled by these 1,500 workers was shifted to North and South Carolina, both right-to-work states and safely outside the geographical scope of the organizing rights agreement negotiated by the union. Verizon's runaway call centers also sent a powerful message to other VZW workers around the country: union activity leads to lost jobs. Not a single VZW worker ever won union representation using the recognition procedure negotiated in 2000.

Verizon's bad-faith bargaining about card check and neutrality was followed by fitful CWA attempts over the next few years to punish the company for its misbehavior. This "leverage campaign" tried to brand VZW as an industry rogue and get labor-friendly customers to switch to more union-friendly Cingular, now known as AT&T Mobility. In the rest of wireless, VZW is not alone in its anti-unionism, however. Other major players include T-Mobile, which has just a single union contract covering fifteen workers. Another longtime union-buster in the field is Sprint. Sprint uses a media-savvy reseller called Credo to lure progressives into signing up for its cellular service by promising to share a small portion of its profits with good causes. Credo's ads claim that AT&T and Verizon are "socially irresponsible" and Credo is not. Non-union Credo is a great source of ad revenue for left/liberal publications. Its own hypocrisy about worker rights reached new heights during the Verizon strike when it sent out an email blast criticizing such "bad corporate actors" for "squeezing money out of their own employees." With a friend like Credo/Sprint, CWA and IBEW members don't need enemies.

This confusing muddle of consumer choices makes "union label" marketing of AT&T quite a challenge. Individual customers also face penalties for extricating themselves from other plans ahead of expiration. One Bay Area union sympathizer who got a strike-related leaflet with the message "Don't Shop @ Verizon Wireless!" quickly discovered that it would cost her $620 to cancel her account with VZW and immediately take her business to AT&T. In the community-labor outreach to customers at VZW stores, actually switching to AT&T was not even mentioned in the leaflets distributed by strikers and their supporters, despite many years of previous CWA investment in that VZW boycott strategy.

On the East Coast, phone customers who are union members and even unions themselves—the usual target audience for product boycotts—have long associated Verizon with high-profile strikes and bargaining, leading many to assume that VZW is unionized as well. Even when informed of the facts, some labor organizations—like SEIU's huge East Coast affiliate, 1199/United Healthcare Workers East—have failed to switch to AT&T. Others stick with VZW out of similar indifference or just plain ignorance about the existence of similarly priced "union label" alternatives.

Inside Pressure

As CWA and IBEW enter the uncharted waters of what could still be a second strike (that is, going back out if bargaining with Verizon breaks down again), continued mobilization on the job and in the community is essential to keep maximum pressure on the company. The creative, militant, and even Facebook-assisted strike activity of IBEW and CWA members must now be translated into "inside strategies" that make the company pay a continued price for its giveback demands and foot-dragging in negotiations. In YouTube videos, newspaper, radio, and TV interviews, and many of their Facebook postings (at We Are One! Ready to Strike at Verizon, 2011, IBEW-CWA), strikers provided their own eloquent and spirited testimony about what's at stake in this ongoing contract struggle—for themselves, their families, and all American workers.

Telephone union activists will have more success organizing the unorganized within Verizon if they tackle this long-term project together with their strike allies and don't let up this time, until more of the job gets done. Unfortunately, that much-needed post-strike collaboration got off to a stumbling start. CWA and IBEW told their growing network of labor and community supporters to suspend public protests directed at VZW. This created confusion and some consternation among local groups just recently asked to "adopt" a local VZW retail store for their continuing attention.

The back-to-work agreement negotiated with Verizon only suspended *striker* picketing at these locations, but the message conveyed to Jobs with Justice chapters and other union members was that "support activities should now end," as UNITE HERE president John Wilhelm put it in a "stand down" message sent to hundreds of activists in his union. From Washington, JWJ national director Sarita Gupta announced that "all leafleting at stores, work sites, and other events" must "cease," when in fact such activity is not completely barred by the back-to-work agreement.

Based on much past Verizon experience, Boston Jobs with Justice leader Russ Davis warned IBEW and CWA about the danger of losing the support campaign momentum developed during the strike. The unions "have the public's attention," he noted, and should continue with store leafleting and other activities, conducted by allies if necessary. In addition, if each already involved local union, inside or outside of CWA and IBEW, plus Jobs with Justice chapters, proceeded with their "adoption" of VZW retail and call center locations around the country, they might be able to build ongoing relationships of solidarity with the non-union workers inside. Over time, this networking and contact making could lead to new VZW organizing and a revived fight for wireless worker bargaining rights. [23]

Tearing Down the Wall

Although mentioned in the unions' pre-strike mobilization materials, the need to "Tear Down the Wall" between IBEW-CWA members and the company's "Wal-Mart" side was not stressed as a public theme, as it was in the 2007–8 Verizon contract fight. As part of that effort, CWA and IBEW waged a model organizing rights campaign and ended up winning contract coverage for 600 technicians employed by Verizon Business (VZB), which serves corporate and governmental customers. Similarly, VZB groups then gained contract protection in other parts of the country.

IBEW Local 2222 in Boston began this fight by educating its membership about the threat posed by VZB's much larger, and still problematic, parallel workforce, which Verizon acquired by taking over MCI/Worldcom. Unlike earlier IBEW-CWA mobilizations against the threat posed by Verizon Wireless, which proved harder to sustain, union agitation and protests about the diversion of bargaining unit work to VZB resonated with union workers. For their part, VZB techs had already suffered greatly due to the financial collapse of their scandal-ridden previous employer. They saw little initial improvement in wages, benefits, or job security at Verizon, so some responded favorably to overtures from CWA and IBEW.

By mid-2007, 150 techs employed in ten northeastern states had formed a VZB organizing committee, backed by both unions, and added their names to a public "mission statement." Even after a majority of their coworkers signed union authorization cards, Verizon spurned all card check demands. Proclaiming its belief in the sanctity of "secret ballot elections," the company insisted that the representation question could only be decided by utilization of NLRB procedures, which, based on its Verizon Wireless track record, management lawyers would then turn into a morass of litigation and delay, before and/or after any vote is held.

The two unions decided instead to make VZB a major issue among rank-and-file members in the run-up to 2008 contract bargaining. Techs from VZB began meeting with their unionized counterparts, one-on-one and in general membership meetings. With help from Jobs with Justice and the AFL-CIO, CWA and IBEW members began to contact VZB's many public sector customers about its denial of union recognition. On the CWA side, this "strategic campaign" was funded with a $6 million allocation from the union's national strike fund. A big chunk of that money was devoted to internal education, in the form of day-long training sessions to create a "stewards army," with 6,000 members better equipped to help "Tear Down the Wall" between themselves and their not-yet-union brothers and sisters at VZB and VZW.

The unions' first priority now is obviously getting a contract for the 45,000 workers it already represents at Verizon in the Northeast during the truce period following their return to work. These members face the short-term challenge of keeping sufficient pressure on the company to fend off the contract concessions they just struck over. Longer term, regardless of how that struggle ends, Verizon must also start paying a higher price for the continued existence of its "wall." That barrier to union progress, or even survival, won't be breached again until union members link up with non-union workers and the day-to-day workforce cooperation on which management depends becomes a much bigger question mark in the future.[24]

POSTSCRIPT

In August 2011, CWA and IBEW did end up throwing the company a curveball but it wasn't by working without a contract so workers could regain and use the right to strike over grievances. Instead, Verizon workers walked out for two weeks and then returned to work while negotiating under a series of contract extensions, which remained in effect for the next year. The unions' chosen strategy was unprecedented at Verizon and its predecessor firms in the Northeast. Yet it was not much discussed beforehand with local leaders and shop floor activists. So there were plenty of post-strike recriminations about the wisdom of declaring a truce and continuing to negotiate, but without the same degree of pressure on management that a strike ideally generates, if successful in its impact.[25]

During the two-week work stoppage, the high level of mass picketing and other forms of militancy resulted in more than 120 strikers being fired or suspended. As part of the initial back-to-work agreement, there was no promise by the company to arbitrate these strike discipline cases. So the forty IBEW and CWA members who were not allowed to return to work in 2011, after their cases were reviewed, filed NLRB charges instead and remained off the job for the next year. Ironically, one objection to the grievance strike strategy was that if workers got fired they would not have access to arbitration and would have to rely on the NLRB, where past cases involving alleged "strike misconduct" have been decided less favorably than by arbitrators.

The unions avoided the cutoff of medical benefits for the 45,000 strikers and their families that Verizon announced would go into effect September 1. Even without paying for extended medical coverage, CWA spent an estimated $10 million on strike assistance for its 34,000 striking members. (IBEW strikers received no similar benefits but did qualify for unemployment benefits in Massachusetts.) CWA also continued to tap its $400 million Member Relief Fund to provide a weekly income of $300 (plus COBRA coverage) for the fired strikers whose cases were not quickly resolved. Large sums were expended trying to revive and sustain public protests directed at Verizon Wireless and businesses with ties to Verizon board members.

In the wake of the strike and nationwide leafleting of VZW stores, one small group of Verizon Wireless sales employees attempted to unionize at a retail location in Bloomington, Indiana. Management conducted a full-blown anti-union campaign and ended up winning the vote, 7–6. This January 2012 election was delayed for two months; when the workers first petitioned for an election, a large majority had signed union cards. In the weeks before the vote, seven top-level VZW executives visited this single store to campaign against CWA. CWA filed objections to the election, seeking to have it overturned, but the NLRB upheld the results.

22—A STEWARDS' ARMY UPRISING

My first contact with union reformers in New York City was nearly thirty-five years ago. They were critics of internal corruption but, like many rank-and-file dissidents before and since, tended to be prophets without honor in their own local. Teamsters Local 282 was at the time one of the most mobbed-up affiliates of a national union notorious for its organized crime ties. The Gambino family's overseer of the local was Salvatore "Sammy the Bull" Gravano, later credited with assisting nineteen murders. My Teamster friends, who drove trucks full of cement to building sites around the city, displayed enormous, almost reckless, courage. They were, after all, tangling with some of the best friends a "wiseguy" ever had inside a big city construction local—and in real life, not on *The Sopranos.*

Understandably, many "ready mix" drivers were afraid to be seen with the dissidents, much less join their opposition group. Other street-wise Teamsters actually looked down on those who challenged John Cody and Bobby Sasso, leaders of Local 282 who were eventually jailed for labor racketeering. To defenders of Cody and Sasso, the reformers were just a bunch of "Boy Scouts" or "enemies of the union" working for "the Feds," an ironic accusation in light of Sammy the Bull's later star turn as a government witness against John Gotti, his own former boss.

The culture of Big Apple unionism has become slightly more dissident-friendly and less mobbed up since then. But institutional loyalty, where it still exists, tends to run deep. When grifters, gangsters, and autocrats hold union office in the five boroughs, they're usually smart enough to deflect any membership criticism of themselves by recasting it as an attack on the union itself. Plus, there's a deep well of local cynicism for incumbents to tap about the permanence of corruption in politics, business, and labor. After all, this is the city where Brian McLaughlin, a big player at the intersection of all three fields, managed to steal more than $3 million while serving simultaneously as a N.Y. State Assemblyman and leader of the nation's largest Central Labor Council (CLC). The victims of his shakedowns or thievery included the state of New York, the CLC, various IBEW contractors, his own reelection committee and even a union-sponsored Little League team in Queens.

In a revealing display of outer-borough solidarity (of the wrong kind), Bronx-born John Sweeney, then national president of the AFL-CIO, urged the federal judge sentencing McLaughlin to be lenient. He cited his friend Brian's "long record of service to the working men and women of New York City." The judge demurred, sending the defendant away for ten years because his "brazen abuse of trust" lent credence to "the harshest critics of organized labor." On the job in lower Manhattan, Verizon technicians Kevin Condy and Al Russo both read about the McLaughlin case. (It was hard to avoid coverage of it in the New York *Daily News* or *Post.*) They often encountered IBEW Local 3 members, whose Little League team lost $95,000. By the time McLaughlin was awaiting sentencing in

2008, Condy and Russo had become more concerned about official mis-behavior in their own union, the Communications Workers of America.

With 7,000-members in Manhattan and the Bronx, Local 1101 is the largest telecom local in the Northeast. In its youth, as a relatively new CWA affiliate, 1101 exemplified labor insurgency in the 1970s. As Aaron Brenner reports in *Rebel Rank-and-File: Labor Militancy and Revolt from Below*, telephone workers in New York battled management and, at times, their national union during a historic seven-month work stoppage: "The 1971–72 strike experience unified one of the most important CWA locals in the country, making it much more effective in protecting work-ers' rights and improving their wages and benefits. A few rank-and-file activists maintained their organization and continued to push the union toward more militancy."[26]

The Bell Wringer

In 1979, proponents of militancy and internal democracy came together during a long legal fight to defend Dave Newman, who was removed as an elected steward in retaliation for criticizing policies of the local leader-ship. Local 1101 had general membership meetings only twice a year and its official newspaper was not very informative. So the group launched a rank-and-file newsletter called *The Bell Wringer*, advertising it as "An Open Forum for Telephone Workers." As Newman explained later, "We would encourage other members to write about what is happening in their shop or garage or office. Or letters criticizing the company or the union or criticizing us."

During the 1980s, *Bell Wring*er volunteers distributed as many as 4,500 copies of each issue. According to switching technician Ilene Winkler, some coworkers would "take a bundle and leave it around the locker room or pass it one-on-one but didn't want to stand in front of their building and do it, because they're afraid. There's a lot of fear in our local." *The Bell Wringer* caucus supported slates that ran for office three times in 1101, getting disqualified once, and gaining 25 and 37 percent of the vote in the other two elections. "The platform," says Newman, "was mostly centered on union democracy issues: direct election of chief stew-ards, regular membership meetings, open committees that members can participate in. We tried to make it clear that democracy wasn't the be-all and end-all but that it was a prerequisite of having a union that can effectively take on the company."

Even with the prodding of *Bell Wringer* supporters, Local 1101 didn't change its ways during the 1989 strike against NYNEX, the union's biggest confrontation with management since 1971. "The local has an entrenched, very bureaucratic leadership that has not held one membership meeting in four months of being on strike," Winkler reported at the time. "It is very distant from the membership. Virtually all the officers have been full-time officials for over 15 years. They are very conservative politically and socially."[27] Nearly two decades later, the same Local 1101 clique was still in power. Like all the key organizers of *The Bell Wringer,* these longtime leaders were now retired from Verizon.[28] But unlike their onetime foes, eleven out of thirteen executive board members were collecting their pensions from the company *and* six-figure salaries from the union. In some cases, they were also enjoying additional forms of personal enrichment, at company and/or union expense, thanks to other questionable practices.

In 2008, forty-four-year-old Kevin Condy and thirty-four-year-old Al Russo decided to rally their coworkers against further union stagnation under the rule of full-time officials no longer even bargaining unit members. Both were serving as chief stewards. Condy was also a "member organizer" who had assisted CWA organizing activity among non-union workers at Verizon. Based on their union volunteerism alone, both were prototypical members of the CWA "stewards' army" that new national union president Larry Cohen tried to summon into being after finally taking office in 2005.[29] In contrast, most Local 1101 officials only paid lip-service to that concept and the earlier national union program of "membership mobilization" that Cohen first championed as CWA's organizing director and public sector leader in New Jersey.

The Local 1101 incumbents preferred running the local like a regular army, with them giving all the orders and those under them loyally following. When Condy and Russo started to put together an opposition slate in 2008, their initiative was regarded as mutiny within the ranks. Soon all the fellow stewards they had originally recruited to run with them decided not to become candidates. The hints or threats of retaliation, combined with patronage promises, from "the hall" were simply too persuasive. Running just by themselves, Kevin and Al lost by about 400 votes out of 1,800 cast. They were up against a well-financed political machine, which controlled the whole election process, from start to finish.

When Condy and Russo appealed the 2008 election results to CWA District 1, also based in New York City, they felt there was little chance of getting a fair shake there either. Local 1101 now had two of its own alumni serving in the top positions at the union's regional office. These District 1 officials still had friends or relatives in the 1101 hierarchy. Concerned about incurring the political disfavor of their own home local, they could be counted on to do very little when 1101 members complained about unfair election practices, poor representation, particularly at an AT&T call center awarded to the local, or even financial improprieties.

Rebuilding 1101

After their election defeat in 2008, Condy and Russo didn't just lay low and lick their wounds. They left their campaign website up, stayed in touch with outside helpers like *Labor Notes* and the Association for Union Democracy, and steadily expanded their network of rank-and-file contacts. None of this was easy to juggle with a full-time phone company job, family and community responsibilities, labor education classes at night, and a spot high on the "shit list" of Verizon managers and 1101 business agents. (Condy is a graduate of the National Labor College and is working on a labor studies master's degree at City University.) Over time, Condy and Russo were able to involve more stewards and chief stewards in a broader reform grouping called "Rebuild 1101." Its whistle-blowing, information-sharing, know-your-rights website became a kind of online reincarnation of *The Bell Wringer* from the 1980s.

By late 2010, the "Rebuilders" had enough political juice to turn out more than 800 fellow workers, two days before Thanksgiving, to challenge the 1101 leadership over by-laws reform. Three months after that extremely rare membership meeting, some Local 1101 insiders blew the whistle on their sticky-fingered, and now estranged, colleagues. They asked CWA president Cohen to put the local under trusteeship, a request that triggered an investigation, conducted by an upstate New York CWA official and visits by an auditor from CWA headquarters. Their reports disclosed that 1101 leaders had granted themselves unapproved perks like un-receipted weekly expense allowances that were costing the treasury $156,000 a year. A Labor Department investigation already under way gained new credibility and momentum.

These and other Local 1101 financial abuses were the basis for trusteeship demands. But the trusteeship record of CWA District 1 was not confidence inspiring. Just three years ago, District 1 removed the elected leader of a CWA-affiliated newspaper union who embezzled $375,000 in dues money. The international union staffer appointed by District 1 to serve as temporary trustee then stole another $60,000 from that same local. One embarrassing scandal and jail sentence led to another. In addition to distrusting the District, 1101 rebuilders saw any trusteeship as delaying the election for local officers and executive board members that would give rank-and-filers an opportunity to clean up the local themselves. Cohen and the CWA executive board declined to take over the local. Instead, they opted to install Patrick Hunt, a retired national union researcher without any District 1 ties, to serve as a "monitor" over the local. Hunt's mandate included financial oversight but, most important, making arrangements for a free and fair union election in 1101.

The two-week strike at Verizon in August 2011 gave Rebuild 1101 candidates the chance to demonstrate picket-line leadership that incumbent officials failed to provide.[30] Even in the middle of a major bargaining breakdown and work stoppage, 1101 leaders were, for the most part, missing in action. In the monitor-supervised mail ballot vote conducted just two months after the strike, turnout was much higher than previously. More than 3,000 members participated. After an expensive and exhausting campaign, the entire 12-member Rebuild 1101 slate was elected. Most of the successful opposition candidates were chosen by a two-to-one margin. Kevin Condy became the local's new secretary-treasurer and Al Russo was elected to serve as one of its three vice presidents. Chief steward and volunteer organizer Keith Purce was the new president.

Rebuild supporter Pam Galpern, a Verizon technician, told *Labor Notes* that the vote vindicated "the principle that an educated mobilized membership is the backbone of a strong union." Another member of the local, now retired and a veteran of the New York Tel strike in 1971, read the results this way: "If you rob the members and try to stack the leadership with relatives and friends, the members will turn against you." But the electoral success of Rebuild 1101 also reminds us that few rank-and-file challenges to a local labor autocracy arise spontaneously. Restoring union accountability and regaining lost workplace power takes a lot of slow, difficult, one-on-one organizing work. It also helps to have that army of shop stewards, who can be deployed either to keep management at bay or, in this case, replace union leaders who've gone astray.[31]

POSTSCRIPT

When Local 1101 Rebuilders took over in January 2012 they and the 45,000 other Verizon workers who struck in August 2011 were still working without a new contract. Local 1101 tried to help revive what appeared to many members to be a faltering mobilization campaign. As new 1101 vice president Al Russo pointed out in *Labor Notes*, mass picketing at Verizon Wireless stores, plus mobile picketing of supervisors doing bargaining unit work, had been the strikers' most effective tactics. Now the challenge was finding other ways to disrupt VZ's business and bottom line. "That's the only thing that'll affect this company," he said.[32]

While negotiations dragged on, Verizon unveiled a plan to leave its unionized landline workforce further in the lurch.[33] The company sought federal regulatory approval for a cooperative marketing scheme with four leading cable TV companies. Rather than compete with these largely nonunion firms, by further expanding its own high-speed fiber optic cable network (called FiOS), Verizon Wireless wants to share revenue with them derived from joint "bundling" of wireless, high-speed Internet, and cable TV services. CWA and IBEW employment in the company's still unfinished FIOS build-out would suffer greatly as a result.

In mid-September 2012 a tentative agreement was finally reached. It called for an $800 ratification bonus and an 8.2 percent pay raise over four years. Health care costs were increased for both retirees and active employees, with the latter required for the first time to make premium contributions for individual or family coverage. Over three years, the worker's share will rise to $110 monthly for family coverage and $55 per month for individual coverage, depending on choice of plan. Employees hired in the future would no longer be eligible for defined-benefit pensions and would instead have 401(k) accounts, with an improved Verizon match. As part of the settlement, nearly all the fired strikers in both unions won their jobs back, but without back pay. Those still seeking NLRB determinations in their favor, which might have led to both reinstatement and back pay, dropped those cases as part of the deal.

CWA president Cohen told the *New* York *Times* that "we've maintained our living standards in this contract" and "the reality of today in America is if you hold your own that's a victory." IBEW leaders in New England, Local 1400 president Don Trementozzi, and all other Verizon bargaining committee members except one, urged acceptance of the agreement. "I think we got scratched up," Trementozzi told a reporter, "but we battled back against huge concessions and it's still one of the best contracts in the business."[34]

In a widely distributed letter, CWA District 1 vice president Chris Shelton warned that rejecting the contract could lead to a strike lasting "longer than our 17-week strike in 1989, maybe six months or more." Shelton also criticized "some members and a handful of local leaders [who] are calling this contract a 'sell-out' and urging we go on strike." Going out again, he suggested, might mean "walking into a trap the company set for us—giving them an opportunity to replace thousands of us and break our union."

The 1101 Rebuilders were not convinced. New Local 1101 president Keith Purce joined CWA's regional bargaining team in January 2012 after his election, and became the sole dissenting vote against the tentative agreement. In a press interview, Kevin Condy angrily ticked off his objections: "It seems that there's nothing that wasn't touched. We gave up the sick time. We've got the two-tier system. Gave up job security language. For medical, they penalize you for using the plan. There's a lot of changes in the contract on a day-to-day basis. [Verizon is] looking to reclaim a lot of things that were won over 50 years."[35]

The local's new mobilization coordinator Pam Galpern expressed similar concern: "This is how contracts are dismantled over time and unions are weakened. It's an incremental process, with the company counting on the fact that members won't fight for the future generation, as long as we can protect what we have. Verizon has a long-term plan to weaken our unions, and they are moving progressively forward on that plan."[36]

Following the lead of their new executive board, Local 1101 members voted 1,382 to 1,105 against acceptance of the new Verizon contract. It was ratified in the eight IBEW locals affected and fifty-five other CWA locals, including Trementozzi's. Just a few months later, Verizon announced that it was relocating the work done at 140 West Street, Condy and Russo's old Lower Manhattan work location, to Brooklyn. This would make the nearly 500 technicians from 1101 now reporting to West Street members of another CWA local. In the spring of 2013, Local 1101's new leaders were thus plunged into yet another Verizon-related fight, defending a key base of support for Rebuild 1101.[37]

PART VI

IS THERE A LEADER IN THE HOUSE?

C. Wright Mills's *The New Men of Pow*er may have been the last hurrah of left scholarship, or of any kind, for that matter, on the subject of U.S. union leadership as "a social and political type." In his classic study of what was then still a predominantly male occupation, Mills saw trade unions, with all their flaws, as key progressive organizations and the only ones capable "of stopping the main drift toward war and [economic] slump."[1] He was critical of the union bureaucratization he saw already developing within the Congress of Industrial Organizations (CIO). Yet his 1948 book reflects considerable optimism about organized labor's role in the postwar era, due to its politicization and infusion of rank-and-file militancy during the Great Depression. Unfortunately, just as *New Men of Power* was published, the CIO began its self-destructive purge of the labor left, which helped propel industrial unionism back into coalition with the conservative American Federation of Labor by 1955. As historian Nelson Lichtenstein notes:

"Mills himself soon abandoned any interest or hope in the radical potential of the labor movement, especially after American trade union leaders seemed to make their postwar peace with corporate America. . . . As the generation of labor leaders who built the new unions in the 1930s retired, labor seemed a stagnant force, largely defenseless against the political and economic hammer blows that befell the rank and file during the 1970s and 1980s."[2]

In more recent decades, these hammer blows have continued, leaving most unions in their own prolonged slump.   As we see in this section, few prominent labor leaders have opposed "the main drift toward war," which now takes the form of an open-ended global "war on terror," waged variously by Presidents Reagan, Bush, Clinton, Bush II, and Obama. In 1995, top officials of AFSCME and SEIU argued, successfully, that the AFL-CIO needed "New Voice" leadership, only to resist their own retirement for so long that they began to look and sound like the "old voices" their reform campaign replaced. Ten years later, Change to Win (CTW) was hailed in some quarters as the cure for labor federation stagnation, but it too failed to create a pole of attraction for any large number of unorganized workers. And even with the lure of lower per capita dues, CTW soon lost several of its original AFL-CIO union defectors. Meanwhile, in labor organizations affiliated with both federations, far too much membership dues money is still being diverted, in very last century-fashion, into "excess compensation" for top leaders, both conservative and "progressive."

At the micro, or local union level, greater leadership diversity alone—as important as that is—does not ensure union transformation. If the leadership potential of rank-and-file members in their own organizations is trampled or ignored in favor of hot-shot saviors from the outside, that's a formula for further labor decline, whatever short-term gains may be achieved. If the full-time officialdom, raised up from within, is just a multicultural, more appropriately gendered modern-day version of Mill's "new men of power," we already know where most in that crowd will end up or have already arrived vis-à-vis the workers they represent.

In their heyday, as Lichtenstein observes, "the great CIO industrial unions—in the steel, auto, rubber, and electrical product industries—contained a remarkable layer of alert, politically conscious militants. They were the shop stewards, the committeemen, the local union officers, and the regional directors who gave leadership to an industrial underclass . . . whose voice had long been mute." Modern-day conditions may not always resemble those that spawned the CIO. But the activity of that same layer of union militants, even if smaller and more dispersed today, is still absolutely critical to the working class finding its voice again.

24—DOES LABOR NEED ANOTHER WIMPY?

One of the great mysteries of organized labor four decades ago, for neophytes first encountering its then-dominant culture of blue-collar machismo, was how anyone known as Wimpy (or "Wimp" for short) could become president of an AFL-CIO union. In the militant 1970s, a moniker like that was not helpful in a shop steward election, much less any more ambitious bid for higher union office. Patrick Halley's new authorized biography of William Winpisinger (titled *Wimpy*, of course) shows how this former leader of the International Association of Machinists (IAM) leader transcended his anomalous nickname during a colorful and unusual forty-one-year career. By the time Winpisinger retired as Machinists' president in 1989, many of his AFL-CIO executive council colleagues certainly resembled J. Wellington Wimpy, the cowardly comic strip pal of Popeye, but labor's real-life Wimpy was an action figure far more in the muscle-flexing mold of the "Sailor Man" himself.

In the vexing circumstances of the Obama era, Winpisinger's political example in the late 1970s is well worth recalling. His outspoken criticism of another disappointing Democratic president, Jimmy Carter, stands in sharp contrast to the tabby-cat role that labor leaders tend to play at the White House today. No matter how much workers get kicked in the teeth by the Obama administration with more job-killing free trade deals, labor law reform fiascos, federal employee wage freezes, stalled NLRB appointments, public school teacher bashing, or health care reform schemes that backfire, most top union officials just can't wait for their next social summons to 1600 Pennsylvania Avenue. In the case of AFL-CIO President Richard Trumka, a chance to watch the Super Bowl in presidential company was reportedly one such invite.

When Carter let unions down on labor law reform and other legislative priorities in the late 1970s, Winpisinger didn't mourn the prospect of lost

White House access. He went out and organized, within the Democratic Party, to challenge Obama's neoliberal predecessor from the left. "To me," he told an IAM conference in 1978, "President Carter is through. He's a weak, vacillating, and ineffective president." Winpisinger became a leader of "the dump Jimmy Carter and dump George Meany forces," since he also had no love for Meany, the eighty-four-year-old AFL-CIO leader whose capitulation to Carter's weakness on labor issues just made things worse, in Wimpy's view.

In 1980, the IAM president backed an unsuccessful presidential primary campaign against Carter by Ted Kennedy. The Massachusetts senator was perceived by many at the time as being more liberal and labor-friendly than the president. In reality, he shared much of Carter's unhelpful enthusiasm for causes such as trucking and airline deregulation that left unions weaker in both industries. Like the much smaller minority of trade unionists who later backed Ralph Nader against Al Gore in 2000, Wimpy had to contend with critics who accused him of creating internal strife that just helped the GOP gain control of the White House for the next twelve years.

But very early in Carter's single term, Winpisinger understood that holding Democrats accountable in Washington wasn't just a difficult balancing act during presidential election years. It required allies all the time. So he urged the AFL-CIO to build more effective ongoing relationships with civil rights groups, feminists, religious leaders, environmentalists, and consumers. When Meany spurned this approach in favor of existing letterhead coalitions dominated by the labor movement, the IAM helped launch the Citizens Labor Energy Coalition (CLEC) to fight Carter's energy policies. In 1978, as Halley notes, "Carter's real number-one legislative priority" was an energy bill that deregulated natural gas prices, rather than fighting for private sector labor law reform in the face of Republican filibustering that proved fatal.

By 1979, Dan Rather was introducing Wimpy to *60 Minutes* viewers as "the only card-carrying radical" on the AFL-CIO Executive Council. "Where older colleagues shied away from the media spotlight, Wimpy basked in it," Halley writes. "Where more cautious labor leaders were still cowed by the stigma of being called a 'communist' and went to great lengths to avoid any hint of socialism, Wimpy proudly claimed the socialist label."

More than three decades later, it's hard to imagine any union lefty of similar rank outing him or herself on national TV today. Union leaders with a less conservative membership base than Winpisinger's wouldn't think of using the *S*-word in public now, for fear of arousing Glenn Beck and other right-wingers who are already prone to see reds under the bed in unions where there are hardly any and surely don't occupy the top job. Not only is the socialist label shunned but, late in his presidency at SEIU, Andy Stern wanted labor to become au courant by downplaying its past ties to welfare state liberalism.

In Stern's futurism-inflected book, *A Country that Works*, he dismissed the New Deal, and its accompanying regulatory regime, as historically irrelevant to the challenges facing workers in the twenty-first century.[3] Stern's timing in the marketplace of ideas was not so good. Two years after this volume appeared, the stock market crashed, a development that the author and many other big income earners failed to anticipate. The Wall Street downturn of 2008–9 was so bad for millions of ordinary workers and homeowners that it quickly brought New Deal ideas roaring back to life inside the Beltway, albeit only briefly during Obama's first term and in watered-down form.

The irony of Winpisinger being, in his day, a far bolder champion of business regulation, Pentagon budget cutting, nuclear disarmament, and economic conversion than almost any current labor leader becomes apparent in Halley's book.[4] Winpisinger's career began inauspiciously in Cleveland, where he dropped out of high school. After serving in the Second World War, he became an auto mechanic, then an IAM local officer, and "Grand Lodge" organizer and rep. On his way up, Wimpy was so much a product of the IAM's conservative business union culture that he actually made his bones as an FBI helper during the McCarthy era.

In the early 1950s, he assisted membership raids on the left-led United Electrical Workers (UE) and fingered "Communist infiltrators" in IAM shops. As late as 1976, when he was serving as national vice president of the Machinists and about to take over as president, he warned about the "motley crew of small splinter groups" spawned by the New Left that were still trying to "infiltrate a few union halls" and make a "nuisance of themselves." Just a few years later, however, he was defending one prominent New Left alumna, Heather Booth, against more virulent red-baiting by

Lane Kirkland, the AFL-CIO apparatchik who replaced Meany in 1979. Surrounded by a coterie of right-wing social democrats, Kirkland spent the 1980s cheerleading for the Reagan administration's bloody meddling in Nicaragua and El Salvador.

By attacking Booth and other lefties in Wimpy's circle, Kirkland was trying to discredit the CLEC, the first of many progressive formations funded by the IAM, including Jesse Jackson's Rainbow Coalition. Despite his lack of formal education, Winpisinger had what Halley calls a "restless intellectual talent," uncommon in the U.S. labor movement. It enabled him to embrace new people and ideas, rethink old organizational positions, and take the political risks necessary to push a broader social agenda on behalf of his own members and other workers. His Washington brain trust included not only Booth but Barbara Shailor (who became a top IAM staffer), Dick Greenwood (his longtime speechwriter and political muse), and activists from Michael Harrington's Democratic Socialists of America (DSA) and the Committee for a SANE Nuclear Policy (SANE).

How much of Wimpy's new worldview was embraced by Machinist locals is another question entirely; some remained as hidebound after him as before, and merely paid lip-service to the national union progressivism he embodied, while he wielded the considerable powers of the IAM presidency. Within the AFL-CIO, he definitely was a much-needed thorn in the side of its still regnant cold warriors. He flouted the federation's ban on U.S. union contact with Communist-led countries by traveling to Cuba and the Soviet Union to discuss issues related to trade, labor, and world peace. But unlike some visiting progressives, he wasn't afraid to criticize KGB treatment of Russian dissidents. "There's no reason in the world organized labor has to be the biggest hawk in the country," he told the *Cleveland Plain Dealer*. "Lane Kirkland is worse than George Meany."

As an IAM-hired biographer, Halley veers off into hagiography here and there. His previous book was *On the Road with Hillary*, a Hillary-friendly account of his nine years spent as an advance man for the former presidential spouse, U.S. senator from New York, and secretary of state under Obama. The less valorous episodes in Wimpy's career, like the 1981 PATCO strike, are downplayed. The 12,000 air traffic controllers fired by President Reagan needed some real solidarity and risk-taking by other union members, particularly those in the airline industry. As former head of the IAM's airline

division, this was a constituency that Winpsinger knew well; he had personally negotiated many big airline contracts earlier in his career.

Unlike the annoyed Kirkland, Wimpy made his personal sympathy for
the strikers clear. "I expect our people to act like trade unionists [and] not
cross a picket line if they confront one," he announced. Yet there was little
serious effort to organize a collective stand by "the 40,000 ramp workers,
mechanics, and maintenance people" without whom "there would be no
airline flights," as Halley notes. The IAM joined the pilots and flight attendants on the sidelines, shifting the blame for everyone's impending defeat
onto PATCO members who "failed to build public support for their
action" or "do the spade work necessary with their fellow trade unionists."
It was a cop-out with lasting consequences that can't just be blamed on the
sclerotic Kirkland administration.

One doesn't have to be a Wimpy-worshiper, and many are quoted in the
book, to appreciate that his union presidency was still better than anyone
else's in the IAM before or since. *Wimpy* is well worth reading at a time
when his brand of progressive, blue-collar iconoclasm is pretty rare, in
his own and other unions. Today's AFL-CIO president, Rich Trumka,
a former coal miner and lawyer for the United Mine Workers, is liberal,
articulate, and tough-talking about the abuses of corporate power. But
you won't hear him inveighing against wasteful military spending, nuclear
weapons, or U.S. intervention abroad, the way Wimpy did in his heyday,
when the federal tax money squandered in Central America amounted to
a tiny fraction of the one-trillion-dollar direct cost of occupying Iraq and
Afghanistan under Bush and Obama.[5]

During Obama's first term, Trumka was touting his new partnership
with the Chamber of Commerce on "job creation," an approach quite
different from Winpisinger's calls for public investment in manufacturing "infrastructure" three decades ago. The idea that factories should be
converted to socially useful and less environmentally destructive forms of
production has finally caught on, differently, as part of labor's embrace of
"Green Jobs."[6] But economic conversion of military to civilian production, as bravely advocated by Wimpy thirty years ago, is rarely on the radar
screen anymore, and not favored by the Chamber, then or now. As a result,
the IAM, UAW, IUE-CWA, and other manufacturing unions are forced to
cling desperately to Pentagon contracts. Some defense projects keep their

members employed making new weapons systems and aircraft that are billions of dollars over budget and clearly redundant.

Like other industrial unions, the IAM's own ranks have been decimated
by automation, free trade, overseas outsourcing, deregulation (in the airline industry), and de-unionization of manufacturing generally. What
Winpisinger called "the delusion that defense spending creates secure
jobs" goes largely unchallenged by any high-ranking AFL-CIO or Change
to Win figure today. The current Machinist president, Tom Buffenbarger,
who comes from a GE plant in Ohio where the UE was ousted, never met
a missile system he didn't like. In 2010, Buffenbarger did incur the disfavor of the Obama White House for his Wimpy-like public criticism of the
Affordable Care Act's future tax on "Cadillac health plans" negotiated by
his and other unions.

Wimpy's own Pentagon budget criticism was sometimes controversial
within the IAM rank and file. In 1983, Halley reports, he got an angry
letter from a machinist at McDonnell Douglas who was critical of his
membership in SANE. In his personal reply, the IAM president politely
rebutted the worker's contention that "without defense work, we would
not have jobs for our families." He supplied the relevant facts and figures
about the relative job-creating impact of different forms of federal spending and argued in his response that a "peacetime economy" was far more
desirable than one organized around endless preparations for war. "The
continuing buildup of more and more and ever more implements of mass
destruction is suicidal, and I intend to go on saying so," he pledged.

Popular or not, that was a promise Wimpy kept until the day he left
office, under his own steam, in 1989. He died eight years later, at age
seventy-three, leaving behind memories that grow fonder the more pres-
ent-day labor leaders fail to speak out on some of his favorite topics.[7]

25—A UNION "HOUSE OF LORDS" WON'T HELP

Every winter, like the southern migration of Canadian geese and others of
their species, members of the AFL-CIO executive council head to Florida.
Their preferred venue these days is Orlando, amid festive theme parks
and lush golf courses. For a long time, Miami and its environs was the

destination of choice. In the era of AFL-CIO president George Meany, that meant hanging out near Miami every February, in full view of the mainstream media. There were so many embarrassing poolside scenes, captured in stories datelined Bal Harbour, that this swank beach-front village became, over time, an indelible symbol of the labor officialdom's lifestyle disconnect from the rank and file.

Under the "new AFL-CIO" of John Sweeney, who took over from Meany's successors in 1995, many things were supposed to change. But some federation habits, like wintertime meetings in Florida, remained the same. Fourteen years after Sweeney became president, and just a few months before of his own retirement, his staff had succeeded in moving the council's deliberations only a few miles away from Bal Harbour. Interviewed by the *New York Times* in the lobby of the Fontainebleau Hotel and Resort, some dissenting members were still expressing "embarrassment" at their latest plush surroundings.

After all, as the *Times* noted, blue-collar unemployment was "soaring and the stock market tanking" in March of 2009. But amid these signs of hard times elsewhere, it was hard not to notice, as Fox News did, that the Fontainebleau has "10 pools and a 40,000-square-foot spa," plus rooms that "often run $400 or more a night." Per usual, Fox was hardly being "fair or balanced" because the AFL-CIO had actually negotiated a much lower group rate, cutting standard room charges to a mere $199 per night. As AFL-CIO communications director Denise Mitchell was quick to point out, this was "less than it would cost for a hotel room in Washington." What Mitchell failed to mention is that if she, Sweeney, and everyone else involved in the council's work had simply stayed home in D.C. and met in the federation's own spacious headquarters on 16th Street, the total savings to our financially troubled U.S. labor movement would have been in the $400,000 range, according to one disgruntled council member.

Wasted dues money aside, an additional problem with this particular AFL-CIO confab became apparent when the *Times* also reported that council members were discussing "whether to create a mechanism to nudge past-their-prime union presidents to retire so unions are not stuck with tired, uninspired leaders." One official involved in this brainstorming "talked of creating an advisory 'Labor House of Lords' to encourage older union presidents to step aside."

Now, I'm all in favor of early, rather than later, retirement by all those who linger long past "their prime" in organized labor. At a much lower pay grade than the AFL executive council, I tried to set a good example myself, by "redeploying" at age fifty-eight, after twenty-seven years of active duty with the Communications Workers of America. One much older candidate for immediate retirement is Brother Sweeney, currently hanging on until the very end of his latest term, which expires in September 2009. Nearing seventy-five, he is already five years beyond the age he once promised to step down as a "New Voice" for labor in Washington. But I don't think a barmy idea like creating a "Labor House of Lords" is going to hasten Brother Sweeney's long overdue departure. Nor does it address the broader labor movement manifestations of the problem he now exemplifies—that is, retiring on, rather than from, the job.

Labor has a larger demographics problem that must also be tackled. Only 4 percent of the workforce under the age of twenty-four belongs to unions. About three-fourths of all U.S. union members are over the age of thirty-five.[8] What passes for "young Turks" or "new blood" among national union leaders today tends to be people, at best, in their late fifties or early sixties, who were, in some cases, originally inspired by the social movements of the 1960s. These include the key organizers and promoters of the Change to Win labor federation, from SEIU and UNITE HERE, who put John Sweeney into office in 1995 and then gave up on him as an agent of change ten years later. Members of their broader generational cohort, including me, went into workplaces or full-time union work very much committed to making union leadership less "pale, male, and stale." While some progress has been made, diversity-wise, on the first two fronts, American labor remains an appallingly geriatric institution. Sixty-five and out—at the top—is not a change we have won in either federation.[9]

Just look at Sweeney's expected successor, Rich Trumka, my onetime colleague at the United Mine Workers back in the 1970s and another guy about to turn sixty. Rich went from being the youngest elected president of the UMW in its history to suffering fourteen years of Prince Charles–like waiting in the wings for Sweeney to retire. Is he likely to support a requirement that AFL-CIO officers or executive council members step down at age sixty-five or even seventy? Don't count on it.[10]

Trumka, I'm sure, feels that he's entitled to a stay in office at least as long as Sweeney's. If his health holds up, expect him to still be president of the AFL-CIO in 2023. If Rich really gets attached to his new job, he might not even step down at seventy-four, since Meany soldiered on until he was eighty-five, serving for twenty-seven years in all. Lane Kirkland, who spent sixteen years as president between the Meany and Sweeney eras, did leave at the ripe young age of seventy-three, but that was under duress. He checked out earlier only because he was facing defeat in the first successfully contested AFL-CIO presidential election in 100 years.

So the already senescent top layer of our U.S. "House of Labor" really doesn't need an additional "House of Lords" wing, where it can put people out to pasture sooner in an "advisory" capacity. Anyone familiar with the composition of the AFL-CIO Executive Council knows that we already have a "Labor House of Lords," which is the council itself. Many of our existing "labor peers" in that body hold cushy high-paid, sometimes chauffeur-driven jobs that they are understandably reluctant to relinquish to their juniors, even when, in the building trades, the "junior" in question might be a blood relative.

Consider, for example, AFSCME's gerontocracy. The American Federation of State, County, and Municipal Employees is often identified as one of labor's more "progressive" unions. AFSCME District Council 37 in New York City is one of its largest and most important municipal worker affiliates, with 125,000 members of all ages. Yet it is headed by a woman who is apparently 83 years old. DC 37 refused to confirm or deny Roberts's exact age, but estimating it, based on old press reports, is not difficult. Executive director Lillian Roberts was in her "prime" back in the 1960s and '70s, when she served as Victor Gotbaum's deputy at DC 37. In 2002, after the council came out of trusteeship for corruption, she returned to DC 37 at the age of seventy-six, after a hiatus of many years, during which she helped administer a Health Maintenance Organization. When disgruntled members of her executive board tried to cut her pay from $250,000 to a mere $175,000 in 2005, she was able to respond with a lawsuit accusing seventeen board members—five of them African American—of race, sex, and age discrimination, a legal trifecta probably only possible in organized labor, since Corporate America rarely employs people in their eighties to direct publicly traded companies.[11]

Roberts has, unfortunately, raised the age bar for AFSCME's two national officers, Jerry McEntee and Bill Lucy, aged seventy-four and seventy-five, respectively. McEntee played an important role in ousting Lane Kirkland from the AFL-CIO presidency at an age when he was slightly younger than McEntee today. In 2008 both Lucy and McEntee decided they were still so invaluable to AFSCME that they should run for another four-year term. When those end in 2012, they'll be almost as old as Roberts is now, but, as noted above, she may still be running DC 37 in New York. In recent years, McEntee has spent a great deal of "work" time in Florida, even when the AFL-CIO executive council was not meeting in the state, since he owns a second home there. Back at the union's Washington headquarters, his top assistant, Paul Booth, has long covered for him. A onetime leader of Students for a Democratic Society, Booth has served the AFSCME president for so long that he's now rumored to be considering retirement himself, except that, at age sixty-six, he's really not old enough to leave yet, at least by DC 37 or AFSCME headquarters' standards.

In my own union, another uncomfortably tethered duo, longtime CWA president Morty Bahr and his secretary-treasurer Barbara Easterling, both remained at their posts until their mid to late seventies. Neither one wanted to leave before the other did. So their retirement standoff delayed the emergence of new national leadership in CWA for a good decade. This tendency to leave successors waiting in the wings is reinforced in the environment of the AFL-CIO executive council. For many of the years that Bahr served on that body, he could come to meetings and see fellow New Yorker Moe Biller, from the American Postal Workers Union. Biller didn't retire until he was eighty-five, in 2001, dying just two years later. But as long as Moe was still around it wasn't hard for other senior citizens in labor, like Morty, to feel they had many "good years" ahead of them too.

Whether such extended job tenure is good for anyone else is another question. One academic expert I consulted on the matter wished to remain anonymous lest labor's septuagenarians take offense over his/her comments. This campus observer believes that the "geriatric culture" of U.S. unions breeds organizational stagnation because longtime officeholders also don't "train successors or build secondary leadership." Instead they adopt a "wait your turn" attitude that keeps younger officials in a frustrated, long-term holding pattern. He/she points out that Canadian,

Australian, and Western European unions generally have mandatory retirement rules that force their sixty-something presidents or general secretaries to move on, allowing younger officials, including women and minorities, to move up sooner than here.

In the United Kingdom, this means that high-ranking retirees do become "labor peers," a form of co-optation that's long been controversial among Labour Party leftists, who favor abolition of the House of Lords. In Canada, where labor also has more social weight and political clout than in the United States, former union leaders have joined international labor organizations, become Canadian ambassadors, academics, or public figures of some other type. They're less likely to lose their prior status and quickly disappear from view just because they're no longer enjoying the perks of high union office. As my subject-matter expert asked: "Where can senior American trade unionists go when they step down? What can they do?"

In the United States, it's also far too lucrative for top officials to remain on the union headquarters payroll, particularly when they control it. Those who cling to their jobs well into their seventies continue to collect hefty six-figure salaries. They're often receiving benefits from one or more generous private pension plans, plus their Social Security check, all of which adds up to a big monthly income that would be substantially reduced if they retired. See, for example, the case of John Sweeney. With total AFL-CIO compensation of nearly $300,000, plus multiple pensions from the federation and SEIU, and his Social Security allotment, Sweeney is one of the most richly rewarded senior citizens in the labor movement.[12]

To create more frequent openings at the top, unions need to embrace mandatory retirement rules and/or the National Education Association solution: term limits.[13] Both are necessary, if not sufficient, reforms; in the UAW, for example, presidential retirements mandated by the ruling "administration caucus" just lead to another, slightly younger member of the same political faction taking over, with little change in union policy or direction. Another priority should be eliminating the myriad financial incentives that keep union oldsters at their posts long past their prime—if they ever had one. One of the first perks to go should be costly winter meetings in balmy climates paid for out of membership dues money. If more Washington-based members of the AFL-CIO executive council

were forced to stay home for its meetings, maybe some would eventually
decide, sooner rather than later, to stay home entirely, taking all future
Florida vacations on their own time and dime.[14]

26—A WISCONSIN WAKE-UP CALL FOR AFSCME?

June 2012 was a bad month for public workers from the West Coast to
the Midwest. Voters in San Diego and San Jose approved retirement benefit cuts for their city employees, which led major newspapers to proclaim
that more "pension reform" of this type is on the way, despite worker and
retiree resistance to it. In Wisconsin, labor and its allies failed to oust
Republican governor Scott Walker who stripped the American Federation
of State, County, and Municipal Employees (AFSCME) and other workers of their ability to negotiate about pensions and other benefits.

Within AFSCME, the rollback of past collective bargaining gains and,
in Wisconsin, the virtual elimination of bargaining itself, has given some
activists a new sense of urgency about shaking up the leadership of their
own 1.4 million–member union. Since the labor-community uprising in
Madison in early 2011, members of Wisconsin Council 40 of AFSCME
have been in the forefront of rank-and-file struggle against public sector
union busting. They circulated petitions to recall Walker and other anti-
union Republicans and went door-to-door again to turn out the labor
vote. Now some of these same activists are headed for an AFSCME convention in Los Angeles, where they hope to do better in a vote on the
union's own leadership.

About 3,500 AFSCME delegates are gathering to decide who takes over
from seventy-seven-year old Jerry McEntee as president of the third-largest U.S. labor organization. McEntee is retiring after more than thirty years
in office. Internal critics of his heir apparent, Lee Saunders, view this hotly
contested election as a rare opportunity to revitalize the union at a time of
great peril for all public workers, including thousands of AFSCME members in California. Sanders has been a national union staffer for more than
three decades. He was narrowly elected secretary-treasurer after his predecessor, Bill Lucy, stepped down two years ago before the end of his term.
McEntee backed Saunders then too, but Lucy, one of the highest-ranking

African Americans in labor and a founder of the Coalition of Black Trade Unionists, favored Danny Donohue. Donohue is president of AFSCME Local 1000, the 200,000-member Civil Service Employees Association (CSEA) in New York State. McEntee became president of AFSCME by defeating Lucy and another candidate in 1981.

In 2010, Donohue ran with the support of AFSCME affiliates upset about McEntee's high-handed decision making and remote control administration of the union from his vacation home in Florida.[15] At a raucous convention in Boston in 2010, which was controversially chaired by McEntee, Saunders received 652,660 votes to Donohue's 649,356. Note that AFSCME delegates cast votes reflecting the relative membership strength of the local unions they represent. The union's district councils are coordinating bodies composed of some or all of the AFSCME locals in a particular city, state, or region.

In this year's rematch for the presidency, both Saunders, a sixty-year-old African American from Ohio, and Donohue, who is white and seven years older, have California allies seeking to become the union's first female secretary-treasurer. On the "Moving Forward Together" ticket, Saunders is running with former home care worker Laura Reyes, who already serves on the AFSCME executive board and as president of Local 3930 in Southern California. Donohue's "One AFSCME" team includes Alice Goff, who is an immigrant from Belize, a former Los Angeles city worker, and five-term president of AFSCME District Council 36.

"We need Danny and Alice to bring back the focus of this international union to the members, to the grassroots," says Anneliese Sheehan, a Wisconsin child care provider who is coming to the convention. At a recent meeting of District Council 40 delegates, Sheehan and other activists in the fight against Walker won a 291-to-7 vote endorsing Donohue and Goff. This action represented a shift in Donohue's favor from two years ago, when the council was evenly split between his and Saunders's supporters.

What made District Council 40 more receptive to Donohue's challenge now? According to Marv Vike, a bearded, burly highway maintenance worker from Rock County, Wisconsin, the intervening political offensive by "right-wing nuts" was a major wake-up call. "We cannot let our guard down, ever again," Vike says. "When members are facing the kinds of attacks we have seen here and around the country, we need rank-and-file leaders, who can help us rebuild this union from the ground up, state by state, city by city, county by county."

Whereas Donohue has stressed his background as a working member of CSEA/AFSCME, before he moved up the ranks into its top elected position in 1994, Saunders has emphasized his role in a series of appointed staff positions, including acting as trustee of AFSCME District Council 37 in New York City after it became mired in corruption in the late 1990s. Saunders pledges to strengthen AFSCME's existing coalitions with non-labor groups "to save pensions, end privatization, and stop budgets cuts around the country." He accuses Donohue of failing to resist CSEA contract concessions sought last year by Governor Andrew Cuomo and not organizing enough new members. Just five years ago, the CSEA teamed up with the American Federation of Teachers to organize 60,000 child-care providers, an expansion of unionized public sector employment in New York that has been thwarted elsewhere by governors like California's Jerry Brown.

Donohue accuses McEntee and Saunders of focusing too much on politics inside the Beltway. As Donohue told *In These Times* reporter Mike Elk, "We haven't done as much as we should have done in developing the capacity of state level affiliates throughout the country. I think some of our political investments at the national level haven't been wise. I don't think we should endorse every Democrat simply because they are Democrat. Sometimes, I think, we should even look at endorsing Republicans on the state and local level when they support us." Since becoming a first-time elected official two years ago, Saunders has tried to raise his own public profile. Like candidates for the U.S. presidency, he has published an election year manifesto, with McEntee as his coauthor, laying out the challenges facing our country and AFSCME. Published by Nation Books, *The Main Street Moment: Fighting Back to Save the American Dream*, describes the proliferating attacks on public workers and seeks "to enlist even more Americans in the struggle to save the soul of our nation and return power once again to the people."

Not everyone in the Donohue and Saunders camps is equally enthusiastic about returning "power to the people" within AFSCME. The competing leadership slates draw their support from the same rival wings of the AFSCME bureaucracy that first squared off against each other in 2010, after many years of mounting top-level disagreement between McEntee and Lucy. As is often the case in union politics, the Donohue-Saunders rematch has led to some unusual alignments at the local level. In Northern California, for example, one frustrated AFSCME reformer, who asked to remain anonymous, contends that he "was attacked by AFSCME international representatives and their small band of entrenched and opportunistic followers" when he and others "tried to bring democracy back" to his 5,000-member state employees' local. Now some of his past union foes are backing Donohue so, in this dissenting member's view, "the more progressive side of this conflict within AFSCME is the Lee Saunders group."

Kathyrn Lybarger, a gardener at the University of California-Berkeley and local labor-left activist, was elected in 2011 as president of 21,000-member Local 3299 on a reform slate called "Members First." As the Detroit-based newsletter *Labor Notes* reported, disgruntled university workers chose her over Lakesha Harrison, a longtime ally of Lee Saunders, because Harrison had negotiated givebacks and lost touch with the rank and file. "With the backing of the AFSCME International, Harrison and her vice president also mounted a campaign to change the local's constitution to concentrate power in their hands," according to *Labor Notes*. After five of six top officers were defeated by a two-to-one margin, Harrison and her allies then tried to lock the winners out of the union office and filed "trumped-up charges aimed at engineering an international trusteeship to restore Harrison."

No trusteeship was imposed; Lybarger was able to take office; and prior to the Los Angeles convention she arranged for Local 3299's new executive board to conduct a 30-minute phone interview with both AFSCME presidential candidates. "Donohue said stuff that I personally thought my board would be responsive to," Lybarger told me. But the decision to endorse Saunders, over his opponent, was unanimous and little debated. "Saunders has actually come through for our local—not just in the last six months but considerably before it," Lybarger said. "There's a lot of rebuilding we need to do. We're also trying to win a huge contract fight with the third-largest employer in the state."[16] When I asked a consultant working for Donohue why newly elected AFSCME reformers, who had ousted a Saunders supporter, were now backing him rather than Danny, this campaign advisor suggested that 3299 just wanted to avoid antagonizing the international union during a contract year.

In Chicago, the president of AFSCME Local 2858 is voting for Donohue, strictly on a "lesser evil" basis, because "Danny is not Gerry McEntee's hand-picked successor." Steve Edwards is a welfare worker, a member of Socialist Alternative, and a longtime dissident within District Council 31, whose top officers, Henry Bayer and Roberta Lynch, are key Donohue backers on the AFSCME executive board and local Democratic Party supporters. At AFSCME's last convention in Boston, Edwards spoke from the floor, criticizing the union's ties to mainstream politicians in Illinois and nationally. He believes that AFSCME's "relationship with the Democrats is so stifling that we are quite unable to debate the most basic questions of importance to the unions—the only range of views that's allowed at our meetings is what's acceptable to one or another wing of the Democratic Party."

Two years later, he finds it encouraging that Donohue "wants to move away from total lockstep with the Democratic National Committee." But Edwards thinks that Donohue's proposal to accept *only* a salary of $295,000 a year if elected president is laughable, because that would still give the CSEA leader a $90,000 a year increase from his current combined pay. Edwards notes that his own salary totaled $62,000 last year, much closer to the average earnings of AFSCME members. In a climate of concession bargaining and public sector austerity, Edwards says he has "no sympathy" for the lavish salaries and perks that his dues money pays for at AFSCME headquarters.

As president, McEntee has long enjoyed the services of a full-time chauffeur for his union car, plus AFSCME has paid for costly charter flights and years of first-class travel back and forth between Washington and his primary residence in Naples, Florida.[17] His total compensation now exceeds $500,000 a year, while Saunders receives $310,000 annually, along with another $123,000 for his expenses and benefits. Even longtime McEntee assistant Paul Booth, a onetime leader of Students for a Democratic Society, makes nearly $240,000 a year, a much larger salary than big industrial unions like the Auto Workers, Steel Workers, and Communications Workers pay their national presidents.

Under Donohue's proposed constitutional change, AFSCME secretary-treasurer pay would drop to a mere quarter of a million dollars each year. When quizzed about this by Council 40 members in April, Saunders refused to say whether he supports convention approval of the top-officer salary reductions, a belt-tightening move that barely qualifies as "equality of sacrifice" when so many AFSCME members are suffering pay cuts or freezes around the country.

As the AFSCME vote nears, both sides in the leadership fight are trading accusations about campaign misconduct, a continuation of the dispute between Saunders and Donohue about convention voting procedures two years ago in Boston. AFSCME national executive board members have spent much time since January personally skirmishing with each other about what the ground rules will be at this gathering. Disagreements have arisen, and some remain unresolved, over election observers, the role of union staffers who serve as delegates, and how individual delegates should be released from "block voting" by their locals if they choose to cast a minority vote for a different candidate. Donohue supporters claim that delegates from some locals, like 3299, will defect to their camp, on an individual basis—if they can—on the convention floor in Los Angeles.

Both contenders for the AFSCME crown have agreed, in principle, to debate each other at the convention, an exercise in democracy that could be a model for other unions to follow, if it does in fact occur. Neither presidential candidate advocates letting the members choose the union's top officers, a form of internal democracy practiced by only a handful of national labor organizations. While a direct mail ballot vote for the leadership presents some problems of its own, this method helped bring about major changes in the United Mine Workers and the Teamsters. It shifts ultimate decision-making power from a few thousand local union delegates at an incumbent-dominated convention and puts it in the hands of the rank and file, or at least those who choose to vote. If the outcome of the Saunders-Donohue bout is the same as two years ago, the losing side may decide it's time to start advocating this election reform.[18]

POSTSCRIPT

At the AFSCME convention shortly thereafter, Lee Saunders defeated Donohue for the presidency by a margin of 54 to 46 percent among the delegates voting. Donohue's running mate, Alice Goff, also lost, though by a narrower margin, to Laura Reyes, who is now the union's secretary-treasurer. Prior to the vote, the candidates for both positions debated the issues in front of the entire convention, a rare occurrence in the U.S. labor movement.

In an election postmortem written for *Portside*, Ray Markey and Greg Heires, both Saunders supporters from District Council 37 in New York, argued that Donohue lost because he failed "to chart an alternative path for the union in the debate" and in his campaign. A longtime AFSCME reformer and retired leader of city library workers, Markey also believes that Donohue "rolled over and played dead to both Governors Patterson and Cuomo" in New York State worker contract negotiations. He objected to the claim by Donohue supporters that their champion was "more progressive simply because he was an opposition candidate." What's so oppositionist, he asked, about "sitting on the AFSCME executive board and voting for 37 straight budgets and probably 99 percent of all resolutions"?

For *Portside*, Donohue delegate Andrea Houtman from AFSCME Local 800 and District Council 36 penned a bloodied but unbowed response to Markey and Heires. She attributed Saunders's victory to his "adopting some Donohue-esque positions" and then "holding sway at the most undemocratic convention to date." She believes Donohue's candidacy forced Saunders to agree "to change our priorities to deal with the severity of the [political] attack" and reduce "the bloated salary for the International President by $90, 000 down to a mere $290,000." Saunders "has been elected, by hook or by crook," Houtman acknowledged. But "the fight for union democracy will continue," she asserted. "That's a promise."

27—WHITHER CHANGE TO WIN?

Most six-year-olds like to have a big birthday bash, with lots of games, presents, balloons, sugary cake, and as much noise as possible. Change to Win, the new kid on labor's block born in 2005, has opted for a quieter approach, much in contrast with the celebratory and self-aggrandizing scene at its festive founding convention in St. Louis six years ago. On that occasion, CTW founders like Tom Woodruff, now its executive director, talked about spending $750 million a year on new organizing drives similar to those launched by the Congress of Industrial Organizations (CIO) in the 1930s. Then UNITE HERE copresident Bruce Raynor, later drummed out of the union office for alleged expense account fiddling, gave a radical-sounding speech calling for the imprisonment of corporate bosses who mishandle workers' pension fund money.

Six years after these rhetorical fireworks, only four of the seven unions that broke away from the AFL-CIO to form CTW remain in the latter camp.[19] The union coalition that sociologist Ruth Milkman and others once touted as "labor's best hope—maybe its only hope—for revitalization" is rarely seen or heard from. At the International Brotherhood of Teamsters (IBT) convention in 2011, leaders of the two largest CTW affiliates—James Hoffa, president of the host union, and Mary Kay Henry, president of the Service Employees International Union (SEIU)—lathered much praise on each other. Yet neither ever mentioned the words "Change to Win," in forty minutes' worth of speechifying about the close working relationship between SEIU and the IBT.

On its own website, CTW recently gave itself a downgrade. It now describes the alliance of SEIU, IBT, United Food and Commercial Workers (UFCW), and the tiny United Farm Workers (UFW) as a "Strategic Organizing Center," not a new labor federation. The participating unions are working on four "innovative organizing campaigns in the private sector economy" involving farm labor, port trucking, warehousing, and Wal-Mart. All four groups of workers were a membership recruitment focus of the UFW, IBT, and/or UFCW respectively long before they left the AFL-CIO and linked up together.[20]

This modest reconception of Change to Win's role is a far cry from earlier claims to be a dynamic, fast-growing alternative to a labor federation forever hobbled by its own dysfunctional bureaucracy and internal protocol. The common denominator of CTW seems to be its affiliates' shared interest in continuing to pay lower per capita dues than the national AFL-CIO requires (now 65 cents per member per month); the four "Strategic Organizing Center" participants pay about half what other cash-strapped unions contribute to the federation now led by Rich Trumka, former president of the United Mine Workers. If the CTW defectors had remained in the main "House of Labor," AFL programs and staff would have received an estimated $150 million more in dues and special assessments since 2005.

At the time of its birth, skeptics argued that CTW was more about the money (as in paying less), than a different kind of labor federation functioning. At most, CTW recalled the Alliance for Labor Action, a short-lived coupling of the Chemical Workers, Teamsters, and Auto Workers in the late 1960s when the UAW and IBT were both on the outs with the AFL-CIO. Critics saw the CTW union defections as a self-serving dues revolt, dressed up as a principled parting of ways between a recalcitrant "old guard," then personified by onetime progressive hero John Sweeney, and Sweeney's frustrated and impatient former backers—Bruce Raynor, John Wilhelm, then co president of UNITE HERE, and Andy Stern, now "president emeritus" of SEIU.

In the parched landscape of American labor, circa 2004–5, CTW shimmered briefly as an oasis in the desert. But its journalistic and campus cheerleaders, like then-UCLA professor Milkman, failed to see that it was a mixed bag at best, more mirage than real, and hardly the second coming of the CIO. Within its ranks were the Carpenters, a union already estranged from the AFL-CIO and detested by other building trades' organizations for poaching on their turf and undermining industry standards. CTW cofounder Douglas McCarron, president of the Carpenters, was George Bush's closest friend in the labor movement and thus not the best advertisement for the new approaches to politics ostensibly favored by CTW. Another unlikely labor movement "reformer" is Teamster president Hoffa, who has professed no interest in realigning union jurisdiction in the ideal fashion favored by Stern, Raynor, and Wilhelm, who were the driving force behind the three-way "New Unity Partnership" (NUP) that preceded the seven-union split from the AFL-CIO. It was an article of faith among them at the time that top-down structuring, assisted by union mergers, was the panacea for labor. Before his departure from the AFL-CIO, Raynor insisted that its fifty-plus affiliates should consolidate into just ten to fifteen mega-unions, with less overlapping jurisdiction and a better focus on "core industries."

To demonstrate how progressive unions could combine quickly and grow faster together, Raynor and Wilhelm formed the 440,000-member UNITE HERE. Within five years, this much applauded "marriage of equals" foundered on the rocks of a messy divorce that proved costly and disruptive for both hotel and garment workers. The meddlesome third party in that troubled relationship was none other than CTW founding father Andy Stern. In early 2009, while simultaneously laying waste to his own membership base in California, Stern wooed a rump group from UNITE HERE, led by Raynor, into SEIU. The resulting conflict between UNITE HERE and the SEIU-affiliated "Workers United" proved to be a carnival of organizational cannibalism. Eighteen months and tens of millions of dollars later, SEIU, by then headed by Mary Kay Henry, sued for peace and not long afterward got rid of new SEIU executive vice president Raynor too.

As *Daily News* columnist Juan Gonzalez explained it all to *Democracy Now!* listeners in July 2009:

> The reformers that were supposed to be the Change to Win unions have become so torn by internal division and attempts by SEIU to dominate the American labor movement that, in essence, the Change to Win federation is—it's not officially dead yet, but some of the existing Change to Win unions will soon be rejoining the AFL-CIO, but probably without SEIU.

As Gonzalez predicted, UNITE HERE and the Laborers soon reaffiliated with the AFL-CIO. The Carpenters also abandoned Change to Win, although its return to unaffiliated status was not acknowledged for more than a year after McCarron stopped paying dues.

In its current downsized condition, CTW is still dominated by SEIU, its largest financial backer. Although UFCW president Joe Hansen has replaced now retired SEIU secretary-treasurer Anna Burger as chair of the group, three of its seven "leadership council" members are SEIU officers or executive board members. One of them, SEIU executive vice president Woodruff, doubles as executive director of CTW. (My information requests for this article were initially fielded by Bob Callahan, a veteran SEIU operative involved in Stern's disastrous 2009–11 trusteeship over United Healthcare Workers-West; he failed to provide any requested data about CTW's current budget, staffing, or dues structure.) When asked to assess the state of Change to Win today, one longtime union staffer likened its current functioning to that of a single AFL-CIO headquarters department, the Food and Allied Services Trades (FAST) group, before the split. Like CTW today, FAST helped coordinate corporate campaigns and organizing by some of the same national unions. After its key affiliates defected to CTW, FAST was disbanded and its talented corporate campaign staff dispersed elsewhere. Younger labor activists who gravitated toward CTW for field staff jobs after the split often ended up disillusioned—and laid off as well.[21]

As one ex-CTW political campaigner told me, "Change to Win was a husk of a federation and always has been. There was not a whole lot there and it was a constant battle to get anyone to work together. It hasn't succeeded by its own measures, or anyone else's." In the early years of CTW, only SEIU displayed much of the promised membership growth CTW was supposed to foster. Between 2006 and 2008, it added 300,000 workers to its ranks. But in 2009 and 2010, thanks largely to the labor civil warfare unleashed by Stern, SEIU's average annual growth slowed to 55,000, even with the addition of disputed members of UNITE HERE. In 2011, SEIU registered a net gain of only 7,000 members and agency fee-payers, probably the lowest growth year in the union's entire history.

Six years after its founding, only a handful of the "5.5 million workers" who, according to the CTW website, "united to create Change to Win" even know what it is or why they are in it. In the 1930s, it was just the opposite. The CIO brand was so strong that even workers unsure about their own union's acronym proudly identified with the broader industrial union movement.

In today's very different environment, similar brand loyalty is not likely to arise from an overblown inside-the-Beltway concoction. As union activists learned from the WTO battle in Seattle in 1999, the mass strike activity over immigrant rights in 2006 and the more recent occupations of the Wisconsin state capitol and Wall Street, putting real movement back in the labor movement requires an upsurge from below, not a reshuffling of deck chairs on a second and even smaller *Titanic*.[22]

POSTSCRIPT

To their credit, Change to Win affiliates did provide support for strikes in 2012 and 2013 by "non-union workers, employed in Walmart stores, in sub-contracted Walmart warehouses, and in fast food restaurants" in a

number of cities.[23] In May 2013, a CTW-backed group called Good Jobs
Nation organized a one-day walkout by hundreds of non-union workers
in government buildings in Washington, D.C., as part of an ongoing campaign to pressure President Obama to improve labor standards for federal
contract employees.[24] Nevertheless, the United Food and Commercial
Workers returned to the AFL-CIO just a few months later, leaving CTW
with only three remaining affiliates.

28—BIDDING ADIEU TO SEIU

Few modern unions have done more outside hiring than the Service
Employees International Union (SEIU), America's second-largest labor
organization. Beginning in the mid-1970s and continuing unabated today,
SEIU and its local affiliates have employed thousands of non-members as
organizers, servicing reps, researchers, education specialists, PR people,
and staffers of other kinds. Though most unions hire and promote largely
from within the ranks of their working members, SEIU has always cast its
net wider.

The union has welcomed energetic refugees from other unions,
promising young student activists, former community organizers, ex-envi-
ronmentalists, Democratic Party campaign operatives, and political exiles
from abroad. One prototypical campus recruit was my older daughter,
Alex, a Latin American Studies major who became a local union staffer for
SEIU after supporting the janitors employed at her Connecticut college.

Many, if not most, of SEIU's outside hires no longer work for the union,
in part because of its penchant for "management by churn." This means
that its network of distinguished alumni today is far larger than its current
national and local workforce, which is not small. And not all of these SEIU
alums have fond memories of their tour of duty in purple, the union's signature color. For an institution that demands great loyalty from its staff,
SEIU is not known for its reciprocal attachment to those who do its bidding. Ex-SEIUers include many dedicated, hardworking organizers who
were useful for a while, until they were not.

In several recent purges, SEIU even managed to forget about the past
services rendered by organizers sometimes described as "legendary." I

refer here to Bruce Raynor, former head of Workers United/SEIU, and Stephen Lerner, a fellow SEIU executive board member who directed the union's Private Equity Project and devised its much-applauded "Justice for Janitors" campaigns two decades ago.

Raynor began his career as an organizer in the 1970s, helping southern textile workers like the one portrayed by Sally Field in the film *Norma Rae*. While still serving as national president of UNITE HERE in 2009, Raynor rather messily defected to SEIU, a fellow Change to Win affiliate. In the face of stiff rank-and-file opposition, he steered about a quarter of UNITE HERE's membership into the far larger union run by his friend, Andy Stern. Raynor was given a new title, executive vice president of SEIU, and continued to earn more than a quarter-million dollars a year. Yet, just two years later, he was drummed out of Workers United/SEIU on disputed charges of billing SEIU for $2,300 worth of "non-business lunches."

Stephen Lerner's fall from grace and loss of his $156,000 annual salary began, more incrementally, in the fall of 2010. Lerner had just unveiled what was supposed to be a global, multiunion SEIU-coordinated bank workers organizing campaign, only to find himself put out on paid administrative leave for three months, after a noisy beef with his new SEIU headquarters boss. Lerner had been an influential publicist for many SEIU causes, including the New Unity Partnership (a predecessor to Change to Win), when his longtime patron, Andy Stern, was still Service Employees president. Under Stern's successor and protégée, Mary Kay Henry, Lerner's contributions were far less appreciated and, soon, no longer wanted at all.

Under president Henry, Lerner's bank worker organizing was shut down. But when his SEIU staff pension and job severance issues were eventually sorted out, he became free to rail, to his heart's content, about Wall Street and "the banksters" bereft of any meaningful union base. Henry then ran, unopposed, for reelection in May 2012 with an "administration slate" cleansed of both Lerner and Raynor.

A Deep Organizer Scorned

Jane McAlevey, author of *Raising Expectations (and Raising Hell): My Decade Fighting for the Labor Movement*, was, in 2007–8, a member of the same national union executive board graced, in happier days, by both men. Whereas the normally vocal Lerner and Raynor have been reticent about their involuntary departure from SEIU, McAlevey is a labor organizer scorned (or unburdened by any non-disclosure agreement?). Her resulting fury, or political frustration, is reflected in many parts of her memoir about being undermined and driven out of a 9,000-member SEIU affiliate in Nevada that she labels "one of the most successful in the nation." Written with the assistance of Bob Ostertag, *Raising Expectations* settles old scores with numerous members of what McAlevey calls "the Stern gang in D.C.," who helped shorten her local union leadership career to less than five years. The book should, therefore, be required reading for anyone hoping to last longer at SEIU—"before the rug is pulled out from under them" by the same "people at the top" who so disdained McAlevey because she wouldn't cop to their "paranoid institutional culture."[25]

Lest anyone think that the author's union employment was a little short term for such a blistering critique of SEIU and other unions, I should note, as the book's subtitle does, that McAlevey actually spent an entire decade trying to straighten out organized labor before concluding it was pretty hopeless. As she writes in the book's final chapter:

> I operated on the assumption that, if you just kept winning in a principled way, the work you were doing would create the conditions for its own continued existence. The people at the top might not like you, they might not understand what you were trying to do, they might consider you a big pain in the ass, but if you consistently succeeded at the assignments they gave you, ultimately they would give you more assignments and the work would go forward.
>
> I was wrong. . . . Past a certain point, winning actually becomes a liability, because the people at the top will feel threatened by the power you're accumulating unless they can control it; they cannot imagine that your ambition would not be to use that power in the same way they use theirs. It took ten years of banging my head on a wall to finally knock that into it.

Forty-eight-year-old McAlevey had a varied non-labor career before she started "winning in a principled way" and power accumulating (without personal ambition) in "the house of labor." She was a student government leader at the State University of New York at Buffalo, an activist in the environmental justice movement at home and abroad, associate director of the Highlander Center in Tennessee, and a program officer for Veatch, a progressive foundation backed by the Unitarian Church.

In 1998, McAlevey was recruited by then-AFL-CIO organizing director Richard Bensinger to head up the Stamford Organizing Project. SOP was a collaborative effort by local affiliates of SEIU, the Auto Workers, Hotel Employees, and Food and Commercial Workers. *Raising Expectations* reports that it "helped 5,000 workers successfully form unions and win first contracts that set new standards in their industries and [local] market." This multiracial, cross-union model wasn't replicated elsewhere, the author suggests, because post-1995 efforts "to reform the national AFL-CIO in Washington, D.C., were shipwrecking." One casualty was the federation's short-lived experiment with Stamford-style "geographical organizing."

Even after she moved on, McAlevey's methods earned high marks from campus fans like Dan Clawson, author of *The Next Upsurge: Labor and the New Social Movements*, who lauded the Stamford project as an expression of new "social movement unionism."[26] McAlevey prefers to call her work "deep organizing" or, in other parts of the book, "whole worker organizing." This approach involves "bring[ing] community organizing techniques right into the shop floor while moving labor organizing techniques out into the community" after conducting "power structure analysis that enables workers to systematically pool their knowledge of their communities and integrate this knowledge with conventional research done by union professionals." Workers themselves, not union staffers or some "union front group," are empowered to decide "when and where to take on 'non-workplace issues,'" like affordable housing, that too many unions fail to address.

After Stamford, McAlevey worked for SEIU in New York, Washington, D.C., Kansas, and California as the union's Deputy Director for Strategic Campaigns at Tenet Healthcare and other companies. Her longest and last stand was in Las Vegas, working as the Andy Stern–installed executive director of 9,000-member Local 1107, a public sector and health care affiliate of SEIU that also represented thousands of non-dues payers. McAlevey variously describes the local she took over in 2004 as "a rat's nest," a "joke," and a dysfunctional "grievance mill."

Las Vegas Challenges

Her opinion of her new home wasn't much higher. It's "a myth" that Las Vegas is a model "union town," she contends. UNITE HERE Local 226 may have done "a stellar job of winning good contracts," but that only means the city has "a union street . . . universally known as the Strip." As for the rest of the place, according to the author, it's "a phony city built on gambling and prostitution" located "in a corrupt right-to-work state" where "the temperature climbs above 110 for days on end." Sin City's one redeeming feature, for McAlevey, was "land so cheap that I could get a little place where my horse could live with me." Her equine companion, a Tennessean named Jalapeno, later came in handy when she tried to bond with local politicos, who also spent off-duty time in the saddle.

Prior to arriving in this desert, McAlevey's headquarters handlers all agreed that she "should present herself as a seasoned hand at negotiating contracts," a major responsibility of her new appointed position. Her actual bargaining experience was shockingly thin for someone who was now representing thousands of workers at Hospital Corporation of America, United Health Services, Catholic Healthcare West, and other large employers. "I had hardly even read a union contract," she admits. "I had never negotiated and there were all sorts of technicalities of the collective bargaining process I had no clue about." (One SEIU headquarters helper reassured her that workers would soon discover how "really talented and terrific" she was anyway.) Fortunately, with much long-distance telephone call coaching from New England 1199/SEIU leader Jerry Brown, McAlevey proved to be a fast learner.

During her first several years as its staff director, McAlevey helped strengthen Local 1107 by overhauling the local's financial and administrative practices, hiring younger staffers, encouraging member involvement in bargaining, better integrating internal and external organizing, and reviving SEIU as a political force in Nevada. Several of the best chapters in *Raising Expectations* describe her jousting with management and provide detailed examples of how open negotiations—what the author calls "big representation bargaining"—can increase rank-and-file participation and restore members' confidence in the union as their workplace voice.

McAlevey now believes that despite this promising beginning and favorable contract results her commitment to "building real worker power"—through "activism on the shop floor"—conflicted too much with the "vested interests" of those "higher up" in SEIU. Her headquarters critics favored labor-management partnering and no longer wanted to deal with members' day-to-day job problems. Her personal string of "who-would-have-believed-it" victories, in a "maverick local," was just too much of an affront to top officials, who frowned on strikes and other forms of worker militancy. Her adversaries in the SEIU bureaucracy made sure she remained politically "vulnerable" and, if necessary, easily discarded. According to McAlevey, "the national SEIU sucked" and was just itching "to derail the little juggernaut we had put together in Vegas."

In reality, the author's political demise was hastened by her role in a failed attempt to remove Local 1107 president Vicki Hedderman and her allies from their elected positions, a campaign assisted by President Stern. A former unit clerk at Clark County Hospital, Hedderman was, in McAlevey's view, too focused on filing grievances and not sufficiently supportive of new organizing. McAlevey depicts her nominal boss as "tenaciously" clinging to the perks of office, while keeping 1107's public sector and health care members at odds, and thwarting the author's ambitious plans for unifying and transforming the local. According to McAlevey, Hedderman and other incumbents "had maintained control of the local by trading their attentiveness to individual grievances for the votes of the workers who filed them."

Forced to Resign

It was not part of McAlevey's formal job description to meddle in the local's internal politics or round up votes a different way. But that's what she did, rather inexpertly and disastrously. She recruited opposition candidates who ended up being covertly financed by out-of-state SEIU donations solicited by Stern. One of these $5,000 gifts, from Ohio SEIU leader Dave Regan, "turned out to be money that technically could not be used for [union] elections." The U.S. Department of Labor intervened, and found other misconduct as well. A membership uproar ensued and much bad publicity was generated. Hedderman survived both McAlevey's original electoral challenge and a hasty rerun ordered by SEIU. To restore peace to 1107, an emissary from SEIU headquarters negotiated the joint resignations of both women, an exit strategy for McAlevey that she now describes as "taking the fall for Andy Stern." The coterie of energetic young staff people she recruited from outside the local soon left as well.

There's a saying, popular among judges: "Ignorance of the law is no excuse." In this most murky section of her book, McAlevey pleads ignorance nevertheless. She claims that her extensive knowledge of "real world election laws" applying to political campaigns and the "labor laws that relate to beating multi-national corporations" just didn't extend to the Landrum-Grifffin Act, which protects workers' rights as union members. "Internal union election law was all news to me," she confesses.

Equally disingenuous is McAlevey's claim to have been victimized by "the pervasive sexism among the men who are most in control of the resources in unions today." Lack of women in the leadership and insufficient nurturing of female rank-and-file activists is indeed a continuing labor problem, notwithstanding the valiant efforts of various women's caucuses. Yet *Raising Expectations* is full of praise for McAlevey's "beloved and invaluable mentors"—almost all of them high-ranking men like Brown and Bensinger; Bensinger's successor at the AFL-CIO, Kirk Adams, who is now a top SEIU official again; and ex-SEIU health care division head Larry Fox, who along with current SEIU secretary-treasurer Eliseo Medina, was responsible for "shoehorning" the author into Las Vegas.

In contrast, almost every personal nemesis we meet in *Raising Expectations* is female, with the exception of McAlevey's two problematic allies, Andy Stern and Dave Regan. First we encounter Mary Kay Henry, who "was clearly not comfortable with me" and failed to return the author's phone calls. Next, "The Queen of Petty," longtime SEIU secretary-treasurer Anna Burger, makes an appearance, blocking McAlevey from speaking to the SEIU executive board (because Jane was "someone she doesn't like to have around"). Then there is Judy Scott, SEIU general counsel, who calls to "browbeat" Jane into "capitulating to Hospital Corporation of America" so "labor peace" in Las Vegas could be traded for "organizing rights" elsewhere.

According to McAlevey, she was continually thwarted and harried by Hedderman, and her "old guard" allies, many of them female public employees or nurses. Among RNs, Local 1107 was also besieged by labor's "self-styled left wing" (aka the California Nurses Association). Under executive director RoseAnn DeMoro, the CNA descended on Reno to woo hundreds of disaffected nurses away from Jane and SEIU. In McAlevey's view, DeMoro is undeserving of her national following among "academic Marxists, student radicals, and others on the margins of unions." According to the author, CNA's craft-union "approach. . . . is completely retrogressive" and "encourages an attitude of elitism rather than solidarity" among nurses in relation to other lower-paid, less skilled hospital workers.

Shallow Mobilizing

McAlevey's criticism of the CNA is secondary to her indictment of Stern, SEIU, and the "vision for American labor that they have come to personify." According to *Raising Expectations*, SEIU's "shallow mobilizing approach" leaves members with "only the most tenuous relationship with their union." As a result, "the political endorsements their unions give to candidates or ballot initiatives mean little more to workers than the endorsements of their bosses or Fox News."

> The union becomes nothing more than the contract and the contract is only engaged when a worker files a grievance. The union becomes an insurance plan, like car insurance, to which workers pay dues "in case you need it." Staff talk to workers like Geico claims adjusters after an accident.

Given Mary Kay Henry's "many years as Stern's loyal protégée, and her role in the events described in this book," McAlevey finds it "hard to imagine she will alter SEIU's course in any significant way." The author takes direct aim at Henry's "Fight for a Fair Economy," a current SEIU campaign much ballyhooed in the blogosphere and in publications like *The Nation*. According to McAlevey, FFE is just another form of "tactical and transactional engagement with the community that involves union staff renting or buying community groups, or simply setting up their own fully controllable ones." As she accurately observes:

> SEIU is spending tens of millions of dollars mobilizing underpaid,
> underemployed, and unemployed workers and channeling anger
> about jobs into action for positive change. What's beyond bizarre
> is that the program is aimed a mobilizing poor people rather than
> SEIU's own base. SEIU looks everywhere except to their own
> membership to gin up popular revolts.

The author's overall report card on SEIU echoes the better-articulated critique developed by its California rival, the new National Union of Healthcare Workers (NUHW). NUHW was born out of a popular revolt that didn't have to be ginned up.[27]

In January 2009 Stern put members of SEIU's third-largest affiliate, United Healthcare Workers-West (UHW), under trusteeship for challenging him at the union's 2008 convention in Puerto Rico, resisting his attempted dismantling of their local afterward, and publicly questioning the same kind of health care industry "growth deals" that McAlevey also found troubling.

Yet McAlevey did not ally herself with UHW when its soon-to-be-ousted president Sal Rosselli and other would-be reformers challenged Stern's consolidation of personal power at the SEIU convention. By 2007, in fact, she had already accepted Stern's appointment to fill a vacancy on the SEIU national executive board, a body that Rosselli was purged from a year later. Holding on to this promotion required that McAlevey distance herself from the vocal minority of 2008 convention delegates who were publicly critical of SEIU's undemocratic practices and lax contract enforcement. (She describes their brave efforts as just "fizzling" out.) In return, Stern made her part of his hand-picked administration slate at the convention. Her full four-year term on the SEIU board was soon cut short, due her forced departure from Local 1107 in late June 2008, and subsequent year-long struggle with cancer.

In *Raising Expectations*, McAlevey's service on the national executive board—an honor accorded to less than eighty people and the pinnacle of her SEIU career—goes unmentioned. She mentions only that she was among the "moderate" SEIU progressives who were quietly "working to build opposition to [Stern's] policies," while avoiding "a frontal assault on Stern's leadership" of the sort launched by the "loud" and "bombastic"

Rosselli. However, among McAlevey's 2008 convention running mates was Dave Regan, whom she now derides as a "Stern loyalist" and "stooge." It was Regan's Ohio "political fund [that] Stern tapped for the money he had promised for our union election in Nevada—the down payment that turned out to be technically illegal." The truly bombastic Regan went on to became Stern's trustee over UHW, a role he has transformed into the highest-paid local union presidency in SEIU (at $300,000 a year, more than Mary Kay Henry makes to head up the entire union).

Reform or Rebellion?

Now representing more than 10,000 workers, NUHW continues to challenge SEIU in California health care units because of the management-friendly deal-making by Regan and others that McAlevey decries in her book. Nevertheless, *Raising Expectations* displays very little respect or sympathy for the dedicated organizers and workplace leaders who created NUHW after Stern slammed the door on their internal SEIU reform efforts. Unlike McAlevey's smaller-scale Nevada tiffs with SEIU headquarters, the California health care workers' rebellion represented a real threat to national union control. That's why SEIU sued twenty-eight NUHW founders for $25 million, ultimately winning a $1.57 million federal court judgment against sixteen of them and their new union.

All we discover about "the resulting war" is that McAlevey opposes "raids" because they're "one of the sleaziest things one union can do to another." In her view, union leaders, not workers, end up "decid[ing] whether an existing union is bad enough to warrant being raided by another union." Left unexplained by the author is why "workers with bad unions" should be denied "the chance to jump to more effective ones," particularly where the alternative choice, NUHW, appears to be more militant, member-driven, and democratic, not to mention backed by McAlevey's most trusted mentor and advisor from Connecticut, Jerry Brown.

In *Raising Expectations*, McAlevey expounds instead on her own preferred community and labor organizing models. She provides little or no practical advice for members still trapped in her old union, other than maybe learning from her mistake of breaking federal law to influence local union election results. A reader who might belong to SEIU and be unhappy with its performance at the local union level today is left with the impression that the only way his or her own affiliate could be changed for the better—as 1107 was briefly—is by hiring McAlevey or some other "deep organizer" from the outside. As a local union reform strategy, that's a bit of a non-starter. Members who want a stronger, more effective union only get some say over staff hiring and other major policy decisions if they run against incumbents and take over the local, a strategy that McAlevey never discusses except in the context of her own Local 1107 election debacle.

As noted earlier, *Raising Expectations'* main strength lies in its several detailed and useful case studies of contract campaigns worthy of emulation in other open-shop states, where membership is voluntary and the challenge of internal organizing never ends. But even here, as in the past, the author is so self-mythologizing and prone to exaggeration that relevant facts are just ignored. In December 2006, even before McAlevey turned to book writing, she boasted to the *Las Vegas Sun* that "Local 1107's membership had grown from 9,000 to 15,000 since her arrival in spring 2004." The newspaper noted that 1107's own most recent "filing with the U.S. Department of Labor reported a dues paying membership of just 9,124."[28]

Halfway through McAlevey's tenure with the local, 40 percent of the workers then represented by 1107 were not members, either in long-established public sector units or hospitals where SEIU had more recently won recognition. In *Raising Expectations*, McAlevey claims that "we were hitting all these records" and "averaging in the high 70s [percentage of workers who were union members]—built up from the 20s." The LM-2 reports filed by Local 1107 during the entire McAlevey era reveal respectable internal and/or external organizing gains, but overall, the real numbers don't match the author's claimed highs or lows. Around the time McAlevey took over, 1107 reported 8,142 dues-payers; by the time she left, that figure had been boosted to 10, 155. The biggest year-over-year membership growth during her tenure was 16 percent. After McAlevey resigned and left, Local 1107's membership slid back to about 8,000—or an estimated 53 percent of those eligible to join. [29]

Why does any of this matter? Well, McAlevey's memoir is not really that of a "left-wing troublemaker" who single-handedly became such a threat to SEIU leaders that they forced her out. It's more the tale of a progressive prima donna, a labor type that's all too familiar, just as likely to be male as female, if not more so, and not really the best leadership model in any union. In contrast, truly effective organizers try to make union building a collective effort, not a one-person show. If successful, their work with rank-and-file members is built to last, not to disappear with little or no trace after they've departed from the scene.

The best grassroots organizers also tend to be long-distance runners, not sprinters or relay team members who have trouble cooperating with others on the squad and maintaining enduring relationships with workers. They keep in mind the difference between being an elected union officer and an appointed staff person. They don't make the project of union renewal so much about themselves or their own heroic endeavors. In the case of those activists still challenging SEIU in California, many have paid a far higher personal price than McAlevey ever did, because their struggle has involved real risk taking, not just self-promotion and literary reinvention as a martyr to the cause of union reform. We have a lot more to learn from them than from the author of *Raising Expectations*.[30]

POSTSCRIPT

Not surprisingly, the author of *Raising Expectations* disagreed with this assessment of her memoir. For Jane McAlevey's response, see: http://www.zcommunications.org/response-to-steve-earlys-review-of-raising-expectations-by-jane-mcalevey. Others who wrote critically about *Raising Expectations* also discussed the need for better models of labor leadership and local union revitalization. See, for example, Joe Burns at http://talkingunion.wordpress.com/2013/01/22/joe-burns-reviews-rising-expectations/; Dana Simon at http://www.socialpolicy.org/index.php/spring-2013/595-review-of-raising-expectations-a-narrative-at-odds-with-the-history; and Michael Yates at http://monthlyreview.org/2013/05/01/who-will-lead-the-u-s-working-class.

PART VII

TWO, THREE, MANY VERMONTS!

This section pays tribute to the Green Mountain State, a small oasis in the desert of U.S. politics whose social democratic tendencies in the modern era have been variously attributed to a post-1960s influx of "flatlanders" and its proximity to Canada. However, for those who believe that geography is destiny, let's keep in mind that all nine U.S. political subdivisions, to the west and east of Vermont—Washington, Idaho, Montana, North Dakota, Minnesota, Michigan, New York, New Hampshire, and Maine—have quite different red or blue state identities, notwithstanding their coexistence with Canada along the same long international border.

I first wandered into the green pastures of Vermont in 1967 as a college student, when the state was still a Republican redoubt. I was able to do some labor work there in the mid-1970s and more between 1995 and 2007, after CWA's telecom membership expanded in Burlington, the state's largest city. Vermont's transformation, over four decades, and accompanying changes in the political orientation of its labor movement, are both worthy of wider emulation. The question is how? Is small too beautiful to be a model elsewhere? Are Vermont politics too much of an exception to the rule of major-party domination to make the state's experience with independent progressive candidacies useful in other, larger-scale and more urbanized environments?

This section profiles some of the key figures and organizations that have helped make Vermont a laboratory for successful third-party campaigning and cutting-edge grassroots organizing around single-payer health care and other issues. Among the catalysts for change we meet is the only socialist ever elected to the U.S. Senate, Bernie Sanders. Since 1981, Sanders's electoral success as mayor of Burlington, U.S. congressman, and now senator has helped create the political space for emergence of the Vermont Progressive Party (VPP). Like Bernie, the VPP has wooed working-class voters away from both major parties by emphasizing economic issues and labor causes less fervently championed by local Democrats.

Part 7 concludes by assessing Vermont's pioneering union-backed effort to create its own Canadian-style single-payer health care system. As discussed earlier in Part 4, the multiyear implementation of President Obama's Affordable Care Act has had the unfortunate effect of sidelining or preempting single-payer campaigning in some political arenas. That's why the fate of "Green Mountain Care" remains vitally important to many non-Vermonters who may never benefit from it directly, except as a model for more fundamental reform in their own states.

29—A GREEN MOUNTAIN POSTCARD

Vermont has always been a good place to get away from it all in August. But in the late summer of 2009 many Democrats in Congress returned home from Washington to find the Tea Party waiting for them. My vacation newspaper, *The Burlington Free Press,* explained what was brewing locally in a front-page story headlined: "Health Care Fight Comes to Vt." The state's leading media outlet reported that "listening sessions" on health care reform had already "erupted into red-faced shouting matches nationwide" because of an emerging right-wing backlash against President Obama's yet-to-be-enacted plan. Taking note of this trend, Vermont Senator Pat Leahy and Congressman Peter Welch wisely scheduled no such constituent meetings during their recess time off. But their always independent colleague, U.S. Senator Bernie Sanders, forged ahead with plans for three town meetings.

The first of Bernie's events was set for Saturday, August 15, in Rutland, located in the heartland of the state and never an epicenter of its greening over the past thirty years. As the *Free Press* noted, "Sanders has held hundreds of town meetings" during that time, but this session was definitely shaping up to be different. Inspired by events elsewhere, local foes of "out-of-control" federal spending were planning to turn out in force. Paul Beaudry, a conservative talk show host in Waterbury, was among those complaining that our national government "shouldn't be providing health care because the Constitution is silent on the matter." In the *Free Press*, Beaudry urged Vermonters to "speak their piece" at Bernie's meeting but warned that Sanders was "going to have union thugs at the front door and he's not going to let us speak, and, if we do disagree, he's going to belittle us."

Beaudry's ominous prediction of union misbehavior certainly roused me from my own Vermont vacation torpor. I've run into a few "union thugs" over the years but none in the Green Mountain State, even before it morphed into the only place in America that would elect a self-described socialist to Congress. And, believe me, whatever one may think of Bernie Sanders, he didn't get elected mayor of Burlington, then a congressman, and now U.S. senator by belittling his fellow Vermonters, much less depriving them of free speech. I set my alarm for 6:30 a.m. on Saturday, so I could make it down the winding mountain roads to Rutland in time for the Tea Party fireworks at nine.

Well before showtime, there are several hundred of us lined up, waiting in the hot early morning sun outside Rutland's Unitarian Universalist Church; folding chairs have been set up on the lawn to handle the expected overflow. The crowd is a good crosssection of the larger eclectic group that polarizes in Vermont around election time. Present to take Sanders down—and berate him publicly for the health care sins of Obama and the Democrats—are angry working-class Tories, small businessmen, retired professionals, and some not very charming right-wing ideologues. Arrayed against them, with equal fervor and lung power (and maybe a sixty-five to thirty-five numerical edge) are still enthusiastic Obama supporters,

Vermont Progressive Party voters, labor and community activists mobilized by the Vermont Workers Center. Also awaiting their chance to speak, in more unscripted fashion, are various individuals with painful personal stories to tell about the consequences of being sick and uninsured.

In the jostling for entry into the 200-seat venue, one Sanders critic, wearing a blue golf shirt and tasseled loafers, irritably insists that he be admitted first because he arrived at 5 a.m. Some of his Tea Party comrades have come dressed as Minutemen (and women), with tricorn hats, long stockings, and buckles on their shoes. They wander through the crowd, sounding the alarm about "Obamacare," like town criers from the eighteenth century. As TV cameras, radio reporters, and print journalists arrive to cover the event, multicolored printed signs demanding "Single Payer Now!," donated by the faraway California Nurses Association, compete for attention with a handful of artisanal ones favoring a ban on abortion, "No Cap & Trade," and "Health Care Reform" but without a "Government Takeover."

Two Rutland cops are stationed at the door to separate all placards from the pieces of wood they are mounted on, in case things get rowdy inside. A nice stack of kindling builds up by the front door as people file in. By the time Bernie arrives, the crowd inside and out is swelling toward its peak of nearly 600. Congressmen elsewhere have been getting death threats. So the Capitol Police in Washington have requested a Vermont state police escort, which accompanies Sanders in plainclothes. Uncomfortable with his highest security ever, Bernie enters the church like a pro fighter being escorted into the ring. His supporters respond in kind, greeting their champion with the chant, "Bernie! Bernie! Bernie!"

Inside the church, the dark wood walls are adorned with big Sanders-supplied posters featuring the famous 1943 painting *Freedom of Speech* by onetime Vermont resident Norman Rockwell. That masterpiece of Americana depicts an earnest Vermont farmer or mechanic standing up and speaking his piece in front of his neighbors on town meeting day. In his welcoming remarks, Sanders invokes this hallowed, if not always carefully observed, tradition of civility in small-town give-and-take about public policy. "You've all seen on TV these ruckuses that are going on and attempts to shout other people down. That is not what the state of Vermont is all about!" he declares to universal applause.

"I will try, uncharacteristically, to be as brief as I can," Bernie promises, as he lays out a batting order that includes: opening remarks from a
prearranged panel of three friendlies, follow-up commentary by him, and
then an open-mike session, alternating between two-minute questions
and/or statements from critics of "Obamacare," lined up on one side of
the pews, and those favoring some kind of left/liberal reform on the other
side. The only "union thugs" in sight so far are both on Bernie's panel
of local experts. First, we hear from Jen Henry, a nurse for two decades
at Fletcher Allen Hospital in Burlington and now president of the state's
largest health care workers' union, and then from Dave Kaczynski, an
unemployed Vermont ironworker, who is short, muscular, and tattooed,
but otherwise quite unthreatening as he explains the health care plight of
"proud, hardworking and blue-collar Vermonters."

In my section of the congregation, two animated Medicare recipients
from Middlebury are still swapping tips about local rheumatologists and
physical therapists, while the perky, ponytailed blond in front of us is
wearing a white T-shirt that declares "We are Tea'd" and "Taxed Enuff
Already." Billy Clark, from Fairfax in northern Vermont, has already
informed one reporter that her three children are "not going to enjoy the
freedoms that I've had if the government keeps getting involved in our
lives." Outside the church, we can hear some of her friends chanting away,
working an air horn, and showing how "Tea'd" off they are, too.

Standing behind the pulpit, Bernie is just getting warmed up, in what
will soon be a Protestant sweat lodge. "Call me what you want but don't
call me some elitist from Washington, D.C.," he shouts, citing the 300 community forums he has held, on weekends and during congressional breaks,
since he was first elected to serve on Capitol Hill nineteen years ago. Before
the question period even begins, we get a vintage Sanders overview of the
sorry state of national politics and the economy. While most Tea Party
adherents sit on their hands and the progressives applaud, Bernie wallops
Wall Street for its "greed, recklessness, and illegal behavior." He disses
"Democrats and Republicans, liberals and conservatives" alike for their
"disastrous trade policies." He launches a preemptive strike against the
mythical federal "death panel" that's allegedly going to snuff Sarah Palin's
parents, plus her son with Downs syndrome. Sanders says we should worry
more about the 18,000 Americans who "die every year because they can't

get to a doctor." Somehow the planetary threat of "global warming" and the necessity of creating "green jobs" also works its way into this peroration, triggering a major outbreak of Tea Party muttering and head shaking.

The first contra who hits the mike is "Paul from Pittsford." In true right-wing radio style, few who try to bust Bernie's chops have a last name. Paul is middle-aged and bearded, dressed in a loud flowered shirt, shorts, and Crocs. Confusingly enough, he confesses to having "voted for Bernie every time—not because I agree with him on everything, but I like him. I think he's a stand-up guy." However, Paul sees something coming from Washington that he doesn't like in the form of an "A-plan for them, and a B-plan for everyone else."

Bernie's answer sets the tone for the day. "I agree," he tells Paul. "You make a damn good point. Our people should have the same health care plan that Congress has." In any debate with conservative populists, Sanders is a master of political jujitsu. He takes the force of a speaker's rhetorical anger or suspicion and deftly redirects it toward his own preferred and more appropriate corporate or governmental targets. As the questioning unfolds, he frequently expresses sympathy for any part of a Tea Party rant or complaint that makes the slightest bit of anti-establishment sense.

Mike, from Rutland City, has brought with him, for dramatic effect, what he claims is all 1,017 pages of a House version of the health care bill. While his main point, based on reading this thick wad of paper three times, is that " 'advanced care planning' really means euthanasia," he also beseeches Bernie "to come up with something that's not so wicked complex." Sanders asserts that he's "not a great fan of complicated" either. When Anne from Poultney says, "I'm disgusted with both sides of the aisle" in Congress, Bernie follows up with his own insider critique "of the absurdities of the [health care reform] process" and the often "dysfunctional" nature of Congress. Sanders supporter Deb Richter, a member of Physicians for a National Health Program, takes the mike to Bernie's left and tries to simplify things, by making the case for "Medicare for All." When Dr. Deb, as she is known, claims that a majority of Americans want single payer, the other line of waiting speakers erupts in a chorus of "No!"

Sanders uses this teachable moment to do a little polling about real existing "100 percent government-controlled health care." He asks how many of us in the church, and outside, "think we should get rid of Medicare." As the *Free Press* later reported, "About three hands went up." Then Bernie goes on down the list. "How many think we should get rid of the Veterans Administration? How many want to do away with the Doctor Dinosaur program here in Vermont?" Hardly anyone seems willing to ditch public coverage for vets or kids either.

By now, Bernie is mopping his brow frequently and working up a real sweat. While the crew-cut state troopers on either side of him remain impressively cool, standing at attention in their dark glasses, ties, and blazers, the Senator himself has been gesturing emphatically, as he always does, and dealing with questions at the high decibel level necessary to be heard inside the church and outside, via the PA system set up for folks on the lawn. Bernie's open-collared blue shirt is stained with perspiration. His shoulders have become stooped a bit, his khaki pants are beginning to sag, and his white hair is getting mussed. It's time for more questions, on an equal-time basis, from the pro and con lines forming outside, so he charges down the aisle and takes up a new position, on the front steps of the church.

After further rhetorical volleys back and forth between the senator and his questioners outside, Bernie returns to the pulpit. "I think I'm earning my salary today," he says. But wide-eyed Diane Donnolly from Essex Junction is at the right mike and she doesn't look very sympathetic. She brandishes a handwritten sign with a favorite quote from Ronald Reagan: "Never fall for the sweet talk of government-run health care. It will be the END OF FREEDOM!" She cites problems with Social Security and "lines at the DMV" as two strikes against single payer. Says Diane, not very sweetly: "I do not want America to turn into a socialistic country . . . with our health care becoming, government-run bull crap!"

Bernie responds in kind, with a hint of sarcasm: "I do not believe that Social Security, Medicare, Medicaid, or Doctor Dinosaur lead to totalitarian government." But Diane's is not the only reference to his personal views. Several other Tea Partiers preface their remarks by declaring their disagreement with Sanders's own "socialistic policies," explaining that's why they never vote for him. But one such voter, John from Pawlet, did thank Sanders for the staff-written replies to his letters on various issues. In contrast, John was displeased with the answers he had received from

Bernie's two missing-in-action Capitol Hill colleagues, finding them to be insubstantial and even condescending. "That is not you, and I appreciate it," he told the crowd, before launching into a diatribe against tort lawyer malfeasance and blaming Bernie for "letting them [the lawyers] get away with it."

This unexpected sword thrust soon has Bernie off and running against a better target—Ben Bernanke. He cites the need for greater accountability and transparency in federal bailout schemes for big financial institutions, blaming the Federal Reserve chief for stonewalling the public in this area. Earlier he had recalled his legendary jousting as a congressman with Alan Greenspan in House Banking Committee hearings. But, for his hard-core critics, Bernie's singular track record as an inside-the-Beltway dissenter is just not their cup of tea. As the Rutland talkfest nears its conclusion, the questioning gets bogged down in back-and-forth arguments about whose taxes have and haven't been raised lately. One of Bernie's last interlocutors, outside the church, is Fred from Fair Haven, a deeply tanned and mustachioed fellow in a muscle shirt. Fred just keeps talking while Sanders tries to parry his complaints about deficit spending, by referencing the views of leading economists. The bottom line, Bernie explains, is that "the only way you can extend coverage to all without raising taxes is via single payer."

Back at the pulpit inside, Bernie pronounces himself pleased with "the dialogue," reassuring us that he doesn't "consider anyone here an enemy." Today, he declares proudly, "We have shown America that we can disagree with each other without being disagreeable." A few minutes later, on his way out the door, he tells a reporter that he hopes "this type of display becomes a model for the rest of the country." As Sanders drives off in a white sedan, one Tea Party stalwart is still on the sidewalk, droning through a bullhorn about "equal distribution of misery." "That's what they want," he claims, "and we don't need it!" One of the hardest-working, most substantive politicians in the nation won't even have time for lunch before addressing another crowd of 500, gathered in a public park in Arlington, Vermont, thirty miles down Route 7. A midsummer experience that proved torturous for many in Congress was just another town meeting day for Bernie.[1]

30—MUSTERING FOR WAR, AT HOME AND ABROAD

Because of its series of progressive mayors, a city council known to embrace controversial causes, and a general vibe of being on the cutting edge of left politics for the last thirty years, Vermont's largest city is sometimes called, by fans and detractors alike, the "People's Republic of Burlington."

Like all labels based on political stereotypes, this one can be misleading. After all, no city is an island, certainly not in the United States. And even when a municipality is located in a state nationally known for its own progressive leanings, that doesn't always tell the whole story about everyone who resides there. For example, in early December 2009, the "People's Republic" had a busy weekend mustering its forces for active duty on two fronts, one at home and the other abroad.

At the University of Vermont (UVM), up the hill from Burlington's lakeside downtown, several hundred labor and progressive activists gathered to plan more effective resistance to job cuts and contract givebacks demanded by local employers. The title of their statewide conference—"Turning Crisis into Opportunity: Building Democratic, Fighting Unions and Defending Public Services in Hard Economic Times"—was almost as long as the full list of domestic challenges facing most U.S. union members.

The very next day, on the same UVM campus, another group of Vermonters, even more predominantly working class, assembled as defenders of a U.S. occupation thousands of miles away. They were the first 298 of nearly 1,500 National Guard members scheduled to depart for Afghanistan. As reported in the *Burlington Free Press*, their unit's largest deployment since the Second World War was celebrated at an "emotional ceremony," attended by friends, neighbors, and family members at an indoor tennis court. Flags were waved, speeches were made, a military band played, and "farewells were the order of the day." To keep things on an upbeat note, one Guard officer proclaimed, to much applause, that "The Green Mountain Boys are coming!"

He was invoking a tradition of militia activity in Vermont that was, in the late eighteenth century, more successful when deployment was closer to home. Under the leadership of Ethan Allen, who died in Burlington in 1789, the original GMBs fared well in the early stages of our colonial struggle for independence from Britain. Using some Taliban-like tactics, Allen's followers kept absentee landlords from New York at bay when they tried to assert Green Mountain land claims. In 1775, the GMBs paddled across Lake Champlain and seized nearby Fort Ticonderoga "in the name of the Great Jehovah and the Continental Congress," as Ethan informed its commander. Heavy cannon from the fortress came in handy several months later when the patriot siege of Boston forced the King's army to flee Massachusetts for the duration of the war.

Unfortunately, GMB overreaching led to a disastrous invasion of Quebec later in 1775. Many in Allen's band were killed and he was brutally imprisoned, first in Canada and then England. There was much Loyalist clamor for his execution as a traitor in both jurisdictions until some savvy prisoner swapping by George Washington secured his safe return home three years later. Allen's last military objective remains, to this day, unconquered by U.S. troops, although some Quebecois have been known to view Canadian soldiers as "foreign occupiers."

In the run-up to the UVM labor meeting, worker skirmishing with modern-day Tories was not going well in Vermont. New England's largest telecom, North Carolina-based FairPoint, had just declared Chapter 11 bankruptcy, throwing 2,500 workers into an uphill fight to defend their jobs and contract. Republican governor Jim Douglas eliminated 580 state government positions through layoffs or attrition, but still projected a $150 million state budget shortfall. Overall joblessness was high enough to leave Vermont's unemployment fund nearly broke.

Under pressure from Douglas, the Vermont State Employees' Association (VSEA) agreed to an unprecedented 3 percent pay cut for its 7,000 members, followed by a salary freeze. Neal Lunderville, a top Douglas administration official, lauded this settlement as "a commonsense approach that should serve as a blueprint for teachers, municipal workers, and others who receive a paycheck from taxpayers." At the labor conference at UVM, rank-and-file militants and campus socialists had a different message for the governor and his fellow concession-seekers. Summed up in a rousing closing session chant, it was: "They say give-back, we say fight-back!"

Throughout their daylong meeting, local teamsters, teachers, telephone workers, nurses, and state employees grappled with the difficult challenge of making this anti-concessions stance more real than rhetorical. Their deliberations were assisted by the conference cosponsor, *Labor Notes*, which publishes a monthly newsletter linking and encouraging "union troublemakers" throughout the country. As a *Labor Notes* activist, I helped out with a presentation that drew heavily on the educational work of U.S. Labor Against the War. USLAW is a union coalition that favors U.S. withdrawal from Iraq and Afghanistan, plus cuts in the military budget to free up more funds for social programs at home.[2]

It wasn't hard to connect the economic dots between the back-to-back events occurring on the same campus over the weekend. As USLAW notes, every private and public sector employer is chanting the mantra that times are tough, money is short, and there must be shared national sacrifice. In Vermont, based on eight years of experience with two wars in the Middle East, that "sacrifice" means working-class people must fight and die in disproportionate numbers. As taxpayers, they must foot the bill for a $550-billion-a-year Pentagon budget, in addition to the $130 billion annual cost of the simultaneous occupations of Iraq and Afghanistan. Then, if they're veterans who return home safely, they must endure cuts in pay, benefits, jobs, and public services, along with other working-class Vermonters.

USLAW's many charts and graphs helped highlight the domestic costs of U.S. military campaigns overseas and what could be better funded at home if federal budget priorities were different. For example, to avoid that 3 percent pay cut for 7,000 Vermont state workers, we could shut down the war in Afghanistan for twenty minutes and, at the current rate of U.S. spending there, raise the $2 million that Governor Douglas extracted from the VSEA through givebacks instead. To close the governor's entire fiscal year 2011 budget gap would, of course, require the additional "sacrifice" of diverting twenty-four hours' worth of Afghan war spending to help keep Vermont state government afloat for another year.

The following morning, down at the Holiday Inn in South Burlington, where many Vermont National Guard families had spent the weekend saying private, pre-deployment good-byes, the logic of USLAW's antiwar math was not lost on an overworked waitress named Dawna. As she restocked the breakfast buffet and provided coffee refills around the room, everyone but Dawna was transfixed by the big flat-screen over the restaurant bar. There, we could watch real-time coverage of the Afghanistan deployment ceremony being held just up the road at UVM. Restaurant staff members could recognize Holiday Inn guests they had just served, in the same room, a few hours before or earlier in the weekend.

Now, these same "citizen soldiers" were standing stiffly at attention, wearing field caps, camouflage, and combat boots. On the platform in front of them, a parade of local politicians, both pro- and anti-war alike, praised their patriotism and devotion to duty. Among them was my Middlebury College classmate from the late 1960s, Jim Douglas. Long before he ascended to the heights of Vermont state government, Jim was a Richard Nixon–loving, Young Republican booster of the Vietnam War, who neither enlisted nor was drafted to fight in it. From his usual "chicken hawk" perch far from the front lines, Douglas was now assuring Guard members that "while you are doing your duty, I promise we will do ours, here on the home-front." He didn't mention that his domestic duties might include slashing state programs or unemployment benefits needed by them or their families.

No fan of Douglas or other politicians, Dawna was simply disgusted by the whole televised spectacle. "I'm tired of seeing a lot of guys marching around in uniforms," she confided. "I wish they'd turn that off and go back to the 'relax your muscles' show"—a bit of self-help programming for sufferers of lower-back pain that was playing before someone switched channels to the Guard event.

By this point in her Sunday morning shift, Dawna did not seem particularly relaxed herself, in her white shirt, bedraggled tie, and sagging black waitress apron. Although only in her thirties, she had the weary, weighed-down look of many trapped in the low-wage service economy of northern New England. Her cousin, the father of three, has been deployed overseas multiple times already. That's why, she informed me, "war is a sore personal subject" for her. "It's ridiculous," she declared. "We have people living on the street, who've lost their jobs, can't pay for their homes. And now we're sending more people over there to fight somebody else's battles?"

Observing the somber family gatherings in the hotel over the weekend had clearly not been easy for some Holiday Inn staff members. Mistaking one mother and daughter in the dining room for a non-military family, Dawna had asked the child how she liked the hotel pool. "I'm here to say good-bye to my dad," the little girl sadly informed her.

"I'll feel better later on, when I get off work," Dawna assured me, as I paid for my breakfast. "You know it's 'out of sight, out of mind,' 'what doesn't kill you, makes you stronger?'" At the same time, she didn't seem very convinced about the truth of these familiar but oddly conjoined aphorisms. One thing was certain: for a few of the guests she had served earlier in the day, their stay in Afghanistan will prove fatal, without making that country safer, America stronger, or workers in Vermont any better off.[3]

31—THE SASKATCHEWAN OF AMERICA?

After years of political frustration, Earl Mongeon had to see it to believe it. Often when he finishes his twelve-hour night shift at IBM in Essex Junction, Mongeon heads home for breakfast and a few hours of brush clearing on his 60-acre lot in Westford. In mid-January 2011, the fifty-five-year-old microprocessor assembler and labor activist hopped into his car and drove in the opposite direction, to Montpelier. There, at the state Capitol, Mongeon joined other supporters of single-payer health care at a press conference jointly convened by U.S. Senators Bernie Sanders and Patrick Leahy, Congressman Peter Welch, and Governor Peter Shumlin.

Vermont's four top officeholders noted that Congress, just the previous year, had enacted President Obama's Affordable Care Act (ACA). The ACA ended up being a mix of costly subsidies for private coverage, some insurance market reforms, Medicaid expansion, and a new requirement that citizens buy coverage if they don't already have it. According to Sanders, Leahy, Welch, and the newly elected Shumlin, this wasn't good enough for the Green Mountain State. They pledged to work together, with those assembled in the room, for something better. "We firmly believe we can be the state that passes the first single-payer system in the country," Shumlin declared.

Mongeon and other single-payer advocates have marched and lobbied for years, most recently under the banner of the Vermont Workers' Center (VWC) and its "Healthcare Is a Human Right" campaign.[4] Their tireless activism had a lot to do with spurring Vermont's singular display of political will to go beyond "Obamacare." Two weeks before the press conference, several hundred VWC supporters descended on the Vermont legislature on its opening day. State House and Senate leaders, including some recent converts to the single-payer cause, paid fealty to the grassroots movement to make health care a human right. Before a boisterous crowd of union members and community activists, seventy-one-year-old Peg Franzen, a VWC leader and disability rights advocate, hailed the "people power" that had persuaded legislators to commission a detailed study of options for universal health care in 2010.

By late January a year later, the Democrat-dominated legislature was mulling over a 203-page report from Dr. William Hsiao, the Harvard health care economist hired to develop a road map for more fundamental reform in Vermont. Hsiao's research proposed a system of universal coverage with equal access and a common benefit package that includes community-based preventive and primary care, as well as control on the escalation of health costs. But Hsiao identified no less than fifteen hurdles to achieving this objective.

Undaunted by the roadblocks ahead, Shumlin's special assistant for health care, Anya Rader Wallack, went before a joint legislative committee to unveil H. 202, "An act relating to a single-payer and unified health system." Wallack spelled out a three-stage reform process, spanning at least four years but beginning with the creation of a Vermont Health Reform Board to control costs and streamline payment methods. Wallack described Vermont's current system of multiple private and public payers as "too complex and misguided," noting that it leaves "more than a quarter of the state's population potentially facing health care bills that send them to bankruptcy." On behalf of the governor, she insisted "this craziness must stop. We have to get insurers out of managing medicine and allow providers to use technology and appropriate quality oversight to get waste out of the system."

The political moment for "Green Mountain Care" arrived just as the wind began blowing rightward elsewhere in the country, against implementation of President Obama's plan. GOP governors in red states filed lawsuits challenging the constitutionality of the ACA's individual insurance mandate. Health care reformers in Vermont aren't happy with that feature of President Obama's scheme, either. They want a social insurance system that will sever the connection between health care coverage and employment and eliminate the need for any of the state's 625,000 citizens to be shopping around for private insurance. Marketplace competition and insurance company profiteering—given a renewed lease on life nationally by ACA—would be phased out in Vermont as soon as possible. If single-payer works there, its backers envision the state becoming the Saskatchewan of America, just as Canada's thinly populated but left-led prairie province paved the way for Medicare-for-all north of our border fifty years ago.

Getting from here to there will not be easy. The Green Mountain State's single-payer initiative will be delayed unnecessarily by the ACA's own complicated implementation timeline. Under Obama's law, every state must have health insurance exchanges in order to get the tax credits and hundreds of millions in new federal dollars required to subsidize private benefits. Unless the ACA is amended, a move only belatedly supported by President Obama, any pilot projects headed in a single-payer direction will be delayed until 2017. Then, Vermont must get a federal waiver to eliminate its insurance exchange. In the now GOP-dominated U.S. House, Representative Welch introduced a bill authorizing Vermont to become "a laboratory for innovation and excellence" in three years, rather than six. But, as the *New York Times* reported in March 2011, Welch's bill had "no Republican co-sponsors, making its prospects for passage uncertain at best." Similar problems could arise in 2017 if the Democrats lose control of the White House, between now and then, and a new Republican president is even less sympathetic than Obama to state-level single-payer experimentation.

Single payer also faces corporate resistance, inside and outside the state. A taste of that was provided six years ago by non-union IBM, which held in-plant meetings for 6,000 workers, including Earl Mongeon, to warn them that an earlier single-payer bill, then pending before the legislature, would require $1 billion in new taxes and force employers to leave Vermont. Governor Shumlin is part owner of a family firm in Putney, Vermont, that made him a multimillionaire, so he has used his own private-sector background to neutralize some small business opposition. He has pitched single payer as a way to make Vermont more "business friendly" by curbing health care costs that have doubled in the past decade. Many of the entrepreneurs affiliated with Vermont Businesses for Social Responsibility do favor decoupling health insurance from employment, although not necessarily through the mechanism of single payer. The more mainstream and politically influential Associated Industries of Vermont rejects any plan requiring new taxes to expand public coverage.

Speaking at a conference of Vermont union members, Mark Dudzic of the Washington-based Labor Campaign for Single-Payer Health Care warned about a deluge of anti-single-payer propaganda during the 2011 legislative session and thereafter. "There will be a massive mobilization of corporate power to smash any state single-payer initiative," he predicted. "Vermont is going to be one of the first battlefields in that fight."[5] Some single-payer advocates worry that not enough is being done to educate and mobilize members, whose own negotiated benefits are currently at risk due to medical cost inflation. In Vermont, as in other states, there's growing taxpayer resentment over paying for public employee coverage that many private-sector workers don't have anymore, whether unionized or not.

At every Vermont-NEA bargaining table, school boards are seeking bigger premium contributions from teachers, part of a larger giveback trend that has triggered several strike threats. No group of union members has a bigger stake in building a viable tax-supported system of universal coverage than public employees. Nevertheless, as state worker Leslie Matthews reports, the Vermont State Employees Association (VSEA) has not been a leader in the single-payer fight because some officers and members are "apprehensive that health care reform could lead to erosion of hard-won benefits." In reality, Matthews argues, "it's the rising costs, increasing inequities and cost shifts in our current health care system that will ultimately bring us down. As union members, our access to affordable health care will only be secure when all working people have access to affordable health care."

Vermont Workers' Center director James Haslam cites greater support from the American Federation of Teachers (which also represents nurses in Vermont), the Communications Workers of America, and the AFL-CIO. All have increased their funding of the VWC's health care reform organizing. Other national groups, like the Universal Health Care Action Network, have created a "Help Vermont Win! Campaign Fund" to channel more resources into the fight. The Physicians for a National Health Program is helping out by send nursing and medical students to Vermont to join the lobbying effort. On May 1, 2011, the Jobs with

Justice–affiliated VWC plans to hold its biggest May Day "March on Montpelier" ever—to push the legislature to adopt the strongest possible version of House Bill 202.

The new governor's commitment to the cause is a case study in how Democrats could behave elsewhere, on health care and other issues, if their party faced more challenges from the left. Before his run for governor, Shumlin's only previous bid for statewide office was a failed campaign for lieutenant governor in 2002. His candidacy, as a Democrat, was undermined when 25 percent of the electorate backed Anthony Pollina, a Progressive Party member and longtime single-payer backer who now serves in the State Senate. In a crowded gubernatorial primary eight years later, Shumlin promoted single-payer health care as his main issue. He won that five-way contest by just 200 votes, even though the Vermont-NEA, VSEA, and state AFL-CIO did not endorse him.

In the 2010 general election, Shumlin faced Brian Dubie, who served as lieutenant governor under outgoing GOP governor Jim Douglas. Dubie is a personally affable moderate Republican who attracted some labor support based on his membership in the pilots association at American Airlines. His brother is a top National Guard commander in the state. Four weeks before Election Day, the race was still very close. That's when Vermont's big-foot independent socialist stepped into the ring. Rallying his own grassroots base, Bernie Sanders held a series of get-out-the-vote events for Shumlin that helped him gain ground among working-class Vermonters who might otherwise have drifted toward Dubie. Shumlin ended up winning by less than 2 percent of the vote.

At a *Nation* book-signing event in Boston a few months later, Shumlin's white-haired, sixty-nine-year-old helper was welcomed by local health care reformers. In his discussion with them, Sanders noted that single payer has become "absolutely mainstream" in Vermont because "we've been talking about the issue for thirty years." But he warned that further grassroots organizing was needed because "this is by no means a done deal." Back in Vermont, the Workers Center and allied groups are taking nothing for granted, either, as they gear up for a spring offensive in Montpelier to keep single payer from getting bogged down in the public policy equivalent of Vermont's fabled "mud season," which has never been kind to new models seeking traction, much less the fast track.[6]

32—OUT OF THE MARGINS, INTO THE FRAY

In 2012, millions of Americans found themselves caught, per usual, between a Republican rock and a Democratic hard place. Our two-party system serves up less than a wide range of ideological choices, even in a good year. The absence of viable third-party alternatives isn't just a longstanding national problem. In too many state and local elections, only major party candidates have the funding, organization, and media visibility to be competitive. As a result, minor parties have had relatively little electoral success since the heyday of the Socialist Party a century ago, when hundreds of its candidates won municipal office and a few even made it into state legislatures and Congress.

One state where left-leaning voters have more choice today—and their own political voice—is Vermont. Going into this year's election, the Vermont Progressive Party (VPP) boasted seven members in the legislature—two senators (out of thirty) and five representatives (out of 150) in the House, some of whom run with Democratic Party endorsement as well. Since Vermonters sent the first "Prog" to Montpelier in 1990, sixteen have served a total of forty-eight legislative terms in the state capitol. Progressives have introduced legislation, served on key committees, and played a catalytic role in public policy formation.

Despite the VPP's loss of Burlington City Hall, where Progressive mayors have been predominant for three decades, the party retains three city council seats (out of fourteen) in Vermont's largest municipality. Since 1981, more than twenty-nine Progressives have served on the council. One newly elected VPP member is Max Tracy, a twenty-five-year-old former student activist at the University of Vermont, who is now involved in organizing campus workers. Tracy won in the city's Old North End section by campaigning for living wage jobs, affordable housing, a sustainable transportation system and greater support for local farmers and gardeners.

In similar fashion, Progressives elected in nonpartisan races in smaller towns serve on local school committees, select boards, and community planning bodies. Plus, they turn out on Town Meeting Day to help pass resolutions in favor of issues like tax reform and overturning the Supreme Court's pro-corporate decision in Citizens United—both the subject of town meeting action in seventy Vermont communities in 2012. While never running as a VPP candidate himself, Vermont's independent U.S. senator, socialist Bernie Sanders, has backed other Progressive candidates for state and local office, while VPP activists have, in turn, ardently supported his statewide races.

Taking a leaf from Sanders's singular 30-year career—as Burlington mayor, then Vermont's lone congressman, and now junior senator—the VPP has distinguished itself from the Democratic Party by focusing, in populist fashion, on economic issues. In areas of the state where working-class voters might otherwise be swayed by cultural conservatism or residual rural Republicanism, the VPP has, like Sanders, won elections by campaigning for labor rights, fair taxes, and single-payer health care far more consistently than the Democrats. The party's statement of principles has a distinct Occupy Wall Street slant. "Democracy," it declares, "requires empowering people not only in government but also in the workplace, schools, and in the overall economy. Society's wealth should not be concentrated in the hands of a few, and a wealthy minority should not control the conditions under which we live."

One measure of the Progressives' local impact is passage of Act 48 in 2011, legislation that one hopes will lead to America's first single-payer plan. Prior health care campaigns failed either because Vermont had a Republican governor, like Jim Douglas, who opposed single payer, or a Democratic governor, like Dr. Howard Dean, who supported the concept when running for office but then turned against it on grounds of fiscal conservatism after getting elected. Despite these setbacks, Sanders and the VPP continued to make this a central political issue. As part of a strong grassroots movement, they kept the pressure on local Democrats at a time when liberal politicians in neighboring Massachusetts were opting for insurance market reforms that later became the model for President Obama's Affordable Care Act. With a Democratic-Progressive majority in both houses of the legislature in 2011, new governor Peter Shumlin followed through on his campaign pledge to introduce a state-level single-payer plan.

As longtime VPP supporter Ellen David-Friedman explains: "We have a homeopathic role in the Vermont body politic. We've managed to create enough of an electoral pole outside of the Democrats to constantly pull them to the left on policy issues, by dispensing an alternative brand of medicine that's become increasingly popular." In many other states, most labor activists like David-Friedman, a former teachers' union organizer, have shied away from third-party activity because they don't want to back political "spoilers" or, short of that, mount losing campaigns with no perceptible impact on major party behavior. Elsewhere in the Northeast, labor-financed Working Families Parties (WFP) were launched so "fusion voting" could be used, where permitted under state law, to reward the friends of union causes by giving cross-endorsed candidates an additional ballot line. Fusion was banned in most of the nation a century ago as part of the corporate counterattack against Populism. It allows major-party candidates in states like New York to garner additional votes on the ballot line of each cross-endorsing minor party.

In theory, if not always in practice, this system gives small parties on the left or right greater leverage because they can punish unresponsive mainstream candidates by withholding their support and running their own competing candidates. New York's union-dominated WFP has proved generally reluctant to do this, however. In 2010, WFP leaders even backed Andrew Cuomo for governor after he proclaimed he would seek public employee benefit cuts and curtailment of labor's clout in Albany. "Our strategy of both challenging and working with Democrats in a different way makes us somewhat unique," says Martha Abbott, a tax accountant from Underhill, who serves as chairperson of the VPP. "The difference between VPP and WFP is that the latter only supports Democrats. We run our own candidates and this makes us more effective at challenging them because they know we can, and have cost them elections."[7]

Abbott recounted how her party's "recent history of trying to negotiate policy commitments from Democrats in return for staying out of some statewide races" has panned out. In 2008, Anthony Pollina, a former Sanders aide and advocate for farmers, ran for governor after the Progressives failed to convince the Democrats to field a mutually agreeable candidate who could unseat incumbent Republican Jim Douglas. Pollina had pulled 25 percent of the votes in the 2002 race for lieutenant governor that left then state legislator Peter Shumlin in second place. In 2008, Pollina ended up with 22 percent, leaving another prominent Democratic state legislator, who proved to be a weak campaigner, in third place.

Douglas's decision to retire two years later gave the VPP another opportunity for making demands on the Democrats. According to Abbott,

"We announced that we would stay out of the governor's race in 2010 if the Democrats would fight hard to close Vermont Yankee's nuclear power plant, fight hard for a single-payer health care system, which they had dismissed as impossible, and not balance the state's broken unemployment benefits fund on the backs of the unemployed." As president of the state senate and then successful candidate for the Democratic gubernatorial nomination, Peter Shumlin did the most on all three fronts so that Abbott, as the VPP nominee, dropped out of the race. After Shumlin's election, he personally lobbied Democratic legislative leaders to put Progressive state rep Chris Pearson on the House health care committee. He also pushed to get Pollina, a newly elected Progressive state senator, added to its Senate counterpart to bolster senate support for his health care plan.

Abbott believes that the VPP's "constantly evolving strategy" and its willingness, when needed, "to be a thorn in the Democrats' side has kept them moving in a progressive direction on issues." The party's "brand is strong," she says, "and we are in no danger of disappearing or being co-opted."

VPP executive director Morgan Daybell argues that the party's more flexible and politically savvy approach has helped it overcome "the negative perception of third parties in general." In contrast, Vermont Greens and what's left of the state's Liberty Union Party—Bernie Sanders's original political home in the 1970s—have suffered the fate of left-wing parties elsewhere. Such formations tend to be ideologically pure, presentable but marginal at best, or just plain eccentric, with little to show, organizationally, for any single-digit share of the vote they garner.

To maintain its own "major party" status under Vermont law, the Progressives must field at least one statewide candidate every two years who garners 5 percent or more of the vote. Its campaign coffers are limited because the party lacks wealthy donors, like the Democrats and Republicans attract, and it rejects corporate contributions, few of which would be forthcoming to Progressives anyway. In Vermont House and Senate races, winning margins are more achievable on a limited budget. So the VPP has focused lately on recruiting and supporting viable contenders for legislative seats. With a population of just 626,000 people, Vermont has electoral constituencies small enough for people with progressive ideas to canvass door-to-door, meet nearly every voter, and drum up enough campaign contributions to be competitive even in the absence of any system of public financing of elections. Chris Pearson, who specializes in tax and budget issues for the VPP, represents one of the state's larger multiseat districts. In 2010, he had to raise only $12,000 for his reelection, campaign spending that wouldn't pay for your bumper stickers in a California or New York state assembly race.

Like Pollina, VPP senatorial hopefuls campaign with the "P/D" or "D/P" label, since no single "P" Prog has ever won a senate seat, even in Chittenden County, which includes Burlington.[8] (Under Vermont law, candidates can only collect votes on a single ballot line, but with multiple party endorsements listed after their name.) Sometimes Progressives have sought mutually beneficial local accommodations with Democrats in races where a strong general election showing by two left-of-center candidates would guarantee Republican victory. Several VPP legislators, including state Rep. Susan Hatch Davis, actually represent districts where their main competition comes from GOP nominees; local Democrats are, in effect, the "third party" there.

During a visit to Montpelier during the 2012 legislative session, I found VPP legislators like Davis and Pollina making their presence felt on many working-class issues. Since Pollina joined Sen. Tim Ashe (D/P) in that body, he has been promoting the idea of a state bank, a bill requiring Vermont to "hire and buy local" when contracting for state services and a budget-related survey of poverty and income inequality. Elsewhere in the same golden-domed building, Pearson was huddled with Reps. Mollie Burke and Sarah Edwards at the weekly meeting where VPP members of the House gather to share information and coordinate legislative strategy. Burke and Edwards are both from the Brattleboro area and much engaged with environmental and public health issues related to decommissioning the Vermont Yankee nuclear power plant in their corner of the state.

On the day of my mid-March visit, Vermont labor lobbyists were trying to overcome Democratic reluctance to grant collective bargaining rights to publicly funded "early childhood educators" who provide home day care. As part of the VPP's continuing bid to strengthen its labor ties, Progressive legislators have strongly supported the American Federation of Teachers child-care organizing campaign. The VPP also defended Vermont State Employees Association (VSEA) members against Shumlin's Cuomo-like public criticism of their contract rights and protections during a recent labor management dispute.

In White River Junction and other communities, Windsor County VPP chair Liz Blum and several elected local VPP officials have been working with the Vermont Workers Center and local Occupy activists to fight U.S. Postal Service contraction. Several hundred union jobs are at stake. And, as Blum explains, these "cuts would be devastating for elderly, rural and low-income Vermonters who depend on the reliability and affordability of the mail, and for whom the post office functions as a social link. It's often the place where people interact with neighbors, petition for ballot measures, and swap news, the kind of space that's made small-town Vermont so famously democratic." Such non-electoral activity on behalf of a key labor and community cause barely registers on the radar screen of Vermont Democrats.

Vermont State Labor Council secretary-treasurer Traven Leyshon, who also serves on the VPP's state coordinating committee, says, "Local labor leaders are now willing to support Progressive candidates over Democrats—when they're credible—because of such pro-labor stances." In some cases, he said, rank-and-filers have had to overrule the safer, more conservative candidate endorsements favored by their own union lobbyists and political directors.

This small insurgency from below, in Vermont's now public sector–oriented labor movement, mirrors the VPP's own trajectory in state politics. In a fashion that one hopes is not too exceptional, Progressives have moved from the margins to Montpelier, from also-ran status to an often influential role in state and local government. If there was more left partying like this going in other states, at least one of our two major parties might feel greater pressure to better represent its own badly treated working-class constituents.[9]

POSTSCRIPT

In November 2012 all Vermont Progressive Party incumbents who stood for reelection won (four House members and two senators). Their Progressive Caucus also grew to include new Vermont House member Cindy Weed, who defeated an incumbent Republican, and former state rep David Zuckerman, who became the third Progressive in the Senate.

Running as a D/P, Doug Hoffer was elected state auditor, the first VPP-backed statewide candidate to win. Cassandra Gekas, who similarly campaigned with both Democratic and Progressive Party backing, received 41 percent of the vote in a losing race for lieutenant governor. Governor Shumlin was elected again without any VPP endorsement but, for the second time, the party fielded no candidate against him to avoid splitting the pro-Act 48 vote and helping the GOP derail single payer.

While VPP candidates were doing well in state races, Bernie Sanders was reelected to the U.S. Senate with 71.2 percent of the vote. In a post-election interview with John Nichols in *The Nation*, Sanders attributed his latest electoral success to "building movements, making progress on progressive issues—you have to talk to people, educate people, organize people." Earlier in 2012, there was some concern about a national Republican effort to draft former governor Jim Douglas to enter the race, backed by right-wing millions, to eliminate Sanders from the Senate. After seriously weighing this new career move, Douglas decided to remain in political retirement. Says Sanders: "Why didn't they think they could come in and shout 'socialist' and 'radical' and take me out? I think they realized they can't roll over someone who has built real connections with people, not with 30-second ads but by holding town meetings, by using newsletters to talk about economic issues, by taking their side when the big fights come."[10]

33—POTHOLES IN THE SINGLE-PAYER ROAD

Imagine the perfect storm for real health care reform, at the state level. Prodded by a strong grassroots movement and a progressive third party—both of which took many years to build—the new Democratic governor and Democrat-dominated legislature of America's most left-leaning state votes to make every citizen eligible for publicly funded universal health care.

Under this new system, private medical insurance would no longer be needed by those who are self-employed, working for a small or large business, or lacking any job at all. Over time, something akin to the "Medicare-for-all" plans administered by each Canadian province would absorb many Vermonters whose health care is already tax-financed because they are old, young, disabled, poor, or working for various government entities. Widely varying or often unaffordable job-based medical coverage would become a relic of the past, just as in Canada.

Unfortunately, the transition from a costly, wasteful multipayer mix to the promised land of Vermont "single payer" can't occur overnight. Phasing out existing insurance arrangements and replacing them with "Green Mountain Care," is projected to take six years. One major speed bump is President Obama's Affordable Care Act (ACA), which requires the creation of state "insurance exchanges." This stage in ACA implementation nationally postpones, from 2014 to 2017, the final day of reckoning for private insurers and employer-controlled plans in any state—and there's only one so far—seeking more fundamental change.

Among Vermont's single-payer planners, on its new Green Mountain Care Board (GMCB), many technical issues have yet to be resolved. In early 2014, Vermont legislators must start deciding just how current health care spending by individuals and private employers will be channeled to Green Mountain Care via some form of equitable taxation on both. Disputes will inevitably arise over the level of coverage in the plan, which is supposed to be no less than the benefits now available through the premium-subsidized Catamount Health plan, created in 2006, to make insurance more affordable for Vermonters through their employer or as individuals. Just as Catamount Health funding has been much debated, how much the state spends on single-payer coverage will be hotly contested.

Rebuffed by legislators in 2011, the local business community, private insurers, and right-wing PACs have regrouped and counterattacked since Act 48 was passed. Vermont Health Care Freedom (VHCF), a key conduit for anti-single-payer propaganda, is among those predicting that Vermont will be running budget deficits in excess of $2 billion by 2018, if Green Mountain Care becomes a reality. Republican politicians are also warning about the new taxes everyone will be required to pay. They know that a lot can change, politically and state-budget-wise between now and 2017, particularly in a state with two-year gubernatorial terms. There's no guarantee that Governor Peter Shumlin will still be around to help single payer make it to the finish.

Fortunately, Shumlin's health care overhaul is still polling well, despite its lack of concrete benefits for a single Vermonter so far—a weakness that conservative opponents are exploiting in their ongoing campaign of dis-information and fear-mongering. A 2012 survey, conducted by several Vermont media outlets, found that nearly 48 percent of all respondents favor single payer; 35.7 percent are opposed; and the rest undecided.

To counter paid media assaults from the right, friends of Shumlin's administration, inside and outside the state, have decided to create a vehi-cle for advertising and door-to-door canvassing called "Vermont Leads: Single Payer Now!" Officially blessed by the governor, this new addition to the existing constellation of local health care reform groups plans to spend more than $100,000 on an initial six-month drive "to engage and activate Vermonters through media and grassroots organizing." Vermont Leads projects even greater spending, just on TV ads, when state legislators con-vene to consider Green Mountain Care financing issues.

Peter Sterling, a respected organizer for the Vermont Campaign for Health Care Security and a onetime campaign manager for Bernie Sanders, has been tapped to head the group. Vermont Leads has a hastily cobbled together board of directors, which includes several individuals long active in health care reform. It also has a single financial backer, the 1.9 million-member Service Employees International Union (SEIU). SEIU has been absent from Vermont since a failed effort to join forces with the still-inde-pendent Vermont State Employees Association, more than a decade ago. It currently represents not a single Vermont worker.

Conspicuously missing from the Vermont Leads game plan is the for-midable grassroots network created by the Vermont Workers' Center (VWC), which actually has been leading the single-payer fight since 2008. The VWC's much admired "Health Care Is a Human Right" campaign is widely credited, both locally and nationally, with spearheading the multiyear community-labor mobilization needed to get Act 48 passed. While working closely with the Democratic governor and key legislators to achieve that goal, the VWC-HCHRC has also been willing to sound the alarm and swarm the statehouse when things get off track. In May 2011, for example, Workers Center organizers brought more than 1,500 Vermonters to Montpelier to thwart a bid by legislative insiders to exclude undocumented workers from the scope of Act 48.

An affiliate of Jobs with Justice, VWC has long been supported by unions with members who live and work in Vermont. These backers include the United Electrical Workers (UE), Communications Workers of America (CWA), and the AFT-affiliated Vermont Federation of Nurses and Health Professionals, which bargains for most unionized health care workers in the state. Their rank-and-file activists and local leaders have been personally involved in much VWC organizing and lobbying activity and some serve on its steering committee. Instead of joining with other unions to help build the Workers Center, SEIU sent Matt McDonald, a top union staffer, to meet privately with the Shumlin administration and create a new group from scratch, with Sterling as its SEIU-funded director. VWC supporters speculate that Shumlin was quite willing to go along with the VWC's exclusion from this process, and may even have insisted on it.

For some, SEIU's sudden return to Vermont, with a wad of cash large by local standards, is cause for some rejoicing, not political suspicion or head scratching. In a message touting Vermont Leads to her friends, former state AFL-CIO president Jill Charboneau noted that she was "not used to working with people who have money!" Another enthusiast is Middlebury College professor Ellen Oxfeld, who has agreed to serve on the Vermont Leads board. SEIU funding is "a gift from heaven," she said. "We want to combat the lies, keep up the momentum for single payer, and organize around the [Act 48] financing package." Dr. Deb Richter, long active in Physicians for a National Health Program (PNHP) in Vermont, gave similar reasons for welcoming the out-of-state union to the fray.

"We've got six more years of fighting to do to keep this on track," Richter said. "We now have the ability to spend more for ad campaigns and literature drops. Instead of using existing groups, it made sense to have this one be a separate entity." As for SEIU, "they've always been single-payer supporters," she asserted. "That's what I've been told."

Nevertheless, others in Oxfeld and Richter's own political circles wonder if this particular gift horse might become a Trojan horse in Vermont's health care reform movement. Like many national unions, SEIU has always passed well-worded resolutions favoring "a single-payer system on both the national and state levels, modeled on an expanded and improved 'Medicare for All' system." (This language was adopted at its May 2012 national convention.) But, even more than other unions, and with far greater impact, SEIU's health care reform practice is quite different than its official rhetoric. From the Clinton to the Obama eras, the nation's largest health care union has too often settled short, pursued its own narrower political agenda, and left single-payer further away as a goal, not closer.

As Esther Kaplan reported in *The Nation*, SEIU undercut the single-payer movement in California, then one of the strongest in the country. In 2007, SEIU president Andy Stern, who has since retired, cooked up a plan with Governor Arnold Schwarzenegger that would have required all Californians to buy private insurance. The bill, reports Kaplan, "set no caps on rates and no floor for minimum coverage; tucked inside were perks for SEIU, such as money for a trust fund for home-care workers' health benefits, to be administered by the union."

According to Michael Lighty of the California Nurses Association (CNA), "SEIU played the leading advocacy role and ultimately the lead compromise role on that bill. Stern went behind the back of the California State Federation to cut the deal. But it didn't even pass in the state senate. It lost the backing of labor. It could not withstand the scrutiny." Even SEIU's largest California health care local, United Healthcare Workers (UHW), disavowed Stern's actions. And this act of defiance—by a local with 65,000 home-care workers—was followed by other forms of dissent over union policy. The rift with Stern deepened until the SEIU president imposed a disastrous trusteeship over UHW in 2009, which weakened and disrupted SEIU throughout the state.

Much closer to Vermont, SEIU affiliates in Massachusetts have done little or nothing to build Mass-Care, the main Bay State single-payer coalition. Instead, SEIU officials worked with Senator Ted Kennedy, then-governor Mitt Romney, and the foundation-funded Health Care for All group to enact the system of mandated private insurance coverage that became the model for Obama's plan. As one Mass-Care critic notes, "SEIU has been completely absorbed with 'Romneycare.' For them, it's all about hospital financing, never about changing the system itself."

In 2009–10, SEIU helped run interference for the Obama administration when it was trying to keep "single payer" off the table inside the Beltway, before a more limited "public option" was jettisoned too. Working with liberal foundations and other labor organizations, SEIU helped raise $40 million for Health Care for America Now (HCAN).

As David Moberg from *In These Times* reported, HCAN's spending swamped that of single-payer groups, while "promoting a strategy closer to Obama's proposal that would include employer- provided or individually purchased private insurance."[11]

In 2009, SEIU played political enforcer right next door to Vermont, when a series of community forums were held in New Hampshire to build public support for the president's plan. SEIU operatives tried to prevent PNHP members from distributing single-payer pamphlets at the meetings.

Matt McDonald's multiple SEIU roles in Vermont has also led some labor activists to question his union's motivation for becoming a single-payer sugar daddy, virtually overnight. McDonald is also heading up SEIU's bid to create a new statewide bargaining unit for 5,000 Medicaid-funded personal care attendants who assist the aged and disabled. To facilitate this organizing, Vermont must start treating its home health aides as employees rather than "independent contractors," a change already made by labor-friendly Democrats in Massachusetts, New York, California, and other states. The governor and/or state legislators must also create a mechanism for union recognition based on card signing or a representation vote so they can negotiate with the state.

In 2012, the Democratic-controlled legislature balked, for budgetary reasons, at creating a similar bargaining unit for child-care providers, despite intensive lobbying by the American Federation of Teachers, the state's largest AFL-CIO union. The likelihood of a similar setback in home care is even greater because the American Federation of State, County, and Municipal Employees (AFSCME), which represents 2,000 government workers in Vermont, already had a home-care worker organizing campaign under way when SEIU announced its own rival drive. Having the inside track with Shumlin would clearly be beneficial if costly inter-union conflict ensues. (Having SEIU vying for bargaining rights with AFSCME could also give the governor and legislators an additional reason not to help either, leaving the affected low-wage workers unorganized.)

"In my personal opinion, SEIU seems to be cultivating a direct relationship with our governor by loyally supporting his health care plan, including all the expected compromises and retreats that may lie ahead," says Traven Leyshon, secretary-treasurer of the Vermont AFL-CIO. "It's their way of buying political leverage so they can freeze ASFSCME out and become the collective bargaining agent for home-care workers in Vermont. This will create real problems for any of us pushing for a stronger, more progressively financed single-payer system than Shumlin favors."

Ellen David-Friedman, a founder of the Vermont Progressive Party (VPP) and past organizer for the UE, AFSCME, and NEA, agrees with that assessment. "SEIU makes very short term and opportunistic calculations," David-Friedman observed. "They will help Shumlin get reelected in exchange for legislation authorizing home-care unionization. My guess is that his position on single payer really doesn't matter much to them, since they've never really fought for it anywhere else."

"When conflict with employers over Act 48 implementation gets more intense, SEIU's past pattern of undermining real health care reform will simply reassert itself," David-Friedman predicted. "Their national money and newly developed local ties will be used to subvert our efforts."

Progressive state senator Anthony Pollina is not just concerned about SEIU "providing cover for the compromise—or demise—of reform." He worries that a pro-single-payer "air war," funded and directed by an out-of-state organization, may "encourage right-wing groups to come in and spend even more money" against Act 48 implementation. According to Pollina, "Things could escalate into a media campaign that leaves citizens on the sidelines, just like past single-payer referendum campaigns that were lost in Oregon or California."

The VWC is currently conducting a big fund-raising drive of its own, to support an energetic staff of eight who coordinate the work of scores of volunteers around the state. Many nationally known figures have signed on to a public statement of solidarity with its "Health Care Is a Human Right" campaign. Among those expressing confidence that "Vermont Can Lead the Way" are Bernie Sanders, Ben Cohen and Jerry Greenfield (better known as just Ben & Jerry), Cornel West, Chris Hedges, Dr. Paul Farmer, CWA president Larry Cohen, Donna Smith from National Nurses United, and many others. In an open letter seeking such support, VWC organizers acknowledge that they will "never be able to outspend giant health care profiteers and other big money groups in an 'air war.' But we can out-organize them on the ground!"

During 2009–10, when the AFL-CIO was scrambling unsuccessfully to get some sort of "public option" included in the ACA, Lighty of the

CNA predicted that if any state succeeded in creating a publicly funded Canadian-style plan, it would "move us closer to a single-payer solution" than labor's thwarted addition to Obama's plan.[12] Among health care reformers in Vermont, there is now justified concern that SEIU may someday play the same role locally that it did nationally during Obama's first term. If this prevents the single-payer movement from accomplishing more in Montpelier than it did in Washington, D.C., the political fallout will be harmful in many other states as well.[13]

POSTSCRIPT

Despite Governor Peter Shumlin's reelection in November 2012 by a far larger margin than two years earlier, he remained phobic about raising taxes on wealthy individuals or corporations. This "Republican-lite" stance did not bode well for future decisions about who pays what for Green Mountain Care (GMC). During the 2013 session of the legislature, the Vermont Workers Center hammered away at its familiar theme: "The costs of financing the [new] system should be shared equitably, which means that richer people—and more profitable companies—should pay proportionately more into the health care system than should poorer people." During a lobby day in Montpelier, VWC supporter Mari Cordes, a registered nurse and Burlington health care union leader, reminded legislators that Vermont is supposed to be transitioning "from treating health care like a business opportunity—as if disease was a commodity—to an actual health system designed to support the health of each person in our communities."

Nevertheless, the funding levels and financing mechanisms established by the Shumlin administration, its GMC planners, and the Democrat-controlled legislature may not be sufficient to keep out-of-pocket costs low for people transitioning from existing state-subsidized medical plans into Vermont's new ACA-mandated insurance exchange. Some of those affected could end up paying more for their medical care. Further down the road, there is a similar danger that the state's promised universal coverage will be inferior to or cost individuals more than some of the job-based plans it will supplant, when and if Vermont gets a federal waiver in 2017 to replace its exchange with a system closer to single payer.[14] According to one longtime Vermont labor activist, as of 2013, "everything about moving ahead on implementing Act 48 is still up in the air and subject to speculation, but anyone paying attention is concerned by Shumlin's behavior and statements thus far."

SEIU continued to fund Vermont Leads, its own health care reform group, rather than join forces with the other unions backing the VWC's Health Care Is a Human Right campaign. After the article above appeared, SEIU did make a onetime $20,000 contribution to the VWC as well. Overall, it spent $200,000, including $100,000 in ad buys and $50,000 in political campaign expenditures. (In 2013, AFSCME spent about $35,000 on Vermont candidates, parties, and legislative lobbying.) SEIU's investment in Vermont proved to be only partially successful.[15]

With encouragement from the VWC and others, SEIU and AFSCME lobbied together successfully for legislation that would allow 7,000 state-funded home-care providers to win union recognition. (A bill backed by the Shumlin administration to facilitate unionization of child-care providers was reintroduced in the legislature but died in the senate without being voted on.) The home-care bill was signed into law by the governor, setting the stage for a costly organizing conflict between the two unions. In late May 2013, AFSCME filed an election petition backed by the signatures of 4,500 home-care workers. At this stage, SEIU appeared to have less rank-and-file support but announced its readiness to "spend in the hundreds of thousands of dollars' range" on advertising, door-to-door canvassing, and direct mail.[16]

On July 31, outgunned on the ground by a union that has been operating in Vermont for sixty years, SEIU withdrew from the contest, "after hearing from many providers that the election was creating a divisive atmosphere and distracting from the important issues that need to be resolved."[17] AFSCME proceeded to win bargaining rights in September 2013. SEIU's future role, if any, in Vermont health care reform campaigning was not immediately clear. One Vermont labor official doubted that SEIU would "continue to spend money in the state since they have nothing to gain by staying."

EPILOGUE—DARE TO STRUGGLE, DARE TO WIN?

"The people must rise to the occasion for change to occur."
—THERRON KING, Kaiser Worker

Thanks to McCarthyism and the Cold War, the old U.S. labor tradition of marching and rallying on May Day lay dormant for many decades.[1] It was gradually revived in the new millennium as a day of mass protest on behalf of undocumented workers. On May 1, 2013, immigration reform of some type was finally under active consideration by Congress. So labor and community defenders of the foreign-born organized events around the country to demand equal rights at work and a clear path to citizenship for those laboring without papers. Outside the Ronald V. Dellums Building in downtown Oakland, a boisterous crowd of native-born Californians and their immigrant coworkers demonstrated in favor of workplace change of a more limited sort. But to them, and the rest of organized labor, it might someday prove to be no less important. Like rank-and-filers who battled company unions and the conservative American Federation of Labor in the 1930s, they showed up wearing red and yearning for a new form of unionism that was more militant, democratic, and member-driven.

It wasn't long before this unusually large worker presence, at a National Labor Relations Board (NLRB) vote count, began to rattle officials of the NLRB and the Service Employees International Union (SEIU), their incumbent union. More then 175 Kaiser service and technical employees had put their names on a list of election observers sent to the NLRB the week before by the National Union of Health care Workers (NUHW), a four-year-old rival of SEIU's 143,000-member United Health Care Workers-West (UHW). At their own expense, many of them skipped work on May 1 so they could be at the federal building when it opened. Some drove as a long as seven hours to get to Oakland. "By 8:00 a.m., nearly 300 NUHW supporters were in long lines that snaked through the building's lobby. As additional groups of NUHW supporters arrived from Fresno, Ventura County, Los Angeles and points south, the crowd erupted in cheers."[2]

The first workers to arrive had already made it through the metal-detector protected entrances and were assembled in the fifth-floor cafeteria. There, they waited their turn to watch, in groups of nineteen at a time, how ballots were going to be handled in the Labor Board's rerun of the biggest private sector union vote in seventy years. As reported by the *Sacramento Business Journal*, that's when "things got nasty and Homeland Security was called."[3] According to one Kaiser worker present, NLRB officials, accompanied by security guards, marched into the cafeteria and announced that "if we didn't shut up and get out, they would stop the count and impound the ballots."

Unwilling to risk further delay in ousting SEIU-UHW, its dissident members evacuated the building. They rejoined those similarly barred outside, for the rest of the day. Only forty pro-NUHW rank-and-filers were permitted to stay and observe the count of more than 32,000 votes that continued until the next afternoon. Unfortunately, the final tally was not what NUHW and its ally, the California Nurses Association (CNA), hoped it would be after organizing two of the biggest anti-concession strikes in the country (as recounted in Part 4 of this book) and after rallying Kaiser workers against $2.1 billion worth of future benefit cuts accepted by SEIU during a period when Kaiser posted profits of nearly $9 billion.[4] On May 2, NUHW support in Kaiser's largest bargaining unit increased by 15 percent over its showing in 2010, when the previous decertification election was held. But SEIU-UHW won again by a margin of 18,844 to 13,101, after criticizing strikes and emphasizing its embrace of labor-management cooperation. (Another 334 workers chose no union.)[5]

Over the years, I've witnessed many sad and deflating scenes among workers who have just been defeated in a union representation election. When the NLRB vote count turns in favor of a management, it's pretty common for the planned post-election victory celebration to become a "pity party" instead. When the trend in favor of SEIU became clear on May 2, the NUHW's scheduled gathering at the headquarters of the California Nurses Association (CNA) a few blocks away from the NLRB headed in a different direction. Some in the crowd danced and sang anyway. Then, several hundred NUHW activists and their nurse allies began an impromptu speak-out about how a militant minority of Kaiser workers, still trapped in a management-oriented union, could continue their struggle to replace it with something better. As posed by one worker, the question facing everyone in the room was "What are we going to do tomorrow?"

Roberto Alvarez, a seventeen-year Kaiser x-ray technician from Southern California, was among those pondering the future of NUHW-CNA activity. "We were hopeful this time would be different than last time," he said. "In Orange County, we tripled the support for NUHW, so it was a great leap forward for us there. My theory is that SEIU has promised Kaiser a lot of stuff, cuts that are coming down sooner or later, now that the election is out of the way. We know what the future is with SEIU, so what we have to do now is keep on fighting." George Wong, a pharmacy technician from San Francisco, and other NUHW supporters expressed similar resolve. Wong was removed as an elected rank-and-file leader of UHW when SEIU president Andy Stern imposed the disastrous 2009 trusteeship that spawned California's continuing health care union wars.[6] He's been working to replace SEIU at Kaiser ever since and encouraged his disappointed coworkers "to stay organized, support each other, and remain defiant."

"There's going to be another day," Wong assured them, "and the fight will continue—because it has to."

Partnering in the Magic Kingdom

While NUHW and CNA grappled with their election setback, Kaiser's predominant labor current—what C. Wright Mills would have called the "main drift"—was flowing south to Disneyland, that well-known parallel universe in Southern California. There, in Anaheim, hundreds of health care workers, their union representatives, labor relations managers, and Kaiser Labor-Management Partnership (LMP) leaders were scheduled to spend a long weekend conferring together in the Magic Kingdom Ballroom of the Disneyland Hotel, which is located in the latter's Fantasy Tower. The SEIU-dominated Coalition of Kaiser Permanente Unions (CKPU) includes twenty-eight local unions, from national affiliates of both the AFL-CIO and Change to Win. They represent nearly 100,000 employees, in nine states, serving 9 million Kaiser health plan members. Unfortunately, participation in the CKPU's coordinated bargaining is limited to unions willing to join Kaiser's Labor-Management Partnership (LMP). As explained on the CKPU's website, the LMP is a joint "strategy for high performance":

> We use the Value Compass, which puts the member at the center of every decision, to guide efforts to improve service, the quality of care and eliminate waste that drives up costs. These achievements are created by unit-based teams that include frontline managers, workers and physicians working together to ensure each patient has the best possible experience. This team environment also makes KP a great place to work.

If Kaiser workers—for example, the majority of its nurses in California—belong to a union that is critical of the partnership approach, they are not welcome in the CKPU. The same has been true for the thousands of workers who voted for NUHW instead of SEIU in decertification elections since 2009. "Under pressure from SEIU, the executive director of the CKPU sent a letter declaring that new unions had no place in the Coalition or in the partnership, threatening that if Kaiser workers voted for NUHW they would bargain alone."[7] Among the speakers present in Anaheim to celebrate "the future of unions and health care partnerships" was CKPU executive director John August, the author of that letter, and Bernard Tyson, the incoming chairman and CEO of Kaiser. The bearded, multimillionaire Tyson offered "his view of partnership and how it can become a strategic differentiator for Kaiser" as the hospital chain meets the "the demands of health care reform."[8]

Warming up the crowd for Tyson was Dave Regan, the SEIU executive vice president from Ohio who moved to California in 2009 to assume control over UHW when it was placed under trusteeship by SEIU. Regan also had his eye on the opportunities soon to be created by the Affordable Care Act (ACA). In pre-conference briefings of Kaiser union officials, he informed them that Kaiser plans to double its revenues in the next decade, and add 90,000 more employees to meet the increased demand for federally subsidized health care. If labor continues to play ball with management, most of the workers in those new jobs would end up "being in the Coalition of Kaiser Unions," Regan predicted. Left unsaid was what kind of additional contract concessions might be required as a quid pro quo for union membership growth.[9]

Now earning as much as some health care managers himself, about $300,000 a year, Regan has bonded not only with his counterparts at Kaiser but also its lobbying arm in Sacramento, the California Hospital Association (CHA). Among the industry causes that Regan has championed is blocking legislation that would require nonprofit hospitals to provide a minimum level of "charity care" to low-income patients who lack insurance. The California AFL-CIO, the Teamsters, Machinists, UFCW, and other major unions all favored this measure. But not SEIU-UHW, which represents many low-wage home-care workers who don't even qualify for the job-based insurance coverage negotiated by their own union and who might someday need subsidized hospital treatment.[10]

By 2012, CHA president Duane Dauner was publicly praising Regan's business-friendly approach, while condemning the more adversarial stance of NUHW and CNA. "They look at management and employers as the enemy," Dauner says. "They draw a line in the sand. Anything management does, they are against. It's just 'give us more and more.'" In contrast, he noted, SEIU leaders "are working with us and we are trying to work with them on health care policy and high-road labor relations."[11]

Complaints about the "High Road"

In 2013, NLRB election competition between NUHW-CNA and SEIU-UHW highlighted broader differences between unions happy to be on the "high road" and those questioning where it leads. The struggle by thousands of workers to oust SEIU put strategy questions facing many other union members in sharp relief. Should unions partner with employers or their associations on legislative and regulatory issues affecting their industry or develop an independent agenda better reflecting broader societal concerns? Can unions best protect past contract gains by acceding to wage and benefit cuts or resist management demands for contract concessions with strikes and other forms of workplace militancy? If unions embrace labor-management cooperation in return for promised membership growth, what becomes of their day-to-day role enforcing the contract and representing existing members who still have job problems and complaints? If reforming a union that's overly wedded to "partnership" becomes impossible, how can a "militant minority" of workers, who remain committed to a different vision of unionism, function most effectively to achieve their organizational goals, longer term and day-to-day? And, finally, can like-minded union foes of concession bargaining stick together themselves, on the job and in the community?

To see how these bigger picture questions were playing out among California health care workers in early 2013, I visited Kaiser's shiny new "campus" in Vacaville, south of Sacramento. It was one of 300 hospitals, clinics, or offices around the state where workers would soon be choosing between SEIU and NUHW-CNA. In a scene replicated at thirty of Kaiser's major medical centers around the state, both unions had information tables set up, just across from each other, in the hospital cafeteria. On the day of my visit, NUHW-CNA officers Sal Rosselli and John Borsos were making a lunchtime stop in Vacaville. So a steady stream of SEIU-represented service and technical unit workers, along with CNA nurses, were meeting or greeting them. Among them were nursing aides, phlebotomists, housekeepers, janitors, clerks, cashiers, respiratory therapists, and x-ray technicians.

Most NUHW-CNA supporters sported their signature red T-shirts. A smaller, less buoyant crowd of purple-clad SEIU activists manned the opposite table, which was filled with literature attacking the two visitors. (SEIU supporters declined to be interviewed and referred all questions to UHW communications director Steve Trossman, who later explained, via email, that his union only responds to queries from "legitimate journalists.") In flyers that appeared to be recycled from the last election,

SEIU-UHW proclaimed that Rosselli, Borsos, and other former UHW leaders had been "caught misusing millions of dues dollars." On the back of one leaflet, SEIU-UHW listed the $1.5 million in monetary damages sought from NUHW and sixteen of its organizers in a costly lawsuit filed by SEIU that was upheld by a federal court of appeals in early 2013.[12]

Other SEIU-UHW campaign material took aim at picketing of Kaiser and Sutter's Alta Bates Summit Medical Center, where "NUHW-CNA has gone on strike 12 TIMES and they still have no contracts and are losing benefits." This flyer also quoted CNA executive director RoseAnn DeMoro as saying at the 2012 Left Forum that "we're always out on strike."[13]

Another SEIU-UHW mass mailer asks Kaiser workers: "Would you rather spend your time fighting or winning?" It assures NLRB election voters that SEIU-UHW takes "a balanced approach, working in partnership with Kaiser management when possible and taking them on strongly when necessary." As a result, "we have bargained the best contract in the hospital industry without losing a day of pay on strike."

In the NUHW-CNA corner of the cafeteria at Kaiser Vacaville, a longtime medical records keeper named Jerry Corpus had a different view of that bargaining history. Corpus, who is now retired, comes from a big extended Kaiser family: his wife is an unhappy SEIU member, his sister a CNA-represented nurse, his mother, brother, son, nephews, and nieces are or have been on the Kaiser payroll. For more than a decade, during his own twenty-three-year hospital career, Corpus was active, as a steward and local bargaining committee member, in the pre-trusteeship UHW (then known, in Northern California, as SEIU Local 250). Why did he curtail a long-planned, post-retirement fishing trip to campaign for NUHW-CNA? "If we stay with SEIU, it will affect my whole family," he explained.

Best Contract in the Industry

According to Corpus, it was the pre-trusteeship UHW leaders, like Rosselli and Kaiser division director Ralph Cornejo, who helped members fight, for two decades, to achieve "the best contract in the hospital industry." Now, he believes, that agreement has been weakened by "so many takeaways" and lack of union enforcement, particularly in the area of job security. Kaiser's elimination of 1,000 jobs, with little regard for seniority, went largely uncontested by SEIU-UHW. [14] Even an AFSCME local in Southern California, which generally follows SEIU's lead at Kaiser, briefly announced a boycott of the LMP to protest these cuts. According to Corpus and others, job security at Kaiser is also being undermined through part-timing and contracting out. Thousands of workers who are entitled to full-time, benefited positions, are forced to work on a per diem or "on call" basis, without health insurance while SEIU makes no effort to enforce existing contract language on conversion of part-time jobs to full-time ones.

"If you're a strong union, you're for the employee, not the employer," Corpus said. "But it doesn't seem like that's happening anymore. The managers now are just walking all over people. When we were Local 250, management respected the union and the union kept us informed. We had steward councils and our local leaders never made a move unless employees first had a voice in the decision."

Corpus hardly fits the stereotype of a strike-happy union militant. He finished up at Kaiser working as a project manager in its Human Resources department. For many years, he was the lead LMP coordinator and trainer at Kaiser facilities in several counties north of San Francisco. He favored "interest-based problem solving" and helped create more than 125 "unit-based teams," one of the basic building blocks of the LMP. Now, Corpus, observes, if Kaiser workers have a job problem, they're constantly reminded by supervisors and their union that "we're in a partnership." In his view, "management and labor now use it as a weapon against us." In 2012, he notes, UHW couldn't even get Kaiser to keep paying for its own labor-management cooperation program. SEIU's 45,000 members now pay nine cents an hour—about $200 per year, if you're a full-timer—to support LMP activities previously financed by their employer. This $6 million annual deduction from wages comes on top of SEIU dues that are 25 percent higher than NUHW's.

While contract bargaining details were important to some workers, NUHW supporter Higinia Alvis was more concerned about individual union representation. Alvis is a patient care technician at Kaiser Vacaville who was fired by Sutter in 2010 at its Alta Bates Summit facility in Berkeley, after eight years of service. UHW filed a grievance on her behalf, arguing that she was wrongly dismissed in a dispute over taking her lunch break in an understaffed area of the hospital, where management pressured work-ers to skip their breaks. After several labor-management meetings on her grievance, Alvis heard nothing about the status of her case for more than a year. She repeatedly left voice-mail messages with her UHW rep seek-ing an update, only to be informed via voice-mail just last month that her grievance was not being taken to arbitration. A promised letter explaining the basis for this decision has yet to arrive. So when I interviewed her, Alvis was still trying to persuade the National Labor Relations Board that SEIU-UHW breached its legal duty of fair representation, a generally futile quest at the NLRB.

According to NUHW, more than 430 other unfair labor practice charges, alleging "failure to represent," were filed by other SEIU-UHW members in 2009–13. More than half came from frustrated workers at Kaiser where, NUHW claims, there are now more than 1,000 outstanding grievances, including 239 unresolved termination cases. In a conference call in February with Dave Regan, even SEIU-UHW stewards were complaining about Kaiser's high rate of unfair dismissals. "They are ter-minating more than they ever have," one steward reported. "They are really trying to get rid of people." According to another, "Kaiser is out to weed out anyone that they don't appreciate." On this invitation-only call, which was secretly recorded by a participant, Regan defended UHW's grievance filing record. He reminded his own concerned shop stewards that "representation is also about what's in your paycheck. Every one of our 45,000 members gets paid every couple of weeks by Kaiser and that's representation, too."[15]

Change vs. the Status Quo

The huge infusion of CNA resources after NUHW's affiliation in January 2013 enabled the anti-SEIU forces to field about 200 organizers, afford mass mailings and ads, and conduct a door-to-door canvass (an exercise repeated by SEIU, with its own labor-intensive house-visiting teams). During the 2010 decertification election, when CNA was officially neu-tral, twenty-seven-year Kaiser veteran Teresa Cosper recalled that she was "pretty much out there by myself" at the Vacaville Medical Center. In the rerun election campaign, "the nurses have added so much punch,"

Cosper said, echoing the appreciation of many pro-NUHW coworkers. "To have them with us, makes a tremendous difference." Organizers from both NUHW and CNA hammered away at the price UHW members elsewhere had already paid in contract concessions that Kaiser would soon be seeking from SEIU. "SEIU has eradicated defined benefit pensions in several of the biggest hospital systems in the country," former SEIU member Marilyn Albert explained to workers at Kaiser in Santa Clara. "It's just helping them achieve their goal of replacing hard-won retirement security with 401(k) plans."[16]

NUHW-CNA's anti-partnership stance was showcased in a costly ad blitz informing the public that these two Kaiser unions, in contrast to others, were "working together to make sure that Kaiser and other big hospitals don't put their wealth ahead of your health." The 30-second election-related TV and radio spots feature Kaiser RNs Catherine Kennedy and Monica Rizo, who discussed the NUHW-initiated state crackdown on the HMO for its managed care deficiencies. "NUHW-CNA members just forced Kaiser to use its record profits to hire more mental health clinicians to reduce long delays in care," the ads reported to a listening and viewing audience far wider than Kaiser workers, patients, and their families.

SEIU-UHW flooded Kaiser facilities with its own army of full-time staff, while SEIU locals in other parts of the country contributed what NUHW claimed was another 800 out-of-state helpers for its own home-visiting program. SEIU's "most successful argument among workers was 'you won't have a contract if you leave. You'll lose everything,'" one NUHW organizer acknowledged. Legally speaking, this isn't true.

Existing contract terms for Kaiser's service and technical workers would remain in effect while NUHW negotiated a successor agreement, just as it has been doing for several years in the five smaller bargaining units that switched from SEIU to its rival in 2010. But it was a threatening claim repeated by Dave Regan on KPFA radio on the eve of the election and, with greater impact, by SEIU organizers in every Kaiser workplace.

What lent credibility to SEIU's claim was the three-year bargaining experience of those 4,000 NUHW-represented employees. The first group to switch was illegally punished by Kaiser, when the hospital chain withheld scheduled raises until the NLRB sought a rare federal court injunction against this unfair labor practice and secured a settlement providing NUHW-represented workers with several million dollars in back pay. Kaiser negotiators then did their best to discredit NUHW by prolonging the negotiations thereafter. Just prior to the May 2013 vote, KP management made what SEIU quickly claimed was a "final offer" to 350 optical workers who had already switched to NUHW. Kaiser's settlement proposal featured inferior raises, health care premium sharing, no defined benefit pension coverage for new hires, and other takeaways, on top of those already accepted by SEIU for its own Kaiser members in 2012. In response, three-quarters of the workers involved signed a petition publicly rejecting these concessions and reaffirming their support for their elected NUHW negotiators. "SEIU-UHW isn't interested in helping us," said Sonia Askew, an optician in South Sacramento. "They're just trying to use us as a publicity stunt in the election."

Bad Faith Bargaining?

In 2005–6, similar bad faith bargaining by Kaiser in first contract negotiations with another non-partnership union, the Communications Workers of America, led to CWA's decertification, by a narrow margin, in a newly organized unit of California call-center workers. In those frustrating talks, Kaiser wouldn't agree to the same contract conditions enjoyed by SEIU members in other nearby centers. By no coincidence, management's similar stonewalling of NUHW created an opening for SEIU to stir up decertification activity among a minority of workers in the optical unit and one other represented by NUHW. In June 2013 Askew and other optical workers beat back the SEIU and management-inspired decertification attempt in their own unit, by a vote of 214 to 103, and returned to the bargaining table.

Yet, in the view of NUHW critics like SEIU-UHW communications director Steve Trossman, the bottom line hadn't changed: "They still don't have a contract. Those workers have lost 9 percent in raises that SEIU got that they would have had if they stayed with SEIU."[17] In late July 2013 Kaiser notified optical workers that it was imposing its "last, best, and final offer" increasing co-pays, eliminating defined benefit pensions and retiree health coverage for new hires, weakening job security language, and making other unilateral changes. NUHW filed NLRB charges alleging that Kaiser's declaration of "impasse" was premature and bad faith bargaining.[18]

In the service and technical unit three months earlier, NUHW-CNA organizers believed that they had made sufficient progress overcoming worker concerns about reopening contract negotiations with Kaiser under a different union banner. A systematic assessment of likely voters was conducted by NUHW-CNA organizers and workplace committee members prior to the start of mail balloting. The results showed that about 19,000 workers favored decertification of SEIU, a finding seemingly confirmed during their GOTV drive. This proved to be an overly optimistic estimate—much to the dismay and bafflement of the experienced organizers involved.

NUHW backers' deep estrangement from SEIU was clearly not shared by enough of their coworkers, who average about $55,000 a year in full-time earnings. A majority again opted for the security of the status quo rather than the perceived risk of changing unions. The health care cost shifting and pension plan changes that NUHW-CNA warned were coming at Kaiser had not yet arrived for active employees represented by SEIU. As of the May 2013 rerun election, the cap on retiree health coverage (accepted by SEIU) had not kicked in yet and those affected were not part of the electorate. Longer service workers upset about the elimination of a lump sum pension option—negotiated away by SEIU, with no membership vote, in 2009—were small in number.[19]

Switching unions, on the other hand, would have affected everyone in the service and technical unit. It would have meant beginning negotiations on a successor agreement right away, with a lot more education, agitation, and workplace organizing than SEIU has encouraged since the 2009 UHW trusteeship. NUHW's call to arms was countered in some workplaces by signs displayed by SEIU supporters, that declared: "NUHW—No Time for That!" This message was not just a way of spurning the overtures of vote-seeking NUHW organizers. It was, for some workers, a telling personal statement of what kind of union they wanted—one that would leave them alone and not demand more membership engagement, commitment, and risk taking. "There was no way NUHW or CNA could convince us to give up our great wages, health coverage, pension and job security, especially since NUHW has been unable to bargain a contract at

Kaiser for more than three years," said Cleto Delizo, a Kaiser worker from Sacramento who favored SEIU.

CNA financial backing for NUHW in 2013 totaled $5 million, on top of the $2 million in loans made to the new union when it was founded in 2009. SEIU's Regan publicly acknowledged that his union spent $4 million to $5 million to retain bargaining rights and claimed that CNA actually devoted $8 million to the failed decertification drive. In several pre- and post-election interviews, Regan deplored the mounting cost of inter-union competition at Kaiser "at a time when unionization is down to 7 percent in the private sector" and "unions are on the verge of oblivion."[20] According to Regan, it was "time for people like the leaders of NUHW and CNA, who call themselves 'progressives,' to focus on organizing non-union workers instead of attacking people who already are in a union and have the best contract in the country."

Hatfields vs. the McCoys?

From one end of the country to another, concerned friends of labor and fellow union activists also bemoaned the big do-over at Kaiser. Before and after the vote, some echoed Regan directly. In a February 2013 exchange in *The Nation*, a group of union experts pondered the latest dip in membership levels and labor's mounting political woes. According to Cornell University researcher Kate Bronfenbrenner, "The worst news this winter is not about numbers, or bad legislation, but rather that some of our most effective union organizers are going to be fighting over already organized workers."[21]

From Washington, D.C., political columnist Harold Meyerson warned *American Prospect* readers that this "hugely expensive jurisdictional battle for the already unionized employees of Kaiser and other California hospitals … will probably drain the unions' treasuries at a time when precious little organizing of unorganized workers is going on anywhere in the country. Indeed, it's conceivable that more resources will go to this union-vs-union battle in 2013 than will go to any other organizing campaign in the nation—and just possibly, given the atrophied state of organizing, to *all* other organizing campaigns in the nation." In Meyerson's view, the conflict was an inter-union "blood feud that puts the Hatfields and McCoys to shame."[22] UC Berkeley professor Harley Shaiken similarly opined that, with more than 93 percent of the private sector not organized, "having these kind of resources poured into decertifying a union within the labor movement, it's hard to see what the positive outcome of it could be."[23] Another local observer, labor attorney Jay Youngdahl, wrote that it was "obscene" to spend health care workers' dues money in this fashion. "The Kaiser workers have spoken—twice. It is time for this fighting to stop."[24] Other experienced observers, like UC Santa Barbara labor history professor Nelson Lichtenstein and former SEIU executive board member Wade Rathke, also weighed in with their own calls for a negotiated peace.

At least Lichtenstein, a critic of the UHW trusteeship and past NUHW supporter, recalled that it was SEIU's own crackdown on internal dissidents that started the fight. "The original effort of SEIU to take over UHW-West, this will be SEIU's Iraq," he told a reporter. "The whole thing was a blunder on the part of the SEIU." Since this big mistake, almost 20,000 health care workers and public employees have defected to NUHW or smaller independent unions in California and Nevada. The once fast-growing SEIU-UHW registered a net loss of 3,000 members in the four years after it was trusteed. And, nationally, SEIU expanded by only 7,000 workers in the entire country in 2011, down from an annual growth rate averaging 100,000 in 2006–8. In 2012, SEIU's membership actually dropped by 43,000—the first such loss in many decades.[25]

"It's always been in SEIU's court to extend their hand to NUHW and resolve this," Lichtenstein observed. "I do think that it will be wise on the part of the SEIU to extend an olive branch to the leadership and the activists of NUHW and end this thing, this internecine warfare." Now serving as editor of *Social Policy* magazine, Rathke urged AFL-CIO president Richard Trumka to intervene. According to Rathke, Camp David–style peace talks should be held leading to new organizing "ground rules and real understandings about turf and targets." SEIU's Mary Kay Henry and CNA's DeMoro should both be pressured "to make a deal and make it stick." NUHW was not mentioned as a participant in such deal making.

"Conflict has to be replaced by competition," Rathke argued, "and the competition has to be to organize the more than 95 percent of all health care workers in the United States who don't have any union protection or advocacy. . . . Sure, NUHW will get bigger and might go from 10,000 members today to 100,000 in the future, but the nurses and SEIU stand to get exponentially larger not only in California, but everywhere, if we can finally get unions to focus on the future opportunities and not the past problems."[26]

Been There, Done That

All of these well-intentioned sermons or conflict resolution scenarios suffered from a certain historical amnesia, not to mention, in the case of Meyerson, near total obliviousness to rank-and-file discontent within SEIU.[27] They also seemed to assume that U.S. union capacity to organize the unorganized, with whatever funding available, is unaffected by recent outcomes at the bargaining table. In reality, if unions don't find ways to achieve better results—by working together in contract negotiations and, where necessary, striking—their recruitment of new members will continue to lag. Many unorganized workers will see little incentive for joining an organization that's taking backward steps, like giving up pension or health benefits, when they can save money on union dues and just let their employer make such changes unilaterally. The only membership growth that will be achieved in the private sector will increasingly be the result of union weakness, not strength. "Bargaining to organize" will become synonymous with undercutting another union or trading away past contract gains and worker protections in return for any management-assisted membership boost, no matter how small.[28]

A truce between SEIU and CNA, which settled differences arising from their previous multiyear conflict, was reached in March 2009. It lasted nearly four years until it became the casualty of its own contradictions.[29] Widely acclaimed at the time, this "no raid" pact helped reduce inter-union strife in California and nationwide, while facilitating non-union hospital organizing in Texas, Florida, and other states. The quid pro quo for détente was, of course, that CNA discontinue its funding of NUHW—which took the form of $2 million in loans or grants extended during the first few months after the UHW trusteeship. None of those labor observers urging that SEIU and CNA reconcile again seem to have noticed that the 2009–12 peace pact eventually had a big downside for California nurses and their hospital coworkers.

SEIU originally extended the olive branch to CNA after Andy Stern put his third-largest affiliate under trusteeship. When SEIU removed Rosselli and other critics of Stern from their elected positions in UHW, RoseAnn DeMoro presciently warned that this "dictatorial receivership" posed a direct threat to "the workplace protections and contract standards of CNA/NNOC members."[30] To meet this challenge, CNA became NUHW's main financial backer, until that role was assumed by UNITE HERE after Stern launched a brazen attack on his fellow Change to Win affiliate later in 2009. In the period immediately following the trusteeship, there were talks between CNA and NUHW about a formal affiliation but no deal was struck (of the sort announced nearly four years later, in January 2013). The 85,000-member CNA reportedly wanted too much control of the fledgling NUHW. Its leaders believed that they could, without a closer CNA connection, liberate large numbers of UHW members from trusteeship more easily than proved to be the case because of the many obstacles that NUHW later encountered in the NLRB decertification election process.[31]

So instead of staying the course with the more like-minded NUHW, CNA veered off in a different direction. After years of costly organizational conflict and mutual denunciations, DeMoro and Stern suddenly announced that "we are burying the hatchet." On March 18, 2009, the two former union rivals unveiled what they called a "transformative cooperation agreement." It was, they claimed, going to boost labor's uphill campaign for the Employee Free Choice Act and aid state-level lobbying for "single-payer health care systems." (SEIU and CNA never ended up working together on either of these projects.) Both parties agreed not to recruit each other's members and CNA promised not to support NUHW anymore, although individual nurses continued to do so at the worksite level.

Rank-and-file supporters of NUHW felt betrayed by CNA's abrupt about-face. Yet, in an interview with *Labor Notes* several months later, CNA copresident Deborah Burger blithely defended the move. She predicted, with less than complete accuracy, that "Andy [Stern] and Sal [Rosselli] will do what they need to survive" and "work out their own deal." In the meantime, "other unions will help NUHW. And we'll all move forward together." Like other top officials of CNA, she argued that her union's truce with SEIU was justified because it was such a great boon for CNA's national ambitions.

According to Burger, SEIU had ceded to CNA "exclusive jurisdiction on all nursing issues in nursing practice," a claim that didn't really correspond to reality since SEIU retained almost all of its existing RN members (a few of whom were traded to CNA). In addition, the AFT, AFSCME, and other affiliated or independent unions continued to represent several hundred thousand nurses nationwide, making CNA's "jurisdiction" anything but "exclusive." Burger also touted the truce on the grounds that CNA would no longer be undercut by SEIU on political issues that affect RNs. Recalling past SEIU efforts to "water down the [California nurse-patient] ratio bill, by putting forward ratios for all health care workers," Burger confidently declared that, in the future, "we won't have anybody undermining . . . our ratios bill."

CNA's truce with SEIU did produce substantial out-of-state membership gains for its National Nurses Organizing Committee (NNOC). But, as California nurses later discovered, it did not end the threat of being undermined by SEIU in both contract negotiations and legislative matters. In 2010–11, CNA-NNOC won the right to represent nearly 6,500 nurses at Hospital Corporation of America (HCA), the world's largest for-profit hospital chain. They were organized at facilities in Florida, Texas, Nevada, and Missouri under the terms of a negotiated neutrality agreement. At Tenet Healthcare, both CNA and SEIU were recognized pursuant to a similar organizing rights deal that brought another 1,500 RNs into NNOC in Texas. As a result of this coordinated multistate effort, SEIU won bargaining rights, in parallel campaigns, for more than 15,000 HCA and Tenet workers. During the same period, CNA also expanded its out-of-state influence by creating National Nurses United (NNU), a network of state nurses' organizations with a total membership of 185,000 and an important focus on RN issues like staffing ratios.

Organizing alongside SEIU in the same hospitals proved easier for CNA-NNOC than coordinating first contract bargaining with HCA. There was little or no joint membership mobilization activity and not even much information sharing between different union bargaining committees dealing with the same employer. SEIU was eager to begin collecting dues, even though its new open shop hospital units had a generally low level of signed-up members. So United Healthcare Workers-East, still better known as 1199/SEIU, the New York City–based SEIU affiliate in charge of the negotiations in Florida, settled months ahead of CNA-NNOC at ten newly organized HCA facilities there. The 1199 SEIU contract left in place much despised "wage caps" that had resulted in some HCA workers going without pay increases for as much as a decade.

According to one NNOC organizer involved, "SEIU had no workplace organization and, as is its practice, clearly had a precooked agreement with the corporation to settle for a substandard contract." SEIU's deal included a "me-too" clause ensuring that, if the nurses negotiated a better health care cost-sharing formula, the same terms would also be extended to SEIU, even though the latter had already settled for less. New members of the NNOC at HCA in Florida finally ratified their first contract in May 2012, after an active contract campaign that enabled them to resist some objectionable contract terms accepted by SEIU, including wage caps. NNOC members took strike votes, conducted whistle-blowing press conferences, and held informational picketing about staffing levels and the quality of patient care. As a result, the nurses also won percentage increases that exceeded SEIU-negotiated raises for lower-paid HCA service workers by about 6.5 percent. Unfortunately, an overly broad "no strike clause" agreed to by SEIU first, and then NNOC as well, limits protest picketing during the life of the contract.

Undercut in California

As described earlier in this book, the lack of solidarity between SEIU and CNA, on the latter's home turf, was demonstrated most starkly when 17,000 nurses took part in the anti-concession strikes at Kaiser in 2011 and 2012. After SEIU-UHW urged its members to cross picket lines set up by CNA and NUHW (who were joined in 2012 by Local 39 of the Operating Engineers), Dave Regan added insult to injury by trying to roll back CNA's most cherished political victory in the Golden State. Working in concert with the California Hospital Association, the SEIU-UHW leader encouraged California legislators and labor federation officials to embrace an industry-backed amendment to the state's safe staffing law, which sets minimum nurse-patient ratios in hospitals. The measure would have suspended, during RN meals and breaks, the nation's first and only ratios law. A much-prized model for yet-to-be-enacted legislation sought by NNU in other states would have been badly weakened.

In an internal message to CNA staffers, DeMoro responded in language reminiscent of her denunciations of SEIU prior to 2009. She called Regan a "management hack" who "may be the most despicable 'labor leader' that we have ever encountered" because "he has climbed so far into bed with the hospital association and employers." According to DeMoro, Regan wanted nurses "to sacrifice their meals and breaks and the safety of their patients to help hospitals save $400 million because the state was in a budget crisis." Meanwhile, as CNA noted, California hospitals were collectively posting $4.4 billion in profits in 2010 alone. Regan's ploy was rejected by the California AFL-CIO and even criticized by a Service Employees local union in southern California that also represents nurses. But that didn't end CNA's problems with Regan's conservative brand of labor-management coalition building.

In San Francisco, SEIU-UHW tried to curry favor with Sutter Health by backing a controversial $2 billion expansion scheme that included curtailing acute care services at St. Luke's Hospital, which serves lower-income people in the city's heavily Latino Mission district. A labor and community alliance, which included CNA and NUHW, put enough pressure on key city officials to force Sutter to modify its plans. CNA activist and Sutter nurse Eileen Prendiville credited this grassroots campaign with "changing the face of health care for San Francisco's future. St Luke's will not only remain open, it will offer more health care services to residents in the community."[32]

SEIU-UHW's conservative business union approach has become another obstacle to overcome in Sutter bargaining. At St. Luke's, SEIU-UHW agreed to pension and health care givebacks but secured a "me-too" clause so that, if other Sutter unions (that is, CNA or NHUW) successfully resisted givebacks, SEIU-UHW members would get the benefit of their better deal instead. After much workplace and community struggle NUHW-CNA did win their own non-concessionary contracts at Sutter's California Pacific Medical Center. So service and technical workers at St. Luke's—like those who had switched from SEIU to NUHW at CPMC—ceased making the hefty health insurance premium contributions required since 2012 due to their UHW-negotiated contract changes.[33]

Elsewhere in the same health care chain, SEIU's bargaining surrenders "emboldened Sutter's already hard line that has provoked a long contract dispute with RNs," according to the CNA. In May 2013, just after the NUHW-CNA election defeat at Kaiser, the CNA was forced to conduct a seven-day strike by thousands of nurses at five Sutter facilities in the East Bay, including Alta Bates Summit Medical Center in Berkeley. Pay, benefits, and patient safety were all at issue in this latest walkout. Citing "changes brought about by the Affordable Care Act," Sutter sought to curtail its insurance coverage of part-timers so nurses who work less than thirty hours per week would not receive company-paid benefits. "We can't think of another industry that gives part time employees full time benefits," a spokesperson for Alta Bates Summit told the *San Francisco Business Times*. The hospital reported it was also seeking RN pay scale changes "to bring them in line with rivals like Kaiser Permanente."[34]

Finding a More Reliable Partner

Faced with this multifront management assault, too often enabled by SEIU's own prior concessions to the same employer, the CNA looked, in late 2012, for ways to build on its Kaiser strike unity with NUHW. A bid by NUHW to win financial backing from the International Association of Machinists (IAM) was, by then, faltering, although the IAM did provide funds that helped lay the groundwork for the second decertification attempt in SEIU's service and technical unit at Kaiser. With NUHW-IAM affiliation talks no longer leading anywhere, CNA and NUHW resumed their effort to create a more reliable and organic "united front against Kaiser and other employers in our upcoming bargaining." In August of 2012 the two formed an "Alliance of Kaiser Unions" dedicated to "raising standards for Kaiser caregivers and protecting Kaiser patients." In its founding statement, the Alliance blasted SEIU and the CKPU for choosing "to partner with Kaiser to increase the corporation's profitability at the expense of their own members and patients."

Six months later, CNA and NUHW took their formal collaboration a step further, unveiling NUHW's formal affiliation with CNA at a press conference in Oakland attended by activists from both unions. "The two unions will remain separate," Rosselli announced, "but we will act like one union when it comes to organizing hospital workers and fighting employers like Kaiser and Sutter Health." There and at other hospital chains, NUHW-CNA hoped to coordinate their resistance to management demands for health care cost shifting, elimination of defined benefit pensions, and various forms of outsourcing. Those plans were, of course, dealt a major blow by the May 2013 election defeat at Kaiser. NUHW-CNA flyers put the best possible face on those results, noting that "together with the 13,000 workers that voted for NUHW in this election, we are 36,000 strong: the majority of Kaiser workers opposes SEIU's cuts and supports NUHW-CNA." But translating that upbeat addition into "a force that will be felt throughout the health care industry and across the nation" would obviously have been easier if NUHW-CNA had supplanted SEIU in the service and technical worker unit at Kaiser. "The people must rise to the occasion for change to occur, and maybe in this case, they must be impacted a little more to acquire that courage," concluded Therron King, a Kaiser worker from Southern California, who posted his post-election assessment on the "NUHW Solidarity" Facebook page.[35] In the 2010 Kaiser election, King was a supporter of SEIU.

CNA executive director DeMoro praised the role that rank-and-file nurses played in the decertification campaign and described it as a "boot camp" for their own 2014 contract struggle. "Nurses gained far greater unity among themselves to fight Kaiser than any bargaining prep would offer," RoseAnn DeMoro said. "We have always needed worker solidarity to defeat the corporate agenda." Sal Rosselli struck a similar hopeful note: "That unity is not going away. It will persist in our workplaces, in the friendships we've made, and in the continued affiliation between NUHW and CNA. It will fuel our continued struggle to stop the cuts that Kaiser is trying to force down our throats with the shameful complicity of SEIU-UHW."

Yet, post-election, some CNA activists expressed private concerns that Kaiser would now feel freer to intensify its "offensive against nurses" in the run-up to their 2014 negotiations. Already, one CNA official reported, RNs face daily hassles over Kaiser's unilaterally imposed and punitive attendance policy, plus increased workloads due to understaffing. In an interview with *Labor Notes*, Deborah Burger, a Kaiser nurse, noted that patient care assistants are "taking on more and more of a workload" as well, but when they're out sick they're not replaced either. "You have a patient waiting in the hallway and you can't get the patient in because the housekeeper hasn't cleaned the room," she reported, "and that's because we are short-staffed."

In a post-election mailing to CNA members, SEIU-UHW tried to stir up discontent among RNs about how much of their dues money was spent trying to unite workers in these different Kaiser job classifications. For their part, CNA leaders displayed little initial enthusiasm for continued funding of NUHW at levels anywhere near their campaign spending from January to May 2013. As a result, NUHW was forced to lay off many of the new staff members hired to assist the attempted ouster of SEIU. NUHW remained affiliated with CNA and resumed its struggle for non-concessionary first contracts covering the Kaiser workers who have decertified SEIU. Among the options under consideration was building for a third statewide strike by NUHW-CNA members and supporters. Such a walk-out might be tied into the nurses' 2013–14 Kaiser contract campaign. One objective would be to involve more of the 13,000 pro-NUHW service and technical workers than the 1,000 or so who dared to become sympathy strikers in 2011 and 2012, despite being actively discouraged and, in some cases, threatened by their own union.

The Labor Strategy Debate

Among U.S. union members, the prevalent strategy for changing the direction of a union or resisting concessions has been to replace the existing leadership and make the union structure more responsive to the rank and file. As reported earlier in this book, workers of all kinds have organized, with varying degrees of success, to elect shop stewards, union convention delegates, bargaining committee members, and national or local leaders willing to wage a more effective fight.[36] After four years of open rebellion against SEIU-UHW, few NUHW supporters at Kaiser believed there was much they could achieve by pursuing reform of this sort within the post-trusteeship structure of their local union. Dissenters on the SEIU-UHW executive board face removal for their NUHW sympathies; a Kaiser worker who ran against Dave Regan for the UHW presidency in 2011 has been suspended from membership for "aiding a rival labor organization."[37] Members must still sign a "loyalty oath" as a prerequisite for even representing their coworkers as stewards. Efforts to remove incompetent and unresponsive SEIU-UHW stewards are routinely thwarted by full-time staffers. Ousting incumbent officials elected on a statewide basis, in a staff-dominated local of more than 140,000, will not be easy in 2014, even if many of the 13,000 dues payers who voted against SEIU, at Kaiser alone, try to "Dump Dave" in that election. [38]

In 2008, thousands of the most active and committed trade unionists in SEIU-UHW rallied behind efforts to reform SEIU at the national level. That effort led to SEIU's retaliatory ouster of all their elected statewide officers and board members, a purge that was followed by the removal or resignation of hundreds of shop stewards and, at Kaiser, some of the union's most experienced "contract specialists." Many of the key union activists sidelined by SEIU's 2009 coup later helped sustain NUHW's shop floor support in hospitals and nursing homes around the state, adding to its base of support at Kaiser in the second big decertification vote there. In some Kaiser medical centers, NUHW has majority support and could easily decertify SEIU if that was legally possible at individual hospitals, as it has been for the 10,000 workers in other Kaiser units and more than a dozen facilities operated by other health care employers.

If the United States were a country like France, Kaiser workers dissatisfied with SEIU would simply quit that organization and make their voluntary dues payments to NUHW instead. In many countries, national labor law does not grant any union exclusive bargaining rights, which means that multiple unions or labor federations can compete for members and play a representational role in the same enterprise or workplace. But Kaiser is not an open shop and this is not how the post–Wagner Act system of labor relations works in this country, for better or worse. Everyone represented by a Kaiser union in California is required to pay dues or, if they become non-members, pay an equivalent amount in agency fees instead. The thousands of workers at Kaiser and other hospitals who want to leave SEIU are forced to remain captive members or fee payers. Their own dues money continues to be used against them, an egregious insult that began when UHW was seized by SEIU in 2009, after more than a year of prior disruption and subversion by the national union.[39]

At a post-election strategy meeting in mid-May 2013, more than 150 Northern California NUHW committee members gathered again at CNA headquarters in Oakland to figure out what to do about this. They came at their own expense, on a Saturday morning of Mother's Day weekend, from Kaiser hospitals in Fresno, Modesto, Roseville, Sacramento, Stockton, San Jose, Santa Clara, Antioch, Hayward, Vallejo, Redwood City, and South San Francisco. The purpose of the gathering was to begin charting a course that might combine elements of past rank-and-file struggles with the "dual union" approach Kaiser workers have already sustained, most impressively, through two decertification campaigns of unusual scale and difficulty. The participants were predominantly female, with African Americans and Latinas heavily represented, along with working-class whites.

"Those who voted for NUHW are still there and are still committed," reported one speaker from Santa Clara, who sought guidance about next steps for her hospital-level committee. Now that there was no immediate prospect of escape from SEIU, a Fremont worker wanted to know "how do we keep everyone together? How do we continue to give our coworkers hope?" A respiratory therapist for seventeen years at Kaiser said of her NUHW campaign role that she had "never been so inspired" by her involvement in anything but needed advice now on "how do you force them [SEIU] to follow the contract?" Another NUHW activist argued that, even after the election defeat, "we can still have a movement about pensions, working conditions, and the dignity and integrity of our work."

As one worker expressed the consensus of the group: "We can be a 'shadow union,' if we stay united." NUHW organizer Ralph Cornejo agreed. "There are lots of different things we can do as 'the union in exile,'" he said, citing the "NUHW Solidarity" Facebook page as one invaluable tool for keeping real union spirit alive, sharing ideas and information, and encouraging ongoing rank-and-file activity at Kaiser.

As the discussion unfolded, one dilemma facing NUHW stalwarts was how to relate to coworkers who had, for a second time, voted differently. "When someone comes to you and says about SEIU, 'I made a big mistake,' don't smash on them," one former UHW steward suggested helpfully. A dynamo for NUHW at Kaiser-San Jose, now known among her coworkers as the "Red Lady" because of her 24/7 union color wearing, reported that she "gets constant calls from coworkers." She planned to continue her practice of answering all contract-related questions, even from "folks still lost in their purple haze." But now, she said, as part of the process of educating her coworkers about their rights and developing the leadership ability of others, she was going to "encourage them to do more things for themselves."[40]

As one participant summed up her unofficial shop floor leadership role, amid widespread union dysfunction at Kaiser Hayward, "We don't get representation. And we need it. The workers need stewards and they need to know who they are, they need to recognize them, they need to trust them. Now we can't find a steward. It's heartbreaking. But I do my best. It's why I get here early, every day I walk the floors. I make connections at lunch time, at five o'clock I walk the floors again."[41] Another NUHW volunteer was even more succinct about the post-election terrain in her hospital: "It's just us and Kaiser—we work in a non-union shop."

But, with NUHW backers still alive and kicking, Kaiser is no de facto "union-free environment" of the ordinary sort. In Fresno, members of an informal workplace grouping known as the "Five O'Clock Gang"— because of its regular meeting time in the hospital cafeteria—announced plans to keep planting the red flag of NUHW at the same time and location. "Create your own 'Five O'Clock Gang,'" one Fresno worker counseled. "Be brave and lead by example." After driving all the way to Oakland from Manteca in the San Joaquin Valley, a rank-and-file leader there insightfully contrasted NUHW's union culture with SEIU's. "They don't have brothers and sisters," she observed. "They have 'me, myself, and I,' everybody out for themselves. We have familyhood and that's the one thing we will always have that they do not." She expressed optimism that "we can convince our coworkers, SEIU members, that they can have power this way too" but predicted, accurately, "there's going to have to be a grassroots movement process we go through."

Militant Minority Unionism?

This brainstorming among Kaiser rank-and-filers occurred not long after the AFL-CIO itself professed high-level interest in assisting "any worker or group of workers who wants to organize and build power in the workplace." At a University of Illinois conference in March 2013 on "New Models of Worker Representation," AFL-CIO president Rich Trumka declared that our "system of workplace representation is failing to meet the needs of America's workers." When workers don't have an effective voice on the job, wage levels drop, there's less retirement security, and other past labor gains are jeopardized. To remedy this situation, Trumka touted "new models for organizing workers" that don't necessarily involve traditional collective bargaining relationships.[42] In preparation for the federation's convention in Los Angeles in September 2013, where such ideas were to be discussed further, Trumka created a committee of labor historians to advise the federation about "new and forgotten methods of organizing."[43] Meanwhile, local central labor councils were encouraged to hold "listening sessions" as part of a "6-month effort to come up with more viable union models."[44]

The "Alt-labor" experiments now being embraced by the AFL-CIO reflect a broader conception of labor organization long championed by the left.[45] Critics of "contract unionism," like Stanley Aronowitz and others, have argued that union membership and functioning should not be defined by statute or confined to formal collective bargaining units. Losing a Labor Board election, lacking enough support to get one, or not having a union contract does not prevent any group of workers from thinking and acting like a union. With or without formal union backing, they can maintain workplace committees and engage in legally protected concerted activity "that improves wages, benefits, and/or working conditions. . . . Minority unions are workplace-based organizations that have not been officially recognized by employers or certified as collective bargaining representatives."[46] At least one well-known law professor, Charles Morris, has argued that the NLRB should sanction union efforts to engage employers in "members-only bargaining," in situations where workers lack the majority support necessary for legal certification.[47]

This approach is a good blueprint for ongoing NUHW functioning, on a wide scale, within the service and technical unit at Kaiser where exclusive bargaining rights have twice been contested, most recently with 40 percent of the voters choosing an alternative union. Of course, in the minds of top AFL-CIO officials, and probably most of their academic helpers, the concept of "minority unionism" is only properly applied in non-union workplaces. The proponents of "new ideas" for organized labor are not likely to endorse it as an organizing model for workers opposed to a labor-management cooperation scheme blessed by the AFL-CIO.[48] And that's true even if "minority union" activity might actually help defend defined benefit pensions, job security protections, affordable health insurance, and other past contract gains now threatened at Kaiser.

Instead, as NUHW organizer Marilyn Albert notes, academics observing the Kaiser conflict from afar have described it "as just two unions fighting over already organized workers." Their assumption is that "thousands of those workers had no agency in this struggle," she says, "but were just being batted around by leaders of SEIU-UHW and NUHW-CNA. In reality, rank-and-file members would not have fought so hard and for so long if they did not think they were defending their very jobs, working conditions, salaries, and hard-won benefits."[49]

The notion that a "militant minority" of workers can still shape events, while swimming against the prevailing tide of their era, is not a new one. Nor is the concept historically limited to the circumstances contemplated by the AFL-CIO today. It was an idea that greatly animated *The Fall of the House of Labor* by David Montgomery who is now deceased and, sadly, not among those academics being consulted by the AFL-CIO today. Like the politically inspired "salts" we met earlier in this book, Montgomery was a college-educated radical who became a blue-collar worker in the 1950s. As an active member of the heavily red-baited United Electrical Workers (UE), he was fired and blacklisted, an experience that eventually altered his career plans. Left-wing labor's loss became academia's gain when Montgomery transitioned, in the early 1960s, from being a machinist to one of the nation's leading labor historians. As one colleague noted after he died in 2011, "Montgomery took his readers into the workplace . . . which he saw as central to shaping workers' consciousness and political struggles. The key to working-class organization and advance lay in the militant minority, in the shop stewards, radicals, ethnic leaders, and itinerant organizers. . . . Clear-eyed about labor's defeats as well as its victories, Montgomery had a firm faith in the power and ingenuity of working people in fighting for better lives and a better society."[50]

In the early 1930s, right after the postwar era of defeat and retreat chronicled in *The Fall of the House of Labor*, U.S. labor was able to revive in rather dramatic fashion. As Staughton Lynd, another radical historian, has documented, rank-and-file struggles, relying heavily on direct action, "were organized from below, by committees of ordinary workers who teamed up with others in their shops . . . and in the community where they all lived." Then and now, the labor officialdom too often discourages worker initiatives that threaten to disrupt the stability of old or new collective bargaining relationships. So, Lynd has argued, "small, informal groups of active and retired workers, and their supporters" should seek to create and sustain forms of "parallel unionism" rooted in the workplace struggles that union contract holders are reluctant to wage, particularly in settings, like Kaiser, where the ideology of "partnership" is so highly developed and unabashedly articulated.[51]

The "parallel union" path at Kaiser is largely uncharted beyond the familiar routines of workplace committee building and representation election campaigning. Hopefully, those with the institutional resources necessary to sustain the next phase of California health care worker struggle will help rank-and-file activists find their way. (Although the CNA spent millions on its new affiliate, NUHW, prior to the second decertification vote in the Kaiser service and technical unit in May 2013, its organizing subsidies dried up immediately thereafter, reflecting CNA shortsightedness for sure.)

In the end, workers who are bravely resisting the Kaiser-SEIU partnership may have to "make the road by walking," just like the worker center members in New York City who organize under that name.[52] But like Make the Road and other community-based workers' centers, the durable NUHW network in Kaiser hospitals is not going to be heavily staffed or financed by any social change foundations. The latter are more enamored with "Alt-labor" initiatives like the "Fight for Fifteen" campaign among fast food workers. That much-applauded effort is, of course, funded primarily by SEIU, a union with perhaps one million members making less than $15 an hour and, at Kaiser, a record of opposing, rather than promoting, strike activity.

The Kaiser union rebels will gain wider solidarity and support only when more advocates of "organizing the unorganized" belatedly realize that the fate of their own troubled project is inextricably tied to the precarious state of workplace organization, contract protection, and rank-and-file morale among the already organized. The goal of "saving our unions" is best pursued in ecumenical fashion, from the bottom up, with no false dichotomy between "external" and "internal" organizing. Activists trying to expand the labor movement by building "alternative institutions" should not neglect or, worse yet, reject the struggles of union members forced to create alternatives to their existing unions. Wherever the traditional route of union reform is blocked and workers remain trapped in labor-management relationships that deprive them of any meaningful, independent voice, the militant minority will soldier on. Its usual friends and allies will continue to lend a hand because they know that the magic kingdom of labor-management partnering is no laboratory for creating a more democratic, inclusive, and social justice–oriented labor movement. It's far more likely that elements of such a movement will emerge from worker resistance to company unionism, where the first glimmers of something better are already visible and inspiring at Kaiser.

NOTES

1. Union security clauses typically obligate all workers represented by a union to pay for the cost of representation by having union dues either deducted from their paychecks or an equivalent amount deducted in "agency fees" if they choose not to join. The strongest form of union security requires everyone in the bargaining unit to become a union member. In September 2013, a county judge struck down Indiana's right-to-work law but the state supreme court was expected to uphold its constitutionality. See Tim Evans, "Indiana attorney general appeals ruling that 'right-to-work' is unconstitutional," *IndyStar,* Sept. 12, 2013.

2. As quoted by Monica Davey, "Michigan Labor Fight Cleaves a Union Bulwark," *New York Time Times,* December 10, 2012. For a follow-up report on how Michigan unions are responding to their new open-shop environment, see Jane Slaughter, "Coping with Michigan Right-to-Work Law," *Labor Notes,* May 2013, 4–5. Before the effective date of the new law, many unions rushed to lock-in dues deduction for one contract term but the quid pro quo, reports Slaughter, was "long, concessionary contracts."

3. Steven Greenhouse, "Productivity Climbs but Wages Stagnate," *New York Times,* January 13, 2013.

4. For a lengthier appreciation and defense of Occupy's resonant political rhetoric, see Michael Yates, " 'We Are the 99%': The Political Arithmetic of Revolt," *New Labor Forum* (Winter 2013): 10–13.

5. Nelson Lichtenstein, "Class Unconciousness: Stop Using 'Middle Class' to Depict the Labor Movement,"*New Labor Forum* (Spring 2012): 11–13. For the most persuasive book-length statement of this argument, see Michael Zweig, *The Working-Class Majority: America's Best Kept Secret* (Ithaca, NY: Cornell University Press, 2000).

6. For the best collective assessment of all aspects of the struggle in Wisconsin, see Michael D. Yates, ed., *Wisconsin Uprising: Labor Fights Back* (New York: Monthly Review Press, 2010). In our contribution to the book, titled "Back to the Future:

Union Survival Strategies in Open Shop America," Rand Wilson and I suggest ways that private and public sector unions in the Midwest may need to change in order to maintain membership in their now besieged bargaining units.

7.   In *The Future of Our Schools: Teachers Unions and Social Justice* (Chicago: Haymarket Books, 2012), education professor and former teacher union activist Lois Weiner describes why and how "building social movement teachers unions" is so necessary at a time when "hostile politicians blame teachers for an astounding list of social and economic problems."

8   In May 2013, CORE-backed Karen Lewis was elected to another 3-year term as president of the CTU with 80 percent of the vote, a strong membership endorsement of her strike leadership the previous year. See Valerie Strauss, "Fiery Chicago Teachers Union President Reelected," *Washington Post,* May 18, 2013.

9.   For more detailed accounts of the CTU struggle, see Lee Sustar, *Striking Back in Chicago: How Teachers Took on City Hall and Pushed Back Corporate Education 'Reform'"* (Chicago: Haymarket Books, 2013); and Micah Uetricht, *Strike for America: Chicago Teachers against Austerity* (New York: Verso/Jacobin Books, 2013). Also, multiple contributors to *Monthly Review* analyzed the Chicago contract fight and related public education trends in the journal's informative special June 2013 edition, "Public School Teachers Fight Back," edited by Michael Yates.

10.   Worker centers are labor advocacy groups that provide organizing help and legal representation to workers who lack union bargaining rights. Their short-term goal is to win workplace improvements or stronger protective labor legislation. Some work closely with unions and receive funding from them, such as the $2.5 million that SEIU gave New York Communities for Change in 2011. Others are more reliant on foundation funding. Union ties to worker centers have come under right-wing Republican scrutiny. See Kevin Bogardus, "Big Business Planning Attaack on Low Wage Worker Organizing," *Popular Resistance,* September 21, 2013.

11.   Josh Eidelson, "Walmart Workers Plan Wednesday Scheduling Showdowns in a Hundred Stores," *The Nation.com/blogs,* April 23, 2013. In early June 2013, just prior to Walmart's annual shareholders meeting in Bentonville, Arkansas, some workers tried to mount a longer work stoppage in several states where OUR Walmart has been strong. See Eidelson, "Walmart Workers Launch First-Ever 'Prolonged Strikes,'" *The Nation.com/blogs,* May 28, 2013. Another series of "Black Friday" protests, including walkouts, was being planned for November 29, 2013, as this book went to press.

12.   Walmart eventually responded to this series of short-duration protest strikes by firing or suspending sixty to seventy members of OUR Walmart, including workers who left their jobs to attend the company's 2013 annual meeting. Jenny Brown, "Retaliation Is Illegal, but Walmart Doesn't Care," *Labor Notes* (September 2013), 14–15. As Brown reports, "some fast-food workers have also been fired for organizing."

13.   Change to Win is the coalition of unions—now numbering only three--that broke away from the AFL-CIO in 2005, with the original intention of creating a rival national labor federation. For more on its formation and subsequent problems, see Part 6 of this book.

14.   See Josh Eidelson, "Surprise Fast Food Strike Planned in St. Louis," *Salon,* May 8, 2013; and "Fast Food Strikes to Expand Massively," *Salon,* August 14, 2013.

For a more sober view of the difficulty of building durable, self-sustaining workers organizations in these sectors, see Arun Gupta, "The Walmart Working Class," forthcoming in *Socialist Register 2014: Registering Class,* ed. Leo Panitch, Greg Albo, and Vivek Chibber (New York: Monthly Review Press, 2014).

15.   Micah Uetricht raises good questions about where the "Fight for Fifteen" is headed in "Fast Food Strike Tactics Debated," *Working In These Times,* August 30, 2013, and "Is Fight for 15 for Real?" *Working In These Times,* Sept.19, 2013.

16.   Steve Early, *The Civil Wars in U.S. Labor: Birth of a New Workers Movement or Death Throes of the Old?* (Chicago: Haymarket Books, 2011).

17.   One exception to this trend is the great work of Chris Hayes, host of the MSNBC show *All In,* who notes that "labor issues are getting more coverage than they've ever gotten before on cable news, first and foremost thanks to Ed Schultz, and then assisted by others of us who've taken up that mantle." Hayes is also encouraged that "there has been a new crop of excellent young journalists writing about labor" and "a lot of really good reporting in the progressive press on workers." See his interview with Amy Dean, "Putting Workers on TV: MSNBC's Chris Hayes on Bringing Labor to Prime Time," *Yes!,* August 16, 2013.

18.   See Michael D. Yates, *Why Unions Matter,* 2nd ed. (New York: Monthly Review Press, 2009).

PART I: REBELS WITH A CAUSE

1.   Rick Fantasia, *Cultures of Solidarity: Consciousness, Action, and Contemporary American Workers* (Berkeley: University of California Press, 1988), 7.

2.   In public employee and service sector unions, however, some observers have noted an encouraging new wave of reform campaign victories. See Mark Brenner, "Reformers Resurgent: A Survey of Recent Rank-and-File Uprisings," *New Labor Forum* (Spring 2013): 79–84. According to Brenner, dozens of reform groups like the Caucus of Rank-and-File Educators in Chicago "have sprouted up across the country in the last five years—to challenge unresponsive leaders, resist concessions, build ties with the community, and promote internal democracy and member control."

3.   Joseph McCartin, "Democracy on the Shopfloor," *New Labor Forum* (Winter 2013): 104–6. For an excellent rebuttal to McCartin, see Brian Walsh, "Battling Business-as-Usual Unionism: Worker Insurgencies and Labor Revitalization," *Dollars & Sense,* May–June 2013. Walsh argues that "union insurgencies—against not only the employers, but often against the workers' own union leadership—are both a key part of the labor movement's history and crucial to its future revitalization." *Labor Notes* director Mark Brenner cites successful reform struggles in large local unions like the 36,000-member New York State Nurses Association (NYSNA), now headed by longtime *Labor Notes* supporter Judy Sheridan-Gonzalez, a working nurse at Montefiore Hospital in the Bronx.

4.   For an excellent history of the AUD's exemplary work, see Herman Benson, *Rebels, Reformers, and Racketeers: How Insurgents Transformed the Labor Movement,* (New York: Association for Union Democracy, 2008).

5.   See Tom Geoghegan, *Which Side Are You On? Trying to Be for Labor When It's Flat on Its Back* (New York: Farrar, Straus & Giroux, 1991); Paul Clark, *The Miners' Fight for Democracy: Arnold Miller and the Reform of the United Mine Workers* (Ithaca,

NY: Cornell ILR Press, 1981); and Paul J. Nyden, "Rank-and-File Movements in the United Mine Workers of America, Early 1960s–Early 1980s," in *Rebel Rank and File: Labor Militancy and Revolt from Below*, ed. Aaron Brenner, Robert Brenner, and Cal Winslow (New York: Verso, 2009), 173–98.

6.   Nyden, "Rank-and-File Movements," 179.

7.   For more on the UMW's 1974 agreement with the BCOA and other MFD accomplishments, see Joseph A. Yablonski, "Jock Yablonski's 1969 Campaign for the UMW Presidency: His Son Looks Back 40 Years after His Assassination," in *Labor and Working Class History Association Newsletter* (Spring 2010): 16–19, available at http://www.lawcha.org/wordpress/newsletters/spring10.pdf.

8.   Ibid., 19. The author bitterly notes "that the name 'Yablonski' does not appear in the historical offerings on the UMW website and rarely, if ever, appears in *The UMW Journal* despite the "ultimate sacrifice [Jock Yablonski] made for UMW members."

9.   For more on the formation and early years of TDU, see Dan LaBotz, *Rank and File Rebellion: Teamsters for a Democratic Union* (New York: Verso, 1990); and Samuel Friedman, *Teamster Rank and File: Power, Bureaucracy, and Rebellion at Work and in a Union* (New York: Columbia University Press, 1982). A more recent assessment by LaBotz of TDU's organizational development and political influences can be found in "The Tumultuous Teamsters of the 1970s" in *Rebel Rank-and-File: Labor Militancy and Revolt from Below*, ed. Aaron Brenner, Robert Brenner, and Cal Winslow (New York: Verso, 2009), 199–226.

10.   Ken Crowe, *Collision: How the Rank and File Took Back the Teamsters* (New York: Charles Scribner's, 1983).

11.   "When Union Outsiders Win" combines material first published in *The Nation*, December 29, 2008 under the title "A Teamster Apart: Ron Carey Remembered," (coauthored with Rand Wilson) and an article entitled "Sometimes A Great Notion: Local Union Reformers Run for National Union Office," which originally appeared in *Social Policy*, February 2012,

12.   Quotes that follow are from these two books: Jean Alonso, *The Patriots: An Inside Look at Life in a Defense Plant* (Charleston, S.C.: Leap Year Press, 2011); and Dana Cloud, *We Are the Union: Democratic Unionism and Dissent at Boeing* (Chicago: University of Illinois Press, 2011).

13.   This chapter was originally published in *WorkingUSA*, June 2012. For subscription information, see http://onlinelibrary.wiley.com/journal/10.1111/(ISSN)1743-4580.

14.   Jefferson Cowie, *Capital Moves: RCA's Seventy-Year Quest for Cheap Labor* (Ithaca, NY: Cornell ILR Press, 1999).

15.   Jefferson Cowie, *Stayin' Alive: The 1970s and the Last Days of the Working Class* (New York: New Press, 2010).

16.   Originally published in *New Labor Forum*, Fall 2011.

17.   UPS road driver Tim Hill was later chosen to represent members of Local 690 on the negotiating committee for the Washington State Rider of the Teamsters' national contract with United Parcel Service. For his account of how 240,000 UPS Teamsters fared in 2013 bargaining, see Tim Hill, "UPS Largest Private Sector Contract, Profitable Employer, Flat Beer," *Labor Notes*, May 20, 2013. Many UPS workers shared Hill's lack of enthusiasm for either the master contract or regional attachments to it. Although the national agreement was narrowly approved by a 53 to 47 percent margin, a TDU-backed "Vote No" movement forced a renegotiation of 18

local supplements and contract riders covering more than 60 percent of all UPS Teamsters. For more on this rebuff to the Hoffa-Hall leadership of the union, see David Levin, "'Vote No' Movement Sends UPS Bargainers Back to Table," *Labor Notes,* June 27, 2013.

18.   *"Viva* Las Vegas" combines two of my Teamster convention reports originally published as "Viva Las Vegas? Teamsters Gather in Sin City for Old School Convention," *Working In These Times,* June 28, 2011; and "Insurgent Sandy Pope Nominated for Teamster Presidency," *Working In These Times,* July 11, 2011.

19.   Steve Downs, *Hell on Wheels: The Success and Failure of Reform in Transport Workers Union Local 100* (Detroit: Solidarity, 2008). Available at http:// www.solidarity-us.org/hellonwheels.

20.   Originally published in *Working In These Times,* December 9, 2009.

21.   Gregg Shotwell, *Autoworkers under the Gun: A Shop-Floor View of the End of the American Dream* (Chicago: Haymarket Books, 2011).

22.   For more on Jerry Tucker's singular career, see Peter Downs, "Organizer and Workers' Advocate," *Against the Current* (May–June 2012): 40–44.

23.   This chapter was originally published in *Labor Studies Journal,* September 2012, 47. For an informative account of more recent UAW membership recruitment in the South, see Roger Bybee, "UAW Battles for Human Rights in Organizing Drive at Mississippi Nissan Plant," *Working In These Times,* February 6, 2013.

PART II: STRIKING BACK OR STRIKING OUT

1.   As Boston labor lawyer Robert Schwartz notes, "workers, both union and non-union, who take part in a short-term strike have the same legal protection as workers who engage in open-ended strikes." See Schwartz, "One Day Strikes," *Labor Notes,* (September, 2013), 12–13.

2.   Stephen Lerner, as quoted in David Moberg, "Thank You, Strike Again: Low-Wage Service Workers Are Changing the Face of Labor," *In These Times,* August 2013, 30–31.

3.   For useful advice on dealing with this new lockout trend and many other strike-related matters, see Robert Schwartz, *No Contract, No Peace: A Legal Guide to Contract Campaigns, Strikes, Picketing, and Lockouts* (Boston: Work Rights Press, 2013). This is an updated version of an invaluable guide originally published in 2006.

4.   For the story of how the Lawrence struggle got its name, see Robert J. S. Ross, "Bread and Roses: Women Workers and the Struggle for Dignity and Respect," *WorkingUSA,* March 2013, 59–68.

5.   Originally published in the *Boston Globe,* January 11, 2012.

6.   Originally published in *The Industrial Worker,* March 2011.

7.   Joseph McCartin, *Collision Course: Ronald Reagan, the Air Traffic Controllers, and the Strike that Changed America* (New York: Oxford University Press, 2011).

8.   Kim Voss and Irene Bloemraad, *Rallying for Immigrant Rights: The Fight for Inclusion in 21st Century America* (Berkeley: University of California Press, 2011), 6–8.

9.   Joe Burns, *Reviving the Strike: How Working People Can Regain Power and Transform America* (New York: IG Publishing, 2011).

10.   David Bacon, *Illegal People: How Globalization Creates Migration and Criminalizes Immigrants* (Boston: Beacon Press, 2008).

11.   Randal Archibold, "Immigrants Take to U.S. Streets in Show of Strength," *New York Times*, May 2, 2006.

12.   Originally published in *Monthly Review*, March 2012.

13.   David Carr, "New Orleans Paper Said to Make Deep Cuts and May Cut Back Publication," *New York Times*, May 23, 2012.

14.   Chris Rhomberg *The Broken Table: The Detroit Newspaper Strike and the State of American Labor* (New York: Russell Sage, 2012).

15.   Originally published in *Dissent*, August 13, 2012.

16.   Seumas Milne, *The Enemy Within: The Secret War against the Miners*, 3rd ed. (London: Verso, 2004).

17.   Ralph Miliband, *Parliamentary Socialism*, 2nd ed. (London: Merlin Press, 2009).

18.   Andy McSmith, "Ralph Miliband: The Father of a New Generation," *The Independent*, September 7, 2010.

19.   Becky Johnson, "Miliband to Attend Durham Miners' Gala," *Sky News*, July 12, 2012.

20.   Martin Wainwright, "Ed Miliband to Speak at Durham Miners' Gala," *The Guardian*, July 13, 2012.

21.   Originally published in *Red Pepper*, July 2012.

22.   This disenchantment with Miliband's leadership extended beyond the ranks of labor in the Labour Party. See Steven Erlanger and Stephen Castle, "Labour Party Finding Fault with Its Leader," *New York Times*, Sept. 20, 2013, A4, A8.

23.   As quoted by Mark Tallentire, "Unite Chief McCluckey Tells Durham Miners' Gala: I'm Ready for Reform," *Northern Echo*, July 13, 2013.

24.   As quoted by Joe Daunt, "Durham Miners Gala: Thousands March as Unions Rally for Labour Party Change," *Sky News*, July 13, 2013. For more skepticism about the likelihood of the Labour Party restoring lost workplace rights in a future Miliband government, see Joseph Richardson, "Trade Unions and the Strike in Britain," *CounterPunch*, January 1, 2013. Tim Strangleman reflects on the party's estrangement from its working-class roots in "What About the Workers?" *Working-Class Perspectives* blog, August 19, 2013, available at http://workingclassstudies.wordpress.com.

PART III: ORGANIZING FOR THE LONG HAUL

1.   The story of 1970s labor insurgency is recounted by various contributors to *Rebel Rank and File: Labor Militancy and Revolt from Below during the Long 1970s*, ed. Aaron Brenner, Robert Brenner, and Cal Winslow (New York: Verso Books, 2012). For an excellent first-person account of "colonizing" in California agriculture, see Bruce Neuburger, *Lettuce Wars: Ten Years of Work and Struggle in the Fields of California* (New York: Monthly Review Press, 2013).

2.   For more on this emerging strata of the workforce, see Guy Standing, *The Precariat: The Dangerous New Class* (London and New York: Bloomsbury Academic, 2011).

3.   See Robert Reich, "Unions, not Manufacturing, Key to Our Economic Revival," *San Francisco Chronicle*, February 26, 2012. Solidarity member Kim Moody disputes this downplaying of the importance of manufacturing in the economy. He points out that, while "the industrial working class has declined as a percentage of the workforce from about half the private sector 40 years ago to 30 percent today, the overall number of industrial workers is down only slightly, from about 22 million in the

1970s to slightly more than 20 million today." See Moody, "The Industrial Working Class Today: Why It Still Matters—or Does It?" *Against The Current,* October, 1995, 27–35.

4.   *Radicals at Work: An Activist Strategy for Revitalizing the Labor Movement* (Detroit: Solidarity, 2005), available at http://www.solidarity-us.org.

5.   See Solidarity internal document, "Reflecting on the Rank & File Strategy: A Draft Discussion paper for the 2002 Solidarity Labor Retreat." (Document in possession of the author.)

6.   Interview with the author, May 6, 2007.

7.   Peter Olney, "The Arithmetic of Decline and Some Proposals for Renewal," *New Labor Forum* (Spring–Summer 2002): 35–44.

8.   Carey Dall and Jono Cohen, "Salting the Earth: Organizing for the Long Haul," *New Labor Forum* (Spring–Summer 2002): 36. Echoing Olney's point, the authors note that "in every era in the history of the American labor movement, where militancy flared, there existed organizers within the ranks agitating for rebellion."

9.   See "Interview with Agustin Ramirez, ILWU Organizer," conducted by Peter Olney in *Social Policy* (Fall 2012): 59–62.

10. For more on UNITE HERE's campus recruitment and organizing culture, see Julius Getman's definitive history of the union, *Restoring the Power of Unions: It Takes a Movement* (New Haven: Yale University Press, 2010). The experience of ex-students hired by UNITE HERE, SEIU, and other unions has been chronicled best by Daisy Rooks in "The Cowboy Mentality: Organizers and Occupational Commitment in the New Labor Movement," *Labor Studies Journal* 28/3 (Fall 2003): 33–61.

11. Interview with the author, October 24, 2007.

12. Liza Featherstone, *Students against Sweatshops* (New York: Verso, 2002) contains more profiles of campus activists who entered the labor movement, such as Steve Strong, via USAS.

13. All Steve Strong quotes are from an interview with the author, October 24, 2007, or subsequent email messages from Strong.

14. UNITE HERE press release titled "UNITE HERE Local 11 Files Unfair Labor Practice Charges against Ritz Carlton Huntington Hotel," August 22, 2007. (Document in possession of author.)

15. For more on this trend, see Jenny Brown, "Hotel Employers Conspire to Deny Permanent Jobs," *Labor Notes* (July 2012): 14–15.

16. For a more detailed description of UNITE HERE's committee building and leadership development methods, see Seth Newton Patel, "Have We Built the Committee? Advancing Leadership Development in the U.S. Labor Movement," *WorkingUSA,* (March 2013): 113–42.

17. See Carinna Aceedo, "Youth Workers Protest Cheesecake, Xpress," October 2, 2005, available at http://www.youngworkersunited.org/article.php?id=71.

18. The strengths and weaknesses of workers' centers are assessed by Steve Early, "Can Workers Centers Fill the Void?," in *Embedded with Organized Labor: Journalistic Reflections on the Class War at Home* (New York: Monthly Review Press, 2009), 193–98.

19. For more on the 2005–6 San Francisco hotel lockout, see David Bacon, "Getting It Right," *New Labor Forum* (Fall, 2007): 2.

20. For an account of this process, see Tiffany Ten Eyck, "Organizing and Involving Young Workers: What Does It Take?" *Labor Notes* (July 2007): 5. After working at

Labor Notes for several years, Ten Eyck went on to become a full-time staff member of UNITE HERE Local 26 in Boston.

21. Daniel Gross and Staughton Lynd, *Solidarity Unionism at Starbucks* (Oakland: PM Press, 2011). For a less sympathetic account of the IWW's organizing at Starbucks, see Kim Fellner, *Wrestling with Starbucks: Conscience, Capital, and Cappuccino* (New Brunswick, NJ: Rutgers University Press, 2008).

22. See also Erik Forman, "Peer-to-Peer Organizing: Seeding the Next Labor Insurgency," a power point presentation at the Labor Research Action Network conference at Georgetown University, June 18–19, 2013 (available from the author at erik.forman@gmail.com). Forman notes that IWW doesn't like the old Communist Party–linked concept of "colonizing." His union refers to the practice as "salting, industrial concentration, peer-to-peer organizing, or seeding."

23. Originally pubished in *WorkingUSA*, September 2013.

24. The *ver.di* delegation's 2012 fact-finding report is available at http://cwafiles.org/ tmobile/201209-veri-di-english-final.pdf. In May 2013, CWA and *ver.di* issued a 25-page document called "Standing Up for Good Jobs in Charleston," based on a public speak-out by T-Mobile workers from multiple work locations in the United States and Germany. Available from Communications Workers of America, Washington, D.C. For more on the ongoing rank-and-file activity at T-Mobile, see http://www.loweringthebarforus.org.

25. For more on Internet use to promote cross-border solidarity activity and global union networking, see Eric Lee and Edd Mustill, *Campaigning Online and Winning: How LabourStart's ActNow Campaigns Are Making Unions Strong,* a guide published in 2013 and available from LabourStart at: https://www.createspace.com/4104805.

26. Lance Compa and Fred Feinstein, "Enforcing European Corporate Commitments to Freedom of Association by Legal and Industrial Action in the United States," in *Comparative Labor Law and Policy Journal* 33/4 (Summer 2012): 635–66. For a shorter survey of recent union experiences, see Michael Fichter, "Exporting Labor Relations across the Atlantic: Insights on Labor Relations Policies of German Corporations in the U.S.," *WorkingUSA* 14 (June 2011): 129–43.

27. This article originally appeared in *Social Policy,* Winter 2013.

PART IV: LABOR'S HEALTH CARE MUDDLE

1. The Laborers International Union was one of the few unions that did not support passage of the ACA because of its potential harmful impact on multi-employer plans in construction and other industries. On July 18, 2013, its president, Terry O'Sullivan, wrote to President Obama reminding him that "we were assured that our plans would not be adversely affected and that, as the law was implemented, the issues unique to our universe would be addressed.... Now, our fears have become reality."

2. In mid-2013, Teamsters at United Parcel Service rejected more than a dozen regional and local contract agreements with the company because of its attempt to impose higher deductibles, co-pays, and annual limits on coverage. "We voted 'no' to save our health benefits and win a better contract," explained Nick Perry, a UPS steward from Columbus Local 413. "They need to get the message that we're not accepting givebacks to a company that made $4.5 billion." As quoted in John D. Schultz, "Back to Bargaining for UPS in Its Thorny Parcel, Freight Contracts," *Logistics Management,* July 18, 2013.

3.   Jenny Brown, "Obamacare Opens for Business, Shuts Out Labor," *Labor Notes* (August 2013): 1–5; and David Moberg, "Obamacare: How It Could Flatline," *In These Times,* July 2013, 20–26. As Brown notes, on July 2, 2013, the Obama administration gave large employers another year to meet the health insurance requirements of the ACA before paying a penalty for not doing so. Not long afterward, the White House postponed the ACA's new limits on out-of-pocket costs for consumers, as reported by Robert Pear, "A Limit on Consumer Costs Is Delayed in Health Care Law," *New York Times,* August 13, 2012. Yet, as of Labor Day 2013, there was no similar sign of White House responsiveness to major union problems with implementation of the law.

4.   Julie Weed, "Questions Abound in Learning to Adjust to Health Care Overhaul," *New York Times,* March 21, 2013. In its own 2013 "white paper" about Obamacare-created problems, the International Brotherhood of Electrical Workers notes that the ACA's failure to penalize small businesses with less than 50 employees "exempts almost all construction industry employers from the ACA employer mandate" and "begins a race to the bottom with respect to benefits." For the full document, see http://www.acawhitepaper.org/The%20Affordable%20Care%20Act%20FINAL. pdf.

5.   John Russo, "More (Bad) Jobs: The Unexpected Consequence of the ACA," *Working Class Perspectives,* February 18, 2013.

6.   UFCW Local 1445 president Rick Charette, quoted by Bruce Vail, "New England Grocery Unions Face Grueling Obamacare Test," *Working In These Times,* March 1, 2013. According to Vail, an estimated 10,000 union-represented part-timers at Stop & Shop in New England "will lose existing coverage" in January 2014, when key provisions of Obamacare go into effect, increasing the cost of coverage for the grocery chain's full-time employees. See Bruce Vail, "Grocery Unions at Stop & Shop Take Obamacare's Leap of Faith," *Working In These Times,* March 29, 2013.

7.   For more on the opting out and its cost impact, see Robert Pear, "Employers with Healthy Workers Could Opt Out of Insurance Market, Raising Others' Costs," *New York Times,* February 17, 2013.

8.   See Robert Pear, "Federal Rule Limits Aid to Families Who Can't Afford Employers' Health Coverage," *New York Times,* January 30, 2013.

9.   Kevin Bogardus, "Unions Break Ranks on ObamaCare," *The Hill,* May 21, 2013. As UFCW President Joe Hansen told *The Hill*: "When [the Obama Administration] started writing the [ACA] rules and regulations, we just assumed that Taft-Hartley plans—that workers covered by those plans, especially low-wage workers—would be eligible for the subsidies and stay in their plans and they're not."

10. See July 2013 letter to Harry Reid and Nancy Pelosi from James Hoffa, president of the Teamsters, Joseph Hansen, president of the United Food and Commercial Workers, and D. Taylor, president of UNITE HERE. Among the "nightmare scenarios" they predict: "Even though nonprofit plans like ours won't receive the same subsidies as for-profit plans, they'll be taxed to pay for those subsidies. Taken together, these restrictions will make nonprofit plans like ours unsustainable, and will undermine the health-care market of viable alternatives to the big insurance companies." (Document in possession of author.) At a White House meeting on February 5, 2013, AFL-CIO president Rich Trumka, Taylor, and other top union officials were informed by Obama "that he would not be offering them subsidies meant for

the uninsured." See Avik Roy, "Behind the Scenes of Obama's Effort to Prevent the AFL-CIO from Resolving to Repeal Obamacare," *Forbes.com*, September 9, 2013.

11.   The Sept. 11, 2013, AFL-CIO debate about Resolution 54 on the Affordable Care Act aired building trades grievances about treatment of Taft-Hartley trusts and gave some speakers the chance to argue for single-payer as the only viable long-term solution. See Steve Early, "Labor's Days in La La Land," *CounterPunch*, September 16, 2013.

12.   Jonathan Gruber, quoted by Reed Abelson, "Bearing Down on Health Costs: Companies Maneuver to Avoid 'Cadillac Tax' on Generous Coverage," *New York Times*, May 28, 2013 For a good account of how employers are using the excise tax to their advantage in bargaining, see Samantha Winslow, "Attack of the Cadillac Tax," *Labor Notes*, September, 2013, 2.

13.   Jonathan Gruber, quoted by Kate Taylor, "Health Care Law Raises Pressure on Public Unions," *New York Times*, August 5, 2013. As Taylor reports, "Under the tax, plans that cost above a certain threshold in 2018—$10,200 annually for individual plans and $27,500 for family plans, with slightly higher cutoffs for retirees and those in high risk professions like law enforcement—will be taxed at 40 percent of their costs in excess of the limit. (The thresholds will rise with inflation after 2018)."

14.   Marcia Angell, "Obamacare Confronts a Fiscal Crisis: The Affordable Care Act Doesn't Add Up," *New Labor Forum* (Winter 2013): 44–46. Angell's predicted collapse of Obamacare does not necessarily translate into something better. One Labor for Single Payer campaigner worries that union disaffection with Obamacare will just lead to "further calls for its repeal and return to the status quo ante." A labor movement "more divided and cozying up to the Republicans to teach the Democrats a lesson" is not likely to find a better way forward, he fears.

15.   Robert Pear, "Expanding Medicaid with Private Insurance," *New York Times*, March 22, 2013. As Pear reports, "The White House is encouraging skeptical state officials to expand Medicaid by subsidizing the purchase of private insurance for low-income people, even though that approach might be somewhat more expensive." In April 2013 the Obama administration also unexpectedly boosted federal payments for the Medicare Advantage program, which will further entrench partial privatization of Medicare and jeopardize its more cost-effective traditional form of coverage for seniors. See press release titled "Obama Administration Intervenes to Give $71.5 Billion to Overpaid, For-Profit Medicare Advantage Plans," Physicians for a National Health Program, April 9, 2013.

16.   UE New England leader Peter Knowlton offers good advice to other union negotiators in "Bargaining under the New Health Law," *Labor Notes*, September 14, 2012. See also Mark Dudzic, "Between a Rock and a Hard Place: The Future of Healthcare Bargaining," March 21, 2013, available at http://www.laborforsinglepayer.org/.

17.   Marie Gottschalk, *The Shadow Welfare State: Labor, Business, and the Politics of Health Care in the United States* (Ithaca, NY: Cornell University Press, 2000).

18.   For a more sympathetic view of Taft-Hartley funds and a succinct explanation of how they work, see James McGee, "Union Health Plans Will Suffer under Obamacare," *Labor Notes* (March 2013): 14–15. McGee administers the Transit Employees Health and Welfare Fund in Washington, D.C.

19.   Colin Gordon, *Dead on Arrival: The Politics of Health Care in Twentieth Century America* (Princeton: Princeton University Press, 2004).

20. Originally published in *The Nation*, July 7, 2003.

21. A 2012 survey found that "40 percent of sick Massachusetts adults reported problematic out-of-pocket medical costs" and "36 percent reported that the cost of medical care caused financial problems for their family" despite the state's new ACA-like requirement that "insurance policies offer certain minimum coverage." A. W. Gaffney, "Underinsured in the Age of Obamacare," *In These Times*, July 2013, 27–29.

22. Two labor researchers sized up the Bay State bargaining situation after Romneycare: "Unions representing higher-wage workers and workers at large employers will continue to struggle with increasing health insurance cost shifting and decreasing quality of health insurance plans, with little relief, at least anytime soon." See Malini Cadambi Daniel and Erica Rafford Noyes, "Obamacare and Collective Bargaining: The Massachusetts Experience," *New Labor Forum* 22/1 (Winter 2013): 37–43. The authors quote a building trades leader who observed that "since the Massachusetts law, there has been no change to the economic landscape in health insurance negotiations." The one sector of labor in which they find some improvement is among "unions representing low-wage workers with few health insurance options."

23. Verizon document in possession of the author.

24. Roger Bybee, "Corporations, Federal 'Reform' Keep Shifting Healthcare Costs to Workers," *In These Times*, May 13, 2011.

25. For more on this troubling legislative history, see "How EFCA Died for Obamacare," in Early, *The Civil Wars in U.S. Labor: Birth of a New Workers' Movement or Death Throes of the Old?* (Chicago: Haymarket Books, 2011), chap. 9. Warnings about the Cadillac tax were also sounded in Steve Early and Rand Wilson, "Why the Health Insurance Excise Tax Is a Bad Idea," *The Nation*, October 21, 2009.

26. Originally published in *Labor Notes*, June–July 2011.

27. In early 2013, for example, California single-payer groups were dismayed to discover that even their longtime ally, the California Nurses Association, was not pushing for reintroduction of a single-payer bill locally. Such legislation has been passed twice in Sacramento but vetoed when the state had a Republican governor. As a result of Governor Jerry Brown's preferred focus on implementation of the ACA, and the CNA's tactical retreat from annual single-payer campaigning in the legislature, not a single Democratic sponsor could be lined up to sponsor a new bill. In addition to having a new Democratic governor in 2013, California also boasted a state senate and assembly with Democratic "super-majorities." See Russell Mokhiber, "Single Payer Up Against It in California," *Single Payer Action*, February 19, 2013; and Tom Gallagher, "Single Payer Health Insurance Bill Orphaned in California," *Los Angeles Review of Books,* April 30, 2013. CNA later launched an ad campaign designed to highlight the emerging shortcomings of Obamacare and the need for tax-supported universal coverage instead. For details, see: http://www.nationalnursesunited.org/page/s/our-taxes-our-health care.

28. For further details on the Labor for Single Payer meeting, see http://www.laborforsinglepayer.org/. The "booby trap" for Taft-Hartley funds is described by James McGee in *Labor Notes*, March 2013, 7–8. "The ACA appears to disadvantage multi-employer funds by permitting competitor employers access to the new health exchanges while denying the funds the same access. The result is that employers will have every incentive to get out of the funds when union contracts expire."

29. For the text of this letter and further details on Labor Campaign for Single Payer campaigning at the 2013 AFL-CIO convention and beyond, see http://www.laborforsinglepayer.org/. The Labor Campaign initiative and the building trades backlash against Obamacare are analyzed in Steve Early, "Labor's Love Lost Over Obamacare?," *HuffingtonPost*, August 30, 2013.

30. Eileen Boris and Jennifer Klein, *Caring for America: Home Health Workers in the Shadow of the Welfare State* (New York: Oxford University Press, 2012).

31. Eileen Boris and Jennifer Klein, "Still Waiting For Obama," *Labor Notes* (September 2012): 4–5. See also op-ed piece by Boris and Klein, "Home-Care Workers Aren't Just Companions," *New York Times*, July 1, 2012.

32. Originally published in *Dollars and Sense*, September–October 2012.

33. Steven Greenhouse, "In Michigan, a Setback for Unions," *New York Times*, November 8, 2012. In May 2013, with help from a Democratic governor, labor in Minnesota won passage of legislation creating a process for 21,000 state-subsidized home care and child care providers to win bargaining rights. AFSCME sought to represent the former and SEIU the latter.

34. See "Home Care Rules in the Home Stretch," *New York Times*, March 1, 2013. The proposed federal rule change would "extend overtime and minimum wage protections to home health aides and personal care attendants in the 29 states that don't cover them. . . . Twenty-one states already include home care workers under wage and hour laws, with modestly good effects." Jenny Brown, "Wage Laws Could Include Homecare Workers, Finally," *Labor Notes* (February 2012): 13.

35. Steven Greenhouse, "Wage Law Will Cover Home Aides," *The New York Times*, September 18, 2013,B1-2.

36. Kaiser contends that CNA sympathy-strike activity violates the no-strike clause of the union's contract with the hospital chain. After the September 2011 work stoppage, management filed a grievance seeking to compel arbitration of this disagreement. CNA communications director Chuck Idelson dismissed the Kaiser lawsuit as "a frivolous legal charade" pursued by an employer who should be trying to "settle its differences with workers and reach a fair contract." Quoted in Kathy Robertson, "Kaiser Sues California Nurses Association over Strike," *Sacramento Business Journal*, November 18, 2011.

37. This chapter is based on articles originally published in *The Nation*, November 22, 2011; and *Labor Notes*, February 2012.

38. See Victoria Colliver, "Kaiser Mental Health Service Reprimanded," *San Francisco Chronicle*, March 19, 2013; and "State Fines Kaiser $4 million over Mental Health Access," *San Francisco Chronicle*, June 26, 2013.

39. See National Union of Healthcare Workers press release, and accompanying letter to the directors of Covered California, "Kaiser Permanente Ineligible to Participate in Obamacare Insurance Exchange in California?," July 31, 2013, available at http://www.nuhw.org/news/2013/7/31/kaiser-permanente-ineligible-to-participate-in-obamacare-ins.html.

40. Unfortunately, unions have sometimes joined forces with the beverage industry against these public health initiatives. See Steve Early, "Getting into Bed with Big Soda: How Labor Helped with a Vote for More Obesity," *HuffingtonPost*, November 7, 2012, http://www.huffingtonpost.com/steve-early/richmond-soda-tax_b_2089732.html.

41. The Obama administration's proposed rules for ACA implementation "include several provisions to prevent discrimination against employees. Employers must, for example, allow workers to qualify for rewards in other ways if it would be 'unreasonably difficult' for them to meet a particular standard" for wellness. See Robert Pear, "Administration Defines Benefits That Must Be Offered under the Health Law," *New York Times,* November 21, 2012.

42. As Lee Sustar reported nine months after the teachers' walkout, internal opponents of the CTU leadership tried to exploit "CTU members' understandable discontent" with the union's new negotiated wellness program. But, as Sustar notes, "CTU negotiators succeeded in their demand that members' contribution to health insurance will be unchanged. That's a better deal than [Chicago] transit workers got: they have both higher health costs and the wellness program." Sustar, "Holding the Line for Chicago Teachers," *Socialist Worker,* May 5, 2015.

43. When more details of this wellness bonus were finally revealed, Kaiser stressed that the plan, scheduled to take effect Jan. 1, 2014, would be "collective and voluntary" for the 133,000 union-represented and non-union employees eligible to participate. According to Kaiser, "there are no penalties to meet health goals ... and all biometric information and results are reported in the aggregate. That means that individual participation and biometric date will remain private and confidential."

   Kaiser estimated that the total cost of the program would be $66.5 million when individual payouts of up to $500 per worker are made in 2015 "if participants in their region collectively lose weight, lower blood pressure, lower cholesterol, and stop smoking." See September 19, 2013, Kaiser Permanente press release entitled "Total Health Incentive Plan Takes Innovative Approach to Workforce Wellness." Posted at: http://share.kaiserpermanente.org/article/total-health-incentive-plan-takes-innovative-approach-to-workforce-wellness/.

44. The NUHW-CNA critique of "Total Health" at Kaiser and similar programs is the subject of a 2013 reported titled "Which Way to Wellness: A Workers Guide to Labor and Workplace Strategies for Better Healthcare." (Document in possession of the author.)

   For good advice on union bargaining about wellness issues, see Jane Slaughter, "Coercive Wellness Programs Create New Headaches," *Labor Notes,* January 2013, http://labornotes.org/2013/01/what-do-when-boss-catches-wellness-fever.

45. In September, 2013, faculty members at Penn State University, who are not union-represented, forced the suspension of a new wellness program "that some professors had criticized as coercive and financially punitive." Their protest led to administration withdrawal of a $100 per month penalty for anyone who failed to complete a survey seeking information about intimate details of their jobs, finances, marital situation, and plans, if any, to get pregnant in the next year. See Natasha Singer, "Healthy Plan Penalty Ends at Penn State," *The New York Times,* September 19, 2013, 2–3.

46. Originally published in *The Nation,* February 26, 2013.

47. Jill Horwitz, Brenna Kelly, and John DiNardo, "Wellness Incentives in the Workplace: Cost Savings through Cost Shifting to Unhealthy Workers," *Health Affairs* 32/3 (March 2013): 468–76.

48. Dan Munro, "RAND Corporation (Briefly) Publishes Sobering Report on Workplace Wellness Programs," *Forbes.com blog,* May 28, 2013. See also U.S. Department of Health and Human Services, "Report to Congress on Workplace Wellness," June 2013, available at http://aspe.hhs.gov/hsp/13/WorkplaceWellness/rpt_wellness.cfm.

49. See September 6, 2013, letter to Richard Trumka from Laneta Fitzhugh, David
     Mallon, Sonia Askew, Clement Papazian, and Turusew Gedebu-Wilson. (Document
     in possession of the author.) For an account of the pre-convention skirmish over
     Kaiser's presence, see Steve Early, "No Instant Recess at AFL-CIO Convention,"
     Labor Notes, September 9, 2013.

PART V: TELECOM LABOR TROUBLES

1.   A flyer issued by National Nurses United in February 2011 called for an emergency
     meeting in Madison "to discuss a strategy for fighting back against concessions in
     Wisconsin and across the U.S." (Document in possession of the author.) On March
     3, NNU organized a follow-up march and demonstration involving 7,000 workers
     bearing signs and banners demanding "No Concessions for Workers."

2.   Richard Trumka, "Scott Walker's False Choice," *Wall Street Journal,* March 4,
     2011. In this op-ed page column, the AFL-CIO president asserted that "it's crucial
     that we sit down at the table together and find a way to grow without taking away
     from the middle class." To jump-start those talks, he reassured *WSJ* readers that
     "working America's message to governors like Scott Walker and New Jersey's Chris
     Christie" is "we believe in shared sacrifice."

3.   As quoted by Michael Cooper and Steven Greenhouse, "Unions Debate What to
     Give to Save Bargaining," *New York Times,* February 28, 2011.

4.   The anti-union behavior of telecom firms that began as cable TV providers contin-
     ues to be the worst of all. There are only 3,000 CWA or IBEW-represented cable TV
     workers in the entire country. For recent examples of union busting in this sector,
     see Mike Elk, "Cablevision CEO's Threats Prompt NLRB Complaint," *Working In
     These Times,* April 9, 2013; and Elk's earlier reporting for WITT on CWA orga-
     nizing struggles among New York City Cablevision workers. The anti-union record
     of Comcast is extensively documented in *No Bargain: Comcast and the Future of
     Workers' Rights in Telecommunications,* a research report produced by American
     Rights at Work, the Washington-based labor advocacy group. Available at http://
     www.americanrightsatwork.org.

5.   See "How Has the Telecom Industry Changed?," *CWA News* (Winter 2012): 4. As
     this article reports, "The digital communications revolution has led to the conver-
     gence of previously separate voice, video, and data sectors.... Cable dominates the
     broadband market, as Digital Subscriber Line service loses customers to cable's
     faster-speed Internet service. One-third of all Americans—and 60 percent of all
     adults—are wireless only."

6.   In recent years, CWA put more emphasis on what it calls "movement building" as a
     supplement to its earlier focus on strengthening workplace organization and mem-
     bership mobilization activity. For handbooks describing the two approaches, see the
     union's longtime internal organizing guide, *Mobilizing to Build Power,* and the more
     recent *Building a Movement for Economic Justice & Democracy,* which comes with a
     related curriculum guide. Both can be ordered from the CWA Education Department
     at http://www.cwamaterials.org/. Regular video reports on "movement building"
     work by CWA activists around the country are posted at http://www.cwavoices.org.
     See also David Moberg, "Labor's Turnaround," *In These Times,* March 3, 2013.

7.   For more on the conduct of and preparation for the 1989 NYNEX strike, see Steve
     Early, "Striking NYNEX," *Labor Research Review* 1/17 (1991): 19–30; or Steve

Early, "Holding the Line in '89: Lessons of the NYNEX Strike: How Telephone Workers Can Fight More Effectively Next Time," a 50-page report issued by the Labor Resource Center, Somerville, MA, September 1990. A good account can also be found in Dan LaBotz, *A Troublemaker's Handbook: How to Fight Back Where You Work—and Win!* (Detroit: Labor Notes, 1991), 84–89.

8.   After the Verizon contract settlement in August 2012 health care premium sharing finally became a reality for CWA and IBEW members employed by that company in New York and New England.

9.   Originally published in *Open Media Boston*, December 20, 2009.

10. As a CWA organizer or representative, I worked with four different Local 1400 presidents between 1980 and 2007. For an account of the important changes made by Don Trementozzi and other newly elected Local 1400 reformers in 2003, see Early, *The Civil Wars in U.S. Labor*, 117–20. In 2011, I assisted Trementozzi's run for CWA secretary-treasurer as a Save Our Union 2011 campaign volunteer.

11. Charles Borchert, Jr., "Small Local Stands Up, and after 18 Months, AT&T Backs Down on Some Concessions," *Labor Notes* (September 2010): 8–9.

12. Originally published in *Labor Notes*, July 12, 2011.

13. Charles Borchert, Jr., "Alone Again: AT&T Coordinated Bargaining Disintegrates," *Labor Notes* (May 2013): 13–14.

14. "Delegates Adopt Constitutional Changes," *CWA Newsletter*, April 25, 2013.

15. The unusual degree of cross-union solidarity displayed by CWA and IBEW members from 1989 to 2012 (and, we hope, into the future) represents a sharp break with earlier relations between the two unions in New York and New England. In 1986, three years before the NYNEX strike, 40,000 CWA members walked out for ten days to defeat health care cost shifting. The IBEW, under soon-to-be-changed telecom local leadership in New England, settled separately and sat out the strike. Its bargaining council agreed to premium sharing but also negotiated a "me-too" clause ensuring that 20,000 IBEW members would get the benefit of any better contract language won by CWA. Thanks to the strike, the IBEW's cost-shifting deal was torn up for the next three years. In 1989, the two unions closely coordinated their contract campaign, bargaining, and strike activity, establishing an enduring partnership that thwarted future divide-and-conquer ploys.

16. This Facebook-based social network of Verizon union activists continues to function, post-strike; see https://www.facebook.com/groups/Verizoncontract2011/?ref=notif&notif_t=group_r2j.

17. See *Broken Connections: An Alternative Annual Report for Verizon*, prepared by CWA for distribution at Verizon's 2012 shareholders' meeting and posted at http://www.verigreedy.com. This report cites the loss of "several thousand jobs overseas" due to "low-wage contracting out of customer sales and service, billing, and tech support."

18. At CWA's 2013 convention, delegates voted to raise weekly strike benefits to $400 for members out more than eight weeks.

19. Borchert, "Small Local Stands Up."

20. Originally published in *Working In These Times*, August 2, 2011.

21. By 2012, much of Verizon's overall revenue (of $115.9 billion) and profit was coming from its 55 percent stake in Verizon Wireless, a joint venture with the equally anti-union UK-based Vodafone, whose minority interest is valued at between $100 billion

and $130 billion. In September, 2013, Verizon bought out Vodafone's share of the company in the third largest takeover in corporate history. For details of that deal, see Michael J. de la Merced and Mark Scott, "Verizon to Pay $130 Billion to Fully Own Wireless Unit," *The New York Times*, Sept. 3, 2012, B1-2.

22. For an overly optimistic post-strike account of the Verizon Wireless organizing rights deal, see Steve Early, "Verizon Strike Highlights New Union Role," *Boston Globe*, September 3, 2000.

23. For an informative oral history of Jobs with Justice's solidarity campaigning on behalf of Verizon workers and many others, see Eric Larson, ed., *Jobs with Justice: 25 Years, 25 Voices* (Oakland, CA:PM Press, 2013). Among the contributors are Massachusetts JWJ Director Russ Davis and national JWJ leader Sarita Gupta.

24. Originally published in *Labor Notes*, August 23, 2011.

25. Massachusetts provides jobless benefits to workers who strike but without any "substantial curtailment" of their employer's business operations. In April 2013 IBEW and CWA strikers in Massachusetts won their claim for unemployment insurance arising from the 2011 Verizon walkout. This state unemployment review board decision illustrates the diminished impact of landline work stoppages at telecom firms with the capacity to take the kind of countermeasures that Verizon does. During the strike, the review board found that "there was no disruption to the flow of FiOS, data, video, or voice or to the copper-line voice or high-speed Internet transmissions. Overall revenue increased during the month of the strike. . . . The percentage of incoming calls that the employer was able to answer dropped only marginally. The calls sent to outside vendors increased by 50% to 100% over the employer's normal rate but never exceeded 30% of the total call center volume." Decision by Massachusetts Executive Office of Labor and Workforce Development Board of Review in U.I. Benefit Appeal M-63772-M-69116, April 24, 2011, 21.

26. Cal Winslow, Aaron Brenner, and Bob Brenner. eds., *Rebel Rank and File: Labor Militancy and Revolt from Below during the 1970s* (New York: Verso, 2010), 278.

27. All Newman and Winkler quotes are from Dan LaBotz, *Troublemakers Handbook: How to Fight Back Where You Work—and Win!* (Detroit: Labor Notes, 1991), 202-4. See also an informative oral history interview with Winkler, recorded by Jane LaTour, author of *Sisters in the Brotherhood* (New York: Palgrave Macmillan, 2008), 236. Winkler recorded her own interviews with other female members of Local 1101, which are posted at the same site: http://www.talkinghistory.org/sisters/winkler.html.

28. After the 1101 Rebuilders took over the local in 2011, Verizon retiree and former *Bell Wringer* organizer Ilene Winkler was asked to lead the Local 1101 retirees organization.

29. For more details on this initiative when first unveiled, see Rand Wilson, "Call for 'Stewards' Army' Opens Door for New Labor Activism," *Labor Notes*, January 27, 2007.

30. Verizon strike veterans in 1101 and other CWA locals also became part of the union contingent that related most closely to Occupy Wall Street, when that movement erupted in lower Manhattan shortly after the return to work at Verizon. See Amy Muldoon, "Zuccotti at Work: Daydreams of a Rank-and-Filer," *New Politics* (Summer 2012): 44-46; and Steve Early, "A Lesson for Labor from Occupy Wall Street," *CounterPunch*, November 15, 2011.

31. Originally published in *Working In These Times*, November 29, 2011.

32. As quoted by Jenny Brown, "Unions Expect Verizon to Impose Terms, Ready to Walk Out Again," *Labor Notes*, July 30, 2012.

33. For more on the implications of Verizon and AT&T's attempted abandonment of their copper-wire network customers, see Bruce Kushnick, "Time to Fight for the Public Switched Network," *HuffingtonPost*, February 20, 2013, and "Shame on Verizon," a blog post by the New Networks Institute at http://www.newnetworks.com/VerizonNYC.htm. Susan Crawford's *Captive Audience: The Telecom Industry and Monopoly Power in the Guilded Age* (New Haven: Yale University Press, 2013) provides an incisive overview of larger industry trends since passage of the 1996 Telecommunications Act.

34. As quoted by Matthew Cunningham-Cook, "Controversial New Verizon contract Divides Union," October 8, 2012, *Waging Nonviolence,* available at http://waging-nonviolence.org/feature/controversial-new-verizon-contract-divides-union.

35. As quoted in ibid.

36. As quoted by Mike Elk, "Concessionary, 4-Year Verizon Deal Sealed, Despite Dissent in the Ranks," *Working In These Times*, October 21, 2012. For one CWA chief steward's post-contract plan, see Dominic Renda, "Viewpoint: How to Make Verizon Hear Us Next Time," *Labor Notes,* July 23, 2013. A Verizon customer-service rep and member of Local 1105 in New York City, Renda advocates organizing more of "our rank-and-file members to become activists so that we can stop what is sure to be Verizon's next round of concessionary demands" in 2015.

37. See Helaina Hovitz and Jessica Mastronardi, "Verizon Wants to Move 1,100 Downtown Workers to Brooklyn," *NYPress.com,* April 3, 2013.

PART VI: IS THERE A LEADER IN THE HOUSE?

1. Stanley Aronowitz, *Taking It Big: C. Wright Mills and the Making of Political Intellectuals* (New York: Columbia University Press, 2012), 85–124.

2. Lichtenstein quote is from his informative introduction to the University of Illinois Press edition of *The New Men of Power*, published in 2001.

3. Andy Stern, *A Country that Works: Getting America Back on Track* (New York: Free Press, 2006).

4. For a sad but typical example of U.S. labor rhetoric on military matters today, see "Manufacturing Essential to Nation's Military Readiness," a May 8, 2013, press release issued by the United Steel Workers of America (USWA) hailing the release of a union-backed report titled "Remaking American Security: Supply Chain Vulnerabilities and National Security Risks across the U.S. Defense Industrial Base." In his press statement, USWA president Leo Girard (a Canadian) worries that "we cannot hope to retain our status as a preeminent world power, economically or militarily," if "America's warfighters" are not supplied by "the best and most reliable products in the world" from domestic manufacturing sources. "It has been clear for decades," Girard declares, "that our national defense needs do not begin and end at the walls of the Pentagon."

5. One non-AFL-CIO union that continues to criticize the military-industrial complex and its related national security apparatus is Winpisinger's old McCarthy-era target, the United Electrical Workers (UE). In addition to calling for Pentagon spending cuts and opposing U.S. military intervention abroad, the UE has urged Congress to

"outlaw political spying and disruption by the FBI and other federal agencies." Says UE Political Action director Chris Townsend: "Our civil liberties must not be lost in the security stampede drummed up by politicians and corporations." As quoted in Sam Adler-Bell and David Segal, "Why NSA Surveillance Should Alarm Labor," *In These Times,* July 24, 2013.

6. The "blue-green" alliance frayed considerably over the controversial Keystone XL oil pipeline project, which received tacit approval from Rich Trumka and the AFL-CIO in early 2013 under building trades pressure. Even USWA president Leo Gerard, a stalwart of coalitions with environmentalists, threw his support behind this questionable form of job creation, "as long as the steel used to make the pipes was produced domestically." Leaders of the CWA, SEIU, ATU, TWU, and the National Nurses United—all with no membership jobs of their own at stake—adopted a more environmentally friendly position on the Keystone project. For further details on that split within labor, see Rebecca Burns, "It's Not Easy Being Blue and Green," *In These Times,* June 2013, 10–12.

7. This article originally appeared online in *The HuffingtonPost*, February 21, 2011.

8. According to John Schmitt, an economist at the Center for Economic and Policy Research, the average unionized worker was forty-five years old in 2010, up from age thirty-eight in 1983. See Kris Maher and Melanie Trottman, "AFL-CIO Seeks Answers in Crisis," *Wall Street Journal,* July 26, 2013.

9. To his credit, one of the three original New Unity Partners who helped lay the groundwork for Change to Win did step down as president of his own union, in 2010, when he was just shy of sixty. However, Andy Stern's post-SEIU career has not been a great boon to labor causes. For more on Stern's controversial second act as a corporate director, foundation board member, and Columbia Business School "senior fellow," see Mike Elk, "Andy Stern Responds to Critics of His Post-SEIU Career," *Working In These Times,* August 2, 2012; or Ryan Grim, "Andy Stern's Bizarre Alliance with Private Equity," *HuffingtonPost*, October 7, 2010.

10. In April 2013 delegates to the CWA convention in Pittsburgh set a new mandatory retirement age of seventy for all full-time elected national officers and executive board members. Under this change, board members who reach that age while in office can complete their existing term but not run for reelection. This is a small step in the right direction not likely to be emulated any time soon by the national AFL-CIO.

11. Since this article originally appeared in 2009, Lillian Roberts has been unanimously reelected to a fifth term as DC 37 executive director, which began in January 2013, a year in which she will be celebrating her eighty-seventh birthday. At the AFSCME convention in 2012, she was also reelected, without opposition, to the union's national executive board for another three years. By 2011, her once contested pay had jumped to $315,000, for overall compensation of nearly $350,000 a year.

12. At the age of ninety-eight, labor educator Harry Kelber announced his intention to run against Trumka for president of the AFL-CIO at its 2013 convention in Los Angeles. Unfortunately, Kelber didn't live long enough to attend the convention. But he did make a campaign issue out of his opponent's compensation. According to Kelber, Trumka "increased his salary of $165,000, which he earned in 1995 as secretary-treasurer, to $293,750, which he began receiving after becoming AFL-CIO president in 2009." In addition to enjoying that 23 percent wage increase, Trumka

is now eligible for a lifetime pension equal to 60 percent of his final pay, itself an incentive to keep those presidential paychecks coming, with periodic cost of living increases included. See Harry Kelber, "Richard Trumka's Salary Grab," posted at his campaign website: http://voteharry.org/richard-trumkas-salary-grab/.

13. As Bill Fletcher, a former assistant to AFL-CIO president Sweeney, notes: "There are no structural guarantees….There are structural mechanisms, such as term limits and reasonable restraints on officer salaries, that can inhibit toxic practices. But the most effective counter to undemocratic practices rests in an educated and active membership." See Fletcher, *They're Bankrupting Us (and 20 Other Myths about Unions)* (Boston: Beacon Press, 2012), 26.

14. Originally published in *CounterPunch*, March 12, 2009.

15. At the 2012 convention, McEntee's long career was applauded in a 174-page hard-cover biography, published by the union and distributed to all delegates. The book has an introduction by Lee Saunders, barely mentions Bill Lucy, and describes McEntee as "America's greatest labor organizer of the late 20th and earliest 21st centuries." See Francis Ryan, *Gerald W. McEntee: The Heart of a Lion* (Washington, D.C.: AFSCME, 2012). A more interesting collective portrait is the author's earlier academic study of AFSCME's evolution in McEntee's hometown. See Francis Ryan, *AFSCME's Philadelphia Story: Municipal Workers and Urban Power in the Twentieth Century* (Philadelphia: Temple University Press, 2011).

16. In May 2013, nearly 13,000 of Local 3299's members staged a two-day strike at University of California medical centers throughout the state. According to the union, "The strike came after nearly a year of stalled negotiations with UC administrators." New AFSCME president Lee Saunders flew out to California to participate in Local 3299 strike rallies.

17. See Kris Maher, "Charter Flights Shadow Union Election," *Wall Street Journal*, June 8, 2012. According to Maher's report, the tab for McEntee's chartered aircraft since 2010 was $325,000.

18. Originally published in *Labor Notes*, June 14, 2012.

19. In September 2013 the CTW camp dwindled to three when the United Food and Commercial Workers (UFCW) returned to the AFL-CIO fold, as Mike Elk was the first to report. As he notes, "The defection of the 1.3 million member UFCW" represents the "biggest loss of membership yet" for CTW. See Elk, "UFCW Expected to Rejoin AFL-CIO," *Working In These Times,* July 10, 2013.

20. In 2012, Change to Win–backed warehouse workers made national headlines with their strike activity directed at Wal-Mart subcontractors. In Los Angeles, a small group of port truckers in Los Angeles won what the Teamsters hope will be a breakthrough first contract with the Toll Group, an Australian logistics company. See Brian Sumers, "L.A. Port Truckers Union Reaches Collective Bargaining with Toll Group," *Los Angeles Daily News*, January 11, 2013.

21. According to longtime SEIU admirer Hal Meyerson, "The synergistic campaigns of multiple Change to Win unions to organize whole industries never got off the ground. . . . By 2007, it was already clear that Change to Win hadn't cracked the code to private sector organizing." See Meyerson, "Another Union Drops Out of the Upstart Change to Win Federation and Returns to the AFL-CIO," *The American Prospect*, August 12, 2013.

22. Originally published in *Working In These Times*, October 10, 2011.

23.   Josh Eidelson, "Non-Union Workers with Taxpayer-Supported Jobs Plan to Strike Today," *The Nation.com/blog*, May 21, 2013.

24.   Updates on this and other Change to Win activities are available at http://www.changetowin.org.

25.   Jane McAlevey, with Bob Ostertag, *Raising Expectations (and Raising Hell): My Decade Fighting for the Labor Movement* (New York: Verso, 2012).

26.   Dan Clawson, *The Next Upsurge: Labor and the New Social Movements* (Ithaca, NY: Cornell University Press, 2003), 111–12.

27.   For two longer accounts of that development, see my own *The Civil Wars in U.S. Labor* (Chicago: Haymarket Books, 2011); and Cal Winslow, *Labor's Civil War in California: The NUHW Healthcare Workers Rebellion* (Oakland: PM Press, 2010).

28.   See Tony Cook and Mike Mishak, "Union Split over Leader," *Las Vegas Sun*, December 3, 2007.

29.   This percentage assumes that SEIU still had bargaining rights for roughly 15,000 workers. After facing decertification elections, among nurses, and then recession-related job cuts in the public sector, the total number of workers represented by Local 1107 may have become smaller by 2011.

30.   Originally published in *WorkingUSA*, December 2012.

PART VII: TWO, THREE, MANY VERMONTS!

1.   Originally published in *ZNet*, August 19, 2009.

2.   For more on the work of U.S. Labor against the War, see www.uslaboragainstwar.org/.

3.   Originally published in *The Progressive Populist*, January 2010.

4.   For more information on the Vermont Workers Center and its health care reform campaign, see http://www.workerscenter.org/.

5.   The activities of the Labor Campaign for Single-Payer Healthcare are described at http://www.laborforsinglepayer.org/.

6.   Originally published in *The Nation*, March 10, 2011.

7.   The Working Families Party approach is now being pursued in Oregon, as well as in northeastern states. For more on its favorable political impact, see http://www.motherjones.com/politics/2012/05/third-parties-working-families-party-oregon-new-york. Information about the New York WFP can be found at http://www.workingfamiliesparty.org/.

8.   For more on who runs as a "P/D," as opposed to a "D/P," and why, see Kevin J. Kelly, "Pragmatism or Purity: Is 'Fusion' Good for the Progressive Party?" *Seven Days*, October 26, 2012. VPP chair Abbott told Kelly that, in her view, only ten of the current Democratic members of the Vermont legislature could qualify for a Prog endorsement. "It's not as though we're going to be supporting lots and lots of Democrats," she assured him. Archived at http://www.7dvt.com/2012pragmatism-or-purity-fusion-good-progressive-party.

9.   Originally published in *In These Times*, May 2012.

10.   For Sanders's full 2012 election postmortem interview with Nichols, see http://www.thenation.com/blog/171599/secret-bernie-sanders-success#.

11.   See Steve Early, *The Civil Wars in U.S. Labor: Birth of a New Workers Movement or Death Throes of the Old?* (Chicago: Haymarket Books, 2011), 255–80.

12.   For a detailed discussion of the multiple ways that the ACA as enacted is likely to fall short, see Marcia Angell, "Obamacare Confronts a Fiscal Crisis: Why the Affordable

Care Act Doesn't Add Up," *New Labor Forum* 22/1 (Winter 2013): 44–46. According to Angell, "Obamacare is simply incapable of what it is supposed to do— provide nearly universal care at an affordable and sustainable cost....Unravel it will, as costs rise and it becomes clear that there are still tens of millions of Americans priced out of the system."

13. Originally published online in HuffingtonPost, June 22, 2012.

14. In the *New England Journal of Medicine*, health researcher Laura Grubb notes that Vermont is still ahead of other states. Although it is one of the smallest states, it will be receiving $250 million for its insurance exchange, the fifth-highest allocation in the nation. According to Grubb, Vermont's expansion of Medicaid "will bring in a lot of federal dollars and will improve coverage of the state's residents. Vermont expanded its program beyond the Affordable Care Act's proposed income eligibility and is expecting to gain $259 million." Laura Grubb, "Lessons from Vermont's Health Care Reform," *New England Journal of Medicine*, April 2013.

15. Paul Heintz, "Divided We Brawl: The Fight to Unionize Vermont Home-Care Workers," *Seven Days*, May 22, 2013.

16. Alicia Freese, "Formerly Allies, Two Unions Now to Compete for Home-Care Workers' Votes," VTdigger.org, May 29, 2013.

17. See "Statement From SEIU Withdrawing from Vermont Home Care Election"; and Terri Hallenbeck, "SEIU Withdraws from Race to Represent Home Care Workers," *Burlington Free Press*, July 31, 2013.

EPILOGUE —DARE TO STRUGGLE, DARE TO WIN?

1. This epilogue draws on reporting that originally appeared in *Working In These Times* and *Labor Notes* in early 2013.

2. Stern Burger with Fries blog, "Report from Day 1 at Kaiser Ballot Count," May 2, 2013, http://sternburgerwithfries.blogspot.com/2013/05/report-from-day-1-at-kaiser-ballot-count.html.

3. Kathy Robertson, "Fireworks Erupt as Kaiser Vote Count on Unions Continues," *Sacramento Business Journal*, May 1, 2013.

4. Between 2009 and early 2013, Kaiser Permanente reported a record $8.7 billion in profits.

5. In a press release issued after the 2013 vote count, NUHW alleged that Kaiser granted "unequal facility access to SEIU-UHW staff and illegally abridged the speech rights of workers supporting NUHW-CNA." NUHW also charged that SEIU prevailed through a "campaign of fear, intimidation, and collusion with management." But the losing union filed no post-election objections of the sort that triggered a Labor Board investigation of SEIU and Kaiser's conduct in the 2010 vote, which led to that election being rerun. NUHW's original attempt to get a decertification election in the wake of SEIU's trusteeship in January 2009 was delayed by the NLRB for more than eighteen months. When NUHW filed for that vote, insiders report that it demonstrated far more support (on petitions and signature cards) than it was able to muster in either subsequent election. See Steve Early, *The Civil Wars in U.S. Labor*, 329.

6. After months of pre-trusteeship skirmishing, SEIU's ultimate pretext for the takeover was UHW's refusal to allow 40 percent of its members to be transferred to a new SEIU local for long-term care workers, without the approval of those affected. After

then-UHW president Sal Rosselli and his fellow dissidents were purged, SEIU president Andy Stern installed his own appointees to run UHW, including Dave Regan, a member of the union's national executive board from Ohio. Thereafter, UHW was never required to transfer members to another local composed solely of home health aides and nursing home workers. As I have argued elsewhere, Stern's real goal was to crush a burgeoning internal reform movement that was anchored by the pre-trusteeship UHW and increasingly critical of national union policies. See Early, *Civil Wars in U.S. Labor*, 173–206.

7. CKPU executive director John August, quoted in Mike Parker, "Who Are the Partners in Kaiser Partnership?" *Labor Notes,* February 25, 2010. In May 2013, right after the CKPU meeting in Anaheim, August resigned his $200,000-a-year position as executive director. For speculation about the reasons for that, see *Stern Burger with Fries* blog, http://sternburgerwithfries.blogspot.com/2013/05/kaiser-coalitions-john-august-is-ousted.html.

8. About a month after SEIU-UHW's Disneyland love-in with Tyson, SEIU Local 1021 urged San Francisco city workers to bombard the new Kaiser CEO with phone and email messages protesting the fact that "the city, its employees, and taxpayers paid $87 million more than it cost Kaiser to deliver health care to union members from 2010 through 2010." As consumers of Kaiser care, these fellow SEIU members were encouraged to "speak out" at a public hearing held by the city's health insurance plan administrator. Local 1021 charged that Kaiser's 15 percent profit margin on its city worker HMO contract was "draining San Francisco taxpayer dollars." See SEIU Local 1021 flyer titled "Say No to Kaiser Price Gouging & Profiteering!," June 2013. One month later, SEIU-UHW president Dave Regan joined Kaiser executives in lobbying city officials to approve Kaiser's proposed $15 million annual rate hike, which was also opposed by other city worker unions. See *Stern Burger with Fries* blog, July 28, 2013, http://sternburgerwithfries.blogspot.com/2013/07/seiu-uhws-dave-regan-sells-out-seiu.html.

9. For more on this scenario, see the blog post "Recording Reveals Secret Deal behind SEIU-UHW's Planned Benefit Cuts at Kaiser Permanente," Stern Burger with Fries, April 9, 2013, http://sternburgerwithfries.blogspot.com/2013/04/recording-reveals-secret-deal-behind.html.

10. California home-care workers in SEIU-UHW and SEIU Local 6434 have to work a minimum number of hours to qualify for coverage and many with part-time schedules are unable to do that.

11. Kathy Robertson, "CHA Leader: Unions, Organizations Need to Work Together," *Sacramento Business Journal,* November 25, 2012.

12. NUHW estimates that SEIU has spent more than $10 million to pursue this case. In March 2013 the U.S. Court of Appeals for the Ninth District upheld the $1.57 million judgment that SEIU won, at the trial court level, against NUHW and sixteen of its original organizers. UNITE-HERE posted a bond to cover NUHW's organizational share of the judgment while it was being appealed. Five defendants decided to pay SEIU, and others have been subject to wage garnishment after SEIU blocked their attempts to declare personal bankruptcy. Some posted bonds to postpone payment during the appeal process but still owe SEIU $40,000 to $80,000 each. In 2010, after the trial, SEIU publicly acknowledged having spent an estimated $5 million on the case, which, if true, still means that any possible recovery will amount to

less than a third of its legal costs. See Steve Early, "Who Will Be the Next NUHW 16?," *ZNet*, August 14, 2013.

13. CNA has been involved in about a hundred strikes in California between 2010 and 2013. See Chris Rauber, "Sutter Health Responds to Threatened CNA Strike, Denies Several Charges," *San Francisco Business Times*, May 8, 2013.

14. As Samantha Winslow reported, "UHW points out that the contract's job security language allows up to a year before Kaiser can eliminate any position, allowing time to place each employee in a new job. But NUHW supporters say Kaiser shouldn't be laying anyone off, and accuse SEIU of secretly agreeing to cuts behind closed doors." See Winslow, "Round Two in High-Stakes California Health Care Vote," *Labor Notes*, April 2012, 1–4.

15. As quoted in audiotape of KPFA interview, available at http://sternburgerwithfries. blogspot.com/2013/03/part-1-of-purple-conference-calls-seiu.html.

16. In her forty years as a nurse and labor activist, Albert has been a steward in the New York City hospital workers union that became SEIU-1199 (United Healthcare Workers-East), an organizer for the CNA in Ohio and Florida, and an organizer for NUHW during the 2012–13 Kaiser decertification campaign. She was referring to deals like the concessionary contract negotiated by SEIU-UHW in 2012 covering 14,000 workers at Dignity Health. During a period when the chain reported $1.7 billion in profits, the union agreed to hundreds of layoffs, a wage freeze, and cuts in pension and health care coverage.

17. Retroactive raises, covering the period of 2010–13 negotiations, were part of NUHW's proposed contract settlement with Kaiser in the optical unit and others.

18. SEIU-UHW, press release, "Huge Losses for NUHW-Represented Workers at Kaiser," July 23, 2013. The release asserts that "NUHW's recent affiliation with the California Nurses can't stop Kaiser from imposing huge health increases, elimination of pensions, no raises, and other major takebacks." According to SEIU-UHW president Dave Regan, the contested optical bargaining results "demonstrated that [NUHW-CNA] simply do not have the strength to be successful at Kaiser, and the workers are suffering as a result." In contrast, he claimed that "SEIU-UHW members negotiated annual raises and maintained all their benefits in bargaining last year."

19. As Kaiser Santa Clara worker Lisa Tomasian reported: "SEIU brought four stewards to meet with Kaiser after the deal was made. They were told to just listen and ask no questions. SEIU appointees claimed that, by including these four people, democracy was served. Meanwhile, our lump-sum payout will get smaller and smaller until it's gone as an option in 2012." As quoted in Early, "SEIU Civil War Puts Labor-Management 'Partnership' in a New Light," in *Real World Labor: A Reader in Economics, Politics, and Social Policy from Dollars & Sense*, ed. Immanuel Ness, Amy Offner, and Chris Sturr (Boston: Economic Affairs Bureau, 2009), 200–203.

20. Kris Maher, "Powerful Union, Upstart Battle over Shrinking Pie," *Wall Street Journal*, April 29, 2013.

21. See exchange in "How Can Labor Be Saved?," *The Nation*, February 13, 2013.

22. Harold Meyerson, "Just What Workers Need: More Labor Civil War," *The American Prospect*, January 7, 2013.

23. As quoted by Joyce Cutler, "In Rerun Election Mirroring First One, SEIU-UHW Retains Kaiser Representation," *Bureau of National Affairs Daily Labor Reporter*, May 3, 2013.

24. Jay Youngdahl, "It's Time for the Union Fighting to Stop," *East Bay Express*, May
     8, 2013. Even some *Labor Notes* readers, an audience generally more sympathetic
     to the NUHW than Youngdahl, argued for a strategy change. Wrote one: "I agree
     that NUHW should stop their divisive war with SEIU and organize unorganized
     workers, that's what they do best. Quit looking at Kaiser as a cash cow and look
     outside that box." According to another, "The correct course of action for the
     45,000 SEIU members is to actively participate in the governance of their union,
     rather than a divisive and costly fight to replace SEIU with NUHW." See reader
     responses to Steve Early, "SEIU Wins Again at Kaiser but Militant Minority Grows,"
     posted online at *Labor Notes*, May 3, 2013, http://www.labornotes.org/2013/05/
     seiu-wins-again-kaiser-militant-minority-grows.

25. SEIU LM-2 filings with the U.S. Department of Labor in March 2012 and 2013 show
     that its active membership dropped from 1,885,728 to 1,842,490. During 2012,
     another 237,000 workers paid agency fees to SEIU but didn't become members. In
     an April 2013 interview SEIU president Mary Kay Henry optimistically predicted that
     her union "would gain 50,000 new members—mainly security guards, janitors, and
     health care workers—in each of the next three years," which would be quite a reversal
     of 2011–12 trends. See Maher, "Powerful Union, Upstart Battle over Shrinking Pie."

26. Wade Rathke, "Kaiser Aftermath: How about Some Competition to Organize Health
     Care Workers?" *Talking Union*, May 7, 2013. In reality, NUHW did use its limited
     resources to organize nearly 1,000 previously non-union hospital and nursing home
     workers after the January 2009 UHW trusteeship, and a majority of those workers
     later gained first contracts.

27. In his *American Prospect* column, Meyerson wrote of SEIU's "alleged concessions to
     management to Kaiser and other California hospitals" as if they were a figment of the
     imagination of SEIU critics rather than a collective bargaining reality easily verified
     by examining the details of recent UHW settlements with Kaiser, Sutter, Daughters
     of Charity, and Dignity Health Systems. As one NUHW-CNA supporter complained
     on a union blog, pundits like Meyerson always "make it seem like a turf war! I wonder
     if that would still be their opinion if they ACTUALLY talked to workers. . . . Or even
     better, took a job in one of our hospital units and see how they like it."

28. For recent examples of this trend, see Steve Early, "Bargain to Organize: From Boon
     to Embarrassment," *Working In These Times*, August 21. 2012. For a longer discus-
     sion of the many potholes on "the high road to union growth" see Early, *Civil Wars*,
     51–80, 332–34.

29. At the peak of this conflict, SEIU protesters tried, unsuccessfully, to disrupt the
     2008 *Labor Notes* conference because CNA executive director DeMoro was a sched-
     uled speaker. To curb such acts of harassment in California, CNA even sought a
     restraining order against SEIU officials.

30. CNA's National Nurses Organizing Committee (NNOC) has bargaining units in
     Missouri, Illinois, Texas, and Florida.

31. A decertification election sought by NUHW supporters at Children's Hospital in
     Oakland was delayed for 1,207 days—from February 2009 to May 2012. The con-
     tested unit of 450 workers at Children's is now NUHW-represented. For more on
     the new union's multiple ordeals at the NLRB, see Benjamin Ward, "Justice Delayed:
     Workers' Struggle for Democracy Inside and Outside of SEIU," May 2013, an
     unpublished Brooklyn Law School paper in the possession of the author.

32. As quoted in CNA press release, "Nurses Reach Agreement with Sutter California Pacific," March 27, 2013. As a result of this settlement, according to the CNA, "the RNs at both hospitals will be under one contract with equal job security and seniority rights for the first time. The pact includes safe patient handling provisions to stem patient falls and injuries to patients and nurses. Additionally it obligates the employer to provide for meal and rest breaks and stipulates that new technology not supplant RN professional judgment."

33. For more details of this settlement, involving CPMC workers who switched from SEIU to NUHW in 2011, see *Stern Burger with Fries* blog, http://sternburgerwithfries.blogspot.com/2013/03/nuhws-contract-settlement-at-cpmc.html.

34. Rauber, "Sutter Health Responds to Threatened Strike." At Sutter's Delta Medical Center in Antioch, California, an administrative law judge for the NLRB found that management violated federal labor law when it declared negotiations with CNA at an impasse: "unilaterally cut paid sick leave, and eliminated all paid health care coverage for registered nurses working less than 30 hours a week." As CNA co-president Deborah Burger said, "We see this decision as vital in the fight against employers nationwide who are attempting to use the Affordable Care Act to reduce employees' hours and avoid providing health care coverage." As quoted in Mark Glover, "Sutter Loses Labor Decision," *Sacramento Bee,* July 27, 2013.

35. In his Facebook post, King went on to speculate about the discrepancy between NUHW's vote tally and its preelection voter assessments: "My belief is that when it came down to putting up or shutting up, a little more than 25% of our solid red pledges did not have the courage to CHANGE. I know this may be hard to swallow for some provided the detailed information we have provided our coworkers over the last one and a half years about Kaiser and SEIU's collusive intentions."

36. Not everyone on the labor left favors this approach. Historian Staughton Lynd has long dismissed union reform campaigns as overly narrow, misguided, and doomed to fail. For different elaborations on this same critique, see Robert Fitch, *Solidarity for Sale: How Corruption Destroyed the Labor Movement and Undermined America's Promise* (New York: Public Affairs, 2006); and Jane LaTour, "In Their Own Words: Insurgents and the Limits of Reform in Organized Labor," *WorkingUSA* (June 2013): 276–82. A former project director for the Association for Union Democracy, LaTour argues, for example, that "reform efforts that stay with the current union structure and paradigm are doomed to failure."

37. At the first meeting of its 300-member executive board after the 2013 Kaiser election, SEIU-UHW created trial committees to investigate members who violated the local's by-laws by supporting NUHW. Three months later, the former candidate for president, Sophia Sims, was put on trial for "gross disloyalty," "conduct unbecoming a member," and "aiding a rival labor organization." She was barred from the union for seven years. See "Dave Regan's Show Trial gainst Election Rival," *Stern Burger with Fries* blog, July 21, 2013, http://sternburgerwithfries.blogspot.com/2013/07/dave-regans-show-trial-against-election.html.

38. One post-election internal issue making Regan potentially vulnerable to another electoral challenge was his attempt to engineer a huge increase in the dues paid by many SEIU-UHW members. See "Early Defeats for Regan's Dues Hike," *Stern Burger with Fries* blog, September 20, 2013, http://sternburgerwithfries.blogspot.ca/2013/09/early-defeats-for-regans-dues-hike.html.

39. According to NUHW, Kaiser has contributed its own substantial resources to help-
     ing SEIU survive two decertification challenges. To prove this claim, NUHW filed
     suit against Kaiser alleging that it violated Section 302 of the Labor-Management
     Relations Act, which prohibits employers from corrupting unions and their officials
     through improper financial support for their activities. In June 2013 a federal judge
     in San Francisco ordered that the case should proceed to trial (and pretrial discovery)
     because of the seriousness of claims that Kaiser intentionally placed large numbers of
     pro-SEIU workers "on lost-time status to campaign against the rival union," which
     was "tantamount to making cash contributions to SEIU-UHW." See Leonard Dube,
     "Court Lets NUHW Pursue Section 302 Claim that Kaiser 'Lost-Time' Approvals
     Aided SEIU-UHW," *Bloomberg BNA Daily Labor Report,* June 17, 2013.

40. The role of other unofficial shop floor leaders, like Angela Glasper at Kaiser Antioch,
     is well described in Winslow, "Round Two in High-Stakes California Health Care
     Vote."

41. Mel Garcia, a medical assistant at Kaiser Hayward, quoted in Cal Winslow, "Nail
     Biting Time at Kaiser," *ZNet,* April 24, 2013.

42. For a summary of this Trumka speech, see Jackie Tortora, "Future of Unions: New
     Models of Worker Representation," AFL-CIO.org blog, March 7, 2013, www.aflcio.
     org/Blog/Organizing-Bargaining/Future-of-Unions-New-Models-of-Worker-Repre-
     sentation.

43. For the always insightful views of one labor historian not asked to be part of this
     committee, see Stanley Aronowitz, "Reversing the Labor Movement's Free Fall,"
     Logos, Spring 2013. While enthusiastic about creating a " ' new' labor movement,"
     Aronowitz asks "why not seek reform of the existing unions?" http://logosjournal.
     com/2013/aronowitz-spring/.

44. Melissa Maynard, "With Big Changes, Can Labor Grow Again?," *Stateline,* April 15,
     2013, www.pewstates.org/projects/stateline/headlines/with-big-changes-can-labor
     -grow-again-85899468193.

45. See, for example, Steve Early, "How Labor Can Play with a Full Deck," *Working
     Papers for a New Society,* August 1982, a thirty-year-old suggestion that AFL-CIO
     unions create "associate membership" programs to expand their reach beyond
     already shrinking collective bargaining units.

46. See "Bargaining for the Future: Rethinking Labor's Recent Past and Planning
     Strategically for Its Future," a discussion paper prepared by Katie Corrigan, Jennifer
     Luff, and Joseph A. McCartin for the Kalmanovitz Initiative for Labor and the
     Working Poor, Georgetown University, 32–33.

47. As Corrigan, Luff, and McCartin note in ibid., the USWA attempted in 2006 to
     use a union-backed "employee council" as "a test case for the legal theory that the
     NLRA allows collective bargaining for minority unions; the NLRB declined the
     Steelworkers' complaint and has yet to take action on two different union petitions
     for minority bargaining rights." For more on how Morris inspired these thwarted
     NLRB rule-making initiatives, backed by multiple unions and labor law experts,
     see Charles Morris, *The Blue Eagle at Work: Reclaiming Democratic Rights in the
     American Workplace* (Ithaca, NY: Cornell ILR Press, 2004).

48. Even after the UHW trusteeship had dramatically changed the labor relations land-
     scape at Kaiser, Trumka's predecessor, John Sweeney, was still lauding the Kaiser
     LMP for "bringing doctors, nurses, technicians, pharmacists, and other caregivers

together on behalf of patients."

49. Meanwhile, ill-informed academic commentary about "raiding" continued for months after the rerun election at Kaiser. "Union rivalry creates bad public relations and shows the seamy underside of the union movement," Clark University professor Gary Chaison said. "Fights between unions seem to contradict the idea of solidarity between all unions and between all workers." As quoted by Alana Samuels, "Labor Union 'Raids' on Rise as Rivals Seek to Boost Membership Clout," *Los Angeles Times*, August 2, 2013. In this article, the attempt by pro-NUHW workers at Kaiser to regain control over their bargaining unit from a national union affiliate fifteen times larger than NUHW is lumped together with examples of Teamster poaching on airline industry members of the Machinists and Transport Workers, unions that are, respectively, half the size of the IBT or ten times smaller.

50. Josh Freeman, "Labor Historian David Montgomery (1927–2011)," *Sidney Hillman Foundation* blog, December 5, 2011. Benjamin Isitt borrowed from Montgomery for the title of his book, *Militant Minority: British Columbia Workers and the Rise of a New Left, 1948–1972* (Toronto: University of Toronto Press, 2011), wherein he describes how West Coast Canadian labor radicals "endeavored to weld their workmates and neighbors into a self-aware and purposeful working class." The early writings of left syndicalist William Z. Foster (later better known as a leading U.S. Communist Party commissar) also stress the role of the "militant minority" in strike organization and new union building.

51. For an example of successful, if small-scale, workplace organizing in a situation where Teamster members such as NUHW supporters represented by SEIU at Kaiser had "formal but little substantive power over union affairs," see Brian Walsh's account of a Vermont bus drivers' "parallel union" activity in "Battling Business-as-Usual Unionism: Worker Insurgencies and Labor Revitalization," *Dollars & Sense*, May–June 2013. All Staughton Lynd quotes are from that article.

52. Jane McAlevey, "Make the Road New York: Success through 'Love and Agitation,'" *The Nation*, May 21, 2013. Founded in 1997 in the Bushwick section of Brooklyn and known originally as Make the Road by Walking, this worker center drew inspiration from a book by the same name, *We Make the Road by Walking: Conversations on Education and Social Change with Myles Horton and Paolo Freire*, ed. Brenda Bell, John Gaventa, and John Peters (Philadelphia: Temple University Press, 1991).

INDEX